Game Theory

A Non-Technical Introduction to the Analysis of Strategy

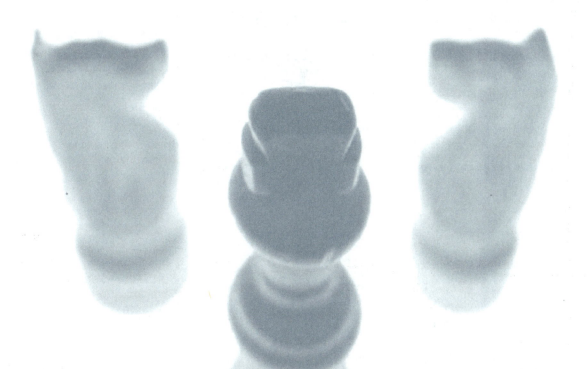

Roger A. McCain, Ph.D.

Professor of Economics
Drexel University

THOMSON

SOUTH-WESTERN

Australia · Canada · Mexico · Singapore · Spain · United Kingdom · United States

Game Theory: A Non-Technical Introduction to the Analysis of Strategy
Roger A. McCain

VP/Editorial Director:
Jack W. Calhoun

VP/Editor-in-Chief:
Mike Roche

Publisher of Economics:
Michael B. Mercier

Acquisitions Editor:
Michael W. Worls

Developmental Editor:
Andrew McGuire

Executive Marketing Manager:
Lisa Lysne

Production Editor:
Tamborah E. Moore

Senior Media Technology Editor:
Vicky True

Media Developmental Editor:
Peggy Buskey

Media Production Editor:
Pam Wallace

Manufacturing Coordinator:
Sandee Milewski

Production House/Compositor:
DPS Associates, Inc.

Printer:
Phoenix Color
Hagerstown, MD

Design Project Manager:
Chris Miller

Internal Designer:
Beckmeyer Design

Cover Designer:
Chris Miller

Cover Photography:
© Getty Images

Library of Congress Control Number: 2003106610

ISBN: 0-324-17572-8
(Core text + Economics Application Card)

ISBN: 0-324-20644-5 (Core text only)

Brief Contents

Part 5
SELECTED APPLICATIONS   285

Contents

Contents

Preface

Game theory is a field of study that was developed in the latter half of the twentieth century. Today, more than ever before, game theory attracts attention for its wide range of applications ranging from business, auctions, and elections to military strategy, biology, and gambling. Game theory received much attention because of the 1994 Nobel Memorial Prize in Economics and the hit 2001 movie based on the life of John Nash, who shared that prize. It is also appreciated as a powerful means of understanding human society. Game theory originated as a branch of mathematics, but research in game theory has included experimental as well as mathematical methods from the first. Thus, game theory has grown to be an interdisciplinary field with applications in economics, political science, philosophy, business, and international relations, among others. Two decades ago, the student who wanted a nontechnical introduction to game theory might have picked up Morton Davis' little book, *Game Theory: a Nontechnical Introduction*, and for intuitive and suggestive applications might have read Schelling's *Strategy of Conflict*. In the intervening years game theory has grown in many ways, but I believe that most of the very important ideas in the field can still be introduced in the same intuitive, nontechnical style that those books exemplify, and that is the purpose of this book.

Thus, the objectives of this textbook are to be interdisciplinary, accessible, clear, and explicit. I aim to teach with examples, beginning each concept with an example and using the example to motivate more general considerations rather than the reverse. I also want to avoid calculus and keep algebra to a minimum. All of these objectives involve trade-offs. As an economist, I have a particular affinity for economic and business examples. I have attempted to control this by including noneconomic as well as economic and business examples in every chapter (except two) and on most topics. An interdisciplinary approach leads naturally to examples that draw on a wide variety of disciplines and other areas: for example, I have examples based on naval conflict (mostly fictionalized), musical comedy, and sports.

Text Organization

Although the book is intended to be elementary, the first two chapters take up the relationship between normal form and extensive form games, a topic not even covered in most other texts. I do this for two reasons. The first (and most important) reason is that, in my opinion, the extensive form is far more intuitive and corresponds more closely to the average person's concept of a game. Thus, under the objective of making the text explicit, I did not feel that I could leave that key relationship implicit. The second reason for taking up the relationship between extensive form and normal form games is that it is often a source of confusion, even in professional-level work. The concept that links extensive form games and normal form games, contingency and contingent strategies, is important in itself and should be a contribution to the students' education even if it were not needed for other purposes in a textbook of game theory.

In Chapter 3 I expand the concept of a prisoner's dilemma, and use the term *social dilemma*. This term is common in Europe and is increasingly common in North America. I think it is a useful term in that it allows us to distinguish between the prisoner's dilemma as a specific example and the more general kind of situation it is an example of. One other departure in that chapter is an example of a game with a dominant strategy equilibrium that is also the cooperative solution. Almost all discussions of dominant strategy equilibrium focus on the social dilemmas, but I think it's important for the student to know that a dominant strategy equilibrium does not have to be inefficient and may indeed be efficient. This is another instance of making explicit what most other textbooks leave implicit.

In Chapters 4 and 5 I introduce the Nash equilibrium in two-person games. The examples in Chapter 4 are fairly novel ones, and I think they illustrate the range of possibilities in Nash equilibrium more systematically than a survey of the classical cases alone would do. In Chapter 5, this includes such familiar two-by-two games as Battle of the Sexes and Chicken, along with the discussion of zero-sum games and the maximin criterion. Moreover, depending on the instructor's purposes, Chapter 5 might be skipped or postponed until some other chapters have been covered.

Some game theory texts have chapters or fairly extensive discussion on three-person games, while others do not. I believe there are two major advantages in discussing three-person games at some length. On one hand, they provide the student with some practice in dealing with games of more than two persons that are still simple enough to be expressed as tables of numbers. I think this is valuable itself. It also gives an opportunity to introduce some of the kinds of phenomena that can arise in multiperson games but not in two-person games. Most other texts do not take full advantage of this. The "spoiler example" is almost the only example of distinct three-person game phenomena found in most texts. In my judgment, however, the most important new phenomenon in three-person games is the possibility that coalitions may form, even in noncooperative games. Conformism, with consequent herding behavior, and nonlinear crowding games are also worth study in three-person games but impossible in two-person games. Thus I regard Chapter 6 as a key chapter.

Since this text is intended for students who may not have background or completed prerequisites in probability and statistics, it seems necessary to introduce some probability concepts, and that is the purpose of Chapter 7. Chapter 8 deals with mixed strategies. Mixed strategies are very counterintuitive and difficult for the average student (in my experience), and I have tried to highlight some of the cognitive difficulties of this topic.

Chapter 9, "Advanced Topics in Noncooperative Equilibrium" is an optional chapter. It begins with the iterative elimination of dominant strategies. This is not an advanced concept in itself, but belongs here because it is closely connected to the distinction of strong and weak dominance, which can be tricky. The chapter then goes on to introduce correlated equilibrium, an alternative to the Nash equilibrium concept that has been a topic of research in the last two decades. I believe it is not found in any other introductory textbook, but I think it belongs here for three reasons. First, it provides a much more satisfactory concept of fully rational behavior in coordination games than the Nash equilibrium does, especially when there is time for "cheap talk" or other arrangements. Second, it illustrates the power of mixed strategies, especially in coalitions in noncooperative games. Third, it provides an answer to "The Blonde Problem" from the movie *A Beautiful Mind*. The movie (and its defects) has just had too much impact to ignore, and it plays a part in several chapters. Another example, from the musical *Guys and Dolls*, further illustrates the point. The examples also serve to illustrate the need for thoroughness, and not to neglect such possibilities as coalitions and mixed strategies.

Chapter 10, on oligopoly pricing models, is also optional and is intended mainly for business and economics students and will probably be skipped by others. It likely suffers more than any other chapter from the avoidance of calculus. In particular, it gives a treatment of Cournot equilibrium in the form of a tabular game in normal form. Many economists will find that strange, but it allows for a far closer parallel to many other game theory examples, including the Edgeworth model. Students will have some difficulty with the differences between the two approaches, but this is another instance where I believe it is better to make the differences explicit by a parallel treatment. The chapter then goes on to develop a very simplified example of a mixed strategy pricing game along lines derived from Ghemawat's recent work. The appendices introduce the familiar calculus-based Cournot and a somewhat more rigorous version of the Ghemawat model along with the smattering of calculus and mathematical statistics that they require. The appendices together might be the equivalent of yet another chapter in the classroom

Chapter 11, on *N*-person games, focuses mainly on some simplifying assumptions that are widely used in applications, especially in economics. Here again, the point is to make explicit what may be implicit in other writing. There is also one minor terminological novelty. One of the two simplifying assumptions uses the representative agent approach, which is very familiar in economics. The other is the use of the term *state variable* to apply to games other than differential games. While this is novel, I think it is a sound extension of the received terminology. We need some term to refer to variables like price, interest, and the frequency of choosing a particular mode of transportation as they play their role in large group interactions.

Chapters 12 and 13 address cooperative solutions to games: in particular, the solution set and the core. This may seem old-fashioned. Most of the competitive textbooks do not discuss cooperative solutions, and one that does it discusses them only at a very advanced level. Also, noncooperative concepts have been far more dominant in recent research, perhaps because of the increasing role of economists in the development of game theory. Economists tend to distrust anything cooperative. Cooperative solutions are a bit more difficult than Nash equilibrium, but I think they are needed in this text for three reasons. First, there are still some appropriate cases for application of the core and the solution set, even though these concepts have not been central to recent research. Cooperative solutions are the right answers and we should teach them. Second, the student needs some understanding of cooperative solutions in order to have a complete understanding of social dilemmas and other Nash equilibria that are contrasted with cooperative solutions. (This applies especially to the solution set.) Third, sequential games that are noncooperative in themselves may have cooperative stages, so that cooperative solutions may play a part in the backward solution of a sequential game. Chapter 12 is intentionally interdisciplinary and thus includes political and international as well as economic and business examples. Chapter 13 is more directed to economic applications and will probably be skipped in courses that are not aimed at economics majors. It would be possible to skip Chapter 13 or both chapters without much loss of continuity for those who prefer to focus quite narrowly on noncooperative solutions.

Chapter 14 introduces sequential games and the subgame perfect equilibrium concept. Chapter 15 applies the principles from Chapter 14 to the study of nested and imbedded games. This is an innovation and I believe it has two major benefits. First, it provides further examples and applications of subgame perfect equilibrium, extending the student's understanding of this somewhat counterintuitive topic. This could be done by other kinds of examples as well, of course. But, second, it introduces the possibility that people may take action to change the rules of the (nested) game. This leads to an interpretation of game theory that is more open to evolution and human creativity, on the one hand, and leads naturally into political applications and mechanism design, on the other. In a terminological innovation, nested games (which are subsets of other games) are distinguished from imbedded games; that is, nested games are proper subgames and thus must be equilibrial in the case of a subgame perfect equilibrium.

Chapters 16 and 17 introduce repeated play, with Chapter 16 assuming a definite endpoint and Chapter 17 assuming indefinite repetition. These chapters conclude the core of the book, which is composed of Chapters 1 through 8, 11, and 14 through 17.

Chapter 18 touches on mechanism design and applications in the law, and includes a discussion of credible threats by authorities, including monetary authorities. This chapter is not meant as a comprehensive survey either of mechanism design or of game theoretic approaches to monetary authority, but rather to make the student aware of the existence of such studies within game theory. Probably two more advanced courses (if not more) would be required for the student who hopes to master these topics!

Chapter 19 attempts to introduce the main ideas in the game-theoretic analysis of voting, perhaps the most important application in the book. It begins with Bowen's analysis of single-peaked preferences in voting, which seems largely lost, and stresses the contrast between strategic and naïve voting and the lack of any voting scheme that always meets standards of reasonableness. This is more of a practical issue than a mathematical one, and the Arrow Theorem is not stressed as the chapter relies largely on examples.

Chapter 20 discusses experimental studies. This very large literature is sampled in a way that is very selective but I hope representative. This chapter stresses the tension between bounded and ideal rationality and between self-interested and other motivations in the experimental literature. Chapter 21 discusses the application to auctions, certainly a key body of applications in the coming-of-age of applied game theory. It should follow the chapter on experiments since experimental studies have played a key role in applied auction theory. The book concludes with a chapter on game theory and evolution, both biological and social. This chapter also looks back to the chapters on experiments and on indefinitely repeated play.

To teachers of game theory I would say one final thing. Game theory is fun to teach and to learn. I hope you enjoy it as much as I do.

Roger A. McCain

Key Text Features

- **To best understand this chapter** Each chapter begins with an introductory box outlining which chapters the student should have already covered. This allows for greater flexibility in assigning chapters, since the box clarifies what can be skipped and what cannot.

- **Heads Up** The "Heads Up" box, positioned toward the beginning of each chapter, introduces the key chapter concepts in order to prepare students for what lies ahead.

- **Definition Boxes** New terms are introduced with boxed definitions that reinforce the text and also provide a handy study tool.

- **Summary** Each chapter ends with a chapter summary that enables students to review the general concepts of the chapter.

- **Exercises and Discussion Questions** A series of exercises at the end of each chapter can be used by students to test what they've learned, or by instructors to work through in-class problems with students.

Key Supplements

- **Instructor's Manual** To assist instructors in teaching the game theory course, an instructor's manual is available that gives an overview of each chapters' objectives, tips for organizing the course (including classroom activities), and answers to end-of-chapter questions.

- **Web site** The text's Web site can be located at *http://mccain.swlearning.com*. The site includes access to Econ Applications Web site, South-Western's acclaimed internet resources. Instructors can also gain password-protected access to quiz questions and answers for each chapter.

- **Economic Applications Web site (e-con@pps) http://econapps.swlearning.com** Complimentary access to South-Western's *e-con@pps Web* site is included with every new copy of this textbook.* This site includes a suite of highly acclaimed and content-rich dynamic Web features developed specifically for economics classrooms: EconNews Online, EconDebate Online, and EconData Online. Organized and searchable by key economic topic for easy integration into your course, these regularly updated features are pedagogically designed to deepen students' understanding of theoretical concepts through hands-on exploration and analysis of the latest economic news stories, policy debates, and data.

- Students buying a used book can purchase access to the site at *http://econapps.swlearning.com*.

Acknowledgements

I am pleased to acknowledge those who aided me in preparing this textbook. Philip Heap of James Madison University was especially helpful as he checked the accuracy of all of the examples and problems within the text. Helpful suggestions and often detailed reviews were also provided by:

Maxim Engers,
University of Virginia

Nick Feltovich,
University of Houston

Joseph E. Harrington, Jr.,
Johns Hopkins University

Philip Heap,
James Madison University

Michael Iachini,
Florida State University

Steven D. Moffitt,
Illinois Institute of Technology

Ed Packel,
Lake Forest College

Matthew Roelofs,
Western Washington University

John L. Scott,
Southern Arkansas University

Martin Shubik,
Yale University

Index of Examples by Topic Area

* End of chapter exercises only.

* End of chapter exercises only.

† Many examples in other categories could be thought of as economics examples, since game theory often follows neoclassical economics in assuming that people are rational in the sense that they maximize something. However, these are example models or issues in economics, and not applied otherwise.

* End of chapter exercises only.

* End of chapter exercises only.

Politics and Government (cont.)	Chapter Number
Pork Barrel*	19
Running for Office*	3
Spoiler	6
U. S. Presidential Election of 1968*	19
U. S. Presidential Election of 1992	19
U. S. Presidential Election of 2000	19

Recreational and Gambling Games

Dice	7, 9
Icosahedral Dice*	7
Lottery*	7
Matching pennies*	1, 4, 5, 8
Mini-checkers*	2
Nim	1
"Rock, Paper, Scissors"	4, 8
Sky Masterson	7

Sport

American Football*	8
Baseball	8
Cricket*	14

Theory‡

Al and George	8
Battle of the Sexes	5, 16
Centipede Game	14, 15, 20
Chain Store Paradox	15
Chicken	5
Dictator Game	2
Hawk vs Dove	5, 11
Heave-Ho Game	4, 5, 20
Make Room Game*	12
Mixed Coordination Game	20
Paradox of Benevolent Authority	18
Payback*	20

* End of chapter exercises only.

‡ Examples in this category have no specific application, or use the application primarily to illustrate an aspect of game theory, or have wider applications, or have been used in experimental studies, or all of these.

Theory (cont.)	Chapter Number
Prisoner's Dilemma	1, 2, 20
Repeated Social Dilemma	22
Ultimatum	20
Urn Problem*	7
War of Attrition*	14

University Life	
Accreditation*	15
Dean's Negotiation*	15
Fraternity Executive Committee	19
GPA	7
Grading Team Projects	18
Impasse in the Faculty Senate*	19
Joe Deadbeat	16
Planning Doctoral Study	15
Sibling Rivalry*	2, 4, 9
Writing a Game Theory Textbook	3, 4

* End of chapter exercises only.

Part 1

Fundamentals

1 Conflict, Strategy, and Games

What is game theory? And what does it have to do with strategy and conflict? Of course, strategy and conflict arise in many aspects of human life, including games. Conflicts may have winners and losers, and games often have winners or losers. This textbook is an introduction to a way of thinking about strategy, a way of thinking derived from the mathematical study of games. The first step in this chapter is to answer those questions—what is **game theory**, and what does it have to do with strategy? To tackle some of these questions, let's begin with some examples. The first one will be an example of the human activity we most often associate with strategy and conflict: war.

The Spanish Rebellion
Puttin' the Hurt on Hirtuleius

Here is the story (as novelized by Colleen McCullough from the history of the Roman Republic):[1]

In about 75 B.C.E., Spain (Hispania in Latin) was in rebellion against Rome, but the leaders of the Spanish Rebellion were Roman soldiers and Spanish Roman wannabes. It was widely believed that the Spanish leader, Quintus Sertorius, meant to use Spain as a base to make himself master of Rome. Rome sent two armies to put down the rebellion: one commanded by the senior, aristocratic, and respected Metellus Pius, and the other commanded by Pompey, who was (as yet) young and untried but very rich and willing to pay for his own army. Pompey was in command over Metellus Pius, which Pius resented because Pompey was not only younger but a social inferior into the bargain. Pompey set out from Rome to relieve the siege of a small Roman garrison at New Carthage, but got no further west than Lauro, where Sertorius caught and besieged him. (See the map in Figure 1.1.) Thus, Pompey and Sertorius had stalemated one another in eastern Spain. Metellus Pius and his army were in western Spain, where Pius was governor. This suited Sertorius, who did not want the two Roman armies to unite, and Sertorius sent his second in command, Hirtuleius, to garrison Laminium, northeast of Pius's camp, and prevent Pius from coming east to make contact with Pompey.

---

1 Colleen McCullough, *Fortune's Favorites*, (Avon PB, 1993) pp. 621–625.

Pius had two strategies to choose from. They are shown by the light gray arrows in the map. He could attack Hirtuleius and take Laminium, which, if successful, would open the way to eastern Spain and deprive the rebels of one of their armies. If successful, he could then march on to Lauro and unite with Pompey against Sertorius. But his chances of success were poor. Fighting a defensive battle in the rough terrain around Laminium, the Spanish legions would be very dangerous and would probably destroy Pius' legions. Alternatively, Pius could make his way to Gades and take ships to New Carthage, raise the siege Pompey had been unable to raise, and march on to Lauro, raising the siege of Pompey's much larger

Here are some concepts we will develop as this chapter goes along:

Game Theory: *Game Theory* is the study of the choice of strategies by interacting rational agents.

A key step in a game theoretic analysis is to discover which strategy is a person's **best response** to the strategies chosen by the others. Following the example of neoclassical economics, we define the best response for a player as the strategy that gives that player the maximum payoff, given the strategy the other player(s) has chosen or can be expected to choose.

Game theory is based on a scientific metaphor, the idea that many interactions we do not usually think of as games, such as economic competition, war and elections, can be treated and analyzed as we would analyze games.

Figure 1.1 | Spain, with Strategies for Hirtuleius and Pius

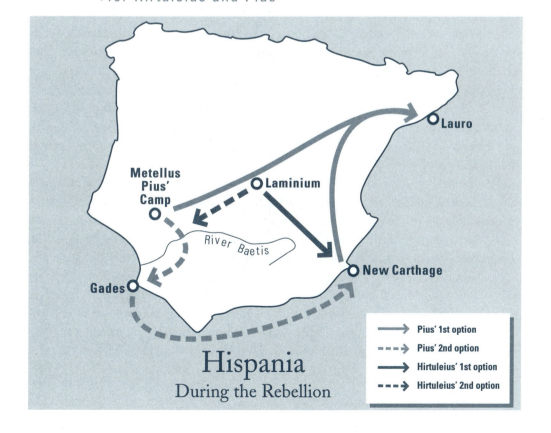

Hispania
During the Rebellion

→ Pius' 1st option
--→ Pius' 2nd option
→ Hirtuleius' 1st option
--→ Hirtuleius' 2nd option

Lauro
Metellus Pius' Camp
Laminium
River Baetis
New Carthage
Gades

forces. To Pius, this was the better outcome, since it would not only unite the Roman armies and set the stage for the defeat of the rebels, but would also show up the upstart Pompey, demonstrating that the young whippersnapper couldn't do the job without getting his army saved by a seasoned Roman aristocrat.

Hirtuleius, a fine soldier, faced a difficult problem of strategy choice to fulfill his mission to contain or destroy Pius. Hirtuleius could march directly to New Carthage and fight Pius at New Carthage, along with the small Spanish force already there. His chances of defeating Pius would be very good, but Pius would learn that Hirtuleius was marching for New Carthage, and then Pius could divert his own march to the north, take Laminium without a fight, and break out to the northeast. Thus, Hirtuleius would fail in his mission.

Alternatively, Hirtuleius could remain at Laminium until Pius marched out of his camp, and then intercept Pius at the ford of the River Baetis. He would arrive with a tired army and would fight on terrain more favorable to the Romans, and so his chances would be less favorable; but there would be no possibility of losing Laminium and the Romans would have to fight to break out of their isolation.

Thus, each of the two commanders has to make a decision: What is the **best response**? We can visualize the decisions as a tree diagram like the one in Figure 1.2. Hirtuleius must first decide whether to commit his troops to the march to New Carthage or remain at Laminium where he can intercept Pius at the Baetis. Begin at the left, with Hirtuleius' decision, and then we see the decision Pius has to make depending on which decision Hirtuleius has made. What about the results? For Hirtuleius, the downside is the simple part. If he fails to stop Pius, he fails in his mission. If he intercepts Pius at New Carthage, he has a good chance of winning. If he intercepts Pius at the ford on the Baetis, he has at least a 50–50 chance of losing the battle. On the whole, Pius wins when Hirtuleius loses. If he breaks out by taking Laminium, he is successful. However, if he raises the siege of New Carthage, he gets the pleasure of showing up his boss as well. But he cannot be sure of winning if he goes to New Carthage.

If Hirtuleius goes to New Carthage, Pius will go to Laminium and win. If Hirtuleius stays at Laminium, Pius will strike for New Carthage. Thus, the best Hirtuleius can do is to stay at Laminium and try to intercept Pius at the river.

Unfortunately for Hirtuleius, his best response was not good enough. In fact, Pius moved more quickly than Hirtuleius had expected, so that Hirtuleius' tired troops had to fight a rested Roman army. The rebels were badly beaten and ran, opening the way for Pius to continue to Gades and transport his legions by sea to New Carthage, where they raised the siege and moved on to raise the siege of Pompey in Lauro, and so Pius returned to Rome a hero. Pompey had plenty of years left to build his own reputation, and would eventually be First Man in Rome, only to find himself in Julius Caesar's headlights. But that's another story.[2]

---

2 Colleen McCullough, *Fortune's Favorites,* (Avon PB, 1993) pp. 621–625.

Figure **1.2** | The Game Tree for the Spanish Rebellion

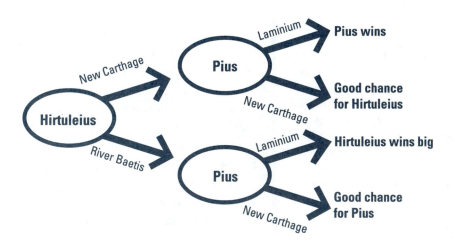

In analyzing the strategies of Pius and Hirtuleius with the tree diagram, we are using concepts from game theory.

Game Theory Emerges

Early in the twentieth century, mathematicians began to study some relatively simple games and, later, much more complex games like chess. These studies were the beginning of game theory. The great mathematician John von Neumann extended the study to games like poker. Poker brings in a new dimension of complexity: In poker, you may not know whether your opponent is "bluffing." Von Neumann's analysis was a step forward in the mathematical study of games. But a more important departure came when von Neumann teamed up with the mathematical economist Oskar Morgenstern. In the 1940s, they collaborated on a book titled *The Theory of Games and Economic Behavior*. The idea behind the book was that many aspects of life that we do not think of as games, such as economic competition and military

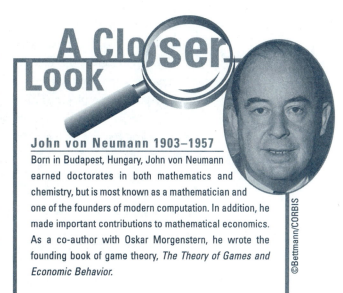

John von Neumann 1903–1957

Born in Budapest, Hungary, John von Neumann earned doctorates in both mathematics and chemistry, but is most known as a mathematician and one of the founders of modern computation. In addition, he made important contributions to mathematical economics. As a co-author with Oskar Morgenstern, he wrote the founding book of game theory, *The Theory of Games and Economic Behavior*.

©Bettmann/CORBIS

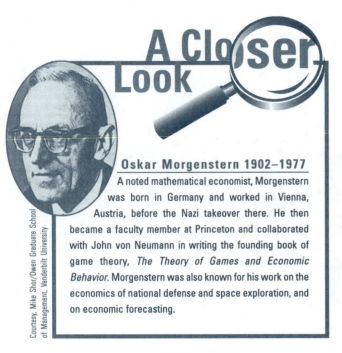

A Closer Look

Oskar Morgenstern 1902–1977

A noted mathematical economist, Morgenstern was born in Germany and worked in Vienna, Austria, before the Nazi takeover there. He then became a faculty member at Princeton and collaborated with John von Neumann in writing the founding book of game theory, *The Theory of Games and Economic Behavior*. Morgenstern was also known for his work on the economics of national defense and space exploration, and on economic forecasting.

conflict, can be analyzed *as if* they were games. Today, game theorists treat all kinds of human strategy choices as if they were strategies for games. It is this scientific metaphor, the idea that all sorts of human strategic problems can be thought of as if they were games, that has led to the great explosion of game theory in the last half century.

As we have said, game theory studies the rational choice of strategies. This conception of rationality has a great deal in common with neoclassical economics. Thus, rationality is a key link between neoclassical economics and game theory. Morgenstern was an economist, but von Neumann was also well acquainted with neoclassical economics, so it was natural that they would draw from the neoclassical economic tradition.

Neoclassical economics is based on the assumption that human beings are absolutely rational in their economic choices. Specifically, the assumption is that each person maximizes her or his rewards—profits, incomes, or subjective benefits—in the circumstances that she or he faces. This hypothesis serves a double purpose in the study of economics. First, it narrows the range of possibilities somewhat. Absolutely rational behavior is more predictable than irrational behavior. Second, it provides a criterion for evaluation of the efficiency of an economic system. If the system leads to a reduction in the rewards coming to some people, without producing more than compensating rewards to others (that is, if costs are greater than benefits, broadly speaking) then something is wrong. Pollution of air and water, the overexploitation of fisheries, and inadequate resources committed to research can all be examples of inefficiency in this sense.

A key step in a game theoretic analysis is to discover which strategy is a person's *best response* to the strategies chosen by the others. Following the example of neoclassical economics, we define the best response for a player as *the strategy that gives that player the maximum payoff, given the strategy the other player has chosen or can be expected to choose*. If there are more than two players, we say that the best response is the strategy that gives the maximum payoff, given the strategies all the other players have chosen. This is a very common concept of rationality in game theory, and we will use it in many chapters that follow in this book. However, it is not the only concept of rationality in game theory, and game theory does not always assume that people are rational. In some of the chapters to follow, we will explore some of these alternative views.

Game Theory, Neoclassical Economics, and Mathematics

In neoclassical economics, the rational individual faces a specific system of institutions, including property rights, money, and highly competitive markets. These are among the circumstances that the person takes into account in maximizing rewards. The implication of property rights, a money economy, and ideally competitive markets is that the individual need not consider her or his interactions with other individuals. Each person need consider only his or her own situation and the conditions of the market. But this leads to two problems. First, it limits the range of the theory. Whenever competition is restricted (but there is no monopoly), or property rights are not fully defined, consensus neoclassical economic theory is inapplicable, and neoclassical economics has never produced a generally accepted extension of the theory to cover these cases. Decisions taken outside the money economy were also problematic for neoclassical economics. Game theory was intended to confront just this problem: to provide a theory of economic and strategic behavior when people interact directly, rather than through the market.

In neoclassical economic theory, to choose rationally is to maximize one's rewards. From one point of view, this is a problem in mathematics: choose the activity that maximizes rewards in given circumstances. Thus, we may think of a rational economic choice as the "solution" to a problem of mathematics. In game theory, the case is complex, since the outcome depends not only on one's own strategies and the market conditions, but also directly on the strategies chosen by others. Still, we may think of the rational choice of strategies as a mathematical problem—maximize the rewards of a group of interacting decision makers—and so we again speak of the rational outcome as the "solution" to the game.

With these concepts in mind, let's look at a real game!

What Does This Have to Do with Games?

The story about the Spanish Rebellion is a good example of the way we ordinarily think about strategy in conflict. Hirtuleius has to go first, and he has to try to guess how Metellus Pius will respond to his decision. Somehow, each one wants to try to outsmart the other one. According to common sense, that's what strategy is all about.

Figure 1.3 | Nim

There are some games that work very much like the conflict between Metellus Pius and Hirtuleius. A very simple game of that kind is called Nim. Actually, Nim is a whole family of games, from smaller and simpler versions up to larger and more complex versions. For this example, though, we will look at only the very simplest version. Three coins are laid out in two rows, as shown in Figure 1.3. One coin is in the first row, and two are in the second. The two players take turns, and each turn a player must take at least one coin. At each turn, the player can take as many coins as she wishes from a single row, but can never take coins from more than one row on any round of play. The winner is the player who picks up the last coin. Thus, the objective is to put the opponent in the position of having to leave just one coin behind.

There are some questions about this game that we would like to answer. What is the best sequence of plays for each of the two players? Is there such a best strategy at all? Can we be certain that the first player can win? Or the second? These are questions you might like to know the answer to if, for example, someone offered to make you a bet on a game of Nim.

Let's say that our two Nim players are Anna and Barbara. Anna will play first. Once again, we will visualize the strategies of our two players with a tree diagram. The diagram is shown in Figure 1.4. Anna will begin with the circle at the left, and each circle shows the coins that the player will see in case she arrives at that circle. Thus, Anna, playing first, will see all three coins. Anna can then choose among three plays at this first stage. The three plays are:

1. Take one coin from the top row.

2. Take one coin from the second row.

3. Take both coins from the second row.

Figure 1.4 | A Tree Diagram for Nim

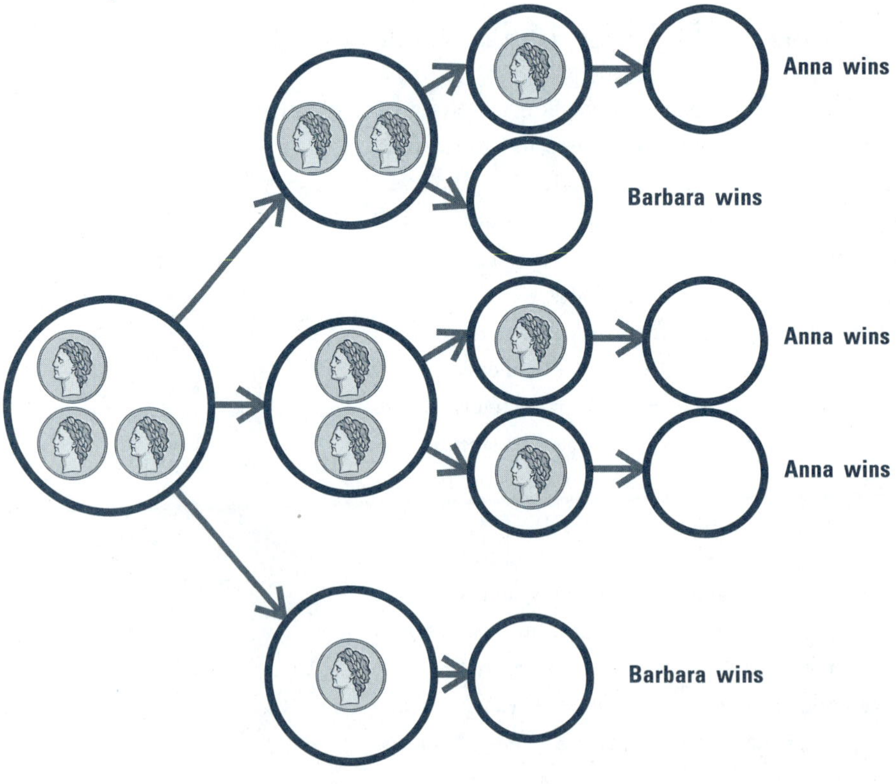

The arrows shown leading away from the first circle correspond from top to bottom to these three moves. Thus, if Anna chooses the first move, Barbara will see the two coins shown side by side in the top circle of the second column. In that case Barbara has the choice of taking either one or two coins from the second row, leaving either none or one for Anna to choose in the next round, as shown in the top two circles of the third column. Of course, by taking two coins, leaving none for Anna, Barbara will have won the game.

In a similar way, we can see in the diagram how Anna's other two choices leave Barbara with other alternative moves. Looking to strategy 3, we see that it leaves Barbara with only one possibility; but that one possibility means that Barbara wins. From Anna's point of view, move 2, in the middle, is the most interesting. As we see in the middle circle, second column, this leaves Barbara with one coin in each row. Barbara has to take one or the other—those are her only choices. But each one leaves Anna with just one coin to take, leaving Barbara with nothing on her next turn, so Anna wins the game. We can now see that Anna's best move is to take one coin from the second row, and once she has done that, there is nothing Barbara can do to keep Anna from winning.

Now we know the answers to the questions above. There is a best strategy for the game of Nim. For Anna, the best strategy is, "Take one coin from the second row on the first turn, and then take whichever coin Barbara leaves." For Barbara, the best strategy is "If Anna leaves coins on only one row, take them. Otherwise, take any coin." We can also be sure that Anna will win if she plays her best strategy.

A Closer Look

Albert Tucker 1905-1995

Born in Ontario, Canada, Tucker arrived at Princeton in 1929 to do graduate work. He returned to become a member of the Princeton faculty and head of the department of mathematics at a time when it was one of the most creative college mathematics departments in the world. In 1950, addressing an audience of psychologists at Stanford University, Tucker created the Prisoner's Dilemma. This example, which can be set out in one page, could be the most influential one page in the social sciences in the latter half of the twentieth century. Tucker is remembered for his contributions to game theory and the mathematics of maximization and minimization.

University Archives. Department of Rare Books & Special Collections. Princeton University Library

The Prisoner's Dilemma

John von Neumann was at the Institute for Advanced Study in Princeton. Oskar Morgenstern was at Princeton University. As a result of their collaboration, Princeton was soon buzzing with game theory. Albert Tucker, the chairman of the mathematics department at Princeton, was visiting at Stanford University, and wanted to give a group of psychologists some idea of what all the buzz was about, without using too much mathematics. The example that he gave them is called the **Prisoner's Dilemma**.[3] It is the most studied example in game theory and possibly the most influential half a page written in the twentieth century. You may very well have seen it in some other class. The Prisoner's Dilemma is presented a little differently from the two previous examples, however.

3 S.J. Hagenmayer, "Albert W. Tucker, 89, Famed Mathematician," *The Philadelphia Inquirer* (Thursday, Feb. 2, 1995, p. B7).

Tucker began with a little story like this: Two burglars, Bob and Al, are captured near the scene of a burglary and are given the "third degree" separately by the police. Each has to choose whether to confess and implicate the other. If neither man confesses, then both will serve 1 year on a charge of carrying a concealed weapon. If each confesses and implicates the other, both will go to prison for 10 years. However, if one burglar confesses and implicates the other, and the other burglar does not confess, the one who has collaborated with the police will go free, while the other burglar will go to prison for 20 years on the maximum charge.

Definition

Payoff Table—A **payoff table** is a table with the strategies of two or three players along the margins and the payoffs to the players in the cells. Each strategy corresponds to a column or row and so the payoffs in a cell are the payoffs for the strategies that correspond to the column and row.

The strategies in this case are: confess or don't confess. The payoffs (penalties, actually) are the sentences served. We can express all this compactly in a **payoff table** of a kind that has become pretty standard in game theory. Table 1.1 is the payoff table for the Prisoner's Dilemma game.

The table is read like this: Each prisoner chooses one of the two strategies. In effect, Al chooses a column and Bob chooses a row. The two numbers in each cell tell the outcomes for the two prisoners when the corresponding pair of strategies is chosen. The number to the left of the comma tells the payoff to the person who chooses the rows (Bob) while the number to the right of the comma tells the payoff to the person who chooses the columns (Al). Thus (reading down the first column), if they both confess, each gets 10 years, but if Al confesses and Bob does not, Bob gets 20 and Al goes free.

Table 1.1 | The Prisoner's Dilemma

		Al	
		confess	don't
Bob	confess	10 years, 10 years	0, 20 years
	don't	20 years, 0	1 year, 1 year

So: How to solve this game? What strategies are "rational" if both men want to minimize the time they spend in jail? Al might reason as follows: "Two things can happen: Bob can confess or Bob can keep quiet. Suppose Bob confesses. Then I get 20 years if I don't confess, 10 years if I do, so in that case it's best to confess. On the other hand, if Bob doesn't confess, and I don't either, I get a year; but in that case, if I confess I can go free. Either way, it's best if I confess. Therefore, I'll confess."

But Bob can and presumably will reason in the same way—so that they both confess and go to prison for 10 years each. Yet, if they had acted "irrationally," and kept quiet, they each could have gotten off with 1 year each.

This remarkable result—that self-interested and seemingly rational action results in both persons being made worse off in terms of their own self-interested purposes—is what has made a wide impact in modern social science. There are many interactions in the modern world that seem very much like that, from arms races through road congestion and pollution to the depletion of fisheries and the overexploitation of some subsurface water resources. These are all quite different interactions in detail, but are interactions in which (we suppose) individually rational action leads to inferior results for each person, and the Prisoner's Dilemma suggests something of what is going on in each of them. That is the source of its power.

Having said that, we must also admit candidly that the Prisoner's Dilemma is a very simplified and abstract—if you will, "unrealistic"—conception of many of these interactions. A number of critical issues can be raised with the Prisoner's Dilemma, and each of these issues has been the basis of a large scholarly literature:

- The Prisoner's Dilemma is a two-person game, but many of the applications of the idea are really many-person interactions.

- We have assumed that there is no communication between the two prisoners. If they could communicate and commit themselves to coordinated strategies, we would expect a quite different outcome.

- In the Prisoner's Dilemma, the two prisoners interact only once. Repetition of the interactions might lead to quite different results.

- Compelling as the reasoning that leads to this conclusion may be, it is not the only way the problem might be reasoned out. Perhaps it is not really the most rational answer after all.

Games in Normal and Extensive Form

There are both important similarities and contrasts between this example and the previous two. A contrast can be seen in the way the examples have been presented. The Prisoner's Dilemma has been presented as a table of numbers, not as a tree diagram. These two different ways of presenting a game will play important and different roles in this book, as they have in the history of game theory.

When a game is represented as a tree diagram, we say that the game is represented in **extensive form**. The extensive form, in other words, represents each decision as a branch point in a tree diagram. One alternative to the extensive form is the representation we see in the Prisoner's Dilemma. This is called the **normal form**. In a normal form representation, the game is shown as a table of numbers with the different strategies available to the players enumerated at the margins of the table.

> **Definition**
>
> *Extensive Form*—A game is represented in **extensive form** when it is shown as a tree diagram in which each strategic decision is shown as a branch point.

> **Definition**
>
> *Normal Form*—A game is represented in **normal form** when it is shown as a table of numbers with the strategies listed along the margins of the table and the payoffs for the participants in the cells of the table.

The normal form representation is probably less intuitive than the extensive form. Nevertheless, it has been very influential and we will rely mostly on the normal form in the next few chapters of this book.

Now let's apply the same approach to an example from that famous movie.

John Nash's Problem in the Movie

In the cinema version of *A Beautiful Mind*, John Nash reaches the insight that leads to his Nobel-Memorial-prize-winning breakthrough by solving what we might call **The Blonde Problem**. The Blonde Problem is defined as follows:

- There are two or more lusty males.

- There are several possibly interested females. There is at least one more female than males.

- Just one female is blonde.

- Every male prefers a blonde to a brunette, and a brunette to no female companion at all.[4]

In the movie, Nash observes that if they all pursue the blonde, they will cancel one another out, the brunettes will be offended, and no one will have a companion, the worst outcome. His proposed solution is that they all forget about the blonde and each pursue a brunette. There are enough brunettes so that no male needs to be frustrated.

Table 1.2 | A Two-By-Two Blonde Problem

		John	
		pursue blonde	pursue brunette
Reinhard	pursue blonde	0, 0	2, 1
	pursue brunette	1, 2	1, 1

To simplify this example and treat it as a two-person game in normal form, we might consider Table 1.2. For simplicity, suppose there are just two lusty males in the bar, John and Reinhard.[5] The values represent benefits received, assuming that the blonde is worth twice as much as the brunette. The movie implies that the solution is that both pursue a brunette for payoffs (1, 1). But this is a little strange, since it means the blonde doesn't get a date and neither of the guys gets his first preference—something of a no-win outcome. In fact, these strategies are *not* best responses! If Reinhard pursues a brunette, John's best response is to pursue the blonde, for 2 rather than 1; and if John pursues a brunette, Reinhard's best response is to pursue the blonde.

What's going on here? Can this be the right answer?[6] Is it really true that good-looking blondes don't get dates because the guys assume they are so busy there is no point in asking? Can this really be the answer that would be given by John Nash's methods? We will have to look into that in later chapters!

---

4 I am indebted to Yvan Kelly of Flagler College, St. Augustine, Florida, for posing the problem in this way, and for some of the discussion here. As Hal Varian observes, the movie version does not treat the women as players, and this is unsound both as game theory and for more general reasons. However, this example follows the movie version. Hal Varian, "What, Exactly, Was on John Nash's Beautiful Mind?" *The New York Times* (April 11, 2002) Business section.

5 John Nash shared the Nobel Memorial Prize in Economics with Reinhard Selten and John Harsanyi.

6 John Nash has said to Professor Kelly, "The movie is fiction and the game theory and economics in the movie are not reliable." (Personal communication, conversation, and e-mail to Kelly forwarded to me, November 2002.)

A Scientific Metaphor

Now, let's return to the question, "What is game theory?" Since the work of John von Neumann (*The Theory of Games and Economic Behavior*, referenced earlier), *games* have been a scientific metaphor for a much wider range of human interactions in which the outcomes depend on the interactive strategies of two or more persons, who have opposed or at best mixed motives. *Game theory is a distinct and interdisciplinary approach to the study of human behavior, an approach that studies rational choices of strategies and treats the interactions among people as if they were games, with known rules and payoffs and in which everyone is trying to "win."* The disciplines most involved in game theory are mathematics, economics, and the other social and behavioral sciences. Among the issues discussed in game theory are the following:

- What does it mean to choose strategies "rationally" when outcomes depend on the strategies chosen by others and when information is incomplete?

- In games that allow mutual gain (or mutual loss), is it rational to cooperate to realize the mutual gain (or avoid the mutual loss), or is it rational to act aggressively in seeking individual gain regardless of mutual gain or loss?

- If the answer to the last question is "sometimes," under which circumstances is aggression rational and under which circumstances is cooperation rational?

- In particular, do ongoing relationships differ from hit-and-run encounters in this connection?

- Can moral rules of cooperation emerge spontaneously from the interactions of rational egoists?

- How does real human behavior correspond to rational behavior in these cases? If it differs, in what direction?

- Are people more cooperative than would be rational? More aggressive? Both?

A Business Case

So far we have seen four examples—cases from war, a recreational game, concealment of a crime, and pursuit of a personal relationship. There are many applications to business, so let us consider a business case before concluding this chapter.[7] We will apply the game metaphor and the representation of the game in normal form. The business example will be very much like the Prisoner's Dilemma.

7 Game theory is important for business and economics, and is valuable also as a link across the disciplines of the other social sciences and philosophy. Thus, part of the plan for this book is that every chapter will include at least one major business case, but also at least one major case from another discipline. The exceptions will be the chapter on industry strategy and prices, which will be pretty nearly all business and economics, and the chapter on games and politics, which will not include a business application.

Before 1964, television advertising of cigarettes was common, but, following the Surgeon General's Report in 1964, the four large tobacco companies, American Brands, Reynolds, Philip Morris, and Ligget and Myers, negotiated an agreement with the federal government. The agreement came into effect as of 1971 and included a pledge not to advertise on television. Can this be explained by means of game theory?

Here is a two-person advertising game much like the situation faced by the tobacco companies. Let's call the companies Fumco and Tabacs. The strategies for each firm are don't advertise or advertise. We assume that if neither of them advertises, they will divide the market and their low costs (no advertising costs) will lead to high profits in which they share equally. If both advertise, they will again divide the market equally, but with higher costs and lower profits. Finally, if one firm advertises and the other does not, the company that advertises gets the larger market share and substantially higher profits. Table 1.3 shows payoffs rating profits on a scale from 1 to 10—with 10 best. The table is read like the table for the Prisoner's Dilemma: Fumco chooses the column, Tabacs chooses the row, and the first payoff is to Tabacs, the second to Fumco.

Table 1.3 | The Advertising Game

		Fumco	
		don't advertise	advertise
Tabacs	don't advertise	8, 8	2, 10
	advertise	10, 2	4, 4

We will find that this game is very much like the Prisoner's Dilemma. Each firm can reason as follows: "If my rival does not advertise, then I am better off to advertise, since I will get profits of 10 rather than 8. On the other hand, if my rival does advertise, I am better off to advertise, since I will get profits of 4 rather than 2. Either way, I had better advertise." Thus, both advertise and get profits of 4 rather than 8.

This is like the Prisoner's Dilemma in that rational, self-seeking behavior leads the two companies to a result that both dislike. It may be difficult for competitive companies, as it is for prisoners in different interrogation rooms, to trust one another and choose the strategy that is better for both. However, when a third party steps in—as the federal government did in the tobacco case—they are happy to agree to restrain their advertising expenditure.

Summary

In this chapter we have addressed the questions "What is game theory? And what does it have to do with strategy and conflict?" We have seen from some examples that game theory is a distinct and interdisciplinary approach to the study of human behavior, based on a scientific metaphor. The metaphor is that conflicts and choices of strategy, as in war, deception, and economic competition, can be treated "as if" they were games. We have seen two major ways that these "games" can be represented:

- In *normal form*—As a table of numbers with the different strategies available to the players enumerated at the margins of the table

- In *extensive form*—As a tree diagram with each strategic decision as a branch point

We have seen that game theory often assumes that people act rationally in the sense that they adopt a best response strategy. Like the neoclassical conception of rational behavior in economics, the assumption is that people are acting rationally when they act as though they are maximizing something: profits, winnings in the game, or subjective benefits of some kind—or, perhaps, minimizing a penalty, such as the number of years in jail. The *best response* is the strategy that gives a player the maximum payoff, given the strategies the other player has chosen or can be expected to choose. These concepts are the beginning point for a study of game theory. In the next chapter, we will explore the relationships among some of them, especially between games in normal and extensive form.

Exercises and Discussion Questions

1.1 **The Spanish Rebellion.** In her story about the Spanish rebellion, McCullough writes: "There was only one thing Hirtuleius could do: March down onto the easy terrain . . . and stop Metellus Pius before he crossed the Baetis." Is McCullouch right? Discuss.

1.2 **Nim.** Consider a game of Nim with three rows of coins, with one coin in the top row, two in the second row, and either one, two, or three in the third row. (a) Does it make any difference how many coins are in the last row? (b) In each case, who wins?

1.3 **Matching Pennies.** Matching pennies is a schoolyard game. One player is identified as "even" and the other as "odd." The two players each show a penny, with either the head or the tail showing upward. If both show the same side of the coin, then "even" keeps both pennies. If the two show different sides of the coin, then "odd" keeps both pennies. Draw a payoff table to represent the game of matching pennies in normal form.

1.4 **Happy Hour.** Jim's Gin Mill and Tom's Turkey Tavern compete for pretty much the same crowd. Each can offer free snacks during happy hour, or not. The profits are 30 to each tavern if neither offers snacks, but 20 to each if they both offer snacks, since the taverns have to pay for the snacks they offer. However, if one offers snacks and the other does not, the one who offers snacks gets most of the business and a profit of 50, while the other loses 20. Discuss this example using concepts from this chapter. How is the competition between the two tavern owners like a game? What are the strategies? Represent this game in normal form.

2 Games in Extensive and Normal Form

To best understand this chapter 2

You need to understand the material in Chapter 1 first. That's probably no surprise, but each chapter from now on will have a box like this to let you know what you can skip and what you had best not.

In the previous chapter we saw two rather different kinds of examples. The examples of Hirtuleius and Pius and the game of Nim were represented in extensive form—that is, as a tree diagram. The Prisoner's Dilemma and the Advertising Game were represented in normal form—that is, in tabular form. There are some other differences between those games, and the representation as a tree diagram or as a table is partly a matter of convenience.

In the early development of game theory, the representation of games in normal form was more common and was very influential. In some more recent work the representation of games in extensive form has played a key role. Following this history, the next few chapters of this book will focus mainly on games in normal form, and later chapters will analyze games in extensive form.

Representation in Normal Form
A Business Case

We have seen that games can be represented in two different ways: extensive and normal form. Although it is sometimes more convenient to represent a particular game in one way or another, there is nothing absolute about this. Any game can be represented in either form. This is not obvious, of course. It was one of John von Neumann's key discoveries. And there is a trick to it. Here is an example, which is also a business case.

According to a study by the McKinsey business consulting organization, deregulation creates a difficult transition for formerly regulated companies.[1] Often these companies have been public utility monopolies. During most of the twentieth century, public utilities were allowed to operate as monopolies, with their prices regulated and profits limited to a "fair rate of return;" but with new competition prohibited by law. However, under deregulation they face the entry of new competition. The monopoly will be tempted to respond to the new entry with a price war, although, according to the McKinsey organization, this is usually an unprofitable strategy.

---

[1] Andreas Florissen, Boris Maurer, Bernhard Schmidt, and Thomas Vahlenkamp, "The Race to the Bottom," *McKinsey Quarterly* (2001), available at *http://www.mckinseyquarterly.com/article_page.asp?tk=293962:1078:21&ar=1078&L2=21&L3=37*, as of November 27, 2002.

Let's illustrate that with an example. Goldfinch Corp. provides telecommunications services in River City, but the telecommunications market has been deregulated. Bluebird Communications is considering entering the River City market. If Bluebird does enter the market, Goldfinch has two choices: Goldfinch can cut prices, entering into a price war, to retain its market share as far as possible and perhaps to punish Bluebird for entering the market and try to drive Bluebird out. (We ignore the possibility that Goldfinch might run into legal problems if it does this). Alternatively, Goldfinch can cut back on its own output, accommodating the new entering firm and keeping the price up. Either way, Goldfinch will expect decreased profits.

Heads Up!

Here are some concepts we will develop as this chapter goes along:

Games in Normal and Extensive Form: A game is *represented in extensive form* when it is shown as a tree diagram in which each strategic decision is shown as a branch point. A game is *represented in normal form* when it is shown as a table of numbers with the strategies listed along the margins of the table and the payoffs for the participants in the cells of the table.

Contingency: A *contingency* is an event that may or may not occur, such as the event that another player adopts a particular strategy.

Contingent Strategy: A *contingent strategy* is a strategy to be adopted only when it is known that the contingent event has occurred.

Information Set: In a game in extensive form (tree diagram), a decision node with more than one branch included in it is called an *information set*.

Rating profits on a scale of 10 for best, payoffs for Goldfinch are 10 if Bluebird does not enter, 5 if Bluebird enters and Goldfinch shares the market, and 2 if Bluebird enters and Goldfinch starts a price war. Bluebird's payoffs are 0 if it does not enter, 3 if it enters and Goldfinch shares the market, and −5 if there is a price war. As the weaker firm, in a financial sense, Bluebird does not profit as much as Goldfinch if the market is shared and will lose out in a price war. (In case the market is shared, total profits in the industry are reduced from 10 to 8, while consumers, who are not part of the game, benefit from lower prices.)

This game is different from the Prisoner's Dilemma and the Advertising Game (but similar to the Spanish Rebellion and Nim) in that one participant, Bluebird, has to go first in choosing its strategy and the other participant, Goldfinch, can wait and see what Bluebird will do before choosing its strategy. It seems natural to represent this game in extensive form (as a tree diagram) as shown in Figure 2.1.

In the figure, Bluebird's choice is shown at node 1 and Goldfinch's choice is shown at node 2. The numbers at the right side show the payoffs, with Bluebird's payoff first. In this case, Bluebird will want to *think strategically*—that is, anticipate how Goldfinch will respond if Bluebird does decide to enter. Goldfinch will want to plan for the scenario—or **contingency**—that Bluebird will enter. Looking just at decision node 2, we see that Goldfinch gets a payoff

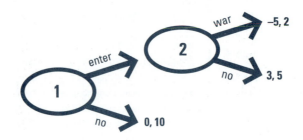

Figure **2.1** | The Game of Market Entry in Extensive Form

<table>
<tr><td></td></tr>
</table>

Definition

Contingency—A **contingency** is an event that may or may not occur, such as the event that another player adopts a particular strategy.

of 5 (hundred million dollars) from the strategy of accommodation, and a payoff of only 2 from the strategy of a price war. Thus, if Goldfinch maximizes its payoffs, Goldfinch will accommodate the new entry, and Bluebird can anticipate that, and will choose to enter for a payoff of 3 rather than staying out for 0. (We will see in later chapters that this sort of commonsense reasoning is very central to game theory, but does not always give quite such commonsense results in more complex examples).

The tree diagram is called the extensive form and here we are examining the game of market entry in extended form. Although it seems natural to express this game in extensive form, it can also be represented in normal form, as a table of numbers like the Prisoner's Dilemma. There is something to be gained by looking at all games in the same way, and von Neumann and Morgenstern selected the normal form as their common framework for looking at all games.

But there is a trick to it. In the game of market entry, Goldfinch's strategies are contingent strategies:

1. *If Bluebird enters, then* accommodate.

2. *If Bluebird enters, then* initiate price war.

Definition

Contingent Strategy—A contingent strategy is a strategy to be adopted only when it is known that the contingent event has occurred.

A **contingent strategy** is a strategy that is adopted only if a particular contingency arises. The phrases in italics in (1) and (2) indicate the contingencies in which Bluebird's strategies are relevant. Like market entry, any game can be represented in normal form, but we may have to treat some of its strategies as contingent strategies in order to do it.

In the game of market entry, as in chess, each participant knows all opponent decisions that are relevant to its own decision. For example, Bluebird must choose first whether to enter, and Goldfinch knows what that decision is when it makes its own decision to retaliate or not.

Bluebird's strategies are

1. Enter

2. Don't enter

Thus, the game in normal form is as shown in Table 2.1. However, game theorists often use a shorthand, leaving out the contingent phrase such as "if Bluebird enters then," and showing Goldfinch's strategies simply as "initiate price war" and "accommodate." This does not cause confusion in a simple case like this, but it can cause confusion in more complex examples, so it is best to be more careful and to keep in mind that the strategies used when we represent games in normal form are contingent strategies.

How will the game come out? First, what is the best response for each company? If Bluebird does enter, accommodate is the better strategy—so there will be no price war, and Bluebird, anticipating this, will enter. (We will have a systematic interpretation of this sort of strategic problem in Chapter 14.) But the McKinsey study warns that deregulated companies, inexperienced in competitive markets, may make the wrong decision in these circumstances, which will harm the profits of both companies.

Contingent strategies play an important role in many business situations. For example, consider this quotation: "All airlines have the grim task of preparing contingency plans in case one of

Table 2.1 | The Market Entry Game in Normal Form

		Goldfinch	
		If *Bluebird enters,* then accommodate; if *Bluebird does not enter,* then do business as usual.	If *Bluebird enters,* then initiate price war; if *Bluebird does not enter,* then do business as usual.
Bluebird	enter	3, 5	−5, 2
	don't	0, 10	0, 10

> ### Definition
>
> *Contingency Plan*—A **contingency plan** is a plan to be put into operation only when it is known that the contingent event has occurred.

their jets should fall out of the sky."[2] A **contingency plan** is a plan to be put into effect if a particular contingency occurs. Contingency planning is not only important in business, but in many other fields as well, such as military affairs (from which the idea originally came) and government. Whenever two or more decision makers are making contingency plans to deal with one another, we have contingent strategies.

Examining the Normal Form

The Prisoner's Dilemma and the Advertising Game examples from Chapter 1 illustrate why game theory has been influential, and highlight some of the issues that arise in more complicated cases. But the way those examples were presented—as tables of numbers—probably is not the way that most of us are accustomed to thinking of games. The table-of-numbers presentation is what the founders of game theory called the game in *normal form*. The game in normal form puts stress on one important aspect of games and other game-like interactions: Each participant's payoffs depend not only on its own strategy but also on the strategy chosen by the other. However, many games seem, on first impression, to be too complex for this treatment—although they might not be very complex games!

A key discovery in *The Theory of Games and Economic Behavior* by von Neumann and Morgenstern is that all games can be represented in normal form. To do this, it will be necessary to view the strategies as contingent strategies. In complex games such as chess and war, with many steps of play, almost all strategies will naturally be thought of as contingent strategies, relevant only if the opponent has already made certain strategic commitments. The number of contingencies that can arise in chess, and thus the number of distinct contingent strategies, are literally inconceivably large, and beyond the computational capacity of any existing computer or any computer in the foreseeable future. Nevertheless, *in principle*, even chess could be represented in normal form.

In principle, all strategies are contingent strategies. In the market entry game, for example, even Bluebird's strategies are contingent: "Whether Goldfinch retaliates or not, enter," and "whether Goldfinch retaliates or not, don't enter." Since Bluebird goes first, and isn't informed whether Goldfinch will retaliate or not, Bluebird has only one contingency for each strategy—so we usually ignore the contingencies for the person who goes first. But, to be quite thorough, we should remember that the contingency is there. This sort of thoroughness is a characteristic that game theory inherits from its mathematical origins and shares with computer programming. We could put it this way: A strategy is an if–then rule, and there must always be something in the "if" part, even if it doesn't make any difference

2 Laurence Zuckerman, "Airline Management Style Honed by Catastrophe," *The New York Times* (November 15, 2001) page C1.

in a particular example. You probably know from experience what a computer does to you if you do not follow the rules *thoroughly*.

For some games that are conveniently shown in extensive form, we will need to know how to convert them to normal form. For example, let's think again about the Spanish Rebellion. If Hirtuleius were to march toward New Carthage, Pius would know, and could march on Laminium unopposed. But Pius would march toward Laminium only if he knew that Hirtuleius had already committed himself to go to New Carthage. The strategy of marching toward Laminium is a contingent strategy.

The Spanish Rebellion

Let's convert the Spanish Rebellion into normal form. As a first step, how many strategies do the two generals have? Clearly, Hirtuleius has only two. Looking at the tree diagram, it is not quite so clear how many strategies Pius has. In fact, Pius has four strategies, and they are all contingent strategies. There are two strategies Pius may choose if Hirtuleius goes to New Carthage, and two others that he may choose if Hirtuleius marches toward the River Baetis.

Using this information, the Spanish Rebellion game is shown in normal form in Table 2.2.

In this case, if we were to leave out the contingent phrases *If Hirtuleius goes to New Carthage*, and *If Hirtuleius marches for the River Baetis*, we might suppose that Pius has only two strategies, and would not take into account his superior information. That could lead to confusion in this slightly more complex game.

Although it is not essential, is often useful in game theory to indicate the results of the game in terms of numbers, as we did with the Prisoner's Dilemma and the advertising game. We will often choose numbers more or less arbitrarily to express the relative desirability or undesirability of the outcomes. Let's see how we might do that for the example of Hirtuleius and Pius.

In the upper right cell of Table 2.2, the outcome is "Pius wins." This is the worst outcome for Hirtuleius and the best for Pius. Let's assign a payoff of 5 for Pius and minus 5 for Hirtuleius. This is shown in Table 2.3, upper right cell, with the payoff for Pius to the left and the payoff for Hirtuleius to the right. As usual, the payoff to the player who chooses the row is to the left, since that player's strategies are to the left. In the next cell, in Table 2.2, the outcome is "good chance for Hirtuleius." We translate that (on a relative scale) as 3 for Hirtuleius and −3 for Pius. In the third and fourth rows, these estimates are more or less reversed, giving us the table of numerical payoffs shown in Table 2.3.

The Dictator Game

Let's try one more example, a new kind of game. The example will be a simple version of the Dictator Game. Amanda is the dictator. She has a candy bar that she has to share with her

Table 2.2 │ Spanish Rebellion in Normal Form

		Hirtuleius	
		(Regardless of Pius' strategy) Go to River Baetis	*(Regardless of Pius' strategy)* Go to New Carthage
Pius	*If Hirtuleius goes to New Carthage,* then go to Laminium; *if Hirtuleius marches for the River Baetis,* then go to Laminium	Hirtuleius wins big	Pius wins
	If Hirtuleius goes to New Carthage, then go to New Carthage; *if Hirtuleius marches for the River Baetis,* then go to New Carthage.	Good chance for Pius	Good chance for Hirtuleius
	If Hirtuleius goes to New Carthage, then go to Laminium; *if Hirtuleius marches for the River Baetis,* then go to New Carthage.	Good chance for Pius	Pius wins
	If Hirtuleius goes to New Carthage, then go to New Carthage; *if Hirtuleius marches for the River Baetis,* then go to Laminium.	Hirtuleius wins big	Good chance for Hirtuleius

little sister, Barbara. (Mother will be angry if she doesn't share at all.) Amanda can share 50–50, or she can keep 90 percent for herself. Barbara's only choice is to accept or reject what she is offered. The tree diagram for this game is shown in Figure 2.2.

In the Dictator Game, Amanda's strategies are 50–50 and 90–10. Amanda's decision is shown by the oval marked A. Barbara's strategies in each case are accept or reject. Her choices

Table 2.3 | Spanish Rebellion in Normal Form with Numeric Outcomes

		Hirtuleius	
		(Regardless of Pius' strategy) Go to River Baetis	*(Regardless of Pius' strategy)* Go to New Carthage
Pius	*If Hirtuleius goes to New Carthage,* then go to Laminium; *if Hirtuleius marches for the River Baetis,* then go to Laminium.	−5, 5	5, −5
	If Hirtuleius goes to New Carthage, then go to New Carthage; *if Hirtuleius marches for the River Baetis,* then go to New Carthage.	3, −3	−3, 3
	If Hirtuleius goes to New Carthage, then go to Laminium; *if Hirtuleius marches for the River Baetis,* then go to New Carthage.	3, −3	5, −5
	If Hirtuleius goes to New Carthage, then go to New Carthage; *if Hirtuleius marches for the River Baetis,* then go to Laminium.	−5, 5	−3, 3

are shown by the ovals marked B. The first payoff is to Amanda, and the second is to Barbara. The game in normal form is shown in Table 2.4. This doesn't look very good for Barbara—perhaps you can see why it is called the Dictator Game. But the main point here is to see how we can translate the game from extensive form to normal form by using the contingent expression of the strategies.

Figure 2.2 | The Dictator Game

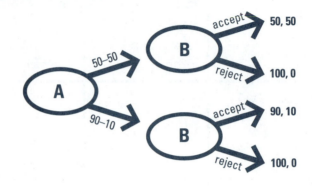

Table 2.4 | The Dictator Game in Normal Form

		Amanda	
		(Whether Barbara accepts or rejects) offer 50–50	(Whether Barbara accepts or rejects) offer 90–10
Barbara	If Amanda offers 50–50, then accept; if Amanda offers 90–10, then accept	50, 50	10, 90
	If Amanda offers 50–50, then accept; if Amanda offers 90–10, then reject	50, 50	0, 100
	If Amanda offers 50–50, then reject; if Amanda offers 90–10, then accept	0, 100	10, 90
	If Amanda offers 50–50, then reject; if Amanda offers 90–10, then reject	0, 100	0, 100

The Prisoner's Dilemma in Extensive Form

For an example of converting a game from normal to extensive form, let's take a look at our old friend, the Prisoner's Dilemma, in extensive form. In Prisoner's Dilemma, both prisoners make their decisions simultaneously, and we have to allow for that. The Prisoner's Dilemma is shown in extensive form in Figure 2.3, and we may suppose that Al makes his decision to confess or not confess at 1, and Bob makes his decision at 2. Notice one difference from Figure 2.1. Bob's decision, in the two different cases, is enclosed in a single oval. That is game-theory

Table 2.5 | The Prisoner's Dilemma

Repeats Table 1.1, Chapter 1

		Al	
		confess	don't
Bob	confess	10 years, 10 years	0, 20 years
	don't	20 years, 0	1 year, 1 year

code, and what it tells us is that when Bob makes his decision, he doesn't know what decision Al has made. Bob has to make his decision without knowing Al's decision. Graphically, Bob doesn't know whether he is at the top of the oval or the bottom. In Figure 2.1, the fact that node 2 gives only one set of arrows means, in game-theory code, that Bluebird knows Goldfinch's decision before Bluebird makes its decision. Recall, Bluebird knows what Goldfinch has decided, but Bob does not know what Al has decided (or will decide).

Because it tells us something about the (limited) information Bob has, node 2 is called an **information set**. Conversely, the extensive form of the game can be useful as a way of visualizing the information available to a participant at each stage of the game.

> **Definition**
>
> *Information Set*—A decision node with more than one branch included in it is called an **information set**.

Figure 2.3 | The Prisoner's Dilemma in Extensive Form

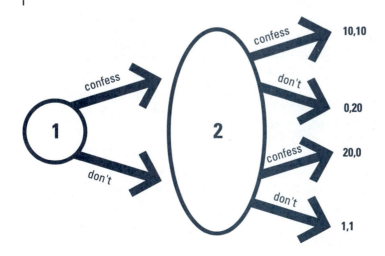

Where information availability is important, we will often want to use the game in extensive form. But for games like the Prisoner's Dilemma, there is no available information, and the game in normal form contains all we need to know about the game.

The Prisoner's Dilemma can be represented in extensive form in two different ways. We have shown it here with Al going first, and Bob following, although not knowing what decision Al made. Since the decisions are made simultaneously, it is equally correct to represent Figure 2.3 with Bob going first and Al following. The important thing is the information that Al and Bob have, or rather, the information they lack. Since each representation shows both men making their decisions without knowledge of the decision the other has made, both are equally correct.

The idea here is nothing more than a visual code. If for any reason a player doesn't know which decision the other player has made, then he does not really know which branch in the tree he is taking. We express that by putting both branches, or all of the branches that he might be making, within a single node in the decision tree. When a game theorist sees two or more branches grouped within a single node, as our oval in Figure 2.3 shows, the game theorist knows that the player lacks information—the player doesn't know which branch he is really at.

An Example from Military History

Let's look at another example, this time an example drawn from military history. By the early twentieth century, heavy, long-range artillery had become a decisive influence in European war. The big cannons were transported by rail, sometimes using special railroads built for that purpose, but also relying on ordinary freight railroads. As a result, in a crisis it was important if possible to be the first to mobilize. Suppose one country moved its cannon into position first. That country would be able to destroy the other country's rail approaches and thus prevent the enemy from moving its cannon into place. The result would be an immediate advantage in the war to follow.

This combination of artillery dominance and limited mobility contributed to the sudden outburst of full-scale war at the beginning of World War I. The crisis came when Gavrilo Princip, a Yugoslav nationalist, assassinated Archduke Franz Ferdinand of Austria. Knowing that a war might follow, Austria, Germany, France and their allies all rushed to mobilize their forces, rather than take a chance that their enemies might mobilize first and leave them at the disadvantage.

The game of mobilization is shown in normal form in Table 2.6, where the two countries are France and Germany. Rating disasters on a scale of 1 to 10, the bloody European war from 1914 to 1918 certainly was a 10. Accordingly, we show a payoff of negative 10 to

Table 2.6   Force Mobilization

		Germany	
		mobilize	don't
France	mobilize	−10, −10	−9, −11
	don't	−11, −9	0, 0

Figure 2.4 | Mobilization

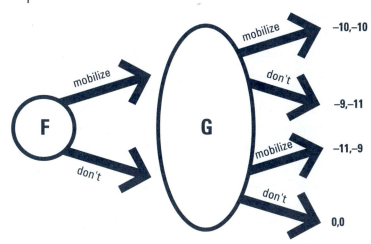

each country if both countries mobilize. If neither country mobilizes, peace continues, and the payoff is zero to each country. If one country mobilizes and the other does not, the country that mobilizes does slightly less badly, with a payoff of negative 9; while a country that does not mobilize does slightly worse, with the payoff of negative 11.

As in the Prisoner's Dilemma, the two countries have to make their decisions simultaneously. Each one has to decide whether to mobilize without knowing whether the other country will mobilize. This lack of information is the crucial point in constructing the diagram of the game in extensive form.

At the same time, and again like the Prisoner's Dilemma, it doesn't matter whether we show France or Germany going first, since they are choosing simultaneously. Let's show the game with France going first. Then we show Germany's choices in a single oval, to express the fact that Germany doesn't know whether France is mobilizing. The diagram is shown in Figure 2.4.

In general, whenever one of the players has to choose without knowing the choices the other player has made, or is making at the same time, we will represent that lack of information by putting all of the branches that the player may be taking in the same node in the tree diagram. This is how the game in extensive form shows information and the lack of information in games.

Summary

One of the early discoveries in game theory was that all kinds of games can be represented in normal form—as a table of numbers with the strategies listed at the margin and the payoffs to the participants in the cells. For some games, some of the strategies are contingent strategies—strategies that are considered only if the other player has already taken some specific action. Contingent strategies and contingency planning are important in themselves, but doubly important in game situations where players may get an advantage from the information they have. On the other hand, when we represent games like the Prisoner's Dilemma (games in which information on the others' moves may be missing) in the extensive form, we have to show what information each decision maker has at each step. When one decision maker does not know what decision the other has made or is making, we put the results of both decisions within a single decision node. In a tree diagram, this will be shown by including two or more branches and a single oval. Such an oval is called an *information set*, since it illustrates what information the decision maker has. To be more exact, it illustrates information the decision maker does not have—that is, which decision the other decision maker will choose.

Our conclusion for this chapter is that the extensive form of a game and the normal form are just alternative ways of looking at games, and each can be applied to any game, so we can use the representation that works best in a particular case. For the next few chapters, we will focus on the normal form.

Exercises and Discussion Questions

2.1 Sibling Rivalry. Two sisters, Iris and Julia, are students at Nearby College, where all the classes are graded on the curve. Since they are the two best students in their class, each of them will top the curve unless they enroll in the same class. Iris and Julia each have to choose one more class this term, and each of them can choose between math and literature. They're both very good at math, but Iris is better at literature. Each wants to maximize her grade point average. The grade point averages are shown in Table 2.E1, which treats their friendly rivalry as a game in normal form.

What are the strategies for this game? Express this game in extensive form, assuming that the sisters make their decisions at the same time. Express this game in extensive form, assuming that Iris makes her decision first and Julia knows Iris's decision when she chooses her strategy.

Suppose Iris doesn't care what her own grade point average is, but she wants to maximize the difference between her grade point average and her sister's—just to show up the little twerp! (But Julia still wants to maximize her grade point average and is not concerned about how her sister does.) Write the table for the game in normal form under this assumption, and redo the last three questions. What strategy will Iris choose if she chooses first?

Table **2.E1** Grade Point Averages for Iris and Julia

		Iris	Iris
		math	lit
Julia	math	3.7, 3.8	4.0, 4.0
Julia	lit	3.8, 4.0	3.7, 4.0

2.2 **The Great Escape.** A prisoner is trying to escape from jail. He can attempt to climb over the walls or dig a tunnel from the floor of his cell. The warden can prevent him from climbing by posting guards on the wall, and he can prevent the con from tunneling by staging regular inspections of the cells, but he has only enough guards to do one or the other, not both.

What are the strategies and payoffs for this game? Express the payoffs in both non-numerical and numerical terms. Express this game in normal form. Express this game in extensive form, assuming that the prisoner and the warden make their decisions at the same time. Express this game in extensive form, assuming that the warden makes his decision first, and the prisoner knows the warden's decision when he chooses his strategy.

2.3 **Checkers.** Figure 2.E1 is a simplified version of the familiar game of checkers.

Mini-checkers is a small-scale version of the familiar game of checkers. It is played on a checkerboard just four squares wide and three deep. Each player has just two pieces. In color, the squares would be red and black, and so would the pieces; but here, red is shown by the lighter gray, and black by the darker gray. As in ordinary checkers, the pieces move diagonally, only on the red squares. Black goes first. As in ordinary checkers again, a piece can "jump" an enemy piece, provided there is an open red square beyond the enemy piece. This is shown in Figure 2.E2.

Figure 2.E1 | Mini-Checkers

Figure 2.E2 | Black Jumps and Wins

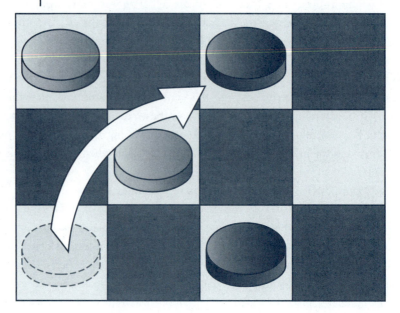

The game ends when either (1) the player whose turn it is cannot move; in which case the player who cannot move loses, or (2) a player advances one of his pieces to the opponent's end of the checkerboard, so that the piece is "kinged;" in which case the player whose piece is kinged is the winner. In Figure 2.E2, black has won by having his piece kinged.

Draw a diagram for the game of mini-checkers in extensive form. Draw the tabular representation of the game of mini-checkers in normal form. Can you determine whether black or red will win at mini-checkers if both sides play their best strategies? Which?

2.4 It's Good to Be da Queen? Queen Elizabeth the First of England faced a difficult strategic problem. On the one hand, if she married, she would no longer have power because, under the customs of the time, her husband would assume all the power of a king. Elizabeth had seen how her father Henry treated several of his queens, with imprisonment or execution. On the other hand, if her nobles had known she would never marry and leave an heir to the throne, they would have seen rebellion as a lesser evil. That's why Liz kept her boyfriend, Dudley, on the string so long.

Treat this problem as a game in which the players are Elizabeth and her nobles. What are their strategies? Express the game in both extensive and normal form. Are there any information sets?

2.5 Nim Strikes Again. Translate the game of Nim (Chapter 1) from extensive to normal form.

Part 2

Noncooperative Equilibria in Normal Form Games

3

Dominant Strategies
and Social Dilemmas

To best understand this chapter   3

To best understand this chapter you need to have
studied and understood the material from Chapters 1
and 2.

The first two chapters have focused mainly on concepts, pointing out that many problems of strategy can be studied as if they were games, and exploring the way the strategies and games are represented. But game theory is particularly interested in the interactions among the people involved in the game. From this point on, we will focus strongly on those interactions.

We want to discover patterns of interaction that are stable and predictable. In economics, a stable and predictable pattern of interaction is usually called an *equilibrium*. Game theorists follow this example (which the economists, in turn, got from chemical engineering) so we can say that we are investigating equilibrium patterns of play in games.

As a first example, we will use a case from environmental policy and environmental economics. This is especially appropriate. Both the words *economics* and *ecology* come from the Greek root word *oikos*, which means a household. Here is the idea: Within a household, the members of the household are in constant interaction, and their interaction is what makes the household work. When we use the words *economic* and *ecological* we are implying that in economic and ecological matters, the interaction is just as constant and crucially important as it is within a household.

The Dumping Game

Figure 3.1 | Two Vacation Plots

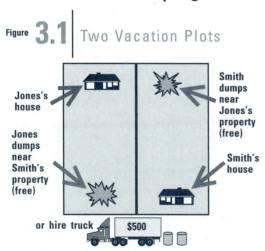

Jones's house

Jones dumps near Smith's property (free)

Smith dumps near Jones's property (free)

Smith's house

or hire truck $500

For this game, we will begin with a story, as we so often do. In this story the characters are two property owners. We will call them Mr. Jones and Mr. Smith. Mr. Jones and Mr. Smith own weekend homes on side-by-side plots of land in a remote area that has no routine garbage collection. They can contract to have their garbage picked up by a trucking firm, but that is rather costly. It would cost either property owner $500 per year to arrange for the garbage pickup. Each one has another possible strategy to get rid of his garbage. Mr. Jones can dump his garbage at the rear of his lot near Mr. Smith's property, and, similarly, Mr. Smith can dump his garbage near Mr. Jones's house. (Figure 3.1).

32

The two landowners will make their decisions simultaneously, so each will not know what strategy the other person is choosing. Therefore, we will want to represent this game in normal form. Each landowner chooses between two strategies: Pay for a garbage pickup or dump the garbage on the neighbor's property. But what are the payoffs in this game?

The benefits the two landowners get from their weekend property are subjective benefits. They consist of the enjoyment the two get from spending their time in this remote and scenic location. But we need to express the benefits in money terms, if only in order to compare them with the dollar cost of the garbage pickup. We can use an idea from economics to do this. We know that the property owners could benefit in other, monetary ways from their property. For example, each one could rent his property out for the season, rather than occupying it himself. We can thus estimate the money value of a person's subjective enjoyment of his property—it is the smallest amount of rent that he would accept in return for giving up his own occupation of the property.

Of course, the subjective benefits depend on whether someone is dumping his garbage on your property. Taking that into account, we will say that each person values his experience at his weekend home at $5,000 per year if there is no dumping, but at $4,000 per year if there is. In other words, if there were no dumping, neither Mr. Jones nor Mr. Smith would give up a year of occupancy for less rent than $5,000; but if there is dumping on the property, each of them would give up the year of occupancy for $4,000.

Using this information, we can represent the dumping game in normal form as shown in Table 3.1.

Heads Up!

Here are some concepts we will develop as this chapter goes along:

Dominant Strategy: Whenever one strategy yields a higher payoff than a second strategy, regardless of which strategies the other players choose, the first strategy dominates the second. If one strategy dominates all other strategies (for a particular player in the game), it is said to be a *dominant strategy* (for that player).

Dominant Strategy Equilibrium: If, in a game, each player has a dominant strategy, and each player plays the dominant strategy, then that combination of (dominant) strategies and the corresponding payoffs are said to constitute the *dominant strategy equilibrium* for that game.

Cooperative and Noncooperative Solutions: The cooperative solution of a game is the list of strategies and payoffs that the participants would choose if they could commit themselves to a coordinated choice of strategies; for example, by signing an enforceable contract. The strategies and payoffs they would choose if there are no enforceable agreements is the *noncooperative solution*.

Social Dilemma: If the game has a dominant strategy solution that is different from the cooperative solution to the game, the game is a *social dilemma*.

Table 3.1 The Dumping Game in Normal Form

		Mr. Smith	
		dump	hire truck
Mr. Jones	dump	4000, 4000	5000, 3500
	hire truck	3500, 5000	4500, 4500

Table 3.2 | Best Responses for Mr. Smith

If Mr. Jones's strategy is	The best response for Mr. Smith is
dump	dump
hire truck	dump

Table 3.3 | Best Responses for Mr. Jones

If Mr. Smith's strategy is	The best response for Mr. Jones is
dump	dump
hire truck	dump

Definition

Dominant Strategy—Whenever one strategy yields a higher payoff than a second strategy, regardless of which strategies the other players choose, the first strategy dominates the second. If one strategy dominates all other strategies (for a particular player in the game), it is said to be a **dominant strategy** (for that player).

Definition

Dominant Strategy Equilibrium—If, in a game, each player has a dominant strategy, and each player plays the dominant strategy, then that combination of (dominant) strategies and the corresponding payoffs are said to constitute the **dominant strategy equilibrium** for that game.

Definition

Dominated Strategy—Whenever one strategy yields a higher payoff than a second strategy, regardless of which strategies the other players choose, the second strategy is dominated by the first, and is said to be a **dominated strategy**.

Now remember, in game theory we focus on "rational" behavior, which means that each player chooses his *best response* to the strategy the other player has chosen or can be expected to choose. First, let's think of Mr. Smith's best response to the strategies that Mr. Jones might choose. These are shown in Table 3.2.

What we see in Table 3.2 is that "dump" is always the best response, regardless of which strategy Mr. Jones chooses. Now let's think through Mr. Jones's best responses to the strategies that Mr. Smith might choose. Since the game is symmetrical, it should come as no surprise that the best response is the same for Mr. Jones as it is for Mr. Smith. That is what we see in Table 3.3.

It seems that both players in the Dumping Game have rather easy decisions. That is because the strategy "dump" is an example of a **dominant strategy**. A dominant strategy is a strategy that is the best response to any strategy that the other player or players might choose. In the Dumping Game, "dump" is a dominant strategy for both players. Since both players in the Dumping Game have dominant strategies, the Dumping Game also gives us a good example of a dominant strategy equilibrium. When each player in a game chooses his dominant strategy, the result is a **dominant strategy equilibrium**. We can also say that the strategy "dump" dominates the strategy "hire a truck." Whenever one strategy yields a higher payoff than a second strategy, regardless of which strategies the other players choose, the second strategy is dominated by the first, and is said to be a **dominated strategy**. In the Dumping Game, the strategy "hire a truck" is a dominated strategy.

Dominant Strategies

When dominant strategies exist in a game, they provide a very powerful reason for choosing one strategy rather than another. You may have noticed that the Dumping Game is very much like the Prisoner's Dilemma. In the Prisoner's Dilemma, "confess" is a dominant strategy both for Al and for Bob; and (confess, confess) is a dominant strategy equilibrium. Similarly, the Advertising Game in Chapter 1 and the Mobilization Game in Chapter 2 are both examples of dominant strategy equilibria. All of these games—the Dumping Game and the other three—are examples of **social dilemmas**. A social dilemma can be defined as a game with a dominant strategy equilibrium in which all players do worse than they would if they adopted nonequilibrium strategies.

> **Definition**
>
> ***Social Dilemma***—A **social dilemma** is a game that has a dominant strategy equilibrium, and the dominant strategy solution is different from the cooperative solution to the game.

Social Dilemmas and Cooperative Solutions

From a mathematical point of view, the dominant strategy equilibrium is a *solution* to the game. That is, it tells us what strategies will be chosen and what the results will be if participants in the game make choices that are "rational" in a certain sense. But from the point of view of the participants in a social dilemma, the dominant strategy equilibrium is more the problem in itself. Let's return to the example of the dumping game. We can be pretty certain that both Mr. Smith and Mr. Jones would prefer the situation where each person chooses to hire a truck rather than the dominant strategy equilibrium. Since both are better off

> **Definition**
>
> ***Cooperative Solution***—The **cooperative solution** of a game is the list of strategies and payoffs that the participants would choose if they could commit themselves to a coordinated choice of strategies—for example, by signing an enforceable contract.

when both hire a truck, we can describe the (hire a truck, hire a truck) outcome as the **cooperative solution** to the dumping game.

Suppose, to continue the example, that Mr. Smith and Mr. Jones come together and negotiate a contract. The contract states that each of them will hire a truck, and that there will be no dumping. After they have signed the contract, they are committed to the strategy of hiring a truck. If either of them should "cheat," the other player can file a lawsuit and force the cheater to comply with the contract. Thus, the institution of contracts provides a solution for social dilemmas in some cases. In this instance it enables the two homeowners to arrive at the cooperative solution rather than the dominant strategy equilibrium.

In fact, contracts of this kind among homeowners are quite common. They are called *covenants*. Many suburban settlements have covenants against dumping and similar nuisances. Of course, legislation serves the same purpose in many incorporated settlements.

In general, we will define the cooperative solution of a game as the list of strategies and payoffs that the participants would choose if they could commit themselves to a coordinated choice of strategies, whether by means of a contract or by any other form of enforcement.

By contrast, the dominant strategy equilibrium we have been considering is a noncooperative solution. A **noncooperative solution** of a game is the list of strategies and payoffs that the participants would choose if there is no possibility of a binding agreement to coordinate strategies. In a noncooperative solution,

> **Definition**
>
> ***Noncooperative Solution***—The **noncooperative solution** of a game is the list of strategies and payoffs that the participants would choose if there is no possibility to commit themselves to a coordinated joint strategy, so that each assumes the other will choose a best response strategy.

each player chooses his own best response to the strategies chosen by the others, and assumes that they do the same, so each player chooses a best response to the best response strategies of the others. This is true in the Dumping Game, for example—each player assumes that the other player will choose dump, so each player chooses the best response to dump.

What defines a social dilemma is the fact that a dominant strategy equilibrium exists and is contrary to the cooperative solution. Thus, for example, in the Prisoner's Dilemma, the two prisoners would certainly prefer to coordinate their strategies, refuse to confess, then serve only one year in prison. The third-degree treatment they receive is specifically designed to prevent them from coordinating their strategies. In the Advertising Game, again, not to advertise is the cooperative solution. When the government threatened to enforce a no-advertising policy, the tobacco companies were in a position to profit by complying. They could profit because, with government enforcement, the choice of a no-advertising strategy would be coordinated—both would adopt it simultaneously. In the Mobilization Game, peace is the cooperative solution. However, the timing limitations that resulted from the reliance on heavy artillery and rail mobility made it impossible for the two sides to coordinate their strategies.

Social dilemmas are a very important category of games, but dominant strategies and dominated strategies will be important in other kinds of games as well. Some games have dominant strategy equilibria and others do not. Also, some games that do have dominant strategy equilibria are not social dilemmas. But a dominant strategy equilibrium does not have to be inferior. Here is a business example that illustrates the possibility of a dominant strategy equilibrium that is not inferior to other strategy combinations.

Collaborative Product Development

Omnisoft Corp. and Microquip, Ltd. are considering a collaborative project of research and product development. Each company has two strategies to choose between: to commit plenty of resources to the project, or to hold back, and commit only minimal resources to the project. A difficulty that can arise in this sort of game is that neither partner can monitor or enforce the commitment of effort and resources by the other. In this case, however, we are assuming that the project has spinoff technologies—that is, technologies that the two companies can put to use profitably even if the collaborative project does not work out, and that will make a difference. The payoffs (in billions) are shown in Table 3.4.

When we examine the game to determine whether there are dominant strategies, we find that there are. Suppose Omnisoft's strategy is to commit. Microquip can then earn $5 billion by choosing "commit" as its own strategy, but only $3 billion by choosing "hold

Table 3.4 Collaborative Product Development

		Omnisoft	
		commit	hold back
Microquip	commit	5, 5	2, 3
	hold back	3, 2	1, 1

back." If Omnisoft's strategy were to hold back, then Microquip can earn $2 billion by choosing "commit" and only $1 billion by choosing "hold back." Thus, "commit" is the dominant strategy for Microquip. By symmetrical reasoning, "commit" is the dominant strategy for Omnisoft as well. Since both players have dominant strategies, this game has a dominant strategy equilibrium. The dominant strategy equilibrium is for each of the two firms to choose commit. This leads to the best possible outcome, with each firm earning $5 billion of profits.

This example contrasts with some of the other ones in that the dominant strategy equilibrium is just the outcome that the two companies want. They could not improve on this outcome even if they merged. The equilibrium at (commit, commit) is not only the dominant strategy equilibrium in this game. It is also the *cooperative solution*; that is, the outcome the players would choose if they could choose any pair of strategies at all. Games like this—in which the dominant strategy equilibrium is also the cooperative solution—do not play a large part in the literature of game theory. Most likely that is because they do not present any problems for people and for society. Game theory is a pragmatic study, oriented toward finding and solving problems. But games in which the cooperative solution is a dominant strategy equilibrium are logically possible, and may even be fairly common in business, since, after all, noncooperative equilibria are barriers to increasing the profits, and (as economist George Stigler observed) "business" consists of all the methods we know for eliminating barriers to increased profits.

A Closer Look

George Stigler 1911–1991

George Stigler was born in Renton, a suburb of Seattle, Washington, and went to the University of Chicago for graduate study in economics. He joined the faculty of the University of Chicago in 1958. He authored work on the history of economics, but it was his path-breaking work on the economics of industrial organization that won him the Nobel Memorial Prize in 1982 and the National Medal of Science in 1987.

©The Nobel Foundation

Cooperative and Noncooperative Games Yet Again

As we have seen, a number of important applications of game theory rest on the contrast of cooperative and dominant strategy noncooperative solutions, but not all games with dominant strategy equilibria are social dilemmas. Cooperative dominant games give no similar problems. Most game theorists would say that noncooperative solutions and equilibria are more fundamental, in that the participants in a cooperative agreement would choose whether to enter into the agreement in very much the way that they decide which strategy to choose in a noncooperative equilibrium.

Let's return to the social dilemma from earlier in the chapter, the Dumping Game. We have seen that one solution would be for the two landowners to sign a contract to have their garbage hauled. Once the contract has been drafted, each landowner must decide whether to accept the contract. If both accept the contract their payoffs are the cooperative solution payoffs: 4500, 4500. If either one refuses, they are back to the social dilemma with its equilibrium

Table 3.5 | An Acceptance Game in Normal Form

		Mr. Smith	
		refuse	accept
Mr. Jones	refuse	4000, 4000	4000, 4000
	accept	4000, 4000	4500, 4500

Table 3.6 | Best Responses for Mr. Smith

If Mr. Jones's strategy is	The best response for Mr. Smith is
accept	accept
reject	doesn't matter

payoff of 4000, 4000. Thus, they are playing a new game, the Acceptance Game, which is shown in Tables 3.5 and 3.6. In this case the noncooperative solution is (accept, accept), and it is also the cooperative solution. The proposal of the contract has transformed the social dilemma into a cooperative-dominant game. [1]

In most of this book (except Chapters 12 and 13) we will focus on noncooperative games and solutions.

A Political Game

Strategic choices have to be made not only in business, waste disposal, recreational games, and war—but also in routine peace-time politics. Let's consider a political example.

For this example, we have two candidates: Senator Blank and Governor Gray. Although the candidates have no personal preferences for one ideology over another, Senator Blank, as a Democrat, can take a position on the political left more credibly than Governor Gray, who is a Republican. Conversely, Governor Gray can take a position on the political right more credibly than Senator Blank. Adopting the left and right political positions are two of the strategies that they can choose. But they both have a third strategy available. Either or both of them can adopt a "middle of the road" political position.

In this case, therefore, we have a game in which each player has three strategies. We can express the game with three strategies in normal form very simply: The table will have three rows and three columns instead of two.

What are the payoffs in this game? We are assuming that the two candidates don't particularly care what positions they take. Their objective is not to advance a particular ideology, but just to get elected. Some German-speaking political economists express this motivation as *Stimmungsmaximieren*—maximizing the vote. That's probably a little bit of an exaggeration. What the candidate needs is not the largest possible vote but a vote over 50 percent. However, a landslide victory (winning by a large margin) can be a big advantage to the winning candidate. In any case, we can express the payoffs as the percentage of the vote the candidate can expect to receive.

---

1 The "accept" strategy does not exactly fit the definition we have given for a dominant strategy, since "accept" and "reject" have the same payoff for Mr. Jones if Mr. Smith chooses "reject." This is a tricky point we will not deal with until Chapter 11. Nevertheless, Smith and Jones should have no difficulty arriving at (accept, accept) as their noncooperative solution to the acceptance game.

Of course, that will depend on where the voters are. We shall assume that the voters are distributed symmetrically, with 30 percent favoring the political right, 30 percent favoring the political left, and 40 percent preferring to vote for a candidate with a middle-of-the-road position. The payoffs are shown in Table 3.7. We are assuming that if both candidates adopt the same middle-of-the-road position, they split the vote 50–50, and the winner is determined by random errors in counting the vote. In that case, each has an equal chance of victory. Likewise, if the Republican takes the right position and the Democrat takes the left, they split the vote 50–50. The candidates will take their voters and will split the middle voters.

Table 3.7 | Vote Payoffs for Two Candidates

		Governor Gray (Republican)		
		left	middle	right
Senator Blank (Democrat)	left	55, 45	30, 70	50, 50
	middle	75, 25	50, 50	70, 30
	right	50, 50	25, 75	45, 55

If the two candidates take different positions, the voters will mostly vote for the one nearest their position. However, not all of the voters on the left will choose the Republican candidate, even if that candidate takes the left position; and similarly, not all of the voters on the right will choose the Democrat if that candidate takes the right position.

If nobody takes the middle position, the middle vote divides equally. Because of this, and because of voter crossover, the payoff if both candidates campaign on the other party's platform is 50–50.

The best responses for Senator Blank are shown in Table 3.8. As we see, the "middle-of-the-road" strategy is a dominant strategy for Senator Blank. And even though the game is not perfectly symmetrical, we can reason symmetrically, and see that the "middle-of-the-road" strategy is also a dominant strategy for Governor Gray. Since both candidates have dominant strategies, we have a dominant strategy equilibrium.

Table 3.8 | Best Responses for Senator Blank

If Gray's strategy is	The best response for Blank is
left	middle
middle	middle
right	middle

This is not a social dilemma. Since the total vote is the same, 100 percent, regardless of which strategies the two candidates choose, there is no conflict between the dominant strategy equilibrium and the cooperative solution in this game. But that is looking at it from the point of view of the candidates, and not from the voters' point of view. This dominant strategy solution might not be a very good one from the voters' point of view. Only one political point of view, the middle-of-the-road viewpoint, is ever expressed. For those on the left or the right—who together are 60 percent of the voters in this case—it might seem that they have been left out entirely. In actual U.S. politics, we do hear this complaint expressed. Many Americans on the right and on the left seem to perceive that the deck is stacked against them. Perhaps this is a symptom that middle strategies are often dominant strategies in U.S. politics.

Table 3.9 | The Dumping Game with Three Strategies

		Mr. Smith		
		dump	hire truck	burn
Mr. Jones	dump	4000, 4000	5000, 3500	4750, 3750
	hire truck	3500, 5000	4500, 4500	4250, 4750
	burn	3750, 4750	4750, 4250	4650, 4650

Games with More than Two Strategies

Most of our example so far in this textbook have been *two-by-two games*—that is, games with just two participants, each of whom must choose between just two strategies. Like the political game, though, most real-world interactions involve more than two participants or more than two strategies or both, and sometimes the number of participants or strategies or both is very large indeed. In future chapters we will consider games with more than two participants. As we have seen, games with more than two strategies are only a little more complicated than two-by-two games, when they are represented in normal form. Only the table has to have more than two rows and columns.

For another example, let's go back to the Dumping Game. We will change it by adding a third strategy: burning the garbage. So now each of the two homeowners will have to choose among three strategies: hire a truck, dump, or burn. Burning will have the same effect on the value of both tracts of land. If one landowner burns, it will reduce the value of both pieces of land by $250, and if both burn, by $350, from what it would be otherwise. The payoff table is shown in Table 3.9. It differs from our previous examples only in that it has one more row and one more column.

As usual, we want to investigate the best responses of each player to the strategies that might be chosen by the other player. The best responses for each are shown in Table 3.10. Once again, we see that "dump" is a dominant strategy for Mr. Smith. By symmetrical reasoning, it is also a dominant strategy for Mr. Jones. So we will again have a dominant strategy equilibrium and a social dilemma.

Table 3.10 | Best Responses for Mr. Smith

If Mr. Jones's strategy is	The best response for Mr. Smith is
dump	dump
hire truck	dump
burn	dump

A Textbook-Writing Game

The concept of a dominant strategy equilibrium is a powerful one, but we will find that not all games have dominant strategy equilibria. Here is an example of a game of three strategies in which there is no dominant strategy equilibrium.

Professor Heffalump and Dr. Boingboing are the authors of rival textbooks of game theory. Their books are of equal quality in every way except length.[2] Both authors know that, given a choice between two well-written books, professors will usually choose the longer book. Each would like to get the larger audience, but writing a longer book is a bigger effort, so neither author wants to write a book longer than necessary to capture the bigger audience. Each of the two authors can choose among the following three strategies: write a book of 400 pages, 600 pages, or 800 pages. The payoffs are shown in Table 3.11.

Table 3.12 shows the best responses for Dr. Boingboing, depending on Prof. Heffalump's strategy choice. What we see is that Dr. Boingboing will want to choose a different strategy when Dr. Heffalump chooses a 400-page text than he will want to choose if Professor Heffalump chooses a 600- or 800-page text. Dr. Boingboing's idea is to write a text just one step longer than Dr. Heffalump's text, if he can. It follows that there is no one strategy that is Dr. Boingboing's best response to each of the different strategies Professor Heffalump might choose. In other words, there is no dominant strategy for Dr. Boingboing. And since the game is symmetrical, we can reason in just the same way and find that there is no dominant strategy for Professor Heffalump, either.

So the textbook writing game gives us an example of a game in which there is no dominant strategy. If we are to find a solution for a game like this one, it will have to be a different kind of solution. We will go on to investigate that in the next chapter. So we set this example aside for now, and will return to it in Chapter 4.

Table 3.11 Writing a Game Theory Textbook

		Prof. Heffalump		
		400 pp.	600 pp.	800 pp.
Dr. Boingboing	400 pp.	45, 45	15, 50	10, 40
	600 pp.	50, 15	40, 40	15, 45
	800 pp.	40, 10	45, 15	35, 35

Table 3.12 Best Responses for Dr. Boingboing

If Prof. Heffalump's strategy is	The best response for Dr. Boingboing is
400	600
600	800
800	800

---

2 This is an unrealistic simplifying assumption, since, of course, this book is far better than any other game theory textbook, page for page, in every way. By now you have probably noticed that we do not hesitate to make unrealistic simplifying assumptions in order to get the point across. Of course, textbooks vary in many ways, including the quality of the writing, the production, and whether the author has a sense of humor.

Summary

One objective of game theoretic analysis is to discover stable and predictable patterns of interactions among the players. Following the example of economics we call these patterns *equilibria*.

Since we assume that players are rational, their choices of strategies will be stable only if they are best-response strategies—the player's best response to the other players' strategies. If there is one strategy that is the best response to every strategy the other player or players might choose, we call that a dominant strategy. If every player in the game has a dominant strategy, and plays the dominant strategy, then we have a dominant strategy equilibrium.

A dominant strategy equilibrium is a noncooperative equilibrium, which means that each player acts independently, not coordinating the choice of strategies. If the players in the game are able to commit themselves to a coordinated choice of strategy, the strategies they choose are called a cooperative equilibrium. It is possible that the cooperative equilibrium may be the same as a dominant strategy equilibrium, but then again, it might not be.

One important class of games with dominant strategy equilibria are the social dilemmas. The familiar Prisoner's Dilemma is a typical example of this class. What the Prisoner's Dilemma has in common with every other social dilemma is that it has a dominant strategy equilibrium that conflicts with its cooperative equilibrium.

We have seen applications to environmental management, advertising, military mobilization, business, partnership, and politics. It seems clear that dominant strategy equilibrium has a wide range of application. Nevertheless, we have also seen that not all games have dominant strategies or dominant strategy equilibria.

Exercises and Discussion Questions

3.1 **Solving the Game.** Explain the advantages and disadvantages of the dominant strategy equilibrium as a solution concept for noncooperative games.

Table 3.E1 | An Effort Dilemma

		Mr. Jones	
		work	shirk
Mr. Smith	work	10, 10	2, 20
	shirk	20, 2	5, 5

3.2 **Effort Dilemmas.** One family of social dilemmas arises where a group of people are involved in some task that depends on the efforts of each of them. The strategy choices are "work" and "shirk." In an effort dilemma, one person's shirking places the burden of increased effort on the other(s). Then the payoff table could be something like Table 3.E1.

Are there any dominant strategies in this game? What? Has this game a dominant strategy equilibrium? What would be the cooperative equilibrium in this game?

In the Pacific Northwest of the United States, in the middle of the twentieth century, between two and three dozen plywood companies were worker owned. The worker-owners controlled the companies by majority rule and hired and fired the managers. However, the managers typically had discretion to assign and discipline work, and were, if anything, more powerful than managers in similar profit-seeking companies. Does the example suggest an explanation of this?

3.3 The Training Game. Two firms hire labor from the same unskilled pool. Each firm can either train its labor force or not. Training increases productivity, but there are spillovers in that the rival can hire the trained workers away. Thus, both firms always face the same productivity net of pay, although the net productivity is higher if more workers are trained. The relation between the proportion trained and net productivity is shown in Table 3.E2.

Table **3.E2** | Training

Proportion trained	Net productivity
0	5
50%	7.5
100%	10

(**Each firm trains either all of its workers or none,** so 0, 50 percent, and 100 percent trained are the only possibilities.) Each firm's profit is the net productivity shown in the table minus training cost. Training cost is 3 if the firm chooses to train its employees and zero otherwise.

Who are the "players" in this game? What are their strategies? Express this as a game in normal form. Are there dominant strategies in this game? If so, what? Is there a dominant strategy equilibrium? If so, what?

3.4 Poison Gas. Allemand and Angleterre are rival nations, often at war, and both can produce and deploy poison gas on the battlefield. In any battle, the payoffs to using gas are as in Table 3.E3.

Are there any dominant strategies in this game? If so, what? Has this game a dominant strategy equilibrium? What would be the cooperative equilibrium in this game? Is this game a social dilemma? If so, why?

Table **3.E3** | Gas

		Angleterre	
		gas	no
Allemand	gas	−8, −8	3, −10
	no	−10, 3	0, 0

Historically, poison gas was used in World War I, but not in World War II, although Germany opposed France and Britain in the second war as it had in the first. The consensus explanation was that if one side were to use gas in a battle, the other side would retaliate with gas in subsequent battles, with the result that the first user would nevertheless be worse off. Discuss the limitations of the dominant strategy equilibrium in the analysis of social dilemmas in the light of this contrast.

3.5 Running for Office. Richard Nixon, a highly successful Republican politician, said that the way for a Republican to be elected to public office was to "run to the right in the primary election, but run to the center in the general election." The political example in this chapter gives an explanation for the advice to "run to the center in the general election." How would you explain "run to the right in the primary?" *Note:* In the political systems of many American states, including California (Nixon's home state), primary elections are held to determine the nominees of the major parties, and are limited to voters registered as members of those respective parties. The nominees selected then compete in a general election. *Hint:* It may be that registered members of the Republican Party are not distributed over the political spectrum as the general population is.

3.6 Happy Hour. Refer to problem 4 in Chapter 1.

Are there any dominant strategies in this game? If so, what? Has this game a dominant strategy equilibrium? What would be the cooperative equilibrium in this game? Is this game a social dilemma? If so, why?

Nash Equilibrium 4

In the last chapter we saw that some games have dominant strategies and dominant strategy equilibria. When a dominant strategy equilibrium exists, it provides a very powerful analysis of noncooperative choices of strategy. However, we also saw that some games do not have dominant strategy equilibria. In order to analyze those games, we will need a different equilibrium concept: Nash equilibrium. The Nash equilibrium concept was named after the mathematician who discovered it, John Nash. Nash's life has had its sad aspects, which are related in a recent biography and movie based on it.[1] Nevertheless, no one has had a greater impact on game theory than John Nash.

As usual, we want to begin with an example. In fact we already have the example from the end of the last chapter: the game of writing a textbook.

A Textbook-Writing Game, Continued

In this game, recall, the players are two professors who are writing rival textbooks of game theory. Each one expects a better payoff if his textbook is longer than the rival textbook. The strategies for each author are to write a book of 400, 600, or 800 pages. The payoffs are shown in Table 4.1. This table is the same as Table 3.11 but is repeated here for convenience.

We already know that this game does not have a dominant strategy equilibrium because Dr. Boingboing's best response strategy depends on the strategy Dr. Heffalump chooses, and vice versa. Table 4.2 shows each author's best response, depending on which strategy the

To best understand this chapter 4

To best understand this chapter you need to have a good understanding of the material from Chapters 1–3. Review the last example from Chapter 3 in particular.

A Closer Look

John Forbes Nash 1928–

John Forbes Nash, a mathematician, was born in Bluefield, West Virginia on June 13, 1928, and lives in Princeton. While a graduate student at Princeton, he proved that the noncooperative equilibrium concept now called "Nash equilibrium" is applicable to nonconstant sum games, for which he shared the Nobel Memorial Prize in 1994. He also developed a mathematical bargaining theory for cooperative games and made other contributions to mathematics. Nash was troubled for many years by mental illness, portrayed in the 2001 movie, *A Beautiful Mind*.

©The Nobel Foundation

---

1 The book is by Sylvia Nasar, *A Beautiful Mind* (New York: Simon and Schuster, 1998).

Table 4.1 | Writing a Game Theory Textbook

Repeats Table 3.11, Chapter 3

		Prof. Heffalump		
		400 pp.	600 pp.	800 pp.
Dr. Boingboing	400 pp.	45, 45	15, 50	10, 40
	600 pp.	50, 15	40, 40	15, 45
	800 pp.	40, 10	45, 15	35, 35

Table 4.2 | Best Responses for Authors of Game Theory Texts

If one author's strategy is	The best response for the other author is
400	600
600	800
800	800

> **Definition**
>
> **Nash Equilibrium**—In any noncooperative game, when each player chooses the strategy that is the best response to the strategies that the other players choose, that is a **Nash equilibrium**.

other author chooses. This is a repeat of Table 3.12, except that it does not matter which author is responding to which.

Looking at Table 4.2, we can see that the 800-page strategy has an interesting property. If both authors choose the strategy of writing 800-page textbooks, each one is choosing his best response to the other author's strategy. Professor Heffalump is choosing his best response to Dr. Boingboing's strategy, and Dr. Boingboing is choosing his best response to Professor Heffalump's strategy. And that is *not* true for any other combination of strategies. For example, if Dr. Boingboing writes a 600-page text, and Professor Heffalump writes a 400-page text, then Dr. Boingboing is choosing his best response to Professor Heffalump's strategy; but Professor Heffalump can do better by increasing the length of his text to 800 pages, for a payoff of 45 (as we see at the middle cell of the right column of Table 4.1). However, at that point, Dr. Boingboing can do better. Dr. Boingboing's best response to a strategy of 800 pages is to increase his own length to 800 pages. Thus, the middle cell in neither the left or right column of Table 4.1 has both players choosing their best response. Only the bottom right cell, where each one chooses a length of 800 pages, has that *interesting property*.

This "interesting property" means that (800, 800) is the **Nash equilibrium** of the textbook writing game. A Nash equilibrium is defined as a list of strategies, with one strategy for each player, such that each strategy is the best response to all the other strategies in the list. In this case, since we have only two players, there are only two strategies in the list: one for Professor Heffalump and one for Dr. Boingboing.

Even though it is not a dominant strategy equilibrium, this Nash equilibrium is the predictable result of rational, self-interested, noncooperative play in the textbook writing game.

Perhaps you have wondered why your textbooks are so long. If so, at least you can see that game theory does have something to do with real life. Actually, it is not so much the number of pages that brings a larger audience to a textbook, as it is the topics and examples the textbook includes. For a textbook author, it is always a worry that if a favorite topic is left out, or a favorite example is omitted, some professors will decide that the textbook is not suitable for their classes, and the text will lose some of the audience it could otherwise gain. So the rule is, "when in doubt, put it in." But more topics and more examples mean more pages.[2]

Nash Equilibrium

The Textbook-Writing Game gives us an example of a game that has no dominant strategies, but does have a Nash equilibrium. We can think of a Nash

Heads Up!

Here are some concepts we will develop as this chapter goes along:

Nash Equilibrium: For any game in normal form, if there is a list of strategies, with one strategy per player, such that each strategy on the list is the best response to the other strategies on the list, that list of strategies is a *Nash equilibrium*.

Coordination Game: A game with two or more Nash equilibria may present a coordination problem, in that the players could have difficulty deciding which equilibrium will occur and thus in coordinating their strategies. This is a *coordination game*.

Schelling Point: In a coordination game, if some clue can lead the participants to believe that one equilibrium is more likely to be realized than the other, the more likely equilibrium is called a *Schelling point*.

equilibrium in general terms as follows: If there are two strategies (or more generally, one strategy per player) such that each strategy is a best response to the other strategy (or strategies), then we describe that list of strategies as Nash equilibrium strategies. If Nash equilibrium strategies exist in a game, and the players choose those strategies, we have a Nash equilibrium in the game.

We see this in the example of the Textbook-Writing Game. The list of strategies is (800, 800)—800 for Professor Heffalump and 800 for Dr. Boingboing. Since 800 is the best response to 800, from the point of view of each of the two authors, this list of strategies is a Nash equilibrium.

Like the dominant strategy equilibrium, the Nash equilibrium reflects rational action on the part of both authors. Neither player can do better by choosing some other strategy as long as the other player persists in the strategy he or she has chosen. The strategies are chosen independently, with no coordination. Also like the dominant strategy equilibrium, the Nash equilibrium is noncooperative. Looking back at Table 4.1, we see that both authors would be better off if they both wrote texts of 400 or even 600 pages. The cooperative solution of this game would be for both to write textbooks 400 pages in length.

However, the concept of Nash equilibrium is more general than dominant strategy equilibrium. Notice that every dominant strategy equilibrium is also a Nash equilibrium,

2 Of course, the author of this book is the unique exception, choosing just those examples and topics you need to master in order to understand game theory—and no others. It's just that I believe every bit of this is really, really, really important.

just as every cocker spaniel is a dog. For example, remember the Prisoner's Dilemma. For each player, "confess" is a dominant strategy, and there is a dominant strategy equilibrium. But it is equally true that when one prisoner chooses "confess," then "confess" is the other prisoner's best response. Each prisoner is choosing his best response to the strategy chosen by the other, so it is indeed a Nash equilibrium. But not every Nash equilibrium is a dominant strategy equilibrium, just as not every dog is a cocker spaniel. Some Nash equilibria are not like dominant strategy equilibria in that the best response strategy for one player depends on the strategy chosen by the other player.

This is illustrated by the Venn diagram in Figure 4.1. A social dilemma is a particular kind of dominant strategy equilibrium, and a dominant strategy equilibrium is a particular kind of a Nash equilibrium, and a Nash equilibrium is a particular kind of noncooperative equilibrium.

Now let's put these ideas to work with another example, applied to a very basic business problem: the choice of a retail location.

Location, Location, Location

For this example, we have two department stores: Gacy's and Mimbel's. Each of the two stores has to choose a location for its one store in Gotham City. Each store will choose one of four location strategies:

Figure **4.1** | Noncooperative Equilibrium Concepts

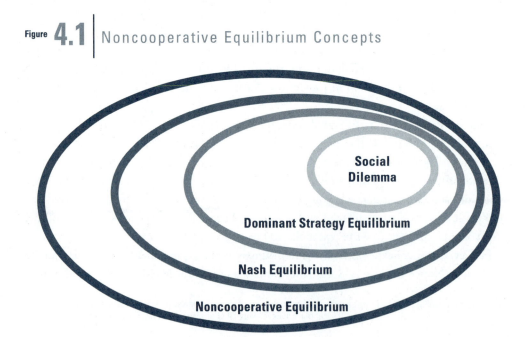

Table 4.3 | Payoffs in the Location Game

		Gacy's			
		Uptown	Center City	East Side	West Side
Mimbel's	Uptown	30, 40	50, 95	55, 95	55, 120
	Center City	115, 40	100, 100	130, 85	120, 95
	East Side	125, 45	95, 65	60, 40	115, 120
	West Side	105, 50	75, 75	95, 95	35, 55

- Uptown
- Center City
- East Side
- West Side

The payoffs for the two companies are shown in Table 4.3. Here are some of the ideas behind the payoffs:

- If both companies locate in the same part of town, they will split the market there. Unless the market is very large, they will make more money locating in different markets.

- Mimbel's stylish reputation sells particularly well on the wealthy East Side.

- Gacy's reputation for value sells particularly well on the middle-class West Side.

- No one does very well Uptown, an area that is, frankly, a bit down at the heels.

- Center City draws its customers not from residents but from commuters, people who have come for shows and restaurants, and people who've come in from the other areas specifically to shop. It can get the largest market, especially if there are no competing department stores in the other areas.

There are 16 combinations of strategies here, so it may take a little time to check them all; but once we have done it we will find that there is just one Nash equilibrium. The Nash equilibrium is found when both stores locate in Center City. Whenever one store chooses to locate in Center City, a location in Center City is the best response for the other one—perhaps because that is the only way that the competing store can draw customers from all four areas in the city. There is no other combination of strategies such that each one is the best response to the other one—no other Nash equilibrium.

Heuristic Methods of Finding Nash Equilibria

Table 4.4 | Writing a Game Theory Textbook with Underlines

Approximately repeats Table 3.11, Chapter 3

		Prof. Heffalump		
		400 pp.	600 pp.	800 pp.
Dr. Boingboing	400 pp.	45, 45	15, <u>50</u>	10, 40
	600 pp.	<u>50</u>, 15	40, 40	15, <u>45</u>
	800 pp.	40, 10	<u>45</u>, 15	<u>35</u>, <u>35</u>

Table 4.5 | The Prisoner's Dilemma with Arrows to Indicate Strategy Shifts

Approximately repeats Table 1.1, Chapter 1

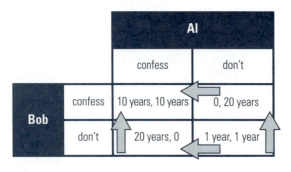

Checking each combination of strategies to find a Nash equilibrium can be tedious as the number of strategies gets larger. There are **heuristic** methods, using visualization, to eliminate nonequilibrium strategies and find the equilibria if there are any. In case the word *heuristic* is new to you, we can say that heuristic methods of problem solving are methods that are informal or inconclusive, by contrast with mathematical solution methods; but are also fast and usually reliable. In this case the methods are informal, involving visualization and a little drawing.

The idea behind the Nash equilibrium is that a strategy will be chosen only if it is a best response. One simple way to highlight the best response is to underline the payoff that is the best response for each strategy. This is illustrated for the Textbook-Writing Game in Table 4.4. As we see, a Nash equilibrium shows up as a cell in which both payoffs are underlined.

Another method that is often used gives a little more information, but is messier. If either player can get a better payoff by changing his strategy, while the other player or players keep their strategies unchanged, then the player will make the change. To visualize this, we can draw an arrow from the old cell to the new one. Draw a left-to-right or right-to-left arrow for the player who chooses the columns, and an up-or-down arrow for the player who picks the rows.

This will be easiest for a two-by-two game, so let's try it with the Prisoner's Dilemma. Table 4.5 shows the Prisoner's Dilemma with arrows to show the direction of strategy shifts. Remember, for the Prisoner's Dilemma, the numbers are penalties and so smaller numbers are preferable to bigger numbers. Thus, for example, if Al did not confess, Bob would shift from don't confess to confess to reduce his time in prison from one year to nothing. The other arrows are interpreted in the same way. Using this approach, we can eliminate all the other possibilities except the equilibrium.

The Textbook-Writing game is a little more complicated, of course. It is shown with arrows as Table 4.6. If you look at the arrows carefully, you will see that there are arrows leading away from every cell except the one at the lower right—the Nash equilibrium cell. Since it is a best response for each player, neither player can improve by moving away, and that's why there are no arrows leading away from it. In this way, the arrows help us to visualize a Nash equilibrium. By drawing the arrows, we see a bit more about the dynamics of the game, and why the Nash equilibrium is at the lower right. The arrows from the first column and row lead to the second, but it is not stable either, because the arrows from the second column and row lead to the third.

Actually, it is probably easier to draw your own arrows than it is to read arrows that have already been put there—they get a bit messy. So give it a try. Make a copy of Table 4.3 and draw in the arrows to visualize the equilibrium in the Location Game.

Table 4.6 | Writing a Game Theory Textbook with Arrows

Approximately repeats Table 3.11, Chapter 3

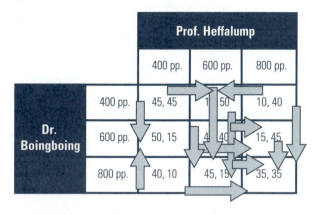

		Prof. Heffalump		
		400 pp.	600 pp.	800 pp.
Dr. Boingboing	400 pp.	45, 45	1, 50	10, 40
	600 pp.	50, 15	4, 40	15, 45
	800 pp.	40, 10	45, 15	35, 35

Choosing Radio Formats

We have had a number of examples of games with unique Nash equilibria. But there are also games with two or more Nash equilibria. Here is an example to illustrate that possibility.

We have two radio stations, WIRD and KOOL. Each station can choose among three broadcast formats: rock-n-roll, country music, and all talk. These are their three strategies. The payoffs for these two radio stations are expressed as the percent of the potential audience they obtain. The biggest audience is for rock-n-roll, with a 70 percent audience share; but if both stations choose that format they will split the audience for rock-and-roll and each be left with only 35 percent of the potential audience. Table 4.7 shows the payoffs for the two stations based on that kind of reasoning.

Table 4.7 | Choosing Radio Formats

		WIRD		
		rock	country	all talk
KOOL	rock	35, 35	50, 40	80, 10
	country	40, 50	20, 20	40, 10
	all talk	10, 80	10, 40	5, 5

Try underlining, or drawing the arrows in, to eliminate all of the non-Nash strategy combinations. Once you have eliminated all the non-Nash pairs, you will find that there are two strategy pairs left—(country, rock) and (rock, country). Examining those two strategy pairs, we find that they are both Nash equilibria: country is a best response to rock, and rock is a best response to country, from the viewpoint of either radio station. In this example, the important thing is to avoid congestion. If both stations choose the same format, they will lose, even if the format is the most popular format, rock-n-roll. As long as they both avoid the unpopular all-talk format, and choose different formats, neither can improve the payoff by choosing a different format strategy. That doesn't mean that they're equally well off in an equilibrium. The station that happens to have the rock format will have the larger audience. But the one with the country format still cannot do any better: if he moves into rock, the rock audience is split; and a move to all talk is simply a disaster.

The fact that there are two Nash equilibria in this game creates a bit of a problem. It is an embarrassment of riches. If we think of the game as a mathematical problem to be solved, we can see why this is an embarrassment. We want an answer to the question: "What strategies will players choose if they act independently, rationally, and with self-interest?" In this case, because there are two equilibria, we don't have a clear answer to that question. That's why we see the possibility that there can be more than one Nash equilibrium as a shortcoming of the Nash equilibrium concept. A good deal of game theoretic research has been devoted to "refining" the Nash equilibrium concept, in the hope that we could always have just one unique solution. But that doesn't really seem possible. It just seems to be in the nature of some game-like interactions that they have more than one best response equilibrium—as in this instance of the game of choosing radio formats—with its strong penalty on congestion.

There is also a parallel problem for the two radio stations themselves. As each one tries to think through its best choice of a radio format, each radio station will find that it cannot make a clear choice unless it has a pretty definite idea what the other station will do. This may or may not be a problem in practice. Suppose that radio station KOOL has been a successful rock station for many years while station WIRD has never played rock before. Then WIRD can reasonably expect that KOOL will continue to play rock, and that gives WIRD a good reason to assume that the (rock, country) equilibrium will be the one realized; and that's a good reason to choose the country format.

In this example, WIRD has gotten a clue from the history of the other station that makes one equilibrium more likely than another. An equilibrium that can be selected on the basis of this kind of clue is called a focal point or a **Schelling point**, in honor of the great game theorist Thomas Schelling.

If there is no clue, however, the existence of two or more Nash equilibria remains an unsolved problem.

> ### Definition
>
> *Schelling Point*—If a game has two or more Nash equilibria, and some clue can lead the participants to believe that one equilibrium is more likely to be realized than the other, the more likely equilibrium is called a **Schelling point**, also known, more generally, as a "focal point."

The Heave-Ho Game

Let's look at another example with more than one Nash equilibrium and think a little further about Schelling points. This will be another two-by-two game—two players, each with two strategies—a bit like the Prisoner's Dilemma. We will call it the Heave-Ho Game. In this game, Jim and Karl are driving down a back road and are stopped by a fallen tree across the road. If they can move the tree out of the way, then they can go ahead. Otherwise, they will have to turn back. In order to move the tree, they will both have to heave as hard as they can to push it out of the road. So each one has a choice of two strategies: heave or don't heave.

If they both heave, they can successfully push the tree out of the road. We will call the payoff in that case 5 to each of them. If one heaves and the other does not, the one who heaves is injured, a minus 10, while the other one has the minor inconvenience of taking the injured party to the hospital: a payoff of 0. If neither man heaves, so that they have to go back, we consider that a payoff of 1 to each. The payoffs are shown in Table 4.8.

Looking at this payoff table, and perhaps drawing a few underlines or arrows, we see that there are two Nash equilibria: (heave, heave) and (don't, don't). However, these two equilibria are different in one obvious and important way. The first one gives each player a better payoff than the second one—and, in fact, a better payoff than any another strategy combination. We express this by saying that the (heave, heave) equilibrium is **payoff dominant**. This unique characteristic seems to make the equilibrium at (heave, heave) a Schelling point. It is so obviously superior (it would seem) that each player could assume that the other player would heave and so would himself choose to heave.

And yet experience might still trump this reasonable line of thought. Suppose Jim knows from past experience that Karl is so lazy that he will never make a real effort. Also, suppose Karl knows Jim's opinion of him. Expecting Karl to shirk and not to heave, Jim will not heave

A Closer Look

Thomas C. Schelling 1921–

Born in Oakland, California in 1921, Thomas Schelling matriculated at the University of California at Berkeley and earned his Ph.D. in Economics at Harvard. His work in government service (1945–53) and at the Rand Corporation (1958–59) seems to have been an important influence on his ideas. He returned to Harvard in 1958, joined the faculty of the Kennedy School of Government in 1969, and has been at the University of Maryland since 1990. Among his many important works on economic and strategic behavior, *The Strategy of Conflict*, 1960, stands out as a key contribution to game theory.

Courtesy, Professor Thomas Schelling

Table 4.8 | The Heave-Ho Game

		Jim	
		heave	don't
Karl	heave	5, 5	−10, 0
	don't	0, −10	1, 1

Definition

Payoff Dominant and Risk Dominant Equilibria—If there are more than one Nash equilibria, and one of the equilibria yields a higher payoff to each player than the others do, it is said to be the **payoff dominant** equilibrium. If one of the equilibria gives the smallest maximum loss to each player, it is said to be the **risk dominant** equilibrium.

The Basis of a Schelling Point Like history or experience, a prominent natural or social landmark can be the basis of a Schelling point. In the 1960s, in his classes at Yale University, Schelling would give his students the following mind experiment: You have to meet your friend in New York on a specific date, but you do not know the time or the place, and neither does your friend. Where will you go to meet your friend, and at what time? Most students answered clearly that they would look for the friend under the clock at Grand Central Station at noon. For students in New Haven, in the middle of the twentieth century, Grand Central Station under the clock was the conventional meeting place. The convention is enough to break the uncertainty and enable the students to come up with the same meeting place. (Other residents of the New York area, or other regions, might have thought of other places. For example, tourists from other American regions might have thought instead of the Empire State Building. Context counts.) And noon, of course, is a prominent landmark on the clock face: both hands straight up. Once again, the landmark is enough to resolve the uncertainty so that the students could come at the same time. It probably would have worked. "Meet me in Manhattan on the first—at the obvious time and place."

either, to avoid the injury and the payoff of minus 10. And Karl can anticipate that. Even if Karl thinks Jim's opinion is mistaken, Karl will not heave for fear that he will get the injury. So we can't be sure that (heave, heave) will be the equilibrium that will occur unless we know something about Karl and Jim's opinions of one another.

Another possibility in this game is that both might choose to avoid the risk of a −10 payoff by choosing (don't, don't). Because it avoids the risk of a large loss, this is called a **risk dominant** Nash equilibrium. This property, too, could attract attention and make (don't, don't) a Schelling point. In experimental studies, both payoff-dominant and risk-dominant strategies can be attractive in different games.

The Heave-Ho Game is an example of a pure coordination game. Both players can get their very best payoff only if they can coordinate their choices of strategies. That seems pretty easy, but as we've seen, they may not succeed if they do not expect to. Success or failure in the coordination game may be partly a self-confirming prophecy.

Market Day

In the medieval European province of Uraltland, each of the towns had a weekly market day. But different towns held their markets on different days—Heimatsdorf had its market on Monday, Freiburg on Tuesday, Kleinstadt on Wednesday, and so on. There seems to be no particular reason for a town to choose one day or another, but each of the towns has had its market day longer than anyone can remember, and none would consider changing. How are we to explain this?

First, it just isn't practical to hold the market every day. With the transportation technology and road system of Europe 700 years ago, a trip of even a few miles to and from the nearby village, laden with goods one way or the other, would take a large fraction of the day, leaving only a few hours for buying and selling and none for working on the farm.

Let's look at it from the point of view of two villagers—one buyer (Simon) and one seller (Pieman). We will think of their problem as a game in normal form. Each can go to market on one of the days of the week (except Sunday), and these six days are their strategies. If they arrive on the same day, then they can trade for mutual benefit and payoffs of (3, 3), but if they arrive on different days, they cannot trade and they bear the costs of travel with no benefits to offset them, leaving the payoffs as the travel costs (−1, −1). Thus, the payoffs look like Table 4.9.

This is a pure coordination game with six Nash equilibria, the six strategy pairs in which the two villagers choose the same day. As before, the problem for the players in the game is which Nash equilibrium will occur? In this case, the logic of the game does not provide a Schelling point. Instead, in each of the towns, it is history that provides the Schelling point: Market day has always been on Tuesday (in Freiburg), that is the custom in Freiburg, and the custom provides the Schelling point for Freiburg. Custom also supplies the (different) Schelling points in Heimatsdorf and Kleinstadt, and all the other towns of Uraltland.

There are two important points here. On the one hand, custom, convention, and tradition can supply the solution to games with multiple Nash equilibria in some cases. On the other hand, Nash equilibria in coordination games can explain how customs and conventions that seem quite arbitrary are nevertheless quite stable: they are Nash equilibria, and therefore self-enforcing.

That Movie, Again

In the first chapter, we looked at an example from the cinema version of *A Beautiful Mind*. In the example, John Nash solves the Blonde Problem by suggesting that each of his companions in the bar should pursue a brunette, rather than "canceling one another out" by all pursuing the

Table 4.9 | Market Day

		Simon (the buyer)					
		Monday	Tuesday	Wednesday	Thursday	Friday	Saturday
Pieman (the seller)	Monday	3, 3	−1, −1	−1, −1	−1, −1	−1, −1	−1, −1
	Tuesday	−1, −1	3, 3	−1, −1	−1, −1	−1, −1	−1, −1
	Wednesday	−1, −1	−1, −1	3, 3	−1, −1	−1, −1	−1, −1
	Thursday	−1, −1	−1, −1	−1, −1	3, 3	−1, −1	−1, −1
	Friday	−1, −1	−1, −1	−1, −1	−1, −1	3, 3	−1, −1
	Saturday	−1, −1	−1, −1	−1, −1	−1, −1	−1, −1	3, 3

Refinements of Nash Equilibrium When a game has multiple Nash equilibria, we might want to narrow the field—ruling some out as being less likely to be chosen. There are a number of concepts in noncooperative game theory called *refinements* of Nash equilibrium that do that—they provide reasonable grounds for excluding some of the plural Nash equilibria and focusing on others. Unfortunately, none has universal application, and so we have to be careful to apply each to the kinds of games for which it makes sense. We will take up a number of refinements in this book.

Table **4.10** | A Two-By-Two Blonde Problem

Repeats Table 1.2, Chapter 1

		John	
		pursue blonde	pursue brunette
Reinhard	pursue blonde	0, 0	2, 1
	pursue brunette	1, 2	1, 1

one blonde in the bar. We now want to ask, is this a Nash equilibrium? The game is shown in Table 4.10.

The movie implies that the solution is (1, 1). But that is not a best-response solution and will not be stable. If Reinhard knows that John will pursue a brunette, then Reinhard's best response is to pursue the blonde, and conversely. This is a coordination game somewhat like the Choosing Radio Formats game. The only Nash equilibria in pure strategies are (1, 2) and (2, 1). As in the Radio Formats game, there are two problems with this. First, the payoffs in equilibrium are unequal, so someone is going to have to settle for the lower payoff for no very good reason. Second, there is apparently no Schelling point in this game, so there is a danger that the two males may guess differently as to which equilibrium will occur. If each one guesses that the other will pursue a brunette, then each will pursue the blonde, and we are back where we started from at (0, 0). It seems that a Nash equilibrium is just what the fictional John Nash in the movie was trying to avoid.

But perhaps that is not the end of the story. We will return to this movie problem one more time in Chapter 9.

An Escape-Evasion Game

Patrolman Pete is pursuing Footpad Fred, a suspected burglar. Fred arrives at a dead end on Riverfront Road, while Pete is out of sight behind him. Fred can turn either north or south. (These are his strategies.) If he turns south, he can take a ferryboat to another jurisdiction and escape. If he turns north, he can hide out in his girlfriend's apartment until she gets a car and drives him to another jurisdiction, where they can escape together. After Fred has made his decision and disappeared, Pete comes to the dead end. Like Fred, he has to decide: north or south. If he turns south and Fred also went south, then Pete can cut Fred off before he boards the ferry and arrest him. If he turns north and catches Fred at the girlfriend's apartment, he can arrest her as an accessory, and bagging them both will get him a modest bonus for initiative. However, if he turns in the wrong direction, he will not catch Fred, and the department will be disappointed in him. Worse, if he turns north and enters Fred's girlfriend's apartment when Fred has gone south, Pete will be reprimanded for harassing the girlfriend.

The payoffs are as shown in Table 4.11.

As the arrows in Table 4.11 show, none of the cells in this game correspond to a Nash equilibrium. No matter which cell we begin with, one or the other of the opponents will want to switch. The unpleasant truth is that some games have no Nash equilibrium whatever in pure strategies.[3]

For another example, we can look at a schoolyard game, a game that I myself played illicitly at Blanchard School in Louisiana in the early 1950s. The game is Matching Pennies. One player is identified as "even" and the other as "odd." The two players each show a penny, with either the head or the tail showing upward. If both show the same side of the coin, then "even" keeps both pennies. If the two show different sides of the coin, then "odd" keeps both pennies. The payoff table is shown as Table 4.12. Once again, we see that Matching Pennies has no Nash equilibria in pure strategies.

It is not surprising that a children's schoolyard game has no simple Nash equilibrium. Probably it is the uncertainty that the game has, because it has no Nash equilibria in pure strategies, that makes it fun to play. For our purposes, these two games serve to remind us that we must not take anything for granted. So long as we are studying games with just a finite list of strategies, we cannot assume that every game will have a Nash equilibrium.

Table 4.11 Payoffs in an Escape-Evasion Game

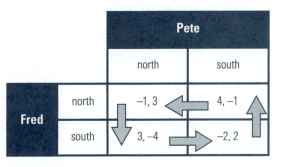

		Pete	
		north	south
Fred	north	−1, 3	4, −1
	south	3, −4	−2, 2

Table 4.12 Matching Pennies

		Roger	
		heads	tails
Barry	heads	−1, 1	1, −1
	tails	1, −1	−1, 1

Summary

In a game that does not have a dominant strategy equilibrium, the strategy choices of all the players will nevertheless be stable, predictable, and rational if every player is playing his best response to the strategies the other players play. In that case, we call it a Nash equilibrium. Remember that a dominant strategy equilibrium is a kind of Nash equilibrium, but there are other Nash equilibria that are not dominant strategy equilibria. A Nash equilibrium is a noncooperative equilibrium, and therefore may or may not agree with a cooperative equilibrium for the game.

Nash equilibria may be found by elimination—that is, by eliminating all strategy pairs that are not both best responses to one another. This can be visualized by drawing an arrow from the cell to another cell on the same row or column that gives a better payoff.

3 The lists of strategies we have been dealing with so far are *pure strategies*. It is possible to combine pure strategies in more complicated kinds of strategies that are not so pure—but we will not get into that until Chapter 8.

Nash equilibrium is a very general rational solution to a game, but it has some shortcomings from that point of view.

- The Nash equilibrium may not be unique. Some games have two or more Nash equilibria. In such a case, the players in the game may find it difficult to determine which Nash equilibrium will occur. This depends on the information they have available. If there is a signal or clue that enables them to see one equilibrium as being much more likely than another, that equilibrium is called a Schelling point. It seems that not all games with multiple equilibria have Schelling points, however.

- Not all games (that have only a finite number of strategies) have Nash equilibria. Thus far, we have looked only at games with a finite list of strategies— usually no more than two, three, or four. Out of that finite list of strategies, there might not be any Nash equilibrium.

Nevertheless, simple games, with all their difficulties, have been applied to a wide range of problems.

Exercises and Discussion Questions

4.1 Solving the Game. Explain the advantages and disadvantages of Nash equilibrium as a solution concept for noncooperative games.

4.2 Location, Location, Location (Again). Not all location problems have similar solutions. Here is another one: Gacy's and Mimbel's are deciding where to put their stores in Metropolis, the town across the river from Gotham City. The three strategies for Metropolis are to locate downtown, in Old Town, or in the Garden District. The payoffs are shown in Table 4.E1.

Does this game have Nash equilibria? What strategies, if so? Which strategies would you predict that Gacy's and Mimbel's would choose? Compare and contrast this game with the location game in the chapter. What would you say about the relative importance of congestion in the location decisions of the firms in the two cases?

Table 4.E1 | Payoffs in a New Location Game

		Gacy's		
		Downtown	Old Town	Garden District
Mimbel's	Downtown	70, 60	60, 120	80, 100
	Old Town	110, 70	40, 40	120, 110
	Garden District	120, 80	110, 120	50, 50

4.3 Drive On. Two cars (a Mercedes and a Buick) meet, crossing, at the intersection of Pigtown Pike and Hiccup Lane. Each has two strategies: wait or go. The payoffs are shown in Table 4.E2.

Discuss this game, from the point of view of noncooperative solutions. Does it have a dominant strategy equilibrium? Does it have Nash equilibria? What strategies, if so? Would you predict which strategies rational drivers would choose in this game? Which? Why? Pigtown Borough has decided to put a stoplight at this intersection. How could that make a difference in the game?

4.4 Rock, Paper, Scissors. Here is another common schoolyard game called Rock, Paper, Scissors. Two children (we will call them Susan and Tess) simultaneously choose a symbol for rock, paper, or scissors. The rules for winning and losing are as follows:

- Paper covers rock (paper wins over rock)

- Rock breaks scissors (rock wins over scissors)

- Scissors cut paper (scissors win over paper)

The payoff table is shown as Table 4.E3.

Discuss this game, from the point of view of noncooperative solutions. Does it have a dominant strategy equilibrium? Does it have Nash equilibria? What strategies, if so? How do you think the little girls will try to play the game?

Table 4.E2 | The Drive-On Game

		Mercedes	
		wait	go
Buick	wait	0, 0	1, 5
	go	5, 1	−100, −100

Table 4.E3 | Rock, Paper, Scissors

		Susan		
		paper	rock	scissors
Tess	paper	0, 0	1, −1	−1, 1
	rock	−1, 1	0, 0	1, −1
	scissors	1, −1	−1, 1	0, 0

4.5 The Great Escape. Refer to Chapter 2, Question 2.

Discuss this game from the point of view of noncooperative solutions. Does it have a dominant strategy equilibrium? Does it have a Nash equilibrium? What strategies, if so? How can these two opponents each rationally choose a strategy?

4.6 Sibling Rivalry. Refer to Chapter 2, Question 1.

Discuss this game from the point of view of noncooperative solutions. Does it have a dominant strategy equilibrium? Determine all the Nash equilibria in this game. Do some Nash equilibria seem likelier to occur than others? Why?

Some Classical Cases in Game Theory

In some ways, Chapter 4 is the key chapter in this book. Nash equilibrium, the topic of that chapter, plays a role in all analyses of noncooperative games, and can enter into cooperative game examples as well. Thus, we will be using those concepts again and again as we continue through the book. In this chapter we consider some special cases in Nash equilibrium and closely related concepts that have played an important role in game theory and continue to motivate much game theoretic work today. These well-understood classical cases are part of the vocabulary of game theory, and so understanding them is an important step toward more advanced work and applications.

A Quiz Game

Olga and Pamela are contestants in a quiz show, but the questions are so easy that both women are confident that they can answer every question. Of course, that isn't the whole story. The rules of the game are as follows:

1.   To answer a question a contestant has to sound a buzzer.

2.   If one contestant buzzes, she gets to answer the question.

3.   A correct answer scores one point.

4.   The contestant who does not buzz is penalized one point.

5.   If neither contestant buzzes, the question is passed, with no score for anyone.

6.   Also (this is the twist) if both contestants buzz, the question is passed with no score for anyone.

The contestants have two strategies: buzz or don't buzz. The payoff table is shown in Table 5.1.

It is easy to see that this game has a dominant strategy equilibrium (buzz, buzz). The result is that both contestants always buzz, and no one ever scores.[1] It is a bit like a Prisoner's Dilemma, but not exactly, since the players would not be any better off if neither of them buzzed—they would be back to the same result.

This game illustrates another concept: The total payoffs for the two players always add up to zero. That means this is a **zero-sum game**. In many of the other games we have explored in this text, the total payoffs depend on the strategies the players choose. These are nonconstant sum or variable-sum games. By contrast, the Buzzer Game is a constant-sum game. So is the Political Game in Chapter 3. Recall, in the Political Game the votes always add up to 100 percent, a constant. In the Buzzer Game, the payoffs add up to 0, which is also a constant!

Equilibrium in constant-sum games, and zero-sum games in particular, can be looked at in another way. To illustrate the point, let's look back at this game strictly from Pamela's point of view. Table 5.2 shows the payoffs just for Pamela. But all of the information in

1 Yes, that would be a really dull quiz game. It would probably be a good idea to make the questions more difficult and penalize only wrong answers. But this would be a bit more complicated, and, for this section, we need a simple example. Obviously, it is too simple to be realistic.

Table **5.1** | The Buzzer Game

		Pamela	
		buzz	don't
Olga	buzz	0, 0	1, −1
	don't	−1, 1	0, 0

Table **5.2** | Pamela's Payoffs in the Buzzer Game

		Pamela	
		buzz	don't
Olga	buzz	0	−1
	don't	1	0
	minimum	0	−1

> **Definition**
>
> ***Maximum and Minimum***—When a player chooses a particular strategy, the payoff depends on the strategies chosen by the other player or players. The smallest and largest of those payoffs are, respectively, the minimum and maximum payoffs associated with that strategy. The strategy that gives the biggest minimum is the **maximin strategy**. The strategy that gives the smallest maximum is the **minimax strategy**.

Table 5.1 is really there, because Pamela knows that whatever makes Olga better off will make her, Pamela, worse off. Thus, Pamela has enough information in this table to figure out what Olga's payoffs and best responses will be. Whatever strategy Pamela chooses, Olga's best response is the strategy that gives Pamela the worst, the **minimum payoff**. This is shown in the last row in Table 5.2. Thus, to choose her best strategy, all Pamela needs to do is choose the strategy that gives the biggest minimum payoff, namely zero. That is, Pamela chooses the strategy that *maximizes the minimum payoff*, the **maximin strategy**, for short. Because Olga can reason in just the same way, she too chooses the strategy that maximizes her minimum payoff, but it is equally the strategy that minimizes Pamela's maximum payoff (the **minimax payoff**).

The study of zero-sum games was important in the early development of game theory. However, many nonzero-sum (and nonconstant-sum) games have also been important. Thinking back over the games you have studied so far in this book, some are zero-sum games and some are not: The Spanish Rebellion and Nim, in Chapter 1, are zero-sum games but the Prisoner's Dilemma and the Advertising Game are not. The new games introduced in Chapter 2 and Chapter 3 are mostly nonconstant sum. The Location, Radio Format and Heave-Ho games are nonconstant sum, while Rock, Paper, Scissors and Matching Pennies are zero-sum.

Here is another example of a zero-sum game. It is a very simplified model of price competition. Like Augustin Cournot (writing in the 1840s) we will think of two companies that sell mineral water. Each company has a fixed cost of $5,000 per period, regardless of whether they sell anything. We will call the companies Coolwater and Springy Springs.

The two companies are competing for the same market and each firm must choose a high price ($2 per bottle) or a low price ($1 per bottle). Here are the rules of the game:

Table 5.3 Payoffs in the Spring Water Game

		Coolwater	
		price = $1	price = $2
Springy Springs	price = $1	0, 0	5000, −5000
	price = $2	−5000, 5000	0, 0

1. At a price of $2, 5,000 bottles can be sold for a total revenue of $10,000.

2. At a price of $1, 10,000 bottles can be sold for a total revenue of $10,000.[2]

3. If both companies charge the same price, they split the sales evenly between them.

4. If one company charges a higher price, the company with the lower price sells the whole amount and the company with the higher price sells nothing.

2 Students who have taken microeconomic principles may realize that we are making a simplifying assumption about the elasticity of demand here. The simplifying example is that the elasticity of demand is exactly 1—and if that is not true, things will not be quite this simple.

5. Payoffs are profits—revenue minus the $5,000 fixed cost.

The payoff table for these two companies is shown in Table 5.3. (Verify for yourself that this is a zero-sum game.)

Let's apply the maximin solution principle. In this game, Coolwater's minimum payoff at a price of $1 is zero, and at a price of $2 it is –$5,000, so the $1 price maximizes the minimum payoff. The same reasoning applies to Springy Springs, so both will choose the $1 price.

Two-person, zero-sum games are in many ways the simplest, most regular class of games. In two-person zero-sum games, the maximin solution is always the same as the Nash equilibrium. However, that simple relationship does not apply to nonconstant sum games, and there are some zero-sum games in which no strategy satisfies the maximin rule.

The Maximin Solution

Let's take another look at the Matching Pennies game. The payoff table for this schoolyard game is repeated in Table 5.4. You should verify that this is a zero-sum game. As we have seen, neither strategy gives a Nash equilibrium for this game. When we apply the maximin solution to this game, we see a hint as to why this happens. The minimum payoff for both strategies for Roger is the same—minus one penny. The same is true for Barry. So, from a mathematical point of view, both strategies satisfy the maximin rule—neither is smaller than the other. The maximin rule does not tell us which one to choose.

A Closer Look

Augustin Cournot 1801–1877

Antoine Augustin Cournot was born in the French district of Franche-Compte in the town of Gray, France. He studied mathematics at the Collège Royal in Besançon, the École Normale Supérieur in Paris, and the Sorbonne, winning recognition from the great mathematician Poisson. In 1838, while inspector general of public education, he published *Recherches sur les principes mathématiques de la théorie des richesses* in which he discussed mathematical economics, and provided the first discussion of demand functions. His theory of duopoly is recognized as an instance of the Nash Equilibrium, so that some game theorists use the term Cournot-Nash equilibrium to refer to it.

Source: *http://slhs.univ-fcomte.fr/rech/philolab/Colloques/Cournot.html*

Table 5.4   Matching Pennies

Repeats Table 4.12, Chapter 4

		Roger	
		heads	tails
Barry	heads	–1, 1	1, –1
	tails	1, –1	–1, 1

So we see that there are some two-person zero-sum games for which the maximin approach does not supply a solution. This is one limitation of the maximin approach. Another limitation is that, when we move to nonconstant sum games, the maximin solution may disagree with the Nash equilibrium. For an example, we can look at an exercise from Chapter 4: The Drive-On Game. Two cars meet, crossing, at the intersection of Pigtown Pike and Hiccup Lane. Each has two strategies: wait or go. The payoffs are repeated in Table 5.5.

For this game, there are two Nash equilibria, each of the strategy pairs at which one car waits and the other goes. But when we apply the maximin approach, we get a different answer.

Constant Numbers—The important point is that the payoffs for the two contestants add up to the same *constant* number regardless of the strategies chosen. If it were a constant other than 0, we would say that the game is a *constant-sum game*. Every zero-sum game is a constant-sum game, but not every constant-sum game is a zero-sum game. Think, for example, of a casino poker game in which the "house" takes a dollar fee out of every pot. Then the total winnings and losses would always add up to minus one dollar. This would be a constant-sum game, but not a zero-sum game.

In all two-person constant-sum games, regardless of whether they are zero-sum games, the equilibrium strategies are the maximin strategies.

For an example of a game that is not a constant-sum game, we do not need to go any further than the Prisoner's Dilemma. In the Prisoner's Dilemma, as shown in Chapter 1, the total payoffs to the two prisoners can range from 2 to 20 (years in prison). Thus, we would say that the Prisoner's Dilemma is a *non-constant sum game*.

Thus, we will contrast zero-sum games with nonconstant-sum games like the Prisoner's Dilemma. This does leave something out—the nonzero constant sum games—and so far as logic is concerned, that group is just as important as any other. But in practice, there are very few applications of nonzero constant sum games.

Table 5.5 | The Drive-On Game

Repeats Table 4.E2, Chapter 4

		Mercedes	
		wait	go
Buick	wait	0, 0	1, 5
	go	5, 1	−100, −100

For the Mercedes, the minimum payoffs are 0 for wait and −100 for go, so wait is the better choice according to the maximin approach. The same reasoning applies to the Buick. Thus, (wait, wait) is the maximin solution to this game.

Where the Nash equilibrium and the maximin criterion disagree, we may want to ask ourselves just what the *rational* choice is. On the one hand, the strategy "wait" is not a best response when the other player chooses "wait," and that is why (wait, wait) is not a Nash equilibrium. On the other hand, since there are two Nash equilibria, in general there is nothing much to assure either driver that the other one will choose "wait." This *uncertainty* is a difficulty with the Nash equilibrium in this case.

To repeat, there is nothing much in general to assure either driver that the other one will choose "wait." In some particular cases, there may be. For example, if there is a stop light, that can provide a Schelling point that makes it clear to both drivers which Nash equilibrium will occur. Uncertainty will not be the problem in that case. Again, if one of the drivers arrives at the intersection a little before the other one, that hint may supply a Schelling point— and the laws of many states say that the first driver in the intersection has the "right of way." However, if there are no clues to establish a Schelling point, uncertainty becomes the predominant motive in the game, and some game theorists would say that there is a strong case for the maximin solution as a rational response to uncertainty.

But we can't push this reasoning very far. To see why, we can look at another game from Chapter 4, the Heave-Ho Game. The payoffs are shown in Table 5.6. This game, also, has two equilibria, but in this case one is better for both players than the other, and this provides a hint that can overcome the uncertainty as to which equilibrium will occur—a possible Schelling point. On this reasoning, (heave, heave) is the most probable equilibrium. But the case looks different when we apply the maximin approach. For each player, the minimum payoff from "heave" is −10, while the minimum payoff from "don't" is 0, so the maximin solution to this game is (don't, don't). This is a Nash equilibrium, all right, but the worse of the two Nash equilibria for this game.

Is the maximin solution a rational solution in nonconstant sum games? There are two answers to that, and some case can be made for each of them. If we understand *rational* to mean "each player chooses the best response to the other player's strategy," then the maximin solution is not, generally, rational in nonconstant

Table 5.6 | The Heave-Ho Game

Repeats Table 4.8, Chapter 4

		Jim	
		heave	don't
Karl	heave	5, 5	−10, 0
	don't	0, −10	1, 1

sum games. If we interpret *rational* more broadly to allow for caution in the face of uncertainty, then maximin may be rational in some nonconstant sum games. But how much caution is rational? The maximin strategy is an extremely cautious strategy! It is possible to carry caution to irrational extremes, and it seems that maximin does just that in a game like Heave-Ho. How much caution is rational? To investigate that, we will need more advanced tools.

The Significance of Zero-Sum Games

Zero-sum games are simple, but, as we have seen, may not be applicable to many real-world interactions. Most of the examples we have seen are in recreational games and war—and even in war, we have the mobilization game from Chapter 2 as an example of a nonconstant sum war game.[3] Apart from their simplicity, what is their significance for the application of game theory to serious human interactions?

By coincidence, there was a good illustration in the morning newspaper the day I was writing this section (*The Philadelphia Inquirer* for Presidents' Day, February 18, 2002). The lead opinion column in the business section deals with proposals for tax reform in Philadelphia and says that the proposed reforms would be a win-win game for Philadelphia government and business.[4] The headline is "Cutting wage tax wouldn't be a zero-sum game for city," and the columnist is warning us not to oversimplify. Some people may assume that,

---

3 Even in recreational games, the zero-sum scoring may not be the whole story. A personal reminiscence can illustrate the point. I played some playground basketball when I was in grade school. I was tall and lanky for my age, but I was also a terrible shooter and medium-slow. As a result, I was a lot better on defense than on offense, so my idea was to do what I could do best and play a really sticky defense. But even my teammates didn't want me to do that. They wanted to have fun running and shooting as much as they wanted to win, if not more. So when I played defense, it actually cut down on the subjective payoffs for both sides. And subjective payoffs are the ones that really count. I have to conclude that my schoolyard basketball was not a zero-sum game, even though there could be only one winner and one loser.

This may tell us why so many coaches stress the importance of *D*—defense. The coach doesn't get to have fun running and shooting anyway, so he just wants to win. Plus, that's what he is paid for.

As for me, I gave up basketball and took up a game in which I could play offense: Bridge.

4 Andrew Cassel, "Commentary: Cutting Wage Tax Wouldn't Be a Zero-Sum Game for City," *The Philadelphia Inquirer* (Monday, February 18, 2002), Section C, pages C1, C9.

in order for tax reform to benefit some people, it must harm others. That would be true in a zero-sum game, but not in a win-win game, since any win-win game is nonconstant sum. Similarly, economist Lester Thurow's book, *The Zero-Sum Society*, focused on the negative results of this sort of oversimplification.[5]

What these examples suggest is that the most important significance of zero-sum games is negative. It is in the contrast to the much richer potential we can find in much of our day-to-day business. It is the warning not to oversimplify. Zero-sum games provide a baseline—important as such, but a baseline we can usually improve upon. To further illustrate the importance of nonconstant sum games, this chapter will continue with some examples of non-constant sum games that have played key roles in the development of game theory. They are classical cases in game theory, too. As you go on in your study of game theory, in this book and beyond, they will be applied again and again.

The Battle of the Sexes

Two-by-two games have been studied extensively in game theoretic research, beginning with the Prisoner's Dilemma. Examples of two-by-two games with more than one Nash equilibrium contrast with the Prisoner's Dilemma, and some are important in ongoing research. One of these is the Battle of the Sexes. Like the Prisoner's Dilemma, it begins with a little story:

Marlene and Guillermo would like to go out Saturday night. Guillermo would enjoy a baseball game, while Marlene would prefer a show. (OK, it's stereotypical, but that's what they like.) Mostly, they want to go together. They can't contact one another because the telephone company is on strike, Marlene's Internet server is down, and the battery is dead in Guillermo's cell phone. Thus, they are just going to try to meet together at the same place. Each one can choose between two strategies: go to the game or go to the show. The payoffs for this game are shown in normal form in Table 5.7.

This game has two Nash equilibria: (game, game) and (show, show). Once again, there is the problem of determining which equilibrium is more likely to occur. In this case, neither equilibrium is better than the other, from the point of view of both players, so we don't have that sort of Schelling point to rely on. In the absence of some other sort of signal or information, there really is no answer. Despite its enigmatic nature—or, actually, because of its enigmatic nature—the battle of the sexes game has played an ongoing part in game theoretic research, and we will see it again in this book, more than once.

Table 5.7 The Battle of the Sexes

		Marlene	
		game	show
Guillermo	game	5, 3	2, 2
	show	1, 1	3, 5

5 Lester Thurow, *The Zero-Sum Society*, (New York: Basic Books, 1980).

Chicken

Another widely studied two-by-two game, at once similar to and different from the others we have seen here, is called Chicken. The Chicken Game is based on some hot-rod movies from the 1950s, or perhaps on the news items that suggested the movies. The players are two hot rodders, whom we will call Mike and Neil. The game is one in which they drive their cars directly at one another, risking a head-on collision. If one of them turns away at the last minute, then the one who turns away is the loser—he is the chicken. However, if neither of them turns away, they both stand to lose a great deal more, since they will be injured or killed in a collision. For the third possibility, if both of them turn away, neither gains or loses anything. The payoffs for this game are shown in Table 5.8.

Table 5.8 | Chicken

		Mike	
		go straight	turn away
Neil	go straight	−10, −10	5, −5
	turn away	−5, 5	0, 0

A little examination shows that this game has two Nash equilibria, one each where one hot rodder turns away and the other one goes straight. But yet again, with two Nash equilibria, and no signal or clue to define a Schelling point, there is no way to say which of the two equilibria is more likely. This is not only a problem for the game theorist, but also a problem for the hot rodders. There seems to be a real danger that they will fall into the mutual disaster of the collision.

The Chicken Game seems to have had some influence on American nuclear policy during the period of tension between the United States and the Soviet Union from the 1950s to the 1980s. Certainly the nuclear standoff, with its "mutually assured destruction" seems to bear some resemblance to a chicken game. And it might have been a chicken game if both sides had had the capability to turn back if the missiles had started to fly. The idea behind "mutually assured destruction" could have been to make the response so automatic that there was never really any possibility for the other side to turn back.

In any case, the Chicken Game also continues to be studied as an example of the problems that can arise in game theory because Nash equilibria are not always unique.

Hawk vs. Dove

Another example of a two-by-two game with two Nash equilibria comes to us from biologists who study animal behavior and its evolutionary basis. It is called Hawk vs. Dove. The idea behind this game is that some animals can be quite aggressive in conflicts over resources or toward prey, while others make only a show of aggression, and then run away. The hawk is symbolic of the first strategy, fighting aggressively, while the dove is symbolic of the second strategy, avoiding a fight.

In population biology, the assumption is that creatures meet one another more or less at random, and dispute over some resource, using the strategies of aggression or running away. The Hawk vs. Dove Game is played out at each meeting, depending on what creatures meet. If two aggressive "hawks" meet, they will fight until both are injured, so both lose even though one of them may come out of the fight in possession of the disputed resource. If two "doves" meet, they will both run away after some show of aggressiveness. Whichever one runs away more slowly will end up in possession of the disputed resource. When a "hawk" meets a "dove," the "dove" runs away, and the "hawk" is left in possession of the disputed resource, at little or no cost.

Table 5.9 | Hawk vs. Dove

		Bird B	
		hawk	dove
Bird A	hawk	–25, –25	14, –9
	dove	–9, 14	5, 5

The payoffs for this game are shown in Table 5.9. These payoffs are derived from assumptions about the benefits of gaining resources and the costs of fighting or pretending to fight, on average. We won't go into the details of that now, however. (Some implications of these particular numbers will be seen in Chapter 9.)

Once again, we see that there are two Nash equilibria: the two combinations in which the birds adopt different strategies. Notice the similarity here to the Chicken Game.

Of course, hawks and doves are unlike human game players in some important ways. The rational human being of game theory is a reflective creature who considers the consequences of his actions, aims to maximize his payoffs, and chooses strategies accordingly. Hawks and doves are not like that. What can it mean to say that hawk-like aggressive behavior is a strategy, or that the hawk chooses it? We will have to leave those questions for later, because the Hawk vs. Dove Game, taken from population biology, is not really a two-person game. It is a game for a population. So we will return to it, in Chapter 11, after we have begun to explore games with a large number of players.

For now, the Hawk vs. Dove Game is of interest as an example from a discipline we might not have associated with game theory: biology. It is also yet another example of a two-by-two game with two Nash equilibria and no information that might serve to define a Schelling point.

Taking the last two games together, we see that they're very much alike, except for the specific numbers in the cells. In fact, in a certain sense, they are the same game. That is another important thing about them.

Expressing Payoffs in Ordinal Numbers

We can make the similarities between the Chicken Game and the Hawk vs. Dove Game more clear if we express the payoffs in a slightly different way. Instead of expressing them in numbers, we can express them in ordinal terms. **Ordinal numbers** express the ordering rather than the quantity, so instead of payoffs we have the best payoff, second best, third best, and worst. When we express the payoffs for the Chicken Game and the Hawk vs. Dove Game in this way we find that they are exactly the same. The payoff table for both games is shown in Table 5.10.

For these games with relatively few strategies, the absolute numbers don't really matter at all. All that matters is the *ordinal* expression of the payoffs: which is best, second best, and so forth. In fact, that is true for any game that has only a finite number of strategies,[6] although of course with millions of strategy combinations we have to enumerate the multimillionth and the multimillionth plus one—a pretty large task.

The point is that any two games with the same ordinal payoffs will have the same equilibria. They are the same game in that sense.

For another example, let's look at our old friend, the Prisoner's Dilemma. An ordinal payoff table for the Prisoner's Dilemma is shown as Table 5.11.

If we look back at all of the social dilemmas we have studied in the previous chapters of this book—the Advertising Game, mobilization in World War I, and the Dumping Game, as well as the Prisoner's Dilemma—we will find that they all have the same payoff table in ordinal terms. In that sense, all social dilemmas are the same dilemma.

Table 5.10 Hawk/Dove and Chicken with Payoffs in Ordinal Terms

		A	
		aggress	avoid
B	aggress	worst, worst	best, 2nd
	avoid	2nd, best	3rd, 3rd

Table 5.11 Prisoner's Dilemma with Payoffs in Ordinal Terms

		Al	
		confess	don't
Bob	confess	2nd, 2nd	worst, best
	don't	best, worst	3rd, 3rd

6 You may be asking, what is the alternative? How can there be more than a finite number of strategies? That will be a topic for Chapter 8.

Summary

This chapter has focused on two different kinds of classical models in game theory—that is, models that have had a great influence on the development of game theory in the past, and to which current work may often refer.

The first is zero-sum games. Games can be divided into two broad categories: constant and nonconstant sum. In constant-sum games, the sum of the payoffs to all players is a constant number, regardless of the strategies chosen. Among the constant-sum games, most examples refer to zero-sum games, in which the sum of the payoffs is zero. However, the same principles apply to both. In any constant-sum game, the Nash equilibrium (if there is one) can be found by the maximin criterion: Determine the smallest or *minimum* payoff for each strategy, and choose the strategy that gives the largest, or *maximum*, value for that minimum: *maximin*. However, when we apply the maximin principle to nonconstant sum games, it represents an extremely cautious stance in response to uncertainty—perhaps irrationally cautious!

The second group of classical cases are two-person two-strategy (two-by-two) nonconstant sum games that have two Nash equilibria. These coordination games include a wide range of possibilities. They can be grouped into families, like the social dilemmas, on the basis of the ordinal ranking of the four possible outcomes. These games—the Battle of the Sexes, Chicken, and Hawk vs. Dove, are landmarks of game-theoretic study to which current research often makes reference.

Exercises and Discussion Questions

5.1 Spring Water. Revise the Spring Water Game with one change in the assumptions: Assume that the fixed cost for each company is $2,000 rather than $5,000.

What sort of game is this? Apply the maximin method to solve this game. What is the Nash equilibrium for this game? Give two reasons why your answer is correct.

5.2 Social Dilemmas. Draw payoff tables for social dilemmas as a class with the payoffs in ordinal terms. In general terms, what are the two strategies in social dilemmas?

5.3 Contrast. Draw payoff tables for the Heave-Ho and Battle of the Sexes games in ordinal terms and contrast them.

Three-Person Games 6

In the book thus far we have considered only games with just two players. In some ways the two-person games are the purest examples in game theory because each person has to choose a strategy with attention to the responses of just one rival. But there are also many applications of game theory with three or more players. It is worthwhile to pause (as von Neumann and Morgenstern did in their book *The Theory of Games and Economic Behavior*) and take a look at three-person games in particular, for two reasons. First, they are simple enough that we can use some of the same techniques that we have used for two-person games, with only a little more complication. Second, many of the complications present in games with more than three persons can be found in three-person games. For example, in a three-person game it is possible for two of the three persons to gang up on the third—a possibility that does not exist in two-person games!

An International Alliance

Runnistan, Soggia, and Wetland are three countries, each of which has a shoreline on Overflowing Bay. They all have military and naval forces stationed on the bay, and depending on how they deploy their forces, two or more of them may be able to control the bay effectively, and use the control to increase their own trade and prosperity at the expense of the third. The strategies for the three countries are the positions at which they station their forces. Runnistan can position its forces in the north or in the south; Soggia can position its forces in the east or in the west; and Wetland can position in its forces offshore on Swampy Island, which Wetland controls, or onshore.

Table 6.1 is read in a straightforward way. There are two panels corresponding to Wetland's

> **To best understand this chapter 6**
>
> To best understand this chapter you need to have studied and understood the material from Chapters 1–4.

Table 6.1 | Payoffs for Three Countries*

		Wetland			
		onshore		offshore	
		Soggia		Soggia	
		west	east	west	east
Runnistan	north	6, 6, 6	7, 7, 1	7, 1, 7	0, 0, 0
	south	0, 0, 0	4, 4, 4	4, 4, 4	1, 7, 7

*Note: The order of the payoffs is Runnistan, Soggia, Wetland. The player who chooses the panel is often listed last, and this chapter will follow that convention.

71

Heads Up!

Here are some concepts we will develop as this chapter goes along:

Coalition: A *coalition* is a group of players who coordinate their strategies. A single player who does not coordinate with anyone is called a singleton coalition.

Spoiler: A player who cannot win, but whose play determines which of the other players will win, is called a *spoiler*.

A Public Good: If a good or service has the properties that everyone in the population enjoys the same level of service, and it does not cost any more to provide one more person with the same level of service, that is what economists call a *public good*.

two strategies. In effect, Wetland chooses the panel, and within each panel, Runnistan chooses the row and Soggia chooses the column. Payoffs are listed with Runnistan first, Soggia second, and Wetland third. Thus, if the three counties choose strategies (south, east, offshore) the payments are 1 to Runnistan, 7 to Soggia, and 7 to Wetland.

In game theory, a group of players who coordinate their strategies is called a **coalition**. Of course, this term came into game theory from politics. In this game, then, there are three possible two-player coalitions—Runnistan and Soggia; Runnistan and Wetland; and Soggia and Wetland. However, that is not quite the whole story. In addition, it is possible for all three countries to get together and coordinate their strategies. In another term borrowed from politics, this would be called a **grand coalition**. Finally, with the single-minded thoroughness that comes into game theory from mathematics, game theorists consider an individual acting independently as a coalition unto himself. The phrase for this sort of coalition doesn't come from politics, though—it comes from card games. A player acting alone is said to be a **singleton coalition**. In this game, then, there can also be three singleton coalitions.

Naturally, coalitions will fit together. If Runnistan and Soggia form a two-country coalition, then Wetland is left in a singleton coalition. In this way, the group of three players is partitioned into two coalitions: a two-country coalition and a singleton coalition. This is called a **coalition structure** for the game. (That's why we have to be thorough and think of a single individual acting alone as a coalition. Otherwise, we would have difficulty in talking about the coalition structure when some players are left out.)

> ### Definition
>
> **Coalition Structure**—A partition of the players in a game into coalitions, including singleton coalitions, is called the **coalition structure** of the game.

Let's list all of the possible coalition structures of this game of international alliances:

(Runnistan, Soggia, and Wetland)

(Runnistan and Soggia); (Wetland)

(Runnistan and Wetland); (Soggia)

(Soggia and Wetland); (Runnistan)

(Runnistan); (Soggia); (Wetland)

If the grand coalition of all three countries were to be formed, it might choose the strategies (north, west, onshore), since that group of strategies would yield a payoff of 6 to each of the countries, the maximum total payoff. But that is not a Nash equilibrium. Since this is a noncooperative game, in that there is no international enforcement mechanism that could force the three countries to deploy their forces in the agreed upon way, this agreement could not be carried out.

However, suppose that Runnistan and Soggia were to form an alliance. They could choose north and east as their coordinated strategies. Given that they choose north and east, Wetland is better off to deploy its forces onshore for a payoff of 1 rather than offshore for payoff of 0. This is a Nash equilibrium, so there is no need for enforcement. Neither

Although coalitions are possible in noncooperative games, they are exceptional. In social dilemmas and many other noncooperative games, only singleton coalitions are stable, and in that case we can ignore coalitions completely—as we usually do in noncooperative game theory. It is only in games with more than one Nash equilibrium, and plenty of opportunity for preplay communication, that we need to allow for coalitions in noncooperative games. But coalitions are very important in cooperative games, as we will see in later chapters, and the terminology is the same.

Runnistan nor Soggia will want to deviate from the agreed upon deployment of their forces.

Similarly, Runnistan and Wetland could form an alliance and deploy their forces north and offshore. With Soggia choosing west, this is a Nash equilibrium. In a similar way, Soggia and Wetland could form an alliance and deploy their forces east and offshore. With Runnistan choosing south, this is, again, a Nash equilibrium, so no enforcement is needed.

In passing, we have noticed that this is one of those games with multiple Nash equilibria. In principle, there could be some mystery as to which of the equilibria will be observed in practice. In this case, though, any treaty of alliance that may exist between two of the three countries provides the Schelling point that resolves the question. On one hand, since there is a Schelling point Nash equilibrium corresponding to every two-country alliance, we can conclude that any of the two-country alliances is a possibility. On the other hand, since there is no Nash equilibrium corresponding to the three-country grand coalition, we would not expect to see a grand coalition in the absence of some system to enforce the deployment strategies corresponding to the grand coalition.

Coalitions can form in noncooperative games with three or more players, as we have seen. However, in the absence of some enforcement mechanism, we will see only coalitions that correspond to Nash equilibria. If there is some sort of enforcement mechanism, or some other effective way that the players in the game can commit themselves to a coordinated strategy, then the possibilities for coalition formation are richer. We are then dealing with cooperative games, and will take them up in Chapters 12 and 13. Some further examples of coalitions in noncooperative games will be seen in Chapter 9.

Continuing this chapter, we will explore examples of three-person games from electoral politics, public policy, and stock markets.

A "Spoiler" in a Political Game

One of the roles that a third party can play is that of a **spoiler**. A spoiler is a player who cannot win, but can prevent another player from winning. Some observers of the election of year 2000 believe that Ralph Nader played the role of spoiler in that election. The same has been said of Ross Perot in 1992 and of George Wallace in 1968. In a closer election, John Anderson might have been a spoiler in 1980. It seems that spoilers are fairly common in American presidential elections.

Table 6.2 Popular Votes for the 2000 Election

Bush \ Nader	Nader run — Gore liberal	Nader run — Gore middle	Nader don't run — Gore liberal	Nader don't run — Gore middle
conservative	45, 50, 1	45, 49, 3	45, 53, 0	45, 52, 0
compassionate	48, 46, 2	46, 47, 3	48, 48, 0	46, 50, 0

Those who think of Nader as a spoiler probably have in mind a game very much like the one shown in Table 6.2. Table 6.2 is read similarly as Table 6.1. Nader, the third party in the game, chooses the panel in which the other two play, and Nader's payoff comes last. Mr. Bush, who was described as a compassionate conservative, chose between the two strategies implicit in that phrase—he could emphasize the conservatism or the compassion. Mr. Gore could run more as a liberal or as a middle-of-the-roader. Nader's strategies are to run or not to run. The payoffs shown are the popular votes. We have to qualify this in two ways. The subjective benefits that motivate the decisions may not have corresponded exactly to the popular vote, in two ways. On the one hand, Nader (and his supporters) might have preferred Gore's election to that of Bush, all other things equal. This does not show up when we record the Nader payoff as his popular vote. But the Nader supporters had reasons for wanting to maximize their popular vote regardless. A larger popular vote would have given them a better chance of competing in future elections. On the other hand, Gore was running with a handicap. We know in retrospect that he had to win the popular vote by more than 1 percent to win the election. Here again, though, the more popular votes he won, the better his chance in the Electoral College.

Nader supporters who were motivated by popular vote had a clear dominant strategy: Nader should run. Otherwise, his popular vote could only be 0. Bush, too, had a dominant strategy. That was to emphasize the compassion, not the conservatism, in his message. Gore did not have a dominant strategy, but given that Bush's dominant strategy was to emphasize compassion, Gore's best response was to run as a middle-of-the-roader.

Thus the Nash equilibrium strategies are (compassionate, middle, run) and the payoffs are (46, 47, 3)—a win for Bush.[1] Notice that, had Nader not run, Bush and Gore would have

---

1 In American presidential elections, the election is decided in the Electoral College, not by the popular vote. Each state has as many Electoral College votes as it has U.S. House and Senate members; the winner of the popular vote in the state takes all the electoral votes for that state.

On two occasions, 1876 and 2000, the winner in the Electoral College has gotten fewer popular votes than his main rival. Nevertheless (we assume), a candidate will seek the largest popular vote he can get as a means of increasing his chances of winning in the Electoral College.

chosen the same strategies, but the Gore advantage in the popular vote would have been wider—four points, if he got all the Green vote. No one can be certain that this popular vote margin would have been enough to win the electoral vote, but it seems probable, and many people are sure it would have. That is what it means to call Nader a spoiler.

Stock Advising

When there are three or more players in a game, there may be some advantage for one of them in going along with the majority. Here is an example of that kind.

Luvitania is a small country with an active stock market but only one corporation, General Stuff (GS), and only three market advisors: June, Julia, and Augusta. Whenever at least two of the three recommend "buy" for General Stuff, the stock goes up, and thus the advisors who recommend "buy" gain in reputation, customers, and payoffs. Whenever at least two of the three recommend "sell" for General Stuff, the stock goes down, and thus the advisors who recommend "sell" gain in reputation, customers, and payoffs.

The payoff table for the three advisors is shown in Table 6.3. We see that there are two Nash equilibria: one where everyone recommends "buy" and one where everyone recommends "sell." Whenever one of the three advisors disagrees with the other two, she loses, and so has reason to switch to agreement.

What does this example tell us about the real world? There are, of course, many more than three stock advisers in the real world. The real world is also more complex in other ways. For example, it is possible for the majority of stock advisors to be wrong, and this has happened from time to time. Thus, stock prices must depend on some other things beside the majority opinions of stock advisors: corporate earnings, for example. However, if stock advisors believe that their advice influences stock price

John Maynard Keynes
1883–1946

John Maynard Keynes was probably the most influential economist of the first half of the twentieth century. With the publication of *The Economic Consequences of the Peace* (1919), he burst (as Joseph Schumpeter wrote in his *History of Economic Analysis*) "into international fame when men of equal insight but less courage and men of equal courage but less insight kept silent." After the disaster of the Great Depression, Keynes was the leading figure in a group of (mostly) younger and very creative economists who attempted to understand and explain the disaster. Borrowing freely from their ideas, Keynes published *The General Theory of Employment, Interest and Money*, which (again quoting Schumpeter) "was a similar feat of leadership. It taught England, in the form of an apparently general analysis, his own personal view of her social and economic situation and also his own personal view of 'what should be done about it.'" Keynes helped found modern macroeconomics.

©Hulton-Deutsch Collection/CORBIS

Table 6.3 | Payoffs for Three Stock Advisors

		June			
		buy		sell	
		Julia		Julia	
		buy	sell	buy	sell
Augusta	buy	5, 5, 5	6, 0, 6	6, 6, 0	0, 6, 6
	sell	0, 6, 6	6, 6, 0	6, 0, 6	5, 5, 5

trends, then a stock advisor will not want to be out of step with the majority unless he has a good reason to think the majority is wrong.

Stock advisors do seem to agree with one another most of the time, when they are wrong as well as when they are right. John Maynard Keynes said that stock markets were a good deal like "beauty contests" sponsored by British newspapers early in the twentieth century. They would publish a page with pictures of 100 (or thereabouts) girls' faces, and invite the readers to vote for the prettiest. Those who voted for the prettiest would get a small prize—and the prettiest was the one who got the most votes! The objective (Keynes said) is not to decide which is prettiest but to decide which one would be thought prettiest by the largest number of others—and stock markets, Keynes said, are like that. In the Luvitania example, the objective is not to predict which way stocks will go, but to predict which way the majority of advisors will predict that stocks will go, much as Keynes said.

The fact that there are two Nash equilibria is important, too. There are two ways everyone can be right—but which will be realized in a particular case? Suppose the first bit of news that comes out during the day is good news—then this good news could provide the "Schelling point" by suggesting to each of the advisors that it is likely that the other advisors will say "buy." So they all say "buy." It often seems that the market overreacts to new information—shifting much more than we can explain by the objective content of the news. Perhaps this occurs because it shifts the financial players to a new Schelling point.

These conclusions are speculations, not facts. We don't really know why the stock markets move as they do—and if I knew why stock markets move as they do, I probably wouldn't need to write this book. But the three-person game suggests a possible explanation for some of the things we observe.

A Crowding Game

We have seen examples of three-person games in which the third person is cut out of a coalition, in which the third person loses unless she conforms to the majority, and in which the third person is a spoiler, in that the player cannot win but can determine by his or her strategy who does. Another possibility is "two's company, but three's a crowd." That is, crowding may become a problem, but only after a certain number of people have joined the crowd. The El Farol game illustrates this.

El Farol is a bar in Santa Fe, New Mexico, where chaos researchers from the Santa Fe Institute often hang out. It is said that the El Farol is at its best when it is crowded, but not too crowded. A key point is that the benefits to bar-goers are nonlinear—as the crowd grows, they increase rapidly up to a point and then decline. Here is a three-person example a little like that. Amy, Barb, and Carole each can choose between two strategies: go (to the bar) or stay home. If all three friends go to the bar, it is just too crowded, and each of the three gets a negative payoff. If just two go, those two get the maximum payoff, but if just one goes, the

Figure 6.1 | Payoffs to Individual Bar-Goers in the Crowding Game

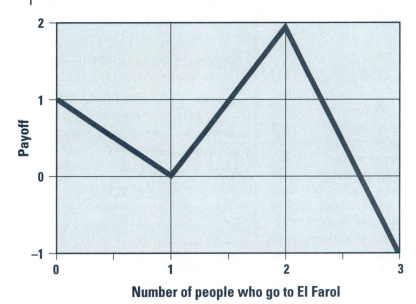

payoff is worse than staying home. The payoffs to bar-goers are shown in Figure 6.1. Notice the three quite different trends as the bar crowd goes from none to one, then two, then three—a contrast that could not be illustrated with fewer than three players. The payoff to those who stay home is always 1.

The payoffs are shown in normal form in Table 6.4. This game has four Nash equilibria. Each strategy triple in which just two go to the bar is an equilibrium. Thus, we may think of it as a coordination game. The fourth equilibrium, in which everyone stays home, is a bit odd. In fact, though—since it is better to stay at home than to be the only one at the bar—it, too, is an equilibrium. Since it is inferior to the other Nash equilibria (in that two women would be better off and none worse off if two were to go to the bar) we might doubt that it would really occur, but no one person can improve on (home, home, home) by changing unilaterally, and in the absence of any other information, each would be uncertain as to which of the other three equilibria could be realized by the shift!

Table 6.4 | Payoffs in a Crowding Game

		Carole			
		go		home	
		Barb		**Barb**	
		go	home	go	home
Amy	go	−1,−1,−1	2, 1, 2	2, 2, 1	0, 1, 1
	home	1, 2, 2	1, 1, 0	1, 0, 1	1, 1, 1

As in the game of international alliances, it is possible that two of the women might form a coalition and go to the bar, leaving the third person with a best-response strategy of staying

What about the odd equilibrium at the lower right? Any two players could form a coalition and shift to one of the other Nash equilibria, and be better off. That would immediately rule the lower right equilibrium out. This Nash equilibrium is not "coalition-proof" since coalitions can form (even in the absence of enforcement) that will shift away from it. It seems that—in games with more than two players and more than one equilibrium—we need to "refine" the Nash equilibrium to allow for strategy shifts by coalitions. There are "refinements" in noncooperative game theory that do this. One is *strong Nash equilibrium.* A Nash equilibrium is strong only if there is no coalition that can benefit, as a whole, by deviating from it. This game has no strong Nash equilibria at all. A less demanding condition is that the equilibrium be *coalition-proof.* To determine if it is coalition-proof, we must ask two questions. First, are there coalitions that could deviate to another Nash equilibrium and be better off? Second, are these coalitions stable in the sense that there are no smaller coalitions within them that could benefit by deviating to yet another Nash equilibrium? Clearly, the lower right equilibrium is not coalition-proof, since any two-person coalition can profit by deviating from it. The two-person coalitions are stable if no smaller (one-person singleton) coalition can benefit by a further deviation. We see that the three other Nash equilibria are stable in this sense, so they are themselves coalition-proof. This gives us some reason to think that the lower right equilibrium is a very unlikely Nash equilibrium in reality.

home. Of course, these sorts of things do happen—coalitions of this kind are often called *cliques* and are reported in just about every high school.

According to people who have been there, though, the essence of the El Farol Game is that the decisions to go or stay home are made at the last minute, without time enough to form a coalition or a clique. There is no communication. The only information people have is from experience, and that can be unreliable. Thus, the problem of uncertainty in coordination games comes to the fore. It often happens that everyone goes to the bar one night, and it is overcrowded, so that they all decide to stay home the following night to avoid the crowd—so that there are too few people for the joint to really rock. Some of the chaos researchers at the institute offer this as an example of mathematical chaos. It is also an excellent example of coordination failures in a coordination game without communication.

A Public Goods Contribution Game

In the economics of the public sector, **a public good** is the term for a good or service (usually a service in fact) with specific properties that make it more suitable for government provision than for private-sector provision.[2] There are two specific characteristics:

1. No one can be excluded from the benefits of the good. In particular, those who do not pay get the same access to benefits as those who do.

2 The indefinite article, "a," is important here. If we speak of "the public good," we are speaking of something much broader. The characteristics that define "a public good" were stated by Paul Samuelson, in the late 1930s, on the basis of a discussion by John Stuart Mill. Social philosophers and others have discussed "the public good" much longer and in many other ways. It would be correct to say that the public good would be advanced if the government were to provide a public good, but the public good might also be advanced in other ways.

2. Although the cost might depend on the level of service, it does not depend on the number of people served—one more person can always be served with the same level of service at no higher cost, and no one can increase his or her own service at the expense of reducing the service to another.

One of the best examples of a public good is broadcasting without commercials or fund appeals. The level of service can be increased by keeping the station broadcasting for longer hours. That will increase costs. But one more person can tune in without increasing the costs or reducing the service available to others. Another example would be uncongested rural roads. Paved roads give a higher level of service, at a higher cost, but (so long as the road remains uncongested) one more person can drive on the road without increasing its cost or depriving others of its service. Other traditional examples are legal protection of personal safety, property, and contracts, and national defense.

Consider the following three-person public goods contribution game:

1. The players are Jack, Karl, and Larry (J, K, and L).

2. Each player may choose to contribute or not contribute one unit of a public good. Players who contribute pay a cost of 1.5 units.

3. If a player contributes, his payoff is the total number of units contributed, minus the 1.5 cost of the player's own contribution.

4. If a player does not contribute, his payoff is the total number of units contributed.

These rules give rise to the payoffs in Table 6.5.

We see that the game has a dominant strategy equilibrium. To contribute is a dominated strategy for Jack, Karl, and Larry. Each of them gets 0.5 greater payoff by not contributing, as compared to contributing. "Do not contribute" all around is the only dominant strategy equilibrium and the only Nash equilibrium of this game.

It is also inefficient. All three of the players would be better off (with payoffs of 1.5 rather than 0) if all contributed. In fact, this is another instance of a social dilemma—a three-person social dilemma.

Table 6.5 A Contribution Game

		Larry			
		contribute		don't contribute	
		Karl		Karl	
		contribute	don't contribute	contribute	don't contribute
Jack	contribute	1.5, 1.5, 1.5	0.5, 2, 0.5	0.5, 0.5, 2	−0.5, 1, 1
	don't contribute	2, 0.5, 0.5	1, 1, −0.5	1, −0.5, 1	0, 0, 0

Another way to think of it is to contrast it with the first game in this chapter, the Game of International Alliances. In that game, two of the countries could benefit by forming a coalition. So let us think of this public-good contribution game in terms of coalitions. Suppose Jack and Karl were to form a coalition and both were to contribute. This would make them both better off than they would be without contributing, although Larry would be helped out even more, as the payoffs go from (0, 0, 0) to (0.5, 0.5, 2). But it won't work, without some sort of enforcement of the agreement, since this is not a Nash equilibrium. For Jack and Karl to form a coalition just reproduces the social dilemma in a two-person game between them.

Indeed, in this game, there is every good reason for the three players to form the grand coalition if they can. But (in this case similarly to the Game of Alliances) the grand coalition strategy of (contribute, contribute, contribute) is not a Nash equilibrium, so it cannot exist without enforcement.

When economists say that public goods are not suitable to be provided in the private sector, this is roughly what they mean: that contributing efficiently to the supply of a public good is a dominated strategy and thus the provision of a public good is a social dilemma.

This reasoning also has application to common-property resources in environmental economics. The classical example is a pasture held in common by the residents of a village, a *village commons*. If all of the villagers put their herds to pasture on the commons, the pasture will be destroyed by overgrazing. The pasture can be preserved if each resident limits his use of it, for example by putting no more than half of his or her herd to graze on the commons. But preservation of the commons in this way is a public good to the villagers, and the dominant strategy is to graze the whole herd on the commons, and get some benefit from it while it lasts. Preservation of the commons is a dominated strategy—and this is called *the tragedy of the commons*. The destruction of the commons is a result of individually rational actions, which lead to a result that makes all worse off.

In the real world, though, there are usually more than three people involved in public goods problems and tragedies of the commons, just as there are more than three stock advisers in the real world. Thus, in Chapter 11, we will consider some ways of analyzing games with many players, including social dilemmas and other kinds of games.

Summary

From some points of view, three-person games are only a little more complicated than two-person games. They can be presented in normal form with tables that are a bit more complicated than those required for two-person games, but still simple enough to get on a single page. From another point of view, three-person games are much more complicated than two-person games. That is, the three-person games bring into game theory many issues that did not arise in two-person games, but do arise in games with more than three players. This combination of simplicity and complication makes three-person games well worth studying.

For example, in a three-person game it becomes possible for two players to form a coalition and cooperate against the third. This is always possible with more than three players, but makes little sense in a two-person game. Of course, in a noncooperative game, not all coalitions are possible. Only those coalitions that correspond to Nash equilibria are stable. Thus, we can observe three-person social dilemmas, in which any coalition of two or more players could make the participants better off; but none is stable as a Nash equilibrium.

Another complication we find in three-person games is the possibility that one of the three players can be a *spoiler*, determining which of the other two can win even though that player cannot win. This seems to have been a pretty common phenomenon in American presidential elections in the latter half of the twentieth century.

In three-person games, too, it becomes possible to model conformism, in which the players each find it advantageous to go along with the majority. We can also find examples in which it is more advantageous to go it alone or in which two's company, but three's a crowd.

Thus, three-person games can be worth studying in themselves, but can also be a source of the ideas to explore in games of more than three persons.

Exercises and Discussion Questions

6.1 Another Water-Selling Game. Tom, Dick, and Harry are all in the bottled-water business. If one or two of them expand their production, they can take business away from those who do not, but if all three expand, they will be back to a break-even situation. The payoffs are shown in Table 6.E1.

Has this game any Nash equilibria? If so, list them and explain. List all possible coalitions in this game. Which coalitions will be stable as Nash equilibria? Compare and contrast this game with the Public-Good Contribution Game and the International Alliance game in the chapter, and with the game in the previous example.

Table **6.E1** Payoffs for Bottled-Water Vendors

		Harry			
		expand		no	
		Dick		**Dick**	
		expand	no	expand	no
Tom	expand	0, 0, 0	1, −2, 1	1, 1, −2	2, −1, −1
	no	−2, 1, 1	−1, −1, 2	−1, 2, −1	0, 0, 0

Table 6.E2 | Payoffs for Eager Frogs

		Flip			
		call		sit	
		Michigan J.		Michigan J.	
		call	sit	call	sit
Kermit	call	5, 5, 5	4, 6, 4	4, 4, 6	7, 2, 2
	sit	6, 4, 4	2, 2, 7	2, 7, 2	1, 1, 1

6.2 Frog Mating Game. Evolutionary biologists use game theory to understand some aspects of animal behavior, including mating behavior. Here is a Three-Frog Mating Game about three lonely frogs: Kermit, Michigan J., and Flip. The frogs are all males who can choose between two strategies for attracting females: the call strategy (call) or the satellite strategy (sit). Those who call take some risk of being eaten, while those who sit run less risk. On the other hand the satellites who do not call may nevertheless encounter a female who has been attracted by another call. So the payoff to the satellite strategy is better when a larger number of other male frogs are calling, so there are more females around who are confused and available for mating.

The payoff table for the three frogs is shown in Table 6.E2, with the first payoff to Kermit, the second to Michigan J., and the last to Flip.

Enumerate all Nash equilibria in this game. Have these equilibria anything in common, so that you could give a general description of equilibria in the game? What is it? Frogs do not form coalitions in mating games. What difference would it make if they did?

6.3 Getting a Sitter. Dr. and Mr. Smith, Professor and Mrs. Jones, and Mr. and Mrs. Hanratty, Esq. and Esq., are members of the Washington, D.C. Babysitting Coöp, an organization through which couples alternate in babysitting for one another. In planning for the coming weekend, each couple has three strategies: (offer to) sit, (plan to go) out, and (do) nothing. The payoffs are shown in Table 6.E3.

The payoffs are listed with Hanratty first, then Jones, then Smith. The idea behind the payoffs is that a match pays 1 for those matched.

How many Nash equilibria does this game have? Give a concise description of the Nash equilibria, indicating what distinguishes them from nonequilibria. Compare this game with the Battle of the Sexes Game.

6.4 Oysterers. Ray, Shari, and Tom are Chesapeake Bay oysterers. They all know an oyster bed off Northeast that other oysterers are unaware of. The oysters will be worth more on the market if they are not harvested until next month, when they are bigger and more mature. However, our three oysterers are considering whether to harvest them now or

Table 6.E3 | Cooperative Babysitters

Hanratty		Smith sit — Jones sit	out	nothing	Smith out — Jones sit	out	nothing	Smith nothing — Jones sit	out	nothing
	sit	0, 0, 0	½, 1, ½	0, 0, 0	½, ½, 1	1, ½, ½	1, 0, 1	0, 0, 0	1, 1, 0	0, 0, 0
	out	1, ½, ½	½, ½, 1	1, 0, 1	½, 1, ½	0, 0, 0	0, 0, 0	1, 1, 0	0, 0, 0	0, 0, 0
	nothing	0, 0, 0	0, 1, 1	0, 0, 0	0, 1, 1	0, 0, 0	0, 0, 0	0, 0, 0	0, 0, 0	0, 0, 0

wait. Those are their two strategies in this waiting game. The payoffs are as shown in Table 6.E4.

The payoffs are listed with Ray first, then Shari, then Tom.

What Nash equilibria does this game have, if any? What kind of a game is it?

6.5 Medical Practice.[3] Traditionally, ob/gyn physicians have provided services that included both obstetrics (delivering babies) and gynecology (general women's health care and surgery). Some older physicians stopped performing obstetric care and mainly concentrated on gynecology. Since obstetricians are on call whenever the baby comes, the exclusive gynecological practice gives the doctor a better lifestyle. In more recent years, younger doctors have also opted for practices limited to gynecology, both for the better lifestyle and under the pressure of increased insurance costs associated with medical liability for obstetric care.

Table 6.E4 | A Waiting Game

Ray		Tom now — Shari now	wait	Tom wait — Shari now	wait
	now	5, 5, 5	7, 1, 7	7, 7, 1	12, 1, 1
	wait	1, 7, 7	1, 1, 12	1, 12, 1	10, 10, 10

3 Thanks to Dr. David Toub, a student in my course on game theory for MBA students, for this example.

Table 6.E5 | Payoffs to Gyn Practitioners

Number of doctors concentrating on gyn practice	Payoff to gyn only practice
1	20
2	10
3	−5

Consider three young ob/gyns: Drs. Yfnif, McCoy, and Spock, who are the only doctors qualified for ob/gyn in the isolated city of Enterprise, AK. Each is in sole practice and can choose between two strategies: limit the practice to gyn or practice ob/gyn. Payoffs to a gyn practice depend on the number of doctors offering gyn services only, as shown in Table 6.E5. Payoffs to an ob/gyn practice are always 5.

Construct the payoff table for this three-person game and determine what Nash equilibria exist, if any. Realistically, the three doctors probably will not establish their practices at the same time. Suppose there is a sequence in which one chooses first, another second, then the third last. What effect would this sequence have on the actual Nash equilibrium? A partnership can be thought of as a coalition. What possibilities for coalitions exist in this game?

Probability and Game Theory 7

Uncertainty plays a role in many games and other human interactions. In games, uncertainty may be created deliberately by throwing dice or shuffling cards. Let's consider the example of throwing a single die. (The word *dice* is the plural of *die*, which means a cube with numbers from 1 to 6 on its six faces. So we say: one die, two or more dice, a pair of dice.) When we throw the die, will it show a number greater than 3? Yes, no, or maybe? Since the answer is uncertain, it is maybe. But can we do better than that?

Probability

In an absolute sense, we can do no better. The statement is either true, false, or uncertain, and in this case it is uncertain. But in a relative sense, some uncertain statements are less likely than other uncertain statements. When we throw the die, for example, the statement that the number will be greater than 5 is less likely than the statement that the number will be greater than 3. The reason is that there are three different ways we can get a number greater than 3—it can be 4, 5, or 6—while there is only one way that we can get a number greater than 5. We can often make these comparisons of likelihood, and we put more confidence in the likelier prediction.

Probability is a way of measuring relative likelihood in numerical terms. A **probability** is a number between 0 and 1, inclusively, in which a probability of 1 corresponds to a certainty and 0 corresponds to statements that are certainly false. Among uncertain statements, the more likely the statement is, the larger the probability number that is assigned to it. Thus we might say that when we throw a die, the probability of a number greater

Definition

Probability—**Probability** is a numerical measure of the likelihood of one of the outcomes of an uncertain event.

than 5 is 1/6, while the probability of a number greater than 3 is 1/2 Thus, the more likely statement has the larger probability.

In some cases we can do better still. We can tie the probability of an event to the frequency with which we observe that event in a whole series of similar experiments. Suppose, for example, that we throw a die one hundred times. We can be reasonably certain that we will

Heads Up!

Here are some concepts we will develop as this chapter goes along:

Probability: A numerical measure of the likelihood of one of the outcomes of an uncertain event, which corresponds to the relative frequency of that outcome if the event can be repeated an unlimited number of times.

Expected Value: Suppose an uncertain event can have several outcomes with numerical values that may be different. The *expected value* (also known as mathematical expectation) of the event is the weighted average of the numerical values, with the probabilities of the outcomes as the weights.

Risk Averse: A person who will choose a safe payment over a risky payment with an expected value greater than that of the safe payment is said to be *risk averse*.

Definition

Limiting Frequency—Let an uncertain event be repeated again and again without limit. At each step, compute the proportion of all trials that have come out in one particular way. If this proportion settles down to a more and more predictable value, that value is the **limiting frequency** of the outcome, and is equivalent to the probability of that outcome on any single trial.

observe a number greater than 5 in approximately one-sixth of all the throws. Similarly, we will observe a number greater than 3 in approximately one half of all the throws. Not only that, but if we throw the die a thousand times, the proportions will be the same, and the approximation will be even better. The proportions remain the same, and the approximations get better, as the number of throws increases. The **limiting frequency** of an event is the number approximated in this way as the number of trials increases without limit. Thus, we identify the *probability* of an event with the *limiting frequency* whenever a limiting frequency makes sense.

In some other important cases, a limiting frequency might not make much sense. Think of the outcome of a research project to find a new technology for automobile engines. Until the research is done, we do not know whether it will be successful. As researchers say, that's what makes it research. But once the research is done and the results are in, that same research project will never need to be done again, nor could it be done again. So a limiting frequency makes no sense in this case. Nevertheless, it seems to me that success in a research project to produce automobile engines using fuel cell technology would be *more probable* than success in a research project to produce automobile engines using nuclear fusion. It would be likelier, so we assign a larger probability number to it. Of course, there is a subjective element in my judgment that success with fuel cell technology is more likely than success with nuclear fusion technology. So there is a subjective element in the probability attached to it. Nevertheless, we will assume that probabilities for unique events like a research project have the same properties as probabilities identified with relative frequencies, despite the subjective element. This is a basic assumption for probabilities in this book (and a common assumption in many applications of probability).

We can also use the relative frequency approach to *estimate* probabilities, when the relative frequencies are observable. Meteorology gives some good examples of this. What are the chances of a white Christmas next year? Although it is too far in the future to know what cold or warm fronts may be passing through, we can look at the frequency of white Christmases over the past decades and use that information to estimate the probability of a white Christmas next year. The records show that about 20 percent of Christmases in the Philadelphia area (where I live) have been white Christmases. So we can say with good confidence that the probability of a white Christmas is about 20 percent.

Throwing a single die is a pretty simple event, and so is a white Christmas. In applications of probability we often have to deal with much more complicated events. To compute the probabilities of very complicated events we may use methods from algebra, logic, and calculus. We will not go into that just now. Some of those methods are important in game theory, but we will get to them when we need them for the game theory. However, there is one method of application of probabilities that we will need throughout the book, and it will be explained in the next section.

Expected Value

Suppose someone were to offer you a bet. You can throw a single die, and he will pay $10 if the die shows 6, but nothing otherwise. How much is this a gamble worth to you? If he would ask you to pay a dollar to play the game, would it be worthwhile? What if he asked for two?

One way to approach this is to think what would happen if you played the game a large number of times—let's say that you played it hundred times. Since we know that the probability of a 6 on each throw is 1/6, you can expect to see approximately one-sixth of 100 sixes in the 100 throws. One-sixth of 100 is between 16 and 17. So you could expect to win roughly 16 or 17 times. If you paid $1 for each game, or $100, and you won 16 or 17 times, you would win approximately $160 or $170. In that case, you would be pretty certain to come out ahead. But if you paid $2 per game, for a total of $200, it doesn't look so good.

But we really want the value of a single play. Each play has two possible outcomes—a 6, which pays $10, and any other number, which pays nothing. The probability of the $10 payoff is 1/6, and the probability of nothing is 5/6. Multiply each of the payoffs by its probability and add the two together. We have $1/6 \times 10 + 5/6 \times 0$ for a total of 1.67. Thus, $1.67 is the value of an individual gamble.

This is an example of the *mathematical expectation* or **expected value** of an uncertain payoff. The expected value is a weighted average of all the possible payoffs, where the weights are the probabilities of those payoffs. Thus, in the game of throwing one die, the payoffs of 1 and 0 are weighted by the probabilities of 1/6 and 5/6 and added together to give the weighted average or expected value.

> ### Definition   **7**
>
> **Expected Value**—Suppose an uncertain event can have several outcomes with numerical values that may be different. The **expected value** (also known as *mathematical expectation*) of the event is the weighted average of the numerical values, with the probabilities of the outcomes as the weights.

Let's try another example of expected value. Joe Cool is taking a three-credit course in game theory, and his grade is uncertain. He is pretty sure that it will be an A, B, or C, with probabilities 0.4, 0.4, and 0.2. His college calculates grade point averages by assigning 4 "quality points" per credit for an A, 3 for a B, 2 for a C, and 1 for a D. What is the expected value of the quality points Joe will get from game theory? If he gets an A he gets $3 \times 4 = 12$ quality points, if a B, 9, and if a C, 6. So we have an expected value of $0.4 \times 12 + 0.4 \times 9 + 0.2 \times 6 = 10.2$ quality points.

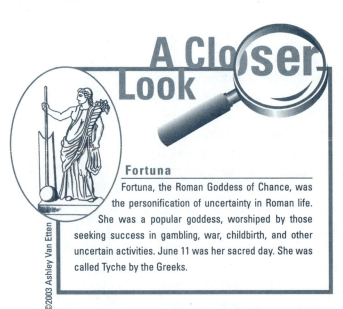

A Closer Look

Fortuna

Fortuna, the Roman Goddess of Chance, was the personification of uncertainty in Roman life. She was a popular goddess, worshiped by those seeking success in gambling, war, childbirth, and other uncertain activities. June 11 was her sacred day. She was called Tyche by the Greeks.

©2003 Ashley Van Etten

Definition

Natural Uncertainty—**Natural uncertainty** is uncertainty about the outcome of a game that results from some natural cause rather than the actions of the human players. In game theory we introduce natural uncertainty by allowing nature to be a player, and assuming that nature plays according to given probabilities.

NOW IT'S YOUR TURN. Suppose a gambler offers to throw one die and pay you the number of dollars shown on the die. What is the mathematical expectation of this payment?

Nature as a Player

In the musical comedy *Guys and Dolls*, a leading character, Sky Masterson, is a notorious gambler. According to a description, he would bet on which of two raindrops dripping down a windowpane would reach the bottom first. This is a good example of natural uncertainty—that is, uncertainty resulting from the complexity and unpredictability of nature. Natural uncertainty plays a part in many games and other human activities. It certainly has ruined a picnic or two of mine.

However, game theory thinks in terms of the interactions of the players in the game. So how do we bring natural uncertainty into game theory? When there is **natural uncertainty**, the convention in game theory is to think of "nature" as a player in the game. Just as the ancient Romans personified Chance as the Goddess Fortuna, so the game theorist makes Chance a player in the game. But "Chance" or "Nature" is a rather strange player. Unlike the human players in the game, she doesn't care about the outcome and always plays her strategies at random, with some given probabilities.

Let's have an example. Suppose that a company is considering the introduction of a new product. Unknown technological and market conditions may be "good" or "bad" for the innovation. This is Nature's play in the game. She decides whether the conditions will be "good" or "bad" and she does so at random, with—for the sake of the example—a 50-50 probability rule. The firm's strategies are go or no-go. The payoffs to the firm are shown in Table 7.1, along with the probabilities of Nature's strategies and the expected values of the go and no-go strategies. Since go pays an expected value of 5, while no-go pays nothing, the firm would choose go and introduce the product.

Table 7.1 | A Game Against Nature

		Nature		expected value payoff
		good	bad	
Decision maker	no-go	0	0	0
	go	20	–10	5
	probability	0.5	0.5	

Table 7.2 The Same Game with Contingent Strategies

		Nature		expected value payoff
		good	bad	
Decisionmaker	if good then go; if bad then go	20	−10	5
	if good then go; if bad then no-go	20	0	10
	if good then no-go; if bad then go	0	−10	−5
	if good then no-go; if bad then no-go	0	0	0
probability		0.5	0.5	

We can apply the expected-value idea (along with contingent strategies) to find out how much the businessperson's ignorance costs him. Here is the mind experiment: Not knowing whether the conditions are good or bad, the decision maker can make a decision based only on probabilities. But suppose that our decision maker can call in a consultant and find out, before making the decision, whether the conditions are good or bad. How much will the decision maker be willing to pay the consultant (i.e., what is the "value of information" that the consultant can supply)?

What, in fact, is the advantage of having more information? The advantage is that, with more information, we can make use of contingent strategies. The game of product development with contingent strategies is shown in Table 7.2. We see that the contingent strategy, "if good then go; if bad then no-go" gives an expected value of 10. By getting the information, and using it to choose a contingent strategy, the businessperson can increase the expected value payoff from 5 to 10. Thus, any consultant's fee less than 5 leaves the decision maker better off in an expected-value sense, and the value of information in this case is 5.

An Example from Naval Conflict

Nature often is a player in war. Here is an example. In 1797, when the British were at war with revolutionary France, Spain joined France as an ally and attempted to bring its navy into the Atlantic to meet with the French navy and together attack the British. The British navy fought the Spanish at the Battle of Cape St. Vincent on February 14, St. Valentine's Day. The

Spanish objective was the port of Cadiz (formerly known as Gades in Roman times, and important also in our example of the Spanish Rebellion!). However, they had been blown out to sea by a storm, and were thus delayed in trying to get to Cadiz. The British intercepted them off the coast of Portugal. The Spanish fleet was divided into two groups, and the British commander, Admiral Sir John Jervis, decided to split the Spanish, sailing between the two groups so that they could not reinforce one another.[1]

The British were much better trained, and if they were able to split the enemy fleet into two parts, they had an excellent chance to defeat them. There was very little wind, and the Spanish had the better angle. (In nautical jargon, the Spanish had the weather gauge). On the one hand, if the wind were to increase, it would help the Spanish more than the British, since the Spanish would be able to reunite their fleet. In that case they had their best chance to defeat the British. On the other hand, if the wind remained light, the British would be able to sail into the gap between the two parts of the Spanish fleet and probably defeat them.

Wind, then, was a source of uncertainty in the Battle of Cape St. Vincent, as it often is for sailors. Nature was a player, and her two strategies were, first, low wind, and second, moderate or high wind. The British strategies were to go ahead and attempt to sail between the two parts of the Spanish fleet or to veer off, and avoid a fight with the bigger fleet. The Spanish strategies were to continue on their course for Cadiz, resisting as best they could, or to veer off for another port. If they did veer off, the British would harass them on the way to the other port, and the Spanish would be likely to take some losses. In that case a stronger wind would work to the disadvantage of the Spanish, since, by turning away from the battle, they would also be giving up the weather gauge.

Table 7.3 shows a reconstruction of the possible outcomes in this game, with a British victory shown as payoffs (1, −1); a Spanish victory shown as payoffs (−1, 1); and a standoff as payoffs (0, 0).

In order to decide which strategy is better, without knowing whether the wind will remain low or increase, the two admirals could compute the expected value of the payoffs for each strategy. (They almost certainly didn't do this consciously, since admirals in those days were not trained in probabilities, but let's see how it would go, anyway.) Suppose the probabilities were 50-50—the probability of increased wind is 50 percent and the probability of

---

1 The British were heavily outnumbered, although they didn't know it. As they got closer, they saw more and more of the Spanish fleet. The admiral's advisers said,

"There are eight sail of the line, Sir John."
"Very well, sir."
"There are twenty sail of the line, Sir John."
"Very well, sir."
"There are twenty-five sail of the line, Sir John."
"Very well, sir."
"There are twenty-seven sail of the line, Sir John."
"Enough, sir, no more of that; the die is cast, and if there are fifty sail I will go through them."

From a British Web site commemorating the two-hundredth anniversary of the battle: *http://www.stvincent.ac.uk/1797/.*

Table 7.3 The Battle of Cape St. Vincent

		Nature			
		low wind		high or moderate wind	
		Spain		Spain	
		go	veer off	go	veer off
British	go	1, −1	0, 0	−1, 1	1, −1
	veer off	−1, 1	0, 0	−1, 1	0, 0
probabilities		0.5		0.5	

continued low wind 50 percent. The expected values on these assumptions are shown in Table 7.4. We see that (go, go) is a dominant strategy equilibrium for this game.

Each side maximizes its expected value by choosing an aggressive strategy—and that is what the two sides did, except for one Spanish ship that left the line of battle and ran for a safe port to the east. In fact, the wind remained light, and the British did split the Spanish line. At that point, miscalculation, luck, desperate improvisation, and heroism played their part, as they do in all battles, but the British won the victory. By the battle's end, four Spanish ships had been captured and Spain had lost 3,000 men. The British lost only 300 men.[2]

Table 7.4 Expected Values for the Battle of Cape St. Vincent

		Spain	
		go	veer off
British	go	0, 0	0.5, −0.5
	veer off	−1, 1	0, 0

Risk Aversion

In a sense, the mathematical expectation is the fair value of an uncertain payment. But that may not be the whole story, since it can be a risky value, and people often prefer to avoid risk.

Here is an example. Karen has bought a painting at an antique show. She got it cheap, and she knows she has a good deal. Karen is pretty certain that the painting is by one of two artists.

2 This example made use of information from two Web sites: *http://www.stvincent.ac.uk/1797/* and *http://www.napoleonguide. com/battle_stvincen.htm*. Some of the interpretation and motivation, and the use of the battle as an example, were suggested by a novel by Dudley Pope, *Ramage and the Drumbeat*. McBooks Press, 2000, first published by Weidenfield & Nicholson, 1967.

One is a well-known nineteenth-century regional artist. If the painting is by the nineteenth-century artist, then it can be resold for $10,000. The second artist is a twentieth-century imitator. If the painting is by the imitator, it is worth only $2,000. From her knowledge of the styles of the two painters, Karen knows that the probability that it is by the nineteenth-century artist is 0.25, so the probability that it is by the twentieth-century artist is 0.75.

Table 7.5 | Money Payoffs of Art Resale

		Expected value payoff		
		19th century	20th century	expected value
Karen	sell for $3,500	3500	3500	3500
	investigate artist	10000	2000	4000
probability		0.25	0.75	

But another person, who arrived at the antique show just after Karen made her purchase, has offered her $3,500 for the painting. Thus, Karen has to choose between a certain $3,500 and an uncertain resale value of the painting that could be as much as $10,000 or as little as $2,000. Karen's strategies are to accept the $3,500 offer or investigate the identity of the artist and perhaps put the painting on the market when the artist's identity has been documented, if possible. The payoffs and probabilities are shown in Table 7.5.

If Karen accepts the deal, she has $3,500 for her painting, with no uncertainty or risk. However, as we see in Table 7.5, the expected value of the "investigate" strategy is $4,000 [(10,000 × 0.25) + (2,000 × 0.75)], which is better. If Karen cares only about the money payoff, she will keep the painting and investigate the author. But Karen might accept the $3,500 offer anyway. The benefits that would motivate Karen to refuse or accept the offer are subjective benefits, and from a subjective point of view, the uncertainty of the resale value of the painting is a disadvantage in itself. Allowing for this disadvantage, the risky resale value isn't really worth as much as its expected value. If this is the way Karen feels, then we would say that Karen is **risk averse**.

> ### Definition
>
> **Risk Aversion**—A person who will choose a safe payment over a risky payment with an expected value greater than that of the safe payment is said to be **risk averse**. A person who chooses a risky payment over a safe payment, even though the risky payment has a smaller expected value than the safe payment, is said to be **risk loving**. A person who will always choose the higher money expected value is said to be **risk neutral**.

Risk aversion seems to be a common fact of human activity. Whenever anyone buys insurance, and whenever an investor chooses a less-profitable investment because it is more secure, these are expressions of risk aversion. Of course, individuals differ, and some might be risk averse while others are not. If a person would choose the risky payment (instead of one that has the same expected value and is certain) we say that the person is **risk loving** rather than risk averse. A person who will always choose the bigger expected value, regardless of the risk, is said to be **risk neutral**.

Now, let's suppose that Karen decided to keep the picture, investigated the artist, and found that the painting really was by the nineteenth-century artist, and therefore worth $10,000. Instead of reselling the picture, however, Karen decided to keep it for herself. In that case, she might consider insuring the picture against loss as a result of fire or theft. Now Karen is involved in yet another game against nature. Nature's strategies are to cause the loss of the picture or not to do so. Karen's strategies are to insure or not insure. Supposing that the probability of a loss is just 1/1,000 and the insurance policy rider would cost $12, we have the payoffs shown in Table 7.6. We see that, if Karen is risk neutral, she will not insure—the expected value of not insuring (with a very small probability of a loss) is greater than the certain cost of the insurance policy. However, if she is risk averse, she might nevertheless choose to insure.

Table 7.6 | Money Payoffs of Insuring Art

		Nature		expected value payoff
		lost	not lost	
Karen	don't insure	−10000	0	−10
	insure	−12	−12	−12
probability		0.001	0.999	

Economists and finance theorists usually assume that risk aversion is an aspect of an individual's tastes. In any case, they would not expect the individual's risk aversion to change very much from one day to the next, since risk aversion is considered to be an aspect of the person's tastes and preferences and tastes and preferences are thought of as being quite stable. But that's an assumption, not a known fact. Most people probably would be less risk averse if they were in a casino than otherwise, so social context does matter. The economist would say that this willingness to take risks in the casino reflects a taste for entertainment, not a change in risk aversion. Stable or not, risk aversion is a key factor whenever human beings confront uncertainty.

Expected Utility

Risk aversion can be linked to other kinds of subjective motivations by means of a concept borrowed from economists, who, in turn, borrowed it from philosophers and mathematicians. The concept is a numerical measure of **utility**. We begin with the assumption that the *subjective* benefits of winning

> **Definition**
>
> *Utility*—**Utility** is a numerical measure of the subjective benefits an individual derives from a particular good, service, income, or payoff.

the game can be measured with a number. This number is called utility, and is the real payoff of the game, from the point of view of the individual player. In general, the utility payoff will differ from the money payoff, but there is a systematic relationship between the two. When the money payoff increases, the utility payoff also increases; but not in proportion.

We cannot really understand this approach completely without using calculus. However, we can illustrate the idea with some examples and visualization. Let's continue with the example of Karen, the art collector. We suppose that Karen evaluates her alternatives in terms of a utility function rather than in terms of the money values. Her utility depends on the money values, and utility increases whenever money payoff does, but not in proportion. Her utility function will have the property economists call diminishing marginal utility. Thus, the more dollars she already has, the less additional utility she gets from one additional dollar.

Figure 7.1 gives a visualization of the changes in Karen's utility as her money payoffs increase—in other words, a graph of the function U(Y). In the figure, the money payoff is shown on the horizontal axis and the corresponding utility, or subjective payoff, is shown on the vertical axis. The dashed gray curve shows the utility, from Karen's point of view, of any money payoff between $2,000 and $10,000—provided the payoff is certain. Her utility varies from 6.7, for a payoff of $2,000, up to 10 for a payoff of $10,000.

One thing we see is that the curve[3] showing the utility gets flatter as the money payoff increases. This is the visual expression diminishing marginal utility. The marginal utility of one dollar more of money, from Karen's point of view, is the slope of the utility curve in Figure 7.1. Thus, the way that the curve gets flatter when the payoffs get larger is a visualization of diminishing marginal utility.

Now, let's apply this to the $3,500 offer Karen had for the picture. Since it is a riskless offer, the utility of the $3,500 is on the gray curve corresponding to $3,500—it is about 7.7. In this case, remember, Karen's utility for a $2,000 payoff is 6.7, and for a $10,000 payoff her

3 Where does this curve come from? In practice, measuring utility functions is pretty much guesswork, although we will say a little more about that later in the appendix to this chapter. In this case, to make the diagram easy to see, I decided that Karen's utility function would be the fourth root of her payoff. If it is new to you, the fourth root is the square root of the square root.

Figure **7.1** | Karen's Utility of Payoffs

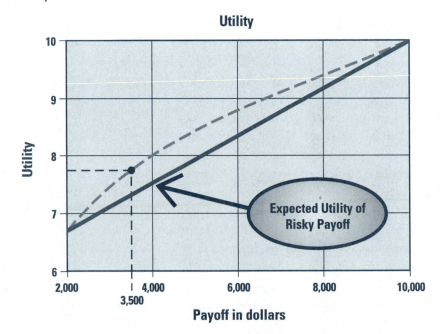

utility is 10. The expected value of the uncertain payoff is $(0.25)(6.7) + (0.75)(10) = 7.5$. So—if Karen's utility function is the one shown in the curve—she would take the offer. The risk-less offer gives more utility, even though less money on the average, than the risky payoff from waiting and investigating the painting.

It turns out that a player who has diminishing marginal utility for payoff dollars will always be risk-averse. Here is the reasoning behind that. We have seen that the expected utility of Karen's uncertain option is $(0.25)(6.7) + (0.75)(10) = 7.5$. We can generalize that for other probabilities. Say that p is the probability of the $2,000 payment and 6.7 utility, so $1 - p$ is the probability of the $10,000 payoff and utility of 10. The expected value of utility is $6.7p + 10(1 - p)$. The main point of this is that the expected value is a *linear* average of the two end-point utilities. All of the expected utilities have to be on a straight line. Specifically, in this case, all of the expected utilities have to be on the solid black line. Notice in Figure 7.1 that the black line is below the gray curve, for every money value from $2,000 to $8,000. That means a riskless payment (gray curve) always gives more utility than a risky alternative with the same expected value in money terms (black line).

> **Rule**
>
> *Utility and Risk Aversion*—A utility function with diminishing marginal utility for the money income corresponds to risk aversion. A utility function with increasing marginal utility corresponds to risk loving. A utility function with constant marginal utility, which means utility is proportional to the money payoff, corresponds to risk neutrality.

This is a general rule. Whenever players have diminishing marginal utility of payoff dollars, they will be risk averse to some extent.

In the previous section, we continued the example by supposing that Karen did actually buy the picture and then had to decide whether to insure it. With the utility function we are using for this example, Karen will not sell the picture, as we have seen. So let's change the rules for the example a little bit. Once she has bought the picture, Karen can examine it more closely before deciding whether to accept the $3,500 offer. Looking at the painting closely, Karen discovers that the painting is signed. Although the signature could be a fake, put there by an unscrupulous dealer, it makes the nineteenth-century artist a bit more likely. With this information, Karen changes her estimates of the probabilities for the two payoffs, as shown in Table 7.8.

Karen's strategies in her game against nature are still the same as they were before: accept the $3,500 offer or investigate further after she has taken the painting home. As we see in Table 7.8, further investigation now gives Karen the greater expected utility. So, with this new information, Karen will refuse the $3,500 offer despite her risk aversion.

Table 7.8 Utility Payoffs of Art Resale with More Information

		Nature		expected utility payoff
		19th century	20th century	
Karen	sell for $3,500	7.7	7.7	7.7
	investigate artist	10	6.7	8
probability		0.4	0.6	

Table 7.9 Utility Payoffs of Insuring Art

Karen		Nature		expected utility payoff
		lost	not lost	
	don't insure	0	10	9.990
	insure	9.997	9.997	9.997
probability		0.001	0.999	

Now we return to Karen's decision whether or not to insure. We are assuming (remember) that after she got home and consulted her reference books, Karen discovered that she had the genuine nineteenth-century painting, worth $10,000. Thus, her choice is to insure against loss of $10,000, or to take her chances. The utility payoffs and expected values of utility for the two decisions are shown in Table 7.9.[4] We see that Karen gets a higher expected value payoff if she chooses to insure. This should not be a surprise. The evaluation in Table 7.6 was based on the assumption that Karen is risk neutral. If risk neutral, Karen would not insure. Now, in Table 7.9, we are assuming that Karen is risk averse, and now, we see, she does insure. The slightly higher payoff to the strategy of insuring is a result of the risk aversion—and risk aversion is one of the reasons insurance companies can make a profit!

Of the three possible cases, risk neutrality, risk aversion, and risk loving, the first, risk neutrality, is the simplest. In that case, utility is proportional to the money payoff, so we can just assume the game player maximizes the expected value of the payoff. For the other two cases, risk aversion and risk loving, the usual assumption is that the game player maximizes the expected value of utility. There is some controversy about this, however, and it is a complication that we can usually avoid in game theory. In most of the examples to follow, when there are probabilities to consider, we will make the simplifying assumption that the player is risk neutral.

Summary

Probability is a way of expressing the relative likelihood of an uncertain outcome in numerical terms. Probabilities range from zero to one, and a larger probability is attached to a more likely outcome. Probability is a large subject in itself, and we limit ourselves in this chapter to a few applications that are very important in game theory.

Probabilities can be helpful in assigning values to uncertain payoffs. If we know that the payoff in a decision or game will be one of several numbers, and we can assign probabilities to the numbers, we can compute the expected value of the payoff as the weighted average of the payoff numbers, using the probabilities as weights.

In game theory, uncertainty is customarily brought into the picture by making Chance or Nature one of the players in the game. Nature plays her strategies with fixed probabilities. When a single individual makes a decision with an uncertain outcome, we think

4 To compute the utility of insuring: Karen's money payoff if she insures is 10,000 − 12 = 9,988, and the fourth root of 9,988 is 9.997, from a trusty spreadsheet.

of that as a game against nature. One possible solution to a game against nature is to maximize the expected value of the payoff.

In other games with two or more human players, nature may also be a player. Here again, one possible solution is for the players to evaluate their various strategies using the expected value of the payoffs, depending on the probabilities of different actions by nature.

But the expected value of the money payoffs may not be the right solution. In the last analysis, the payoffs that motivate human choices of strategy are subjective payoffs. From the subjective point of view, uncertainty may in itself be undesirable. When uncertainty is undesirable, we say that the player or decision maker is risk averse. One way to show risk aversion in the game is to think in terms of the utility function. The player chooses the strategy that gives a maximum for the expected value of the utility of the money payoff. Utility increases with a larger money payoff.

However, utility may increase less than proportionately with the money payoff. On one hand, a player who maximizes the expected value of utility will be risk averse. On the other hand, a player who simply maximizes the money payoff is said to be risk neutral.

Probability and expected value are used widely in game theory, and will play important roles in many chapters to follow. In most cases, we will make the simplifying assumption that players in our games are risk neutral, so that they will maximize the expected value of the money payoff. This is the assumption we have made throughout the previous chapters. In a few cases, where risk aversion is very important, we will apply the idea of an expected utility and assume that the players maximize the expected value of the utility of the money payoff. This complication will be unusual, and the student will be clearly warned when we come to these applications.

Appendix A
Measuring Utility

Using this relationship between the expected utility of money and the expected value of utility of payoffs, von Neumann and Morgenstern proposed a way of measuring the utility of payoffs. Suppose we want to know the utility Karen attaches to a riskless payment of $4,000. We will offer her a lottery, in which the payoff is $10,000, with a probability p, and 0, with a probability 1 – p. We offer Karen a choice between the lottery and the riskless payment of $4,000. She will choose the lottery or the riskless payment, depending on whether the lottery ticket gives her more utility than the riskless payment. So we negotiate with Karen, carefully adjusting the probability p until she doesn't care (is indifferent) which alternative she gets. That means the expected utility of the lottery is the same as the utility of $4,000.

To measure the utility of $4,000, or any other amount, we need to agree on units of measurement and on the zero point. We will assign a zero payoff a utility of zero. That's just as arbitrary as any other zero point, but it is easy to remember. Rating utility on a ten-point scale, we will assign 10 to the payoff of $10,000. Therefore, when Karen is indifferent between the two alternatives (doesn't care whether she gets the lottery or the riskless $4,000), the expected

A Closer Look

Reverend Thomas Bayes
1702–1761

Born in London, England, Bayes was a mathematician and theologian whose work extended from advances in mathematical probability to an attempt to prove the benevolence of God. He is best remembered for his work on probability in "Essay Towards Solving a Problem in the Doctrine of Chances" (1763), published posthumously in the *Philosophical Transactions of the Royal Society of London.*

Courtesy, International Society for Bayesian Analysis

utility of the lottery is $10,000p + (1 - p)(0) = 10,000p =$ utility of \$4,000. Suppose we try the experiment and find that the probability that does the trick is 0.795. Then we say the utility of \$4,000 is $10 \times 0.795 = 7.95$.

In general, according to the von Neumann and Morgenstern approach, the first step in measuring utility is to establish payoffs corresponding to an arbitrary zero point and an arbitrary unit of measurement. Then we can measure the utility of any amount X between the lower and upper limits by finding the probability that makes the person indifferent between X and a lottery that pays either the upper or lower limit. The probability is used to measure the utility of X.

Appendix B
Bayes' Rule

One of the more advanced methods of probability analysis widely used in advanced game theory is *Bayes' Rule*, named after statistician Thomas Bayes. This method will be mentioned in passing in a few of the remaining chapters, but we will not give applications of it in this introductory text. Here is a single example to get the idea.

Suppose that Karen the collector is examining a painting she might buy. Because of its distinctive style, she thinks it might be by Himmelthal—Karen knows that 25 percent of all the paintings in that style are Himmelthals. Looking more carefully, Karen discovers that the painting is signed "Himmelthal." Himmelthal did not sign all of his paintings—Karen knows from her reference books that he signed 90 percent of them. But there are forgeries, too, and 35 percent of all paintings in this style (counting forgeries) are signed Himmelthal. Thus:

p_1 = the probability that a painting in this style is a Himmelthal = 0.25
p_2 = the probability that a Himmelthal is signed "Himmelthal" = 0.90
p_3 = the probability that a painting in this style is signed "Himmelthal" = 0.35

But none of those is what Karen wants. She wants p_4 = the probability that a painting in this style *and* signed Himmelthal *is* a Himmelthal, taking forgeries into account. To get that, she applies Bayes' rule:

$$p_4 = p_2 \, p_1 / p_3 = (0.9)(0.25)/(0.35) = 0.64$$

7.1

The probability that it is a Himmelthal is slightly less than 2/3.

In general, Bayes' rule says:

> **7.2**
>
> probability that A is true if X is observed =
>
> $$\frac{(\text{probability of } X \text{ if } A \text{ is true})(\text{probability of } A \text{ independently of } X)}{(\text{probability of } X \text{ independently of } A)}$$

John Harsanyi shared the Nobel Memorial prize with Nash and Selten in honor of his work exploring the application of Bayes' rule to game theory. In Harsanyi's approach to game theory, the players maximize the expected value of their payoffs, given their estimates of the probabilities that others play particular strategies; and they keep revising their estimates of the probabilities of the others' strategies, using that approach, until no one wants to change either the estimated probability or the strategies any further.

For an approachable explanation of Bayes' rule, see Alan S. Caniglia, *Statistics for Economics, an Intuitive Approach* (New York: HarperCollins, 1992), pp. 69–72.

A Closer Look

John Harsanyi 1920–2000

Born in Budapest, Hungary, John Harsanyi was originally educated as a pharmacist, as his parents wished. Harsanyi switched to philosophy in 1946. Scheduled to be sent to a concentration camp in 1944, he escaped from Nazi confinement and was hidden for a year in the basement of a Jesuit monastery. To leave Communist Hungary in 1950, Harsanyi and his fiancee walked through marshes to cross the border illegally.

After moving to Australia, he had to do factory work at first, but later shifted to a new field, economics, and obtained his Ph.D. at Stanford in 1959. He joined the faculty of the University of California at Berkeley in 1964. His breadth of interests and experience are reflected in contributions to game theory and other fields that focus on the nature of rationality, especially in circumstances of missing information.

©The Nobel Foundation

Exercises and Discussion Questions

7.1 **Icosahedral Dice.** Icosahedral dice are used in some magic role-playing games. Each die is an icosahedron—that is, a solid with 20 equal sides. The sides are numbered from 1 to 20, so that when an icosahedral die is thrown, the uppermost side may show a number between 1 and 20, with equal probabilities. The probability of any specific number is 1/20.

When an icosahedral die is thrown, what is the probability that the number showing is greater than 7? What is the expected value of a bet that pays $5 dollars if the number showing is greater than 7? What is the expected value of the number showing when an icosahedral die is thrown?

7.2   Country Risk. Investors who invest in other countries may be concerned about changes in the countries in which they invest that have an impact on their profits. This is called *country risk*. Of course, country risk is complicated, and the probability of loss is at least partly subjective. Here is a list of countries you might invest in. For each country, estimate the probability that political changes could lead to a serious investment loss. If you do not know anything about the country, take a few minutes with an encyclopedia or on the World Wide Web to learn a little, and then make your best subjective estimate.

A. Pakistan

B. Belgium

C. Ghana

D. Mexico

7.3   Urn Problem. You are to draw one ball at random from an urn containing 50 white balls and 100 black balls. What is the probability that you will draw a white ball? *Hint:* If you were to draw 150 balls, what proportion would be white?

7.4   Lottery. You have tickets in a lottery. The lottery will be decided by drawing a ball from an urn. There are a thousand balls in the urn, numbered from 1 to 1,000. The tickets are also numbered from 1 to 1,000, and the person holding the ticket with a number corresponding to that on the drawn ball will be the winner. The winner will be paid a thousand dollars. You hold all the tickets numbered 1 through 20.

What is the probability that you will win? What is the expected value of your payoff from this lottery?

7.5   Investment in Research. You have an opportunity to invest in a company that is working on a research project. If you invest, you will have to put up $1 million. If the project is successful, the result will be a new kind of product that will yield a return of $6 million for your investment. The probability of success is 1/5.

What is the role of nature in this game? Construct a table to represent your choice of whether to invest as a game, using your answer to the previous question. Compute the expected value of the payoff to your investment. Assuming that you are risk neutral, and you had the million, would you decide to invest or not to invest?

7.6   Risk Aversion. Reconsider your answer to the previous question, assuming that your utility function is $SQRT\sqrt{Y + 1,000,000}$ where Y is the payoff of either 0 or $6 million as the case may be, minus the $1 million you have to put up. Now will you make the investment?

Mixed Strategy Nash Equilibria

To best understand this chapter 8

To best understand this chapter you need to have studied and understood the material from Chapters 1–4 and 7.

We have seen how game theory uses the concept of expected values to deal with uncertainty from natural sources. But the players may deliberately introduce uncertainty into the game because it suits their purposes. There are some games in which the best choice of strategies is an unpredictable choice of strategies. The concepts of probability and expected value can help us to understand that. A good example is found in the great American game of baseball.

Keeping Them Honest in Baseball

Baseball comes down, on every pitch, to a confrontation between two players: the pitcher and the batter. To keep things simple, we consider a pitcher who has just two pitches: a fastball and a change-up. The change-up is a slower ball that would be easy to hit if the batter knew it was coming. But the change-up may be used to fool a batter who is expecting the fastball. These two pitches will be the pitcher's two strategies. The batter is good—he can hit the fastball and knock it a long way, but only if he commits himself to swing before he has seen the ball. If he waits until he can see the ball he will miss the fastball, but he will hit the change-up for a chance at a single. We suppose the count is three balls and two strikes—"three and two" in baseball jargon. For nonbaseball folks, that means this is the last chance (ignoring the possibility of foul balls) for both the pitcher and the batter. The payoffs are shown in Table 8.1.

It may seem that the pitcher should always throw his best pitch, especially in a crucial situation such as this. The problem is that if he does, the batter will always swing early, and will get a lot of hits and a lot of home runs. Even if the pitcher throws his fastball predictably only in three-and-two situations, that will make easier for the batter to decide how to swing. He can just swing early on every three-and-two situation.

Table 8.1 | Payoffs for Baseball

		Pitcher	
		fastball	change-up
Batter	swing early	10, –10	–5, 5
	swing late	–5, 5	3, –3

Heads Up!

Here are some concepts we will develop as this chapter goes along:

Pure Strategies: Every game in normal form is defined by a list of strategies with their payoffs. These are the *pure strategies* in the game.

Mixed or Randomized Strategies: In a game in normal form, a player who chooses among the list of normal-form pure strategies according to given probabilities—two or more of which are positive—is said to choose a *mixed strategy*.

Mixed Strategy Equilibrium: A Nash equilibrium in which one or more of the players chooses a mixed strategy is called a *mixed strategy equilibrium*.

It is very much the same from the point of view of the batter. If he swings predictably—for example, if he just swings early on every pitch—then the pitcher has an easy job. He can just throw a change-up on every pitch. So the batter, too, needs to be unpredictable.

Assuming, as usual, that they are both rational, each of the two baseball players will choose unpredictably between their two strategies. *Unpredictably* means that there is a random element in the choice of strategies. Each will choose one strategy or the other with some probability. This is called a **mixed strategy**, since it mixes the two **pure strategies** shown in the table. Part of the job of the player who calls the plays—pitcher and catcher in baseball, quarterback in football, point guard in basketball—is to "mix them up," to be unpredictable, so that the opposition cannot guess which strategy is coming and prepare accordingly. This is one of the toughest jobs in sports—it really isn't easy for a human being to choose at random.

To restate, a pure strategy is one of the strategies shown in the normal form of the game, picked with probability one (certainty). A mixed strategy is the randomized choice of one pure strategy or another according to given probabilities. The strategies are mixed in the proportions of the probabilities.

But what probabilities will they choose? To figure that out, we have to consider it from both points of view. From my point of view, the key idea is to prevent the other player from exploiting my own predictability. So I want to choose a probability that will keep him guessing. Let's look at it from the point of view of the batter. Let p be the probability that the pitcher throws a fastball. Table 8.2 shows the payoffs to the batter's two strategies, in terms of the probability p. (Of course, we use the expected value concept, since the strategies are unpredictable.) If p is large enough, swinging early will pay better than swinging late. In that case, the batter will choose to swing early. On the other hand, if p is small enough, then swinging late will pay better. In that case, the batter will swing late.

Now let's switch to the pitcher's point of view. To limit his losses, and keep the batter guessing, what the pitcher needs to do is to adjust p so that neither of the batter's strategies pays better than the other. We can express that with a little algebra. To say that neither payoff is bigger than the other is to say that

Table 8.2 Expected Value Payoffs for Batter Strategies

swing early pays	$10p - 5(1-p) = 15p - 5$
swing late pays	$-5p + 3(1-p) = 3 - 8p$

$$15p - 5 = 3 - 8p \qquad \boxed{8.1}$$

Solving that for p,

$$p = 8/23$$

8.2

So the pitcher throws the fastball with probability 8/23. Now, let's look at the batter's strategy choices, from the point of view of the pitcher. Let q be the probability that the batter swings early. Table 8.3 shows the expected value payoffs for a fastball and a change-up. The batter will try to adjust the probability q so that neither of those strategies gives a better expected value payoff than the other. This is expressed by Equation 8.3:

Table 8.3 | Expected Value Payoffs for Pitcher Strategies

fastball pays	$-10q + 5(1 - q) = 5 - 15q$
change-up pays	$5q + 3(1 - q) = 8q - 3$

$$5 - 15q = 8q - 3$$

8.3

Solving Equation 8.3, algebraically, we find a probability of 8/23. That is the probability that the batter will swing early:

$$q = 8/23$$

8.4

We now have the probabilities: The pitcher will throw a fastball with a probability 8/23 and the change-up with a probability 15/23, and the batter will swing early with a probability of 8/23 and swing late with a probability of 15/23. Each one chooses a *mixed strategy*, and in each case the mixture is the player's best response to the mixture chosen by the other player. Remember the definition of a Nash equilibrium: Each player chooses a strategy that is his or her best response to the other players' strategies. It seems that when the two baseball players choose probability mixtures 8/23 and 15/23, we have a Nash equilibrium.

This may be easier to understand if we separate it into two stages. At the first stage, for example, the batter decides whether to randomize, and at the second stage the batter chooses the specific probabilities. So long as the pitcher chooses the mixed strategy with probabilities 8/23 and 15/23, the batter is indifferent between his two strategies. Swing early and swing late both give the same expected payoff. The batter may as well randomize. But, from the point of view of expected payoffs, the batter could choose any probabilities—50-50, 90-10, 100-0, any other. So how does he choose the probabilities? He realizes that if he does not choose the probabilities 8/23 and 15/23, the pitcher will not randomize.

Thinking It Through

There is a sort of intellectual jujitsu involved in the mixed strategy equilibrium idea, and it can be confusing. It may seem odd that the pitcher is balancing the expected value payoffs for the *batter* and equalizing them. But in doing so he is maximizing his own expected value payoff. The pitcher's objective is really to force the batter to randomize *his* hitting strategy.

A person might not want to randomize, reasoning as follows: "I'm not going to randomize, because that's giving up. I'm going to stay a step ahead of the other guy, and choose the right strategy to beat him." But if the other guy is randomizing his strategy, it is no use—he will choose the probabilities so that all of your strategies give you the same expected value, and it doesn't matter which you choose. You just can't out-think the other guy—unless he is trying to out-think you! "You can't con an honest man" and you can't con a randomizer, either.

In game theory we assume *common knowledge of rationality*; that is, not only that both players are rational but that each one knows the other is rational. This is especially important for mixed strategies.

So I reason as follows: "My opponent knows that he cannot out-think me, so he will not try. He will randomize, unless I act irrationally and predictably and so give him an opportunity. He will prevent me from out-thinking him by choosing probabilities that make the expected values of my strategies equal. So I may as well randomize anyway—but with what probabilities? I want to choose the probabilities that will put him in the worst situation, that will prevent him from out-thinking me—and the way to do that is to choose probabilities that make the expected values of his strategies equal."

There is another, somewhat more intuitive approach to mixed strategies, and it is called *Bayesian learning*. Although intuitive, it is also more mathematically advanced. Perhaps I do not think my opponent is rational, and I just rely on experience to estimate the probabilities that he will choose this strategy and that. Meanwhile, he is doing the same with me. This is called *Bayesian learning* after Thomas Bayes, a statistician who proposed a good rule for revising evidence on the basis of experience. (See Appendix B to Chapter 7). In an example like the baseball game, Bayesian learning will eventually lead both players to adopt the rational mixed strategies that game theorists derived from the "common knowledge of rationality" assumption, but there may be exceptions in more complex games. John Harsanyi shared the Nobel Memorial prize with Nash and Selten in honor of his work exploring Bayesian learning in games.

Table 8.4 shows the results of three possible probabilities the batter might choose. If he chooses 7/23, then the pitcher can get an expected payoff of 0.43 by throwing a fastball, but only –0.56 for a change-up, so in that situation, the pitcher will not randomize, leaving the hitter with an expected value payoff of –0.43. If the batter chooses a probability of 9/23, the pitcher can get –0.87 expected value from a fastball, but 0.13 from a change-up, so again he will not randomize but throw the change-up, leaving the hitter with a –0.13 expected value. Only the exact probability 8/23 leaves the pitcher indifferent between the fastball and the change-up, and so leads the pitcher to make the best of his bad situation and randomize—leaving the hitter with his best expected value possibility, 0.21.

In game theory this kind of Nash equilibrium is known as a **mixed strategy equilibrium**. In fact, the mixed strategy equilibrium is the only equilibrium in this game. If you look back

Table 8.4 | Expected Value Payoffs with Alternative Probabilities

probability of swing early	expected payoff to fastball	expected payoff to change-up	batter's expected payoff
7/23	0.43	−0.57	−0.43
8/23	−0.22	−0.22	0.22
9/23	−0.87	0.13	−0.13

at Table 8.1 you can see for yourself that there is no Nash equilibrium in pure strategies. No matter which combination of pure strategies is chosen, one player or the other will want to depart from it. But there is an equilibrium in terms of mixed strategies, and so long as each player chooses an equilibrium mixed strategy, neither player will want to deviate from it independently.

Pure and Mixed Strategies

What we have seen in the previous example is that human beings may make strategic use of uncertainty by choosing mixed strategies rather than pure strategies. Remember that the pure strategies are the list of strategies that define the normal form of the game or its extensive form. A mixed strategy is a policy of choosing one of two or more pure strategies according to some probability. We have also seen that a game may have an equilibrium in mixed strategies even though it does not have an equilibrium in pure strategies.

> ### Definition
>
> **Pure and Mixed Strategies**—Every game in normal form is defined by a list of strategies with their payoffs. These are the **pure strategies** in the game. However, the player has other options, namely to choose among the strategies according to given positive probabilities. Every such decision rule is called a **mixed strategy**.

Moreover, we have seen from a number of examples that not all games have Nash equilibria in pure strategies. This is a well-known shortcoming of the Nash equilibrium concept. However, when we allow for mixed strategies as well as pure strategies, that is no longer true. John Nash discovered that every two-person game in normal form has an equilibrium in mixed strategies, even if it does not have an equilibrium in pure strategies. Von Neumann and Morgenstern showed that this is true for an important subclass of two-person games, the *zero-sum games*, and John Nash extended this by showing that all two-person games have Nash equilibria in mixed strategies if not in pure strategies. Of course, that's why we call it a Nash equilibrium. Nash shared the Nobel Memorial prize for that discovery.

A Blue-Light Special

Let's look at another example of mixed strategies. Some economists have applied mixed-strategy reasoning to the scheduling of sales by retail merchants. This would not apply to all sales. Some sales are scheduled quite predictably, for example, on holidays. But some sales do seem to be unpredictable—for example, there may be a sale without any notice when a blue light is turned on. Why would a retailer want her sales to be unpredictable? This might be a mixed strategy. If the consumer knew when a sale is to be held, she would make a point of coming on those days. But the consumer might also want to be unpredictable. If the retailer knew which days the consumer would be coming, then the retailer would never schedule sales on those days.

Could this kind of reasoning really lead to a mixed strategy? Let's look at a specific example and see. To make things very simple, we will treat it as a two-person game. The seller is one player and the consumer is the other player. The seller's strategies are to schedule a sale today or tomorrow. The consumer's strategies are to visit the store today or tomorrow. The payoffs for the two players are shown in Table 8.5.[1]

Now look at the payoffs from the point of view of the seller and let p be the probability that the consumer visits the store today rather than tomorrow. The expected values for the seller's two strategies are shown in Table 8.6.

If one of these numbers is greater, then the consumer is making it too easy for the seller to pick a date for a sale when the consumer will not be there. Therefore, the consumer will adjust p so that the two values in Table 8.6 are equal. This is solved algebraically in Equation (8.5):

Table 8.5 | Payoffs for a Sale Game

		Consumer	
		shop today	shop tomorrow
Seller	sale today	5, 10	8, 4
	sale tomorrow	10, 5	4, 8

Table 8.6 | Expected Value Payoffs for Seller Strategies

sale today pays	$5p + 8(1 - p) = 8 - 3p$
sale tomorrow pays	$10p + (1 - p)4 = 4 + 6p$

$$8 - 3p = 4 + 6p$$
$$p = 4/9$$

8.5

So we conclude that the consumer will come today with probability 4/9 and tomorrow with probability $(1 - 4/9) = 5/9$.

Now look at the payoffs from the point of view of the consumer and assume that q is the probability that the sale is today rather than tomorrow. The expected value payoffs to the

---

1 Generally, benefits and profits now or in the near future are worth more than payoffs further in the future, so both of these players put a higher value on benefits they get today than tomorrow. In economics this is called *time preference*. This common tendency has been exaggerated a bit in the example, for simplicity—usually the difference between payoffs only a day apart would be much smaller.

consumer for her two strategies are shown in Table 8.7. If one of those is greater than the other, the consumer will find it easy to pick a better day with a good chance to get the benefits of the sale.

Accordingly, the seller will adjust q so that the customer's expected values from coming tomorrow and from coming today are the same, as shown in Equation (8.6):

$$5 + 5q = 8 - 4q$$
$$q = 3/9, \text{ or } 1/3$$

8.6

We conclude that this seller will schedule a sale for today with a probability 1/3 and for tomorrow with a probability 2/3.

Of course, this example is very simplified. In effect, it assumes that there are only two dates on which the two people can do business, today and tomorrow, and thereafter the seller will go out of business. The game is also overly simple in allowing for only one seller and one consumer. Nevertheless, it shows us how the scheduling of sales could be a mixed strategy equilibrium; and indeed, we can find mixed strategy equilibria in much more complicated and realistic games of scheduling sales, allowing for the reality that there may be many sellers and consumers and that they may continue to do business at any date in the future.

Table **8.7** | Expected Value Payoffs for Consumer Strategies

shop today pays	$10q + 5(1 - q) = 5 + 5q$
shop tomorrow pays	$4q + 8(1 - q) = 8 - 4q$

Equilibria with Mixed and Pure Strategies

The games of Baseball and Unpredictable Sales have equilibria in mixed strategies but not in pure strategies. However, some games have both kinds of equilibria. Here is an example. We have two guys who are very polite—excessively polite. Let's call them Al G. and George B. They are trying to pass through a door just wide enough for one, and each is too polite to pass through the door before the other. They just keep exchanging courtesies, each one telling the other "After you, Al;" "No, no, after you, George." They never got through the door.[2]

Here is a game based on the plight of Al and George. Of course, Al and George are the players. They have to pass through a door, the door is not wide enough for both of them to pass through at the same time, and that leads to the payoffs shown in Table 8.8. Each one chooses between two strategies: wait and go.

Table **8.8** | Payoffs for Al and George

		George	
		wait	go
Al	wait	0, 0	2, 3
	go	3, 2	−1, −1

2 This example is based on a vaudeville skit from the beginning of the twentieth century. For more information see the Web sites "A Brief History of Ethnicity in the Comics," *http://www.balchinstitute.org/museum/comics/brief.html*, and "Vaudeville Memories" *http://personal.nbnet.nb.ca/muldrew/vaudeville2.htm*. These were both accessed on Feb. 21, 2002. At that date there was a video clip of the skit available at *http://memory.loc.gov/cgi-bin/query/r?ammem/varstg:@field(NUMBER(1453))*.

If both go at the same time, they bump into one another, and each gets a payoff of –1. If both wait, as in the vaudeville skit, they do not get through the door, for a payoff of 0. If one goes and the other waits, they both get through the door. The one who goes first get a payoff of 3, and the one who waits and follows gets a payoff of 2.

Using methods from earlier chapters, we can see that this game has two Nash equilibria in pure strategies. This is a coordination game and is much like other coordination games. Whenever one player goes and the other waits, we have a Nash equilibrium. However, this game also has a mixed strategy equilibrium. Looking at it from Al's point of view, let p be the probability that George chooses "wait" as his strategy. Then the expected value payoffs for Al are as shown in Table 8.9. (Since the game is symmetrical, we get the same results from George's point of view.)

Table 8.9 | Expected Value Payoffs for Al's Strategies

wait pays	$0p + 2(1 - p) = 2 - 2p$
go pays	$3p - (1 - p) = 4p - 1$

Thus, if George adjusts p so that the expected value payoff of the two strategies for Al are the same, we have

$$2 - 2p = 4p - 1$$
$$\text{solving,}$$
$$p = 3/6 = 1/2$$

8.7

Since the game is symmetrical, both players can reason in the same way and each plays wait with probability 1/2 and go with probability 1/2.

So this game has three Nash equilibria, two in pure strategies and one in mixed strategies.

Table 8.10 | Equilibrium Expected Value Payoffs for Al's Strategies

wait pays	$2 - 2(\frac{1}{2}) = 2 - 1 = 1$
go pays	$3(\frac{1}{2}) - (1 - \frac{1}{2}) = 1.5 - 0.5 = 1$

It is easy to see that Al and George can do no worse than a payoff of 2 in a pure-strategy Nash equilibrium. By comparison, how do they do in the mixed strategy equilibrium? To answer that question, we compute the expected value of payoffs when the two players play the mixed strategy equilibrium. We can substitute the p = 1/2 back in either of the expected value computations in Table 8.9 (since the whole point of the 1/2 probability is that it makes them the same). Thus, we have Table 8.10.

So Al and George do worse in the mixed strategy equilibrium! That's not surprising, since the mixed strategy equilibrium means there is always some probability that they will bump into one another and some probability that they will not get through the door, but the mixed strategy equilibrium does seem a bit strange in this case.

Here is another example of a game with both pure and mixed strategies, an environmental policy example. Two small towns, Littleton and Hamlet, get their drinking water from wells. They can draw from two aquifers. One aquifer is shallow, so a well to reach it is cheap, but will supply only enough water for one town. If both drill for the shallow aquifer, they will deplete it and neither will have enough water. The other aquifer is deeper, so it costs more to drill down to it, but it can provide enough water for both towns, and, consequently, they can share the costs. Each town has two strategies: deep or shallow. The payoffs to the two towns are shown in Table 8.11. Notice that there are two Nash equilibria in pure strategies, and notice also that neither is the cooperative solution, which occurs when the two towns share the deep aquifer and payoffs total 20.

Take Littleton's point of view and let p be the probability that Hamlet plays deep. Then the expected values for Littleton's strategies are shown in Table 8.12. Doing the algebra, we find that the equilibrium probability of choosing "deep" is 3/8. Since the game is symmetrical, this is the same for both towns.

The expected value of payoffs from the mixed strategy is 5.625. This is better than the payoffs to a town that independently digs a deep well, but one that digs the only shallow well can do still better. Thus, there are three Nash equilibria once again: two in pure strategies and one in mixed strategies.

Table 8.11 Payoffs for Littleton and Hamlet

		Hamlet	
		deep	shallow
Littleton	deep	10, 10	3, 15
	shallow	15, 3	0, 0

Table 8.12 Expected Value Payoffs for Littleton's Strategies

deep pays	$10p + 3(1 - p) = 11 - 3p$
shallow pays	$15p - 0(1 - p) = 15p$

Graphics for Mixed Strategies

We can get a clearer idea of what this mixed strategy means by doing a bit of graphics. First, let us do a graphic analysis of the baseball example from earlier in the chapter. We will take the batter's point of view. Figure 8.1 shows the expected value payoffs for the batter. The probability that the pitcher throws a fastball is on the horizontal axis.

The expected value payoff when the batter chooses "swing early" is shown by the black line, and the payoff when the batter chooses "swing late" is shown by the gray line. Students who have taken a course in the principles of economics know that something important usually happens when two lines cross. That's true in game theory as well. The intersection of the two lines shows the equilibrium probability *for the pitcher*. At any other probability, one or the other of the hitting strategies pays better, so the batter will choose the one that gives the better payoff, and make the pitcher worse off. Therefore, the pitcher wants to choose the probability so that neither one is greater than the other—where the lines cross—and, as we know, that is 8/23. Since this game is not symmetrical, the diagram for the expected value payoffs to the pitcher will look a bit different, and we will not show it here.

Notice what happens if the pitcher throws a fastball with a probability slightly more than the equilibrium probability of 8/23. Suppose he chooses a probability of 0.4. Then the batter can get an expected value of 1 by swinging early with probability 1, and if he swings

Figure **8.1** Expected Value Payoffs for the Batter in Baseball

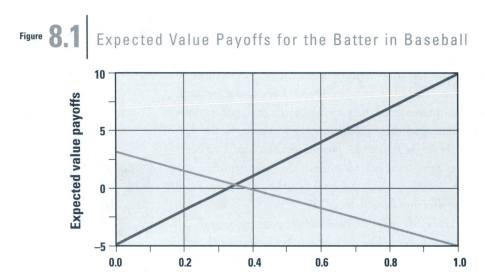

early with any probability less than 1 he will get less; so his best response is to swing early with probability 1. But then the pitcher's best response is to pitch the change-up. This pair of strategies isn't stable either, though. As we know, this game has no equilibrium in pure strategies. Thus, the two athletes will keep shifting their strategies and things will not settle down again until they arrive back at the mixed strategy equilibrium. (*Exercise:* Construct the pitcher's diagram for yourself and use it to follow through the same reasoning about the pitcher's strategies.)

Now, return to the Al and George game. The expected value payoffs for the two strategies for Al and George are shown in Figure 8.2. The probability that George (Al) chooses "wait" is shown on the horizontal axis. The expected value of payoffs is shown on the vertical axis. The payoff to "wait" for Al (George) is shown by the black line, and the payoff to "go" is shown by the gray line. As before, the intersection of the two lines corresponds to the equilibrium probability of "wait," since that is the probability at which the expected values of the two strategies are equal. Since the game is symmetrical, the diagram will look the same from either point of view.

Now, suppose that George chooses "wait" with a probability somewhat greater than 1/2—for example, 0.6. The diagram shows us that, in that case, the expected value of strategy "go" for Al is 1.4, while the expected value for "wait" is 0.8. Thus, Al will choose "go" with a probability of 1. But in that case, Al's best response is to choose "wait" with a probability of 1, and then we have the pure strategy Nash equilibrium (go, wait). Once again, suppose that George chooses "wait" with a probability somewhat less than 1/2—for example, 0.4. The diagram shows us that, in that case, the expected value of strategy "go" for Al is 0.6, while the expected value for "wait" is 1.2. Thus, Al will choose "wait" with a probability of 1. But in that case, George's best response is to choose "go" with probability 1, and then we have the pure strategy Nash equilibrium (wait,

Figure 8.2 | Expected Values for Al and George

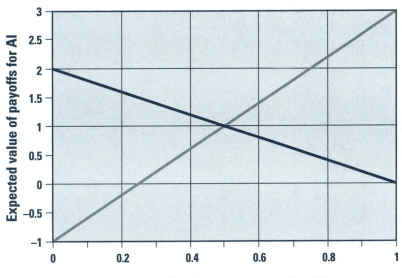

Probability George chooses "wait"

go). We see that any deviation from the equilibrium probabilities, however small, will lead immediately to one of the pure-strategy Nash equilibria. In that sense the mixed strategy equilibrium in this game is unstable. The mixed strategy in the well-drilling game between Littleton and Hamlet is also unstable. In general, coordination games with two Nash equilibria in pure strategies will have a third equilibrium in mixed strategies, and the third equilibrium is unstable.

For another contrast, let us do a graphic analysis of a social dilemma—the Advertising Game from Chapter 1. The two players are two rival companies selling the same product, and their strategies are to advertise or not to advertise. If both advertise, their advertisements largely offset one another. The payoffs for this game are shown in Table 8.13, which repeats Table 1.3. In this game, we recall, (advertise, advertise) is a dominant strategy equilibrium.

This is a symmetrical game, so the analysis will look the same whether we take the viewpoint of Tabacs or Fumco. In Figure 8.3, then, the horizontal axis shows

Table 8.13 | The Advertising Game

Repeats Table 1.3, Chapter 1

		Fumco	
		don't advertise	advertise
Tabacs	don't advertise	8, 8	2, 10
	advertise	10, 2	4, 4

the probability that Tabacs (Fumco) chooses the strategy "don't advertise." Then the black line shows the payoffs to "don't advertise" and the gray line shows the payoffs to "advertise" for

Figure **8.3** | Expected Value Payoffs in the Advertising Game

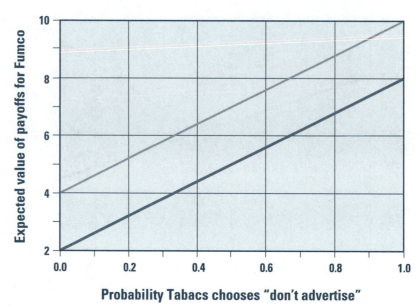

Probability Tabacs chooses "don't advertise"

Fumco (Tabacs). What we see is that the payoff to "advertise" is always greater than the payoff to "don't advertise." That is to say, "advertise" is dominant, not only over the pure strategy "don't advertise," but over all possible mixed strategies as well. This applies to social dilemmas in general: The dominant strategy is dominant over mixed as well as pure strategies.

Now it's your turn. Show that the mixed strategy equilibrium for the well-drilling game between Littleton and Hamlet is unstable.

Summary

Uncertainty may come from the human players in the game, as well as from nature. A game in normal form, we recall, begins with a list of pure strategies for each player. But it may be that playing in the one pure strategy predictably will make the player vulnerable to exploitation by an opponent. In that case, the rational player will attempt to be unpredictable, choosing among the pure strategies with probabilities carefully adjusted to neutralize the opponent's opportunities for exploitation. When strategies are chosen in this way, we call it a mixed strategy.

Since the payoffs to a mixed strategy are uncertain, we evaluate them using the concept of *expected value*. The best response is the strategy (or probabilities for choosing among strategies) that maximizes the expected value of the payoff. For *best responses* defined in this way, all two-person games have Nash equilibria, including those that have no equilibria in pure strategies.

Some games may have more than one equilibrium, including equilibria in both pure and mixed strategies. This is true of coordination games, but the mixed strategies in coordination games are unstable.

Mixed strategies will be especially important in Chapter 10 on duopoly strategies and pricing.

Exercises and Discussion Questions

8.1 Matching Pennies. As we noted in exercise 3, Chapter 1, matching pennies is a schoolyard game. One player is identified as "even" and the other as "odd." The two players each show a penny, with either the head or the tail showing upward. If both show the same side of the coin, then "even" keeps both pennies. If the two show different sides of the coin, then "odd" keeps both pennies.

Verify that matching pennies has no Nash equilibrium in pure strategies. Compute the mixed strategy equilibrium for matching pennies.

8.2 Rock, Paper, Scissors. In exercise 4, Chapter 4, we considered the common schoolyard game called Rock, Paper, Scissors. Two children (we will call them Susan and Tess) simultaneously choose a symbol for rock, paper, or scissors. The rules for winning and losing are:

- Paper covers rock (paper wins over rock)

- Rock breaks scissors (rock wins over scissors)

- Scissors cut paper (scissors win over paper)

The payoff table is shown as Table 8.E1.
Compute the mixed strategy equilibrium for Rock, Paper, Scissors.

Table 8.E1 Rock, Paper, Scissors

		Susan		
		paper	rock	scissors
Tess	paper	0, 0	1, −1	−1, 1
	rock	−1, 1	0, 0	1, −1
	scissors	1, −1	−1, 1	0, 0

8.3 More Mixed Strategies. Compute mixed strategy equilibria for the Heave-Ho (Chapter 4), Battle of the Sexes, Chicken, and Hawk vs. Dove (Chapter 5) games. Compare.

Table 8.E2 | Payoffs in an Escape-Evasion Game

Repeats Table 4.11, Chapter 4

		Pete	
		north	south
Fred	north	−1, 3	4, −1
	south	3, −4	−2, 2

8.4 Escape-Evasion. Recall the Escape-Evasion Game from Chapter 4, with the payoff table shown in Table 8.E2.

We observed in Chapter 4 that this game has no equilibrium in pure strategies, but we know it must have at least one equilibrium when mixed strategies are included. Compute the mixed strategy equilibrium for this game.

8.5 The Great Escape. Refer to Chapter 2, exercise 2.

Does this game have Nash equilibria in pure strategies? Why or why not?

Compute the mixed strategy equilibrium for this game.

8.6 Punic War. In the Second Punic War, 218–202 B.C.E., the Romans faced a powerful army, with elephants as shock troops, led by one of the great strategic generals, Hannibal.

Table 8.E3 | Payoffs in a War of Delay

		F	
		north pass	south pass
H	north pass	5, −5	0, 0
	south pass	0, 0	5, −5

For most of the war, the Romans followed the strategy of Fabius Cunctator, (i.e., "Fabius the Delayer"). They avoided combat with Hannibal's army in Italy while undermining his base of support in other parts of the Mediterranean. Here is an Escape-Evasion Game in that spirit. Generals F and H have to choose between two mountain passes. If they choose the same one, there will be a battle and F, whose army is much weaker, will lose. The payoff is shown in Table 8.E3.

What Nash equilibria, if any, does the game have?

8.7 Football. In American football, the objective for the team on offense is to carry the ball across the goal line, advancing toward the goal line by running with the ball or throwing ("passing") it forward on successive plays. The objective of the defense is to prevent this by "tackling" (physically restraining) the ball carrier or preventing a pass from being caught.

American football, unlike baseball, is a game of coordinated attack by the entire team of 11 players. Crucial as the quarterback may be, he can do little without linemen to block, running backs, and pass receivers. The defense is also coordinated. As a result, there are many plays in the typical playbook for a football team, ranging from "student body right or left," in which a halfback and blocking linemen attempt to run around the end of the defensive line, to the "flea flicker," in which the quarterback throws the ball backward to a halfback who fakes a run and then throws a forward pass to the quarterback, who has run down the field in the meantime.

To keep this example simple, we will limit it to two offensive plays. The plays will be the drop-back pass and the draw play. Both plays develop from the same initial motion, in which the offensive blocking linemen move backward from the *line of scrimmage* dividing the offense from the defense, and the quarterback moves about 10 yards behind the line of scrimmage. From that motion, in a drop-back pass, the blockers form a "passing pocket" to protect quarterback from defensive tacklers and to allow the play time to develop. On a draw play, by contrast, the quarterback hands the ball off to a halfback, and fakes the pass, while the blocking linemen form a blocking screen for the halfback who runs with the ball.

Defense against the drop-back pass often consists of sending the linemen forward rapidly to break down the passing pocket and pulling the faster defensive backfield back toward their own goal to prevent a pass from being caught and to protect against a large gain if it is caught. But this defense is particularly vulnerable to the draw play, since it leaves the line of scrimmage undefended.

Thus, the offense will choose between two strategies: pass or draw play. The defense will choose between defending against the pass and defending against the run. The payoff for the offense will be the expected value of yards gained and the payoff for the defense will be the negative of that number. The payoff table is shown as Table 8.E4.

Compute the mixed strategy equilibrium for this game. What is the expected value of the number of yards gained per play in equilibrium?

Table 8.E4 | Payoffs in American Football

		Offense	
		pass	draw play
Defense	pass defense	−1, 1	−3, 3
	run defense	−4, 4	1, −1

9 Advanced Topics in Noncooperative Equilibrium

Noncooperative game equilibrium concepts have proven themselves in many simple applications and some complex applications. This chapter considers some examples, each of which has something of a twist. First, the concept of a *dominant strategy* seems very clear and compelling, but there are some subtleties with the concept that we may need to keep in mind in order to avoid confusion over tricky examples. Second, even when we seem to have a clear equilibrium when individuals choose pure strategies that are best responses, we should double-check whether there might be a superior alternative with mixed strategies or coalitions or both—a point that arises from the cinema version of *A Beautiful Mind*, the biography of key game theorist John Nash.

The Location Game, Again

Recall the Location Game from Chapter 4. It is shown in Table 4.3 and is repeated (with some emphasis added) in Table 9.1 in this chapter. This game has a Nash equilibrium where

Table 9.1 The Location Game with Dominated Strategies Shaded

Approximately repeats Table 4.3, Chapter 4

		Gacy's			
		Uptown	Center City	East Side	West Side
Mimbel's	Uptown	30, 40	50, 95	55, 95	55, 120
	Center City	115, 40	100, 100	130, 85	120, 95
	East Side	125, 45	95, 65	60, 40	115, 120
	West Side	105, 50	75, 75	95, 95	35, 55

each store chooses Center City. We can show this by considering all 16 combinations of strategies and eliminating all the others. Could there be a more systematic way to find the Nash equilibrium?

Even though this game has no dominant strategies, it does have some *dominated* strategies. (That's *dominated*, not *dominant*.) We recall that, if one strategy always gives a better payoff than a second strategy, regardless of which strategy the opponent chooses, the second strategy is dominated by the first. There are some **dominated strategies** in this game. For Mimbel's, both Uptown and the West Side are dominated by a Center City location. For Gacy's, Uptown is dominated by Center City, and also by the West Side.

There is no reason for a rational decision maker ever to choose or even consider a dominated strategy. Thus, we can eliminate the dominated strategies from the game. This is a key to a somewhat quicker way to find the Nash equilibrium. Table 9.1 shows the payoffs for the Location Game again, with the dominated strategies shaded. We can eliminate these dominated strategies without changing the game. Thus, we really don't need to examine all 16 possible combinations of strategies—only those that are not dominated.

Once we have eliminated the dominated strategies, we see the payoff table shown in Table 9.2, with

Heads Up!

Here are some concepts we will develop as this chapter goes along:

Strongly and Weakly Dominated Strategies: Whenever one strategy yields a payoff strictly greater than that of a second strategy, regardless of which strategies the other players choose, the second strategy is *strongly dominated* by the first. If the first strategy yields a payoff that is not less than the second strategy, and sometimes more, then the second strategy is *weakly dominated* by the first.

Iterated Elimination of Dominated Strategies: If a game has a strongly dominated strategy, the game created by the elimination of that dominated strategy has the same Nash equilibria as the original game. This elimination can be done step by step until there are no more dominated strategies, and the resulting game has the same Nash equilibria as the original game.

Correlated Equilibrium: A *correlated equilibrium* is an arrangement that assigns probabilities to the joint strategies in the game that correspond to Nash equilibria of a coordination game.

Definition

Dominated Strategy—Whenever one strategy yields are higher payoff than a second strategy, regardless of which strategies the other players choose, the second strategy is dominated by the first, and is said to be a **dominated strategy**.

Table 9.2 | A Reduced Location Game with Its Dominated Strategies Shaded

		Gacy's		
		Center City	East Side	West Side
Mimbel's	Center City	100, 100	130, 85	120, 95
	East Side	95, 65	60, 40	115, 120

Table 9.3

A Further Reduced Location Game with Its Dominated Strategies

		Gacy's		
		Center City	East Side	West Side
Mimbel's	Center City	100, 100	130, 85	120, 95

Method

Iterated Elimination of Dominated Strategies—If a game has a dominated strategy, the game created by the elimination of that dominated strategy has the same Nash equilibria as the original game. This elimination can be done step by step until there are no more dominated strategies, and the resulting game has the same Nash equilibria as the original game.

Table 9.4

The Location Game with All Dominated Strategies Iteratively Eliminated

		Gacy's
		Center City
Mimbel's	Center City	100, 100

just six combinations of strategies to consider. This smaller game is equivalent to the original location game, since the strategies we have eliminated would never be considered by a rational player anyway. But this smaller game also has a dominated strategy. For Mimbel's, the East-Side location strategy is now dominated by Center City. This is shown in Table 9.1 by shading the East-Side strategy.

So now we can eliminate the East-Side strategy for Mimbel's. Gacy's knows perfectly well that Mimbel's will never choose it, so Gacy's doesn't need to take that strategy option into account. When we eliminate this dominated strategy, we obtain the equivalent game shown in Table 9.3. But this game, too, has some dominated strategies. For Gacy's, both the East-Side and West-Side strategies are now dominated by Center City. Once again, this is shown by shading those strategies in Table 9.3.

Accordingly, once again, we eliminate the dominated strategies. This leaves the game shown in Table 9.4. In a sense, this game is equivalent to the original Location Game—it has the same equilibrium. But the game in Table 9.4 has only one strategy for each player: Center City.

What we have seen here is an example of a method of analysis of games in normal form called the **iterated elimination of dominated strategies** (IEDS). We can conclude that the strategies (Center City, Center City) constitute the unique Nash equilibrium for this game. Of course, we already knew that from examining the 16 possibilities separately. But the method of iterated elimination of dominated strategies is a powerful technique for simplifying large, complicated games in normal form.

For another example, we can again draw on Chapter 4. Recall the game of Choosing Radio Formats, given in Table 4.7. It is shown again in Table 9.5 with the dominated strategies shaded. Once we eliminate them, we are left with the game shown in Table 9.6. We cannot take elimination of dominated strategies any further in this case, because the reduced game has no dominated strategies; but at least we have reduced the number of cases we need to examine from nine to four. We recall that this game has two Nash equilibria: the two cases where the stations choose different formats.

Table 9.5 | Choosing Radio Formats

Approximately repeats Table 4.7, Chapter 4

		WIRD		
		rock	country	all talk
KOOL	rock	35, 35	50, 40	80, 10
	country	40, 50	20, 20	40, 10
	all talk	10, 80	10, 40	5, 5

Table 9.6 | Reduced Choosing Radio Formats

		WIRD	
		rock	country
KOOL	rock	35, 35	50, 40
	country	40, 50	20, 20

Iterated Elimination of Dominated Strategies

The method of iterated elimination of dominated strategies can be usefully applied to many games in normal form. *Iterated* means step by step. At each step, we eliminate the strategies that wouldn't be considered anyway, and will never be chosen. This produces a new game that is equivalent to the original game in the sense that it has the same Nash equilibria that the original game has.

But there is a complication we need to be careful about. Remember the definition of a dominated strategy from the previous chapter:

> Whenever one strategy yields a higher payoff than a second strategy, regardless of which strategies the other players choose, the second strategy is dominated by the first, and is said to be a dominated strategy.

But we can distinguish two closely related concepts, depending on how we interpret *higher payoff* in that definition. If the payoff to the first strategy is always strictly greater than the payoff to the second strategy, we say that the first strategy *strongly* dominates the second strategy. All of our examples so far are examples of **strongly dominated strategies**. The other possibility is a **weakly dominated strategy**. The

> **Definition**
>
> ***Strongly Dominated Strategy***—Whenever one strategy yields a payoff strictly greater than of a second strategy, regardless of which strategies the other players choose, the second strategy is strongly dominated by the first, and is said to be a **strongly dominated strategy**.

> **Definition**
>
> ***Weakly Dominated Strategy***—Whenever one strategy yields a payoff not less than a second strategy, regardless of which strategies the other players choose; and the payoff to the first strategy is strictly greater than the payoff to the second strategy for some strategies the other players might choose, the second strategy is weakly dominated by the first, and is said to be a **weakly dominated strategy**.

first strategy *weakly* dominates the second strategy if the payoff to the first strategy is at least as great as the payoff to the second strategy, and sometimes, but not always, strictly greater.

Let's have an example with a weakly dominated strategy, to make the definition a little clearer. For this example, the players are two sisters, Iris and Julia. They are students at Nearby College, where all the classes are graded on the curve. Since they are the two best students in their class, each of them will top the curve unless they enroll in the same class. Iris and Julia each have to choose one more class this term, and each of them can choose between math and literature. They're both very good at math, but Iris is better at literature.

Their game is shown in Table 9.7. Notice that, for Julia, mathematics and literature give the same payoff, 3.8, if Iris takes the math course. However, if Iris takes the literature course, Julia gets the better payoff by taking the math course. Therefore, for Julia, the strategy of taking the math course weakly dominates the strategy of taking the literature course. From Iris's point of view, the literature course gives the same payoff regardless of whether Julia picks math or literature, but the math course gives a worse payoff, 3.8, if Julia chooses math. Therefore, for Iris, literature weakly dominates math.

What Nash equilibria does this game have? Certainly when Julia chooses math and Iris chooses literature, and they both get 4.0 averages, that is a Nash equilibrium. But what if they choose the other way around—Julia choosing literature and Iris math? In that case, we have another Nash equilibrium. But it is a rather odd equilibrium. Common sense suggests that there is something wrong with it. Wouldn't it make sense if Julia and Iris chose their failsafe (weakly dominant) strategies instead? And if we eliminate the weakly dominated strategies, we are left with (Julia:math, Iris:lit). But, in fact, (Julia:lit, Iris:math) is a Nash equilibrium, since each is choosing her best (there is no other better) response to the other's strategy.

Table **9.7** Grade Point Averages for Iris and Julia

Repeats Table 2.E1, Chapter 2

		Iris	
		math	lit
Julia	math	3.8, 3.8	4.0, 4.0
	lit	3.8, 4.0	3.7, 4.0

The game between Julia and Iris is an illustration of weakly dominant strategies. The point, really, is a negative one. Iterated elimination of dominated strategies (IEDS) doesn't work very well with weakly dominated strategies. It should really be IESDS—iterated elimination of strongly dominated strategies. Accordingly, we might wish to restate the **method**: **Iterated elimination of dominant strategies**—If a game has a strongly dominated strategy, the game created by the elimination of that dominated strategy has the same Nash equilibria as the original game. This elimination can be done step by step until there are no more dominated strategies, and the resulting game has the same Nash equilibria as the original game. If weakly dominated strategies are present, we must be more cautious.

Refinement
A Trembling Hand

As we have seen, the Grade Point Game between Iris and Julia has two Nash equilibria, but one of them makes more sense than the other. The strategies (math, lit) give both girls perfect 4.0 averages, while the other Nash equilibrium, (lit, math), leaves Julia with only a 3.8. This is a strange equilibrium—not so much because Julia is worse off but because neither girl has a positive reason for choosing these strategies. If Iris unilaterally switches to lit, she is just as well off, with a 4.0; and, similarly, if Julia switches unilaterally to math, she is no worse off either, with a 3.8. Nevertheless it is a Nash equilibrium, since each student is choosing her best response (there is no better response) to the strategy chosen by the other.

This is a fairly common problem in more complex applications of game theory. Where there are two or more Nash equilibria, some of them may seem unreasonable. This is possible because the definition of Nash equilibrium captures only one aspect of rationality, the *best response* criterion. We might be able to add some other rational considerations that would eliminate the unreasonable Nash equilibria. These additional tests of rationality are called *refinements* of Nash equilibrium, and refinements of Nash equilibrium fill a large and important category of advanced game theory.

In this case, the additional test of rationality is the fail-safe test—why choose a strategy that can do worse, but can never do better, than another? In other words, why choose a weakly dominated strategy? In the grade point game, the choice of a lit course could make Julia worse off (with a 3.7) if Iris made the mistake of enrolling in the lit course at the same time. But Julia doesn't have to worry about that, because Julia knows Iris is rational and will not make a mistake that reduces her (Iris's) GPA. Perhaps it would be more realistic for Julia to assume that it is *very probable* that Iris will choose the equilibrium strategy, but not quite certain. Suppose, for example, that the probability that Iris will choose her best response is 95 percent, but there is a 5 percent probability that she will choose the wrong strategy. In that case, Julia's expected payoff is $(0.95)(3.8) + (0.05)(3.7) = 3.798$. On the other hand, by choosing math, Julia can do no worse than 3.8, so she will choose math.

Assuming that Julia allows for a very small probability that her opposite number will make a mistake, the unreasonable Nash equilibrium is eliminated. This assumption is called the **trembling hand assumption**. The idea is that the agent may *tremble* when choosing the best response, accidentally choosing a wrong response. It is a good example of a refinement of the Nash equilibrium, since it assumes a slightly different kind of rationality and, as a result, narrows the possibilities to a single equilibrium that seems to be more reasonable than the other.

> ### Definition
>
> ***Trembling Hand***—A player who might, with very small probability, choose a wrong strategy is said to play with a **trembling hand**. In games with more than one Nash equilibrium, some of the equilibria may be risky when the players have trembling hands. In some cases we refine the concept of Nash equilibrium by ruling out just those equilibria.

Let's see what happens if Iris assumes that Julia could have a trembling hand—Iris guesses that Julia will choose an equilibrium strategy with 90 percent probability and the wrong strategy with 10 percent probability. Then the expected value for Iris if she chooses math is $(0.9)(4) + (0.1)(3.8) = 3.98$, but Iris can guarantee herself a 4.0 by choosing lit—so she chooses literature, and the two students each get their 4.0.

In general, if each player in the game assumes that the other players will very probably choose their best responses, but assigns some small positive probability to the possibility that they might make a mistake, and each player then chooses the strategy that gives her the highest expected value payoff; we have a trembling hand equilibrium. If we make the probabilities of mistakes small enough, the trembling hand equilibrium will be one of the Nash equilibria in the game. This is a **trembling hand Nash equilibrium**. The trembling hand Nash equilibrium "refines" the Nash equilibrium concept by allowing the players to choose fail-safe strategies as well as best responses.

A Confession Game

Table 9.8 | Payoffs in a Confession Game

		Dave			
		confess		don't	
		Barry		**Barry**	
		confess	don't	confess	don't
Rog	confess	−1,−1,−1	−1,0,−1	−1,−1,0	−1,0,0
	don't	0,−1,−1	0,0,−1	0,−1,0	−2,−2,−2

Rog, Barry, and Dave are members of the notoriously mischievous Blanchard School boygang, and they have been at it again. As a Halloween stunt they TP'ed the principal's house. Everybody knows they are the likely villains, so they will all be punished severely—if nobody confesses. On the other hand, if one or more of the boys confesses to the mischief, he will get a reduced punishment, and the others will get off. Counting a severe punishment as −2, a reduced punishment as −1, and getting away with it as 0, the payoffs are shown in Table 9.8.

This is a three-person coordination game. There are three Nash equilibria—the three cells in which just one boy confesses and the others go unpunished. As we have seen before, there could be a problem with a coordination game. If the boys have no clue as to which Nash equilibrium will occur, they may guess wrongly. For example, if Rog and Barry assume that Dave will confess, but Dave assumes that Rog will confess, they all choose "don't" and all get severe punishments, the −2 payoff. Unless they have some clue, some *Schelling point*, there is a real danger that they might fail to get any efficient equilibrium at all. Each boy might be tempted by the fail-safe (risk-dominant) strategy of volunteering to confess, but if all three of them do it, this is inefficient and not a best-response equilibrium. In addition, there is a feeling that it is unfair for one boy to be punished for what all three did.

But these naughty boys have a solution. They will "draw straws" to determine which boy is to confess. Three straws of different length are held by one of the boys so that only one end is showing and the others cannot tell which straw is shortest. Then the other two boys each draw one straw, and the boy who held the straws is left with the other one. The boy who draws the shortest straw must confess. This way, each boy has an equal chance of being the one to be punished.[1]

This solution to the problem is interesting in several ways.

- It is very much like a mixed strategy, in that the decision is made at random, assigning probabilities to strategies.
  - The probabilities of $(-1, 0, 0)$, $(0, -1, 0)$ and $(0, 0, -1)$ are each 0.333.
  - The probabilities of all other outcomes are 0.

- It is different from mixed strategy Nash equilibria in that the probabilities are assigned to joint strategies, whereas in a Nash equilibrium, players assign probabilities independent to their own strategies.
  - For a mixed-strategy equilibrium, each boy chooses a probability of 0.293 for "confess."
  - As a result, there is a probability of more than 1/3 that none will confess, resulting in severe punishments all around.

- Once the straw is drawn, it provides a Schelling point—all have the same expectations as to who will confess. Suppose, for example, that Rog draws the short straw. Rog cannot benefit by cheating on the agreement. The other boys are expecting Rog to confess, so they will not confess, and that means that if Rog cheats by not confessing, he will get a -2 payoff instead of a -1. So Rog's best response is just to put some newspapers down the seat of his pants and march off to take his punishment. Similarly, the other two boys have nothing to gain by confessing, since that would get them -1 instead of 0.

- Before the straw is drawn, each boy has an expected value payoff of $-1/3$—better than he can get by volunteering to confess, the fail-safe strategy.

- Since each boy has the same probability of having to confess and the same expected value payoff, this solution is "fair" in a way that the pure strategy Nash equilibria are not.

- Even if the probabilities would not have been equal, the result would still have provided a Schelling point for the original game. Suppose, for example, that Barry held the straws and was able to cheat, so that Rog had a higher probability of getting the short straw. Even if Rog suspected what was going on, once he had the short straw confession would still be his best response. The probabilities could be anything, fair or unfair, and it would still "work."

Drawing straws in this game is an example of a **correlated equilibrium**. A correlated equilibrium is a new kind of solution to a noncooperative game. In

> ### Definition
>
> **Correlated Equilibrium**—In a game with more than one Nash equilibrium in pure strategies, a group of players may form a coalition to choose their strategies jointly, in such a way that one or more of the Nash equilibria is chosen with some probability. This is a **correlated equilibrium**.

---

1 The boy who holds the straws has a strong incentive to really conceal which is shorter. If he is careless and holds the straws so that the others can see which is shortest, he will certainly be left with the short straw and be punished.

general, a correlated equilibrium is an arrangement that assigns probabilities to the joint strategies in the game that correspond to Nash equilibria of the game. Of course, the probabilities of choosing the joint strategies have to add up to 1. If there is only one equilibrium (for example, as in the Prisoner's Dilemma) then that equilibrium is also the only correlated equilibrium, since the probability assigned to it must be 1. If one equilibrium dominates the others, as in the Heave-Ho Game, once again, the dominant equilibrium will be the only correlated equilibrium, since there is no point in assigning any probability to a dominated Nash equilibrium. However, correlated equilibria can make a big difference in a coordination game like the Confession Game.[2] Since (as we have seen) each player is choosing her or his best response in a correlated equilibrium, a correlated equilibrium is a noncooperative equilibrium; and in a game with two or more Nash equilibria in pure strategies, there will be infinitely many correlated equilibria, corresponding to different assignments of the probabilities (although it may be that only one way of assigning the probabilities will be recognized as fair by the players).

This is important because it increases the role of **coalitions** in noncooperative games. We saw in Chapter 6 that a coalition may form in a noncooperative game of three or more persons, provided that the joint strategy of the coalition consists of best-response strategies for the individuals. That is, the coalition forms to enforce one out of a number of possible Nash equilibria. What Barry, Dave, and Rog have done in this example is to form the grand coalition in their game, in order to avoid the danger of inconsistent guesses in their coordination game. The coalition has chosen a correlated, probabilistic joint strategy rather than a joint pure strategy, because it seems to them to be more fair—otherwise it would be harder to come to an agreement.

A Symmetrical Noncooperative Solution to the Blonde Problem

Table 9.9 | A Two-By-Two Blonde Problem

Repeats Table 1.2, Chapter 1

		John	
		pursue blonde	pursue brunette
Reinhard	pursue blonde	0, 0	2, 1
	pursue brunette	1, 2	1, 1

In two earlier chapters, we have looked at a problem from the movie version of *A Beautiful Mind*, the Blonde Problem. We recall that the problem can be shown as a two-person game in normal form, as shown in Table 9.9. In the movie, the fictional John Nash suggests that the young men in the bar (Reinhard and John, in the two-person version) should each pursue a brunette, so that they would avoid "canceling one another out" in pursuit of the blonde. But this is not actually a Nash equilibrium! This game is a coordination game, and the only Nash equilibria in pure strategies are (blonde, brunette) and (brunette, blonde).

2 A World Wide Web search on the keywords "short straw," "burnt bannock," or "Lindow man" will give other examples of correlated equilibria in practice long before the beginnings of game theory. But these examples can be pretty gruesome, so don't do the search unless you have a pretty strong stomach.

There is a mixed strategy equilibrium, with both males playing strategies with probabilities 1/2, 1/2. The mixed strategy has expected-value payoffs of 1. It is unstable and no better than (brunette, brunette).

Risk aversion might make a difference. If we assume that this is a competitive game and that both players must move simultaneously, why would either player choose to pursue the blonde when they may wind up with 0? Why wouldn't they take the safer strategy and select a brunette? Because they don't know what the strategy of the other is, perhaps they would indeed wind up at payoffs (1, 1). This is a common intuitive response to coordination games. It is the maximin solution to the game. In addition to its appeal to risk aversion, the maximin solution is symmetrical in this case, and the Nash equilibrium in pure strategies cannot be—which, in turn, poses the difficulty (for the players) of predicting what equilibrium will occur.

Maximin was John von Neumann's solution to zero-sum games. Maximin is also the independent best-response equilibrium in zero-sum games, so Nash's equilibrium concept is generally considered an extension of the von Neumann solution, but in some games, including those like Chicken, the two concepts disagree. This is one example. However, (1) in a non-constant sum game such as this one, the maximin solution is applicable only in a context of quite extreme uncertainty or risk aversion or both, and (2) it is hardly plausible that Nash would have offered the von Neumann solution at the moment of his breakthrough. Also, it appears in the context of the movie that Nash proposes a symmetrical solution, but clearly none of the Nash equilibria in pure strategies for the Blonde Problem is symmetrical.

There is a symmetrical noncooperative equilibrium for the Blonde Problem, though. It is a correlated equilibrium.

First, a coalition of males is a possibility in this game. In a noncooperative game (as we saw in Chapter 6), the possibilities for coalition formation are limited, since there can be no enforcement of the agreement to form the coalition. (If there were enforcement, it would be a cooperative game). But some coalition agreements can be self-enforcing, as two-country alliances are in the Game of International Alliances in Chapter 6. If the agreement is itself a Nash equilibrium, there is no need for enforcement. This is particularly likely in a game like this one that has multiple Nash equilibria in pure strategies.

Second, coalitions, like individuals, can choose mixed (randomized) strategies. Suppose, then, that the males form a grand coalition (an agreement of all N) to coordinate their strategies in the following way: First, they assign different roles among themselves. One of them will be "it" and the others will all be "non-it." The roles are assigned by some method that gives each male an equal probability of being "it," such as drawing straws. Second, the one who is selected as "it" has a free pass to approach the blonde. All of the others are expected to court the brunette of their respective choice.

As with the Confession Game, no one can improve his payoff by a unilateral switch of strategies. First, consider "it." His payoff following the agreed strategy is 2. Otherwise it is 1. He has no reason to deviate. What about a "non-it?" If he were to deviate by pursuing the blonde, he can be certain of facing competition from "it." In that case, his payoff would be 0.

However, by playing the strategy assigned to him at the first stage, he can assure himself of a payoff of 1. Thus, the agreement is self-enforcing. This should not be surprising, as it is one of the pure strategy equilibria of the game, chosen at random. Notice that, unlike the conventional (uncorrelated) mixed strategy equilibrium, there is no possibility of an impasse in which two or more males pursue the blonde and thus the payoffs are (0, 0).

Why would the agreement be realized, rather than one of the N arbitrary pure strategy equilibria, without randomization, or indeed another correlated randomized strategy with unequal probabilities? The equal-probability agreement could provide a Schelling point—one Nash equilibrium among several that has some special property that attracts attention to it and leads each player to expect that the other players are particularly likely to choose it. The special property in this case is *symmetry*. Moreover, the solution is risk-free and clearly dominates the maximin solution.[3]

Perhaps this is the sort of solution the fictional John Nash was thinking of. Unfortunately, in the real world, correlated equilibrium was discovered more than 30 years later, in the 1980s. But now, let's look at a slightly more complicated problem from another movie—*Guys and Dolls*.

The Nathan Detroit Dilemma

Guys and Dolls is a stage play and movie, a musical comedy about gamblers and their girlfriends. Although the love stories are the major plot line, the gamblers' strategies and schemes are full of gaming and lend themselves to interpretation in terms of game theory. For that matter, there is a good deal of "gaming" in the love stories—and that should be no surprise, since scheming lovers and their strategies have been driving themes in comedy since Roman times, if not longer. In this example we explore Nathan Detroit's problems in organizing a dice game.

Nathan Detroit, a lead character, is the proprietor of "the oldest established permanent floating crap game in New York," according to one song. Detroit's crap (dice) game "floats" from one location to another to evade the police, since gambling is illegal. As Benny Southstreet, one of Detroit's henchmen, observes, this "sounds like a very difficult thing to do."

As a first step, though, we want to think about *why* Nathan does the work of organizing the game. Why don't the shooters who want to get into a crap game just get together on their own and have a game?[4] Thus, to begin the example, we leave Nathan out and think of the problem as a game among the gamblers and the police. To keep it simple, we will think of it as a three-person game with two crapshooters and one policeman.

---

3 Many coordination games will, in principle, have solutions along these lines. For example, the Drive-On Game from Chapter 5 could be solved in this way. However, it seems unlikely that the drivers of two cars coming into an intersection will have time to get out and flip a coin to decide who is to go first. Thus, the solution is logically *valid*, but practically *inapplicable* to the Drive-On Game and to some other coordination games.

4 Here are some vocabulary items for those new to American dicing. The game of dice is known as *crap* or *craps* because of one outcome—certain combinations result in an immediate loss, and when this happens, the gambler has *crapped out*. Thus, throwing dice is *shooting crap* or *shooting craps* and gamblers at dice are *crapshooters* or just *shooters*. I am indebted to my crapshooting grandfather, the late Hal Fessler, for this information.

The payoff table for this three-person game is shown as Table 9.10. Lt. Brannigan is the policeman and the gamblers are Harry the Horse and Scranton Slim. The two possible locations are Biltmore's Garage and McCloskey's Bar, and these are the two strategies for each of the three players. The payoffs are listed as Slim first, then Harry, and Brannigan last. If all three agents go to the same location, Lt. Brannigan will be able to break up the game and take the gamblers to prison, which is the best outcome for him and the worst for the gamblers, so the payoffs are (−1, −1, 2). If the two gamblers go to different locations, they do not have a game, and this is a no-reward result for them and a moderate success for Lt. Brannigan, resulting in payoffs (0, 0, 1). If the two gamblers go to the same location and Lt. Brannigan goes to the other, then the gamblers have their game without incident, and Lt. Brannigan fails to prevent illegal gambling, resulting in payoffs of (2, 2, 1).[5]

Table 9.10 | Payoffs for Gamblers and Police

		Lt. Brannigan			
		Biltmore's Garage		McCloskey's Bar	
		Harry the Horse		Harry the Horse	
		garage	bar	garage	bar
Scranton Slim	garage	−1, −1, 2	0, 0, 1	2, 2, −1	0, 0, 1
	bar	0, 0, 1	2, 2, −1	0, 0, 1	−1, −1, 2

There are eight possible strategy combinations, and simple elimination will show that none of them are Nash equilibria in pure strategies. This is because, in a sense, there are two different games going on here. Look at Table 9.11, which simplifies Table 9.10 by eliminating Lt. Brannigan as a factor in the game. That is, it eliminates all possibilities for Lt. Brannigan to break up a crap game, treating the game as if it were a two-person game between the two gamblers. This is a pure coordination game, and it has two Nash equilibria in pure strategies where the two gamblers choose the same locations. We know that this sort of game poses a problem for the players, a problem that might be solved by a Schelling point—one particular site might come to be known to everybody as the conventional site for the crap game.

Table 9.11 | The Game Among the Gamblers

		Harry the Horse	
		garage	bar
Scranton Slim	garage	2, 2, −1	0, 0, 1
	bar	0, 0, 1	2, 2, −1

But that won't work in the three-person game, since if there is a conventional site known to everybody it will be known to Lt. Brannigan, and he will break up the game every time. Look at Table 9.12, which shows the game as if it were a two-person game between the gamblers, as

5 Since some of the gamblers will win and some lose at the crap game, we should think of the payoffs to the gamblers as expected value payoffs, including the enjoyment of the game as well as their winnings and losses. The enjoyment of the game makes it a positive-sum outcome.

Table 9.12 | The Game Between the Gamblers and the Police

		Lt. Brannigan	
		garage	bar
Gamblers	garage	–1, –1, 2	2, 2, –1
	bar	2, 2, –1	–1, –1, 2

a group, and the police. This is an escape-evasion game, and like other escape-evasion games, has no equilibria in pure strategies.

Games without Nash equilibria in pure strategies do have equilibria in mixed strategies, and this game has a mixed strategy in which the gamblers and the police each choose between the two strategies with probabilities of 1/2.[6] But individual mixed strategies do not give good results in the three-person game. If each gambler and the police choose a location with probabilities of 1/2 for each, there will be a probability of 1/2 that the gamblers choose different locations, so that there is no game. The expected value payoff to the gamblers in this case is

$$\frac{1}{2}(0) + \frac{1}{4}(-1) + \frac{1}{4}(2) = \frac{1}{4}$$

9.1

All the same, Table 9.12 gives us the hint we need to solve the game. The gamblers' rational solution is to form a coalition and jointly choose a mixed strategy, a correlated mixed strategy. Thus, they have a 50-50 chance of an undisturbed game, so that their expected value payoff is $^1/_2(-1) + {}^1/_2(2) = {}^1/_2$ and they can do no better than that. But for a group of individuals, choosing a correlated mixed strategy "sounds like a very difficult thing to do."

That's where Nathan Detroit comes in. He acts as an agent for the coalition of gamblers, choosing a location for them as a mixed strategy. In the story there are more than two locations (the gym at Public School 84 is mentioned), so the odds are a bit better for the gamblers, and there are many more than just two gamblers. Nathan's job is to choose the location "where it's always just a short walk," and communicate that to the gamblers while keeping the police in the dark. (In the movie, the gamblers wear red carnations so they can be identified and informed of the location).

(In the story, Nathan's problem is complicated by a lack of working capital, which is solved when a new, free location becomes available: the Salvation Army mission. But it is available only once, and Nathan, his working capital restored, renews the game at Biltmore's Garage. And Lt. Brannigan raids it, winning out after all.)

This example provides another example of the importance of coalitions and correlated strategies, even in noncooperative games. In some applications, it may not be possible to put them into practice—there might not be enough time to form a coalition or agree on correlated strategies, or "the heat may be on" so much that there is only one possible choice of strategies, so mixed strategies are out. From the perspective of rational action, however, our analysis is never complete until we have explored the possibilities for coalitions and/or correlated strategies.

6 We are treating the gamblers' payoffs as the average; i.e., –1 or 2, not the sum, –2 or 4.

Summary

The theory of games in normal form provides a rich toolkit for the analysis of strategic interactions.

As is always the case, powerful tools need to be used with caution. Even when there is no dominant strategy equilibrium, strategy dominance can be helpful in analyzing games. Strongly dominated strategies can be eliminated, and this may produce a reduced game that again has dominated strategies that can be eliminated. In some games, this process—iterated elimination of dominated strategies, or IEDS—leads to a unique Nash equilibrium, and it is a very quick and powerful method of finding unique Nash equilibria when they exist. Even when there are multiple Nash equilibria, IEDS can reduce the total number of strategies to be examined for possible Nash equilibria. However, when we allow for weakly dominated strategies, the case is less clear, and IEDS with elimination of weakly dominated strategies can lead to confusing results. On the other hand, we might be able to refine the concept of Nash equilibria by allowing for a very small probability that the players may choose

wrong strategies. If each player allows for that possibility, assigning a very small probability that the other player will have a "trembling hand" and choose the wrong strategy, then they will avoid weakly dominated strategies and some unreasonable Nash equilibria will be eliminated. This is a good example of *refinement* of Nash equilibrium, an important area of research in advanced game theory.

Coalitions can play a part in noncooperative games, but only if all members of the coalition are choosing their best responses. The coalition may choose a joint mixed strategy, however. This is a correlated equilibrium, and it requires that the members of the coalition find some method of jointly choosing strategies with specific probabilities at random. Some traditional methods are choosing the short straw or allocating scarce resources by lottery. In some cases it may make sense for the coalition to designate one person to choose for them. Correlated equilibria may provide symmetrical solutions to coordination games in which the payoffs would otherwise be unequal, as in the Blonde Problem.

Exercises and Discussion Questions

9.1 Location for Complementary Services. Here is yet another location problem. John is planning to build a new movie theater, and Karl's plan is for a brewpub. Note that, instead of competitors, these are complementary services—some customers will have dinner or a drink at the brewpub before or after their movie. Each can choose among several suburban malls for their construction projects. However, Salt-Lick Court already has a brewpub and The Shops at Bitter Springs already has a movie theater. The payoff table is Table 9.E1.

Table **9.E1** Payoffs with Location Strategies for Complementary Services

		Karl		
		Sweettown Mall	Sourville Mall	The Shops at Bitter Springs
John	Sweettown Mall	10, 10	3, 5	2, 12
	Sourville Mall	4, 3	12, 10	3, 8
	Salt-Lick Court	11, 4	5, 3	10, 12

Table 9.E2 | Payoffs in a Crowding Game

		Carole			
		go		home	
		Barb		**Barb**	
		go	home	go	home
Amy	go	−1, −1, −1	2, 1, 2	2, 2, 1	0, 1, 1
	home	1, 2, 2	1, 0, 1	1, 0, 1	1, 1, 1

Apply the method of IEDS to simplify this game. Propose a solution to this game based on a correlated equilibrium.

9.2 El Farol. Refer to the Crowding Game in Chapter 6. The payoffs are shown in Table 9.E2. Propose a correlated equilibrium solution to this game.

9.3 Getting a Sitter. Recall Exercise 6.3. Professional couples are trying to arrange for sitters. The payoffs are shown in Table 9.E3.

Table 9.E3 | Cooperative Babysitters

		Smith								
		sit			out			nothing		
		Jones			**Jones**			**Jones**		
		sit	out	nothing	sit	out	nothing	sit	out	nothing
Hanratty	sit	0, 0, 0	½, 1, ½	0, 0, 0	½, ½, 1	1,½, ½	1, 0, 1	0, 0, 0	1, 1, 0	0, 0, 0
	out	1, ½, ½	½, ½, 1	1, 0, 1	½, 1, ½	0, 0, 0	0, 0, 0	1, 1, 0	0, 0, 0	0, 0, 0
	nothing	0, 0, 0	0, 1, 1	0, 0, 0	0, 1, 1	0, 0, 0	0, 0, 0	0, 0, 0	0, 0, 0	0, 0, 0

The payoffs are listed with Hanratty first, then Jones, then Smith. The idea behind the payoffs is that a match pays 1 for those matched.

Can you apply the method of IEDS to simplify this game? Discuss. Propose a correlated equilibrium solution to this game.

9.4 Medical Practice. Recall Exercise 6.5. Doctors are considering whether to practice as ob/gyns or to limit their practices to gyn. Propose a correlated equilibrium solution to this game.

Duopoly Strategies and Prices · 10

To best understand this chapter · 10

To best understand this chapter you need to have studied and understood the material from Chapters 1–4, 7, and 8. Some knowledge of the principles of economics will also be useful.

One of the objectives of John von Neumann and Oskar Morgenstern in their great book, *The Theory of Games and Economic Behavior*, was to solve an unsolved problem of economic theory: oligopoly pricing. *Oligopoly* means "few sellers," and this suggests that a simple supply-and-demand approach would probably be too simple. With only a few sellers, the sellers may have some ability to cut back on production and raise the price and the profit margin, as a monopoly would do. But to what extent? Would the oligopolists raise the price all the way to the monopoly level? From their point of view, that would be the *cooperative* solution to the game; but if they act *noncooperatively* or competitively, the price might fall below the monopoly target, and might even fall to the competitive price level.

The problem was already of long standing. Since duopoly—a market with just two sellers—is the most extreme form of oligopoly, many studies focused on duopoly pricing. If that problem could be solved, then—probably—it would be fairly easy to move on to three, four, or N sellers. In this chapter, we will survey some of the traditional duopoly models, reinterpret them in game theory terms, and then explore some recent game theoretic work on duopoly pricing.

Cournot Models

The first contribution to our understanding of duopoly pricing came from a French mathematician, Augustin Cournot, in 1838. Cournot assumed that each firm would decide how much product to put on the market, and the price would depend on the total. In twentieth-century economics, the Cournot model is associated with the idea of an industry demand curve. (That was an idea that Augustin Cournot invented, though some English-speaking economists probably came up with the idea independently several years later.) An example is shown in Figure 10.1.

Definition

Demand Curve or Function—The relationship between the price of a good and the quantity that can be sold at each respective price is a demand relationship. It can be shown in a diagram as the **demand curve**, or mathematically as the **demand function**.

Heads Up!

Here are some concepts we will develop as this chapter goes along:

Duopoly: An industry in which just two firms compete for customers is called a *duopoly*.

Cournot Equilibrium: When two firms each put a certain quantity of output on the market, and sell at the price determined by the market, the output is the strategy and the resulting Nash equilibrium is a *Cournot equilibrium*.

Bertrand-Edgeworth Equilibrium: When two firms each set a price, and the firm with the cheaper price dominates the market, the price is the strategy and the resulting Nash equilibrium is a *Bertrand-Edgeworth equilibrium*.

Mixed Strategy Pricing Equilibrium: If prices are the strategies as in Bertrand-Edgeworth equilibrium, but firms have limited production capacities, there may be no equilibrium in pure strategies, and we may see a mixed strategy Nash equilibrium for prices.

An *industry* is a group of firms selling the same or closely substitutable products. Thus, the total output of all firms in the industry is shown on the horizontal axis and the price prevailing in the industry is shown on the vertical axis. The downward-sloping line is the *demand curve*, and it can be interpreted—equally correctly—in two ways. First, given the total output of all firms in the industry, the corresponding point on the demand curve shows the price that will prevail in the industry. This is the interpretation used in Cournot models. Second, given the price in the industry, the distance from the vertical axis to the demand curve shows the maximum amount that can be sold in the industry. With either interpretation, the demand curve demonstrates the idea that a higher price will correspond to a smaller output sold.

Our duopoly industry will consist of two computer firms, MicroSplat and Pear Corp. The Cournot approach assumes that the two firms in the duopoly each decide how much to sell, put that

Figure 10.1 | The Industry Demand Curve

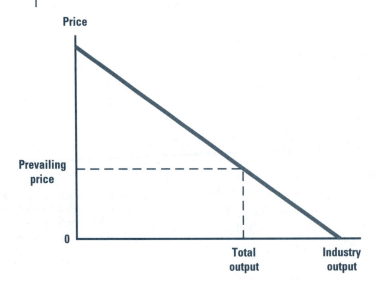

quantity on the market, and sell it at whatever price results along the demand curve.[1] Thus, each firm has to make a guess—a **conjecture**—as to what the other firm will sell. Looking at Figure 10.2, suppose that Pear Corp. conjectures that MicroSplat will put Q_1

units of output on the market. Then Pear can assume that it will have the segment of the industry demand curve to the right of Q_1 as, in effect, its own demand curve. Based on its conjecture about MicroSplat's plans, Pear understands that its demand curve has a 0 point that corresponds to Q_1 on the industry demand curve. In effect, Pear's demand is the residual, what is left over after MicroSplat maximizes its profits. Then Pear's problem is to adjust its output so that the industry price gives it the greatest possible profits.

Cournot approached that problem using calculus, while basic economics textbooks often use a graphical approach. We need not worry about the details here, but will just assume that the two duopolists know how to adjust the output so that the profits are maximized, if they know what their demand curve is like.[2]

---

1 Notice that there is a hidden assumption here. The hidden assumption is that the products sold by the two firms are *homogenous*, that is, one firm's product is a perfect substitute for the product sold by the other. Often this is not true in reality—the products are not homogenous but *differentiated*. In Cournot's original example, he wrote about mineral water. Yet mineral water is not homogenous. Mountain Valley is produced in Arkansas, in the south where I was born and raised, so I feel some traditional loyalty to it; but San Pelligrino brings back memories of sipping mineral water in a café beside a Venetian canal. How could one substitute for the other? One advantage of the Cournot model is that it can be extended to allow for product differentiation. This will be briefly discussed in an appendix to the chapter.

2 This will be discussed in a little more detail in an appendix to the chapter.

Figure 10.2 | Firm 2's Conjecture and Estimated Demand Curve

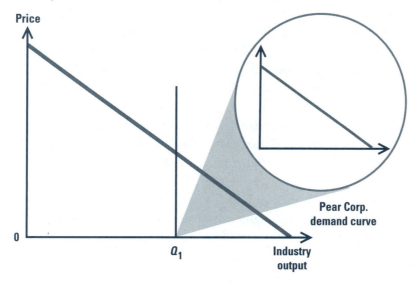

Of course, MicroSplat will also have to try to conjecture about how much Pear will produce, and determine its own demand curve and profit-maximizing output in a similar way. Cournot's idea is that both companies are thinking in the same way, making a conjecture about the output the other one will sell, taking the remainder of the industry demand as their own, and choosing their profit-maximizing output accordingly.

In the history of economic theory, this Cournotian approach has been interpreted in two ways. One interpretation is that it is a step-by-step adjustment process. Suppose that, once Pear has chosen its output, MicroSplat finds that Q_1 does not maximize its profits. Then MicroSplat changes its output to Q_2 in order to increase its profits. But then Pear finds that it has been mistaken—it had conjectured that MicroSplat would produce Q_1, but MicroSplat actually produced Q_2. So Pear changes its conjecture, and that changes its estimate of its own demand curve and therefore its output decision—which means that MicroSplat finds that its conjecture about Pear's output was mistaken, and so MicroSplat changes its conjecture and its output decision, and so it goes until (perhaps) each company maximizes its profits by choosing the quantity the other company conjectures that it will choose. When that happens we say that the two companies have **consistent conjectures**. (The term *consistent conjectures* was not used by Cournot but was first used in the 1980s).

> ### Definition
>
> ***Consistent Conjectures***—When two or more decision makers each base their decisions on conjectures about the decisions of others, and the conjectures lead each decision maker to make the decisions the others had conjectured that she would—so that everyone turns out to be right—we have a case of **consistent conjectures**.

This is not the approach of Nash equilibrium theory, however. Recall that Nash equilibrium theory assumes common knowledge of rationality. Thus, the second interpretation is that the two duopolists understand one another well enough that each can figure out what the other one's profit-maximizing output will be, so that each conjectures correctly that the other one will choose the output that maximizes profits in the circumstances. Thus, they have consistent conjectures right from the start, without any step-by-step series of mistakes.

Both interpretations have influenced game theory. When game theorists think about how people learn to choose equilibrium strategies, the term *Cournot dynamics* refers to a learning process in which each player responds to the action the other player took in the step just past. But we are not concerned with learning, here, so the second interpretation is the one we want to focus on. What the second interpretation says is that each duopolist chooses the output that is the best response to the output chosen by the other. That seems pretty definitely to be what Cournot had in mind, and it is so clearly an instance of a Nash equilibrium (a century before John Nash) that some economists use the term **Cournot-Nash equilibrium** in place of just *Nash equilibrium*.[3]

Thus, in game theory terms, Cournot outputs are a Nash equilibrium in which the quantity sold is the strategy. Each seller assumes the following:

---

3 But—so far as I know—there is no movie about the life of Augustin Cournot. Too bad.

- The other seller will choose the *best-response strategy* (since they are both rational and have common knowledge of their rationality); so

- the other seller's output is given.

- Thus, each seller assumes it has the rest of the market to itself.

Nash Equilibrium in Cournot Models

We do need to say something about maximizing profits in order to go forward with Cournot models. Rather than use calculus or graphics, however, let's look at a numerical tabular example, much like the Prisoner's Dilemma and so many other game-theory examples, to get the idea. The industry demand function will be

$$Q = 11000 - 1000 \times p$$

where Q is the total output of both companies and p is the market price. The demand curve looks like Figure 10.3.

As usual, the price is on the vertical axis, and the total quantity demanded for both firms is on the horizontal axis. We assume that the cost for each firm is $5 per unit. To make things a little simpler, we will limit MicroSplat and Pear Corp. to just four strategies each: outputs of 1,000, 1,500, 2,000, 3,000. (Outputs could be in units of thousands or millions to make the example more realistic!) Each firm will choose to produce one of those four quantities, and the total amount for sale, on the industry demand curve, is the sum of the two quantities. For

Figure 10.3 | Industry Demand

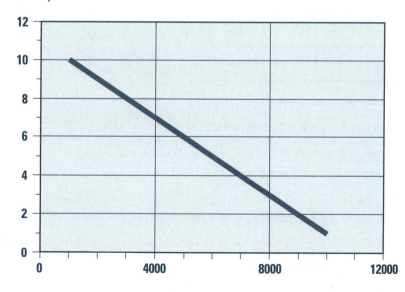

Table 10.1 | Prices and Strategies for MicroSplat and Pear

		MicroSplat			
		1,000	1,500	2,000	3,000
Pear Corp.	1,000	9	8.5	8	7
	1,500	8.5	8	7.5	6.5
	2,000	8	7.5	7	6
	3,000	7	6.5	6	5

Table 10.2 | Payoffs to MicroSplat and Pear

		MicroSplat			
		1,000	1,500	2,000	3,000
Pear Corp.	1,000	4, 4	3.25, 5.25	3, 6	2, 6
	1,500	5.25, 3.5	4.5, 4.5	3.75, 5	2.25, 4.5
	2,000	6, 3	5, 3.75	4, 4	2, 3
	3,000	6, 2	4.5, 2.25	3, 2	0, 0

example, if MicroSplat chooses to produce and sell 2,000, and Pear chooses to produce and sell 1,000, the industry total is 3,000, and, looking at Figure 10.1, we see that the price in the industry will be $8. Table 10.1 shows the price that will result from every pair of output strategies the two firms may choose. Table 10.1 *is not a payoff table*, but it gives us information we need to get a payoff table for this game.

To get the payoffs for each firm, we multiply that firm's quantity strategy by the price minus the $5 marginal unit cost; that is, payoff = $Q(p - 5)$ where Q is the quantity strategy and p is the price. For example, if MicroSplat chooses to produce and sell 2,000, and Pear chooses to produce and sell 1,000, with the resulting price of $8, MicroSplat's payoff and profit is $2,000(8 - 5) = 6,000$ and Pear's payoff is $1,000(8 - 5) = 3,000$. The payoff table for the two firms is shown in Table 10.2.

Payoffs are profits in thousands, and the first number gives the payoff to Pear. Looking at these tables, we can make the following observations:

- Industry profits are maximized—with a total of $9 for both firms—whenever the total output for both firms is 3,000.

- Correspondingly, the monopoly price is $8.

- The competitive price is $5, which is equal to the "marginal cost."

- Accordingly, if both sellers act "competitively," as we understand it in the supply-and-demand approach, their outputs would be 3,000 each.

- However, the Nash equilibrium for this game is at (2000, 2000). All other strategy combinations can be eliminated because they are not best responses for one or both firms.

- Thus, the Cournot equilibrium price is $7—less than the monopoly price of $8 but still more than the competitive price of $5.

This result can be generalized in several ways. We can get rid of some of the simplifying assumptions—marginal cost does not have to be constant, and the demand relationship can be more complex, and the two firms need not be identical—and we still see the equilibrium price somewhere between the competitive and monopoly prices. The model can also be extended to three, four, or more firms—and the more firms we have in the marketplace, the closer the price comes to the competitive price at the marginal cost. Best of all, this agrees qualitatively with the evidence. When we observe different industries and compare them, we do seem to find that, on the whole, oligopoly prices are lower than monopoly prices. The more competitors there are, the closer the price comes to the marginal cost.

Cournot's model thus was not only the first, but a very successful model in many ways. All the same, it had its critics, who raised questions about its logic and assumptions.

Bertrand and Edgeworth

In a book review, Joseph Bertrand (1883) asked why the sellers would focus on the *outputs* rather than compete in terms of prices. In game theory terms, Bertrand is suggesting that the prices, and not the outputs, would be the strategies among which the sellers would choose. The key point is that if one seller cuts his price below the other, the seller with the lower price gets the whole market. If they charge the same price, the simple guess is that they split the market. In our example of MicroSplat and Pear, this leads to payoffs as shown in Table 10.3. Once again, what makes this table different from Table 10.2 is that *prices, not quantities, are the strategies!* For example, a combination of prices (8, 8) in Table 10.3 corresponds to output quantities of (1,500, 1,500) in Table 10.2.

Table 10.3 Prices as Strategies and Payoffs to MicroSplat and Pear

		MicroSplat			
		6	7	8	9
Pear Corp.	6	2.5, 2.5	5, 0	5, 0	5, 0
	7	0, 5	4, 4	8, 0	8, 0
	8	0, 5	0, 8	4.5, 4.5	9, 0
	9	0, 5	0, 8	0, 9	4, 4

We have looked at games a bit like this before. We can eliminate every strategy except the lowest prices allowed, $6 and $6. In a game of this kind, as long as there is any margin of price over marginal cost whatever, the best response is always to cut price below the other competitor. If fractional prices were allowed in this example, the price would keep dropping toward the marginal cost, and competition would eliminate profits entirely, as it does in a perfectly competitive model!

Francis Edgeworth (1897) agreed with Bertrand's criticisms of Cournot, but Edgeworth pointed out two complications. First, the sellers might have limited production capacity. At a price of $6 the total output sold is 5,000. If each company is limited to production of

2,000, then the price will not fall below $7, at which a total output of 4,000 can be sold. That's the supply-and-demand equilibrium price. Second, Edgeworth argued that a supply-and-demand price of $7 would not be stable, either. Since each seller is selling all it can, the seller who charges a higher price will not lose customers to the lower-price seller and may increase its profits by raising its price. Thus, no price is stable—either at or above the supply-and-demand level—and Edgeworth concluded that there will be no stable price, but rather, price will be unpredictable and may fall anywhere over the whole range, from the monopoly price down to the supply-and-demand price.

Figure 10.4 | Edgeworth's Reasoning

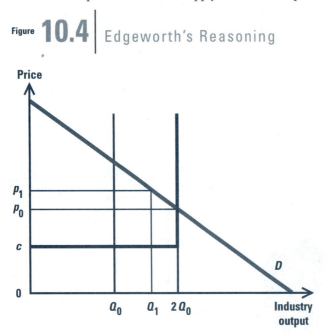

Edgeworth's reasoning is illustrated by Figure 10.4. Downward-sloping line D is the industry demand curve that the two firms share. Each firm can produce up to a capacity limit of Q_θ units of output, at a cost of c per unit. The capacity limit for the industry as a whole is $2Q_\theta$. Thus, the industry supply curve is the right angle formed by the cost line at c and the dark vertical line at $2Q_\theta$, and the supply-and-demand equilibrium price is p_0.

Now suppose that both firms are charging a price of p_1. Industry sales at that price are Q_1, so they split that output between them, each one selling $Q_1/2$ units of output. But if one of the two firms were to cut its price just slightly below p_1, it would be able to sell its entire capacity, Q_θ, increasing its sales by $Q_\theta - Q_1/2$. This lump increase in sales at the cost of a tiny cut in price will increase profits, so the best response to any price above p_0 will generally be a slightly lower price. It follows that no price above p_0 will be a Nash equilibrium. But p_0 might not be a Nash equilibrium, either. At p_0, each firm is selling its capacity limit. If one firm increases its price above p_0, the other firm will be unable to take advantage of that by increasing its output—since it is already at its capacity limit—and, therefore, the firm that raises its price can act essentially as a monopolist with whatever is left of the market, and maximize its profits by restricting its output to less than Q_θ. Edgeworth concluded that there may be no *predictable* price for a duopoly with a capacity constraint. Interpreting this in terms of game theory, we say that there is no Nash equilibrium in *pure strategies*, since every pure (price) strategy opens the firm to a counterstrategy that it, in turn, will want to counter. But we have seen that games without any pure strategy equilibrium may have mixed strategy equilibria. (In fact, Nash proved that two-person games always do have equilibria in mixed if not in pure strategies.) Accordingly, we go on to explore whether the oligopoly pricing game with capacity limits might have an equilibrium in mixed strategies.

A Mixed Strategy Pricing Game[4]

The discussion of Edgeworth's reasoning above suggests that we apply the following assumptions to our numerical example of MicroSplat and Pear:

- If both firms choose the same price, they split the industry demand equally at that price.

- If one firm chooses a higher price, the firm that chooses the lower price sells the entire industry demand or sells out its capacity, whichever is less; and the firm that chooses the higher price sells the industry demand minus the other firm's capacity—the residual demand as in a Cournot model.

For example, suppose MicroSplat and Pear each has a capacity of 2,500 units. Suppose MicroSplat prices at $8 and Pear prices at $7. At a $7 price, 4,000 can be sold, but Pear can sell only 2,500. That leaves 1,500 to be sold by MicroSplat at $8. (No one able to buy at $7 buys at $8; but the demand relationship tells us that there are 3,000 who are willing to buy at $8 if necessary—more than enough.) Thus, selling 2,500 units at $7, Pear's profits are 2,500(7 − 5) = 5,000. MicroSplat sells 1,500 at a price of $8 for a profit of 1,500(8 − 5) = 4,500. A series of similar computations gives us the payoff table shown as Table 10.4.

NOW IT'S YOUR TURN. Confirm at least three of the other cells in Table 10.3 by similar computations.

4 This analysis is suggested by work of Pankaj Ghemawat. *Games Businesses Play, Cases and Models* (Cambridge, Mass: MIT, 1997). Of course, Ghemawat's approach is more mathematically sophisticated than the one used here.

Table 10.4 | Prices as Strategies with a Capacity Constraint

		MicroSplat			
		6	7	8	9
Pear Corp.	6	2.5, 2.5	2.5, 5	2.5, 7.5	2.5, 10
	7	5, 2.5	4, 4	5, 4.5	5, 6
	8	7.5, 2.5	4.5, 5	4.5, 4.5	7.5, 2
	9	10, 2.5	6, 5	2, 7.5	4, 4

Table 10.5 | Prices as Strategies with a Capacity Constraint and Underlines

		MicroSplat			
		6	7	8	9
Pear Corp.	6	2.5, 2.5	2.5, 5	2.5, 7.5	2.5, <u>10</u>
	7	5, 2.2	4, 4	<u>5</u>, 4.5	5, <u>6</u>
	8	7.5, 2.5	4.5, <u>5</u>	4.5, 4.5	<u>7.5</u>, 2
	9	<u>10</u>, 2.5	<u>6</u>, 5	2, <u>7.5</u>	4, 4

The first step is to find out whether there are any Nash equilibria in pure strategies. In Table 10.5, we explore that by putting underlines in the diagram to represent the best responses to various combinations of strategies. We can eliminate every cell—there is no Nash equilibrium in pure strategies.

What about mixed strategies? Remember, a mixed strategy means that two or more strategies are chosen with positive probabilities, in such a way as to keep the other player uncertain about which strategy he should choose. Payoffs have to be computed in expected value terms. Rather than going through the algebra—a little more complex in this game than in the ones we studied in Chapter 8—let's just look at some of the possibilities as shown in Table 10.6. The expected value payoffs are for Pear Corp., and they reflect the probabilities chosen by MicroSplat, but since the two companies are identical in this example—meaning that it is a symmetrical game—those points of view could be reversed without making any difference.

Suppose, for example, that MicroSplat chooses prices of $7, $8, and $9 with probabilities 0.6, 0.4, and 0. Then the expected value (for Pear) of choosing a price of $8 is 4.5, while the other two strategies give expected values of 4.4. Thus, Pear's decision based on those probabilities will be to choose a price of $8, a pure strategy. Suppose instead that MicroSplat chooses prices of $7, $8, and $9 with probabilities 0.4, 0.6, and 0. Then the strategy of pricing at $7 gives

Table 10.6 | Some MicroSplat Probabilities and Corresponding Expected Value Payoffs for Pear

Probabilities			Expected Values			Decision
Price of $7	Price of $8	Price of $9	Price of $7	Price of $8	Price of $9	
0.6	0.4	0	4.4	4.5	4.4	p = 8
0.5	0.5	0	4.5	4.5	4	Mix 7 and 8
0.4	0.6	0	4.6	4.4	3.6	p = 7

Pear a payoff of 4.6, greater than the other two strategies. Pear's decision is to choose a price of $7 as a pure strategy. Suppose yet again that MicroSplat chooses prices of $7, $8, and $9 with probabilities 0.5, 0.5, and 0. Then the strategy of pricing at $9 is inferior to the other two—it will not be chosen. But the expected values of p = 7 and p = 8 are equal, so that Pear doesn't care which of them it chooses. It will choose a mixed strategy consisting of those two pure price strategies.

To find out what probabilities Pear will choose, we have to turn the points of view around, and find out what probabilities will make MicroSplat undecided about which strategy to choose. Since the game is symmetrical, we already know the answer—0.5, 0.5, and 0. Probabilities 0.5, 0.5, and 0 constitute the mixed strategy equilibrium for this game. Notice that, since the price is now a random variable, we cannot use the price in any *particular* transaction as a measure of the overall cheapness of the good sold. Here, again, we must use expected value concepts—and compute the expected value of the price. In this case, it is 0.5 × 7 + 0.5 × 8 + 0 × 9 = 7.5—just halfway between $7 and $8. Of course, all of this would change if we were to change the assumptions, including the assumption that the two firms each have capacities of 2,500.

In fact, the mixed strategies do depend on the capacities—with a bigger production capacity, for example, the firm that underprices will be able to sell more, in most cases, since that firm is usually limited by its capacity rather than demand; while that will reduce the amount sold by the firm that is underpriced. As it turns out, the relationships are a bit complex. There is a different payoff table for each capacity limit, of course; but these can be constructed in a spreadsheet and the probabilities found by equation-solving software. There will not be space to go through the details in the book, but the results are shown by Table 10.7.

Table 10.7 shows some of the characteristics of equilibrium mixed strategies for examples in which each firm has a capacity of 2,000 . . . 3,000. All these numbers show some general trends:

- *On the whole*, the expected value of the price declines as capacity increases.

- *On the whole*, the expected value of profits declines as capacity increases.

- There are some exceptions to both of the above tendencies!

- The lowest price, p = $7, is never chosen at a capacity less than 2,300, but the probability that this price will be chosen increases with every subsequent increase in capacity until it is chosen with certainty at a capacity of 3,000.

- The price of $8 is chosen with certainty if the capacity is less than 2,300, and never chosen if the capacity is more than 2,800.

Thus, it seems we may say that, as the capacity of each of the two firms increases, the pricing in the industry becomes more competitive, *on the whole*. This is probably what an economist would predict. But we can also say that the details are quite complex, sensitive to the exact numbers in a particular case, and computationally difficult. And all of this is true, despite the fact that I have made this example as simple as I could! If the capacities or costs

Table 10.7 | Equilibrium Mixed Strategies by Capacities

Capacity	Equilibrium Probabilities			Expected Values of Payoffs by Strategy			Expected Value of the Price	Expected Value of the Profits
	$p=7$	$p=8$	$p=9$	$p=7$	$p=8$	$p=9$		
2000	0	1	0	4	4.5	4	8	4.5
2100	0	1	0	4.2	4.5	3.6	8	4.5
2200	0	1	0	4.4	4.5	3.2	8	4.5
2300	0.083	0.917	0	4.55	4.55	3.13	7.9	4.55
2400	0.27	0.73	0	4.58	4.58	3.49	7.7	4.58
2500	0.5	0.5	0	4.5	4.5	4	7.5	4.5
2600	0.68	0.29	0.03	4.38	4.38	4.38	7.34	4.38
2700	0.73	0.18	0.08	4.37	4.37	4.37	7.35	4.37
2800	0.77	0.08	0.14	4.36	4.36	4.36	7.37	4.36
2900	0.82	0	0.18	4.33	4.28	4.33	7.36	4.33
2950	0.9	0	0.1	4.18	3.7	1	7.19	4.18
3000	1	0	0	4	3	4	7	4

of the two firms were different, or the firms were not symmetrical in other ways, or if the cost and demand relationships were more complicated, or the model were more realistic in many other ways, then new dimensions of complexity would be introduced.

Put yourself in the position of a business manager who is considering expanding the business's capacity, or perhaps considering reducing it by phasing out some plants. What the example tells us is that such a change of capacity can change the whole competitive landscape for pricing strategy—that a small change, for example, can make a mixed strategy optimal where a pure strategy had been optimal before.

What we can conclude without doubt from this example is that mixed strategy equilibria can be rational in duopoly pricing, and it makes a great deal of difference when we consider mixed strategy equilibria as an alternative to pure strategy pricing.

Applicability

The previous example, complex as it is, rests on a number of simplifying assumptions. Accordingly, it will not always be applicable. Perhaps we can say a little about the limits on its applicability.

- The mixed strategy model makes sense when sellers make independent, take-it-or-leave-it offers to individual buyers. Not all industries fit that description equally well. Big-ticket capital goods, such as electric-power generators, may well be sold pretty much in that way. Where the price is essentially determined by a price list, though, there seems to be less room for mixed strategies. On the other hand, simply because there is a list price does not mean that transactions take place at that price. It is well understood that most transactions take place below list price. The list price typically sets an upper limit from which the price offers begin.

- The quantity put on the market may depend on more than just the production capacities of the sellers. Where sellers carry inventories, they probably will put more on the market when their inventories are higher. On the other side, some industries operate with order backlogs, so that buyers have to go on a waiting list and take delivery after a wait of weeks or months. That will influence price competition as well. Mixed strategy pricing models can be adapted to allow for these things, and this is a promising line of research, since casual observations suggest that inventory fluctuations can have a disproportionate impact on price offers, which is hard to explain by other kinds of pricing models. However, as yet we really know very little about this.

- In all of the pricing strategy models in this chapter, we assume that the rival firms sell identical products. In many industries, however, this assumption is not applicable. Different firms may sell products that are not perfect substitutes, so that some customers prefer one product over another. This is called **product differentiation,** and can be as important as pricing in the market strategies of many firms. Cournot models have been extended (at the cost of a little calculus) to allow for product differentiation, but product differentiation is less well understood in the Bertrand-Edgeworth models.

> **Definition**
>
> **Product Differentiation**—When different firms sell products or services that are not perfect substitutes, and make the distinction among the products a basis of promotion or an aspect of market strategy, we refer to this as **product differentiation**.

- In the Bertrand-Edgeworth and mixed strategy pricing models, there is no customer loyalty—customers always buy from the lower-price seller when they can. Thus, these models are not applicable to markets in which there is customer loyalty, whether the loyalty is a result of product differentiation or any other reason. In order to extend Bertrand-Edgeworth models to markets with customer loyalty, it would be necessary to have a much more complete understanding of how customer loyalty and prices influence consumer decisions in each transaction.

Summary

It seems we have to acknowledge that the best pricing strategy will always depend a great deal on the specifics of the industry and its situation. There is no "architectonic," overarching model of rational pricing and output decisions. But there are principles that will have application in many cases, and so are part of the toolkit of any economist or businessperson concerned with pricing strategy.

First, the concept of Nash equilibrium itself—that the rivals will each choose a strategy that is the best response to the other's strategy—will be applicable to all cases of price competition among rational, profit-seeking rival firms. Second, where the firms have control of the quantities they offer for sale but little control over the price, Cournot models are the best starting point. Where product differentiation is important, more advanced Cournot models, which we have not covered in this chapter, also seem to be the best starting point. Where price competition is strong, the Bertrand model offers important insights, but limitations on productive capacity (or on inventories) may have profound and complicated impacts on pricing strategy.

Appendix A
A Mathematical Treatment of the Cournot Model

This appendix gives a discussion of the Cournot model in terms of calculus and marginal analysis, which is the more conventional way of discussing it in economic theory. In addition, we show how the model is generalized to allow for differentiated products. To understand this appendix, the student needs some understanding of ordinary and partial differentiation and of the indefinite integral in calculus.

For the Cournot model in the main text of the chapter, the price prevailing in the industry is a function of the total output:

$$p = f(Q_A + Q_B)$$

10.A1

where Q_A is the output of Firm A and Q_B is the output of Firm B. To allow for product differentiation, we instead assume

$$p_A = f_A(Q_A, Q_B)$$

10.A2a

$$p_B = f_B(Q_B, Q_A)$$

10.A2b

Here is the idea: Since the outputs of Firms A and B are not perfect substitutes, it seems that an increase in the output of Firm B might have less impact on the market price for Firm A than an equal increase in Firm A's output would have. Conversely, Equation 10.A1 is a special case of 10.A2, in which both functions are the same and Q_A and Q_B are combined by the sum operator.

Assume the costs are determined by Equation 10A.3a and 3b:

$$C_A = g_A(Q_A)$$ 10.A3a

$$C_B = g_B(Q_B)$$ 10.A3b

Each firm aims to maximize its profit:

$$\Pi_A = p_A Q_A - C_A$$ 10.A4a

$$\Pi_B = p_B Q_B - C_B$$ 10.A4b

When we apply calculus to the problem of finding a maximum, we rely on "necessary conditions" using the derivative. The intuition behind this is illustrated by Figure 10.A1. The plot shows how variable y changes as x changes. We want to find x_0, the value that corresponds to the largest value of y. We recall that the derivative of x with respect to y can be visualized as the slope of a tangent to the curve. At the top of the curve, the tangent is flat—that is, it has a slope of zero. So, for a simple case like Figure 10.A1, the *necessary condition* for a maximum is that $dy/dx = 0$. There could be other values of x for which the slope is zero, but y is not at a maximum—for example, the slope would also be flat when y is at a minimum. So the necessary conditions are not sufficient: we need some additional "sufficient" conditions. However, for the rest of this appendix we will not bother about that complication and will explore only the implications of the necessary conditions.

Maximization of Equation 10.A4 is a little more complicated. Without going into details, the necessary conditions are shown in Equation 10.A5.

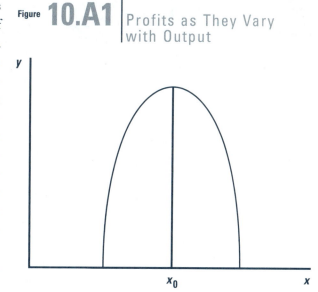

Figure **10.A1** Profits as They Vary with Output

$$p_A - Q \frac{\partial f_A}{\partial Q_A} - \frac{\partial g_A}{\partial Q_A} = 0$$

10.A5

In terms of economic theory,

$$\frac{\partial g_A}{\partial Q_A}$$

is the firm's marginal cost, MC_A, and the marginal revenue is

$$MR_A = p_A - Q \frac{\partial f_A}{\partial Q_A}$$

so Equation 10.A5 is equivalent to the familiar formula from economics, MC = MR.

Figure 10.A2 shows the industry and individual firm demand curves as in Figure 10.2 in the text, with the individual firm's marginal cost and marginal revenue curves added in a slightly darker gray. The marginal revenue curve is the downward-sloping line and the marginal cost curve is the upward-sloping curve. Thus, as we would see in microeconomics, the firm will choose to produce Q, corresponding to the point where the marginal revenue curve cuts the marginal cost curve.

The profit-maximum condition is similar for Firm B. Solving Equation 10.A5 for Q,

$$Q = \frac{p_A - \dfrac{\partial g_A}{\partial Q_A}}{\dfrac{\partial f_A}{\partial Q_A}} = \frac{p_A - MC_A}{\dfrac{\partial f_A}{\partial Q_A}}$$

10.A6

Figure 10.A2 | Diagram for the Calculus-Based Cournot Model

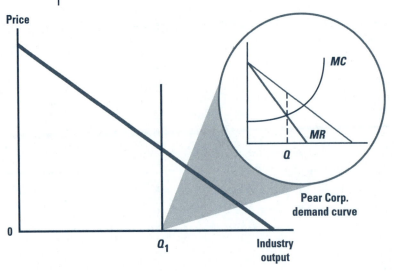

Since

$$\frac{\partial g_A}{\partial Q_A} = MC_A$$

Differentiating Equation 10.A5, we have Equation 10.A7:

$$\frac{dQ_A}{dQ_B} = -\left[\frac{Q_A \dfrac{\partial^2 f_A}{\partial Q_B \partial Q_A} - \dfrac{\partial f}{\partial Q_B}}{(Q_A + 1)\dfrac{\partial^2 f_A}{\partial Q^2_A} - \dfrac{\partial f}{\partial Q_A}} \right] \qquad \text{10.A7}$$

and, integrating this expression, we have the *reaction function* for Firm A,

$$Q_A = b_A(Q_B) \qquad \text{10.A8}$$

Figure 10.A3 shows the reaction function for two firms. The Cournot equilibrium is at Q^*_A and Q^*_B, the intersection of the reaction functions. (We assume that the equilibrium is stable without investigating the conditions under which it will or will not be stable).

This method—deriving *reaction functions* and finding the quantities at which they intersect—is an application of the Nash equilibrium. At every point along Firm A's reaction

Figure 10.A3 | Reaction Functions for Two Firms

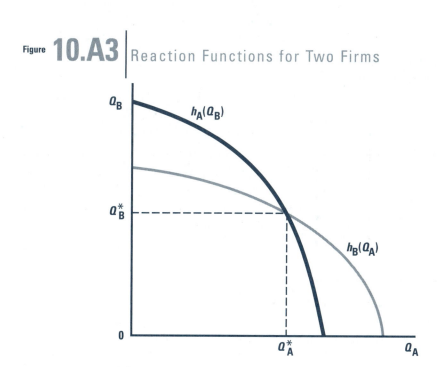

function, Firm A is choosing its best response to Firm B's strategy, and conversely, at every point along Firm B's reaction function Firm B is choosing its best response to Firm A's strategy. Where the reaction functions intersect, each firm is choosing its best response to the other's strategy—a Nash equilibrium.

Appendix B
A Calculus-Based Mixed Strategy Pricing Model and Business Case

The mixed strategy pricing model was introduced by Ghemawat. His analysis is more general and realistic in that it allows for the fact that there is a (price) number between any two (price) numbers. In mathematical terms, prices are drawn from a continuum. What that means in terms of economics is that it is always possible for one firm to undercut a price offer by the other, even if by ever so little. However, his analysis requires two concepts from calculus, so it is too advanced for the main text of this book. For the use of students who have some background in calculus, the appendix gives some details, illustrating them with some results from Ghemawat's study of price competition between General Electric and Westinghouse in the market for large turbine electrical generators.

One of the calculus elements we need is the cumulative density function. The cumulative density function is a way of expressing the probabilities of different observations on a random variable. The idea is clearest (although less useful) if the random variate can take only a finite number of values. Let us think of a random variate, x, that can take only the values 1, 2, 3, 4, and 5. The probabilities of observing these values are shown in Table 10.B1.

The second column contains the probabilities of the values 1, 2, 3, 4, and 5. The cumulative distribution function for this variable, $F(x)$, is the answer to the question "How probable is it that the value I observe will be no greater than x?" Thus, for example, for $F(3)$, the answer is the sum of the probabilities for 3, 2, and 1, (i.e., $0.4 + 0.2 + 0.1 = 0.7$). The CDF for this function is shown in the right-hand column of Table 10.B1. The table illustrates two things about the CDF: (1) it can only increase, never decrease, as the value of x increases, and (2) the CDF always approaches an upper limit of 1.

Table **10.B1** | A Distribution Function

x	Probability	CDF
0	0	0
1	.1	.1
2	.2	.3
3	.4	.7
4	.2	.9
5	.1	1

So the CDF for x is the sum of all the probabilities of all values up to and including x. More generally—when there is a continuum of (probability) numbers—we can say that the CDF is the integral of the probabilities of all values of the variable up to x. Conversely, the probability of x is the difference, p = (F(x) − F(x − 1)). Remember how we compute the expected value of x. It will be (0.1)1 + (0.2)2 + (0.4)3 + (0.2)4 + (0.1)5 = 0.1 + 0.4 + 1.2 + 0.8 + 0.5 = 3. We can either obtain the probabilities from the middle column or—if we were not given the middle column—we could get the probabilities by taking the differences, 0.1 = 0.1 − 0, 0.2 = 0.3 − 0.1, and so on. When x varies over a continuum, so that we cannot get the expected value by adding up a finite number of terms, we can express the expected value as a definite integral. Suppose that x varies from a minimum of a to a maximum of b. Then the expected value, EV(x), is

$$EV(x) = \int_a^b x \frac{dF}{dx}\, dx$$

As the example in Table 10.B1 shows, the cumulative distribution function doesn't *have* to be continuous, but in many of the more useful examples, it is continuous. Figure 10.B1 shows a continuous probability (density) function that approximates Table 10.B1, and the corresponding CDF.

For this case, we would have to use some calculus to compute the expected value of x, but we can always approximate by a numerical computation like the one above. In the example that follows, we will use the CDF of a price to represent a firm's mixed strategy in choosing the price of its product.

The Large Turbine Generator Industry

We will apply the concepts of the CDF and mixed pricing strategies to price competition in the short run between two firms. The large turbine generator industry was dominated during 1951 to 1963 by three large firms, General Electric, Westinghouse, and Allis-Chalmers, with market

Figure 10.B1 | A Continuous Density Function

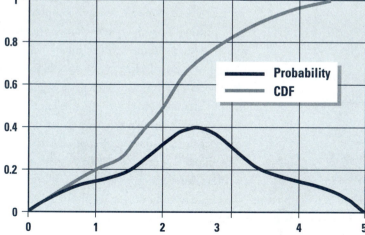

shares of 61 percent, 32 percent, and 6 percent, respectively, averaging over the period. Generators were produced to order, and order backlogs of one to three years were the norm. It has been estimated that marginal costs were roughly constant up to the limit of productive capacity.

Assumptions about Cost

Figure 10.B2 | A Hypothetical Supply Relationship

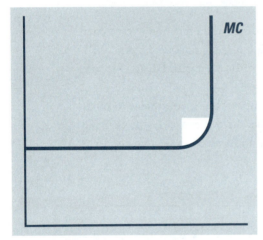

Figure 10.B3 | A Simplified Supply Relationship

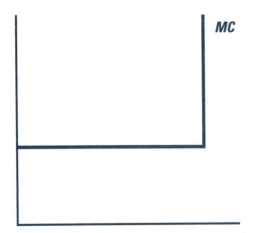

Evidence suggests something like Figure 10.B2.

Following a great deal of literature in applied economics, Ghemawat approximates with a supply relationship that has a constant unit cost up to capacity, like that shown in Figure 10.B3.

Domestic electrical utilities accounted for about 90 percent of industry demand and demand was highly inelastic as long as the cost of producing electricity with large turbines was no higher than that of producing electricity by other means. We will simplify the demand relationship, as Ghemawat does. We suppose that the market will pay a price of u for any quantity up to Q, but will not buy any quantity greater than Q. That leads to a "right-angle" demand curve like angle D in Figure 10.B4. We might think of that as an approximation to a conventional demand curve like angle DD in Figure 10.B4.

During the 1950s, there were some discussions among the sellers of turbine generators about fixing their list price, and some of the data used come from antitrust hearings, but the evidence indicated that pricing was in fact competitive, and 88 percent of all transactions were at prices below list. Accordingly, we need to think a little further about game theory and competitive prices.

Putting the simplifying assumptions together, we have a supply-demand model like that shown in Figure 10.B5. Thus, we are dealing with the kind of competition Edgeworth had in mind. At a price of c the maximum total output offered is R, while buyers will not buy more than Q. Suppose each firm's production capacity is R/2. The marginal cost, c, is the *supply-and-demand equilibrium price*. The monopoly price would be u. With two or more competitors, however, a price of u would not be stable, since either competitor could sell out its own capacity and increase its profits by cutting price below the other. Indeed, no price between c and u would be stable, for the same reason. But a marginal cost price of c would not be stable, either. Since a marginal cost price means no profits (in this simple model), neither seller has anything to lose by raising price above marginal cost. Thus, we have a case for the mixed strategy equilibrium.

For a numerical example, let u be 10 and Q be 80. We will suppose that the two sellers are identical. Each can produce up to a capacity limit of 50 at a cost of 5 per unit produced. If one firm undersells the other, the firm with the lower price, p_1, can sell out its productive capacity, selling 50 units at a profit of $(p_1 - 5) \times 50$. The firm with the higher price, p_2, sells only to those customers who could not get the product at the lower price (i.e., $80 - 50 = 30$ units of output at a profit of $(p_2 - 5) \times 30$). The solution will be a mixed strategy, with all of the prices

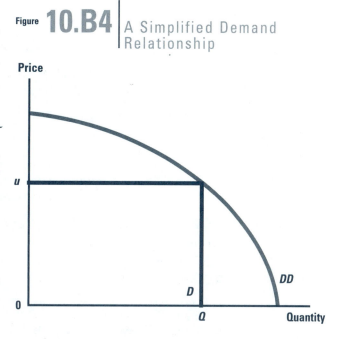

Figure 10.B4 A Simplified Demand Relationship

between 5 and 10 as possibilities. To describe a mixed strategy over the whole range of prices from 5 to 10, we will use the *cumulative distribution function* (CDF). For Firm j, for example, the CDF is

$$F_j(p) = \text{the probability that Firm j's price } p_j \text{ is less than or equal to } p.$$

$F_j(p)$ will be 0 when p is 5, since the firm will never price below 5, and will be 1 when p is 10, since no firm will price above 10. But what will it be in between?

Remember the condition for a mixed strategy equilibrium: Firm j's probabilities must be assigned so that Firm i gets the same expected value of profits no matter which price Firm i charges. If there were any price that leads to higher profits, then Firm i would choose that price, and we would not have a mixed strategy equilibrium. So let's figure out Firm i's expected profits for an unknown price p. No calculus is necessary at this stage—algebra will do the job.

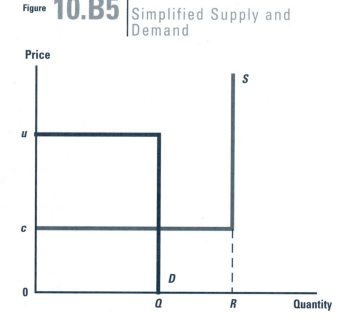

Figure 10.B5 Simplified Supply and Demand

If $p > p_j$, Firm i will sell only 30, for a profit of $(p-5) \times 30$.
The probability of this is $F_j(p)$.

If $p < p_j$, Firm i will sell 50, its capacity, for a profit of $(p-5) \times 50$.
The probability of this is $(1 - F_j(p))$.

(The probability of the exact match $p_i = p_j$ is so small we can ignore it.)

Thus the expected value is

$$EV = F_j(p) \times (p-5) \times 30 + (1 - F_j(p)) \times (p-5) \times 50$$
$$= (p-5) \times [50 - F_j(p) \times (50-30)]$$
$$= (p-5) \times (50 - F_j(p) \times 20)$$

The definition of a mixed strategy equilibrium tells us that EV must be a constant for all values of p that Firm i chooses with a positive probability. What is the constant? Suppose p = u. Then Firm i will almost certainly be underpriced and sell only 30 for a profit of $(10-5) \times 30 = 150$. Thus for any p with a positive probability, we have

$$(p-5) \times (50 - F_j(p) \times 20) = 150$$

since Firm i will never choose a price that will give profit less than they can get by pricing at u. We can solve that for $F_j(p)$ and we get

$$F_j(p) = [50 - (150/(p-5))]/20$$

if $[50 - (150/(p-5))]/20 > 0$ and 0 if $[50 - (150/(p-5))]/20 < 0$.

Figure 10.B6 The Cumulative Probability of a Price Charged by Either Firm

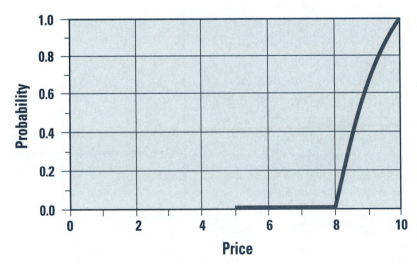

Figure 10.B7 | The Cumulative Probability of the Price Charged if Each Firm Has a Capacity of 70

It means that $F_j(p)$ is the curve shown in Figure 10.B6, and since the two firms are identical, $F_i(p)$ is the same.

What we see here is that no one will charge any price below $8, but that between $8 and $10, the probability that either firm will charge a price no higher increases pretty steeply to 1. We cannot say exactly what the price will be at any time—Edgeworth was right about that—but we can compute the expected value of the price, and in this case it is 8.83—quite close to the monopoly price of $10, "all the market will bear."

But this depends on the production capacities we have chosen for our example. Suppose, instead, that each of the two firms had a capacity of 70—so that either one could come close to supplying the market all alone. Then the probability curve for prices charged would look like Figure 10.B7 and the expected value of the price would be 6.62. Having greater capacities, relative to the market, the firms are "more competitive" and so the price is lower.

The closer we come to a situation where each firm can serve the entire market, the lower the expected price will be. This is shown in Table 10.B2.

Thus, we see that more competition (in that the two firms contest the limited market more hotly) leads to lower prices, on the whole.

Table 10.B2 | One Firm Capacity and Expected Value of Price

Capacities	Expected value of price
45	9.93
50	8.83
55	8.28
60	7.74
65	7.19
70	6.62
75	5.96

In his study of price competition in the market for large turbine generators, Ghemawat uses this overall approach, ignoring Allis-Chalmers, to focus on GE's price relative to that of Westinghouse. However, the analysis is a bit more complex in that the two firms were not symmetrical. They are of different sizes, and the demand and order backlogs varied from time to time. GE was able to charge a premium price, but the margin varied from time to time. Ghemawat derives the mark-up premiums rather than the actual prices.

The Math

Assume the following:

- Leading firm (GE) capacity x_1
- Follower capacity (Westinghouse) x_2
- Demand is Q units at any price no higher than u

Then there are *multiple regimes*:

So long as $x_2 < Q < x_1$ (implies GE can serve the whole market, but Westinghouse cannot)

or

$x_1 < Q < x_1 + x_2$ (implies that neither firm can serve the whole market but both together can) the leader will be the less aggressive price setter.

Using the approach we have just discussed, the cumulative distribution function for Westinghouse, the price follower, will be

$$F_2(p) = [u(Q - x_2) - px_1]/[p(Q - x_1 - x_2)]$$

This gives us a lower limit on Westinghouse's price of

$$p_0 = [u(Q - x_2)]/x_1$$

Thus, GE will always capture the market or sell out its capacity when it prices below p_0. Using that fact, we compute the cumulative distribution for GE to be

$$F_1(p) = \{[u(Q - x_2) - px_1]/[p(Q - x_1 - x_2)]\}\{x_2/x_1\}$$

Both prices are determined probabilistically, with the "distribution functions" something like Figure 10.B8.

Figure 10.B8 shows the functions for actual prices (assuming marginal cost for both firms is $15 per kilowatt hour capacity), so subtract 15 to get the mark-ups derived as $F_1(p)$ and $F_2(p)$ above. Other assumptions for this diagram are that u, the maximum price, is $40 and that Q, the quantity demanded, is 72 percent of the total capacity of both firms but 108 percent of GE's capacity. Thus, for this diagram, demand is relatively slack. The diagram tells us that GE charges the maximum price of $40 with a probability of 50 percent (since the curve for GE jumps discontinuously from 0.5 to 1 at p = $40), and that for any lower price

Figure 10.B8 Rough Relation of Cumulative Probability of the Price Charged for the Two Firms in the Case of Slack Demand

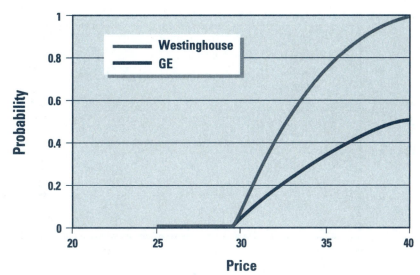

between $30 and $40, the probability of Westinghouse charging the lower price is greater. Computing the expected value of the price, we have $37 for GE and $34 for Westinghouse, to a close approximation.

Figure 10B.9 shows an example that is similar except that Q, the quantity demanded, is 94 percent of the total capacity of both firms but 142 percent of GE's capacity. Thus, for this diagram, demand is relatively tight. The prices charged by the two firms are closer together. Computing the expected value of the price, we have $39.59 for GE and $39.17 for Westinghouse. The overall conclusion is that the larger firm prices less aggressively than the smaller firm—that is, the larger firm is less likely to undercut; and the difference is greater when demand is slack. We may say that the big firm puts a *price umbrella* over the small firm when demand is slack.

Ghemawat offers evidence for his theory in the case of the market for large turbine generators in the form of a statistical study. He considers large-order backlogs as evidence of tight demand. He estimates

$$GEPREM = 1.5437 - 0.7114 \times backlogs$$
$$(0.3078) \quad (0.1248)$$

with standard errors in parentheses and adjusted R^2 of 36.8. GEPREM is the premium of GE's price over that of Westinghouse. This negative coefficient indicates that the game-theoretic interactions were the predominant influence on GE's price premium relative to Westinghouse. As the mixed strategy equilibrium approach indicates, tight demand led to smaller premia on the average.

Figure 10.B9 Rough Relation of Cumulative Probability of the Price Charged for the Two Firms in the Case of Tight Demand

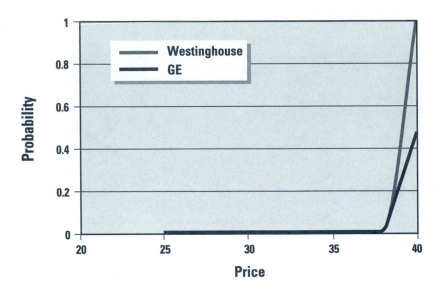

Exercises and Discussion Questions

10.1 Price Competition. In the 1950s Warren Nutter translated Bertrand's critique of Cournot into game theory. Thus we have a Nutter (not Nuttier!) pricing game. Here is a game between Acme Widgets[5] and Widgeon Widgets. The idea behind the game is that if both companies charge the same price, they split the market equally; while if one company charges the lower price, that company gets most of the market share and profits. The payoff table is Table 10.E1.

What sort of a game is this? Why? Does it have a Nash equilibrium in pure strategies? If so, what is it? Does it have a solution in mixed strategies? Explain. Are there any dominated strategies in this game? What? Compare this game with the Bertrand-Edgeworth game in the text.

Table 10.E1 Payoffs in a Nutter Game

		Acme Widgets		
		$p = 1$	$p = 2$	$p = 3$
Widgeon Widgets	$p = 1$	0, 0	50, −10	40, −20
	$p = 2$	−10, 50	20, 20	90, 10
	$p = 3$	−20, 40	10, 90	50, 50

5 A widget is an anonymous manufactured good. Widgets were the product in the musical comedy *How to Succeed in Business Without Really Trying,* and probably found their way into economics in McConnell's introductory text. A widgeon is a colorful little duck.

10.2 Price Competition with Inelastic Demand. Here is another game of price competition. Once again, if both firms charge the monopoly price, they will be able to get high profits of 12 each, but in this case demand is highly inelastic, so a cut in price by one firm lowers both firms' profits. The payoffs are shown in Table 10.E2.

Find all Nash equilibria for this pricing game.

Table **10.E2** | Price Competition Payoffs

		Firm 1	
		low	high
Firm 2	low	5, 5	10, 1
	high	1, 10	12, 12

11 | *N*-Person Games

For applications of game theory to real problems, we will often need to allow for more than three players, and sometimes indefinitely many. Many of the "games" that are most important in the real world involve considerably more than two or three players—for example, economic competition, highway congestion, overexploitation of the environment, and monetary exchange. So we need to explore games with many players. This can get very complicated. For example, if we have ten players, there are 10! = 3,628,800 relationships between them.[1] We will need to make some simplifying assumptions to make analysis of games with many players feasible.

The Queuing Game

Table **11.1** | Queuing Game Payoffs

Order served	Gross payoff	Net payoff
first	20	18
second	17	15
third	14	12
fourth	11	9
fifth	8	6
sixth	5	3

Here is an example of a game with six players. As usual, we will begin with a story. Perhaps you have had an experience like the one in this story. Six people are waiting at an airline boarding gate, but the clerks have not yet arrived at the gate to check them in. Perhaps these six unfortunates have arrived on a connecting flight with a long layover. Anyway, they are sitting and awaiting their chance to check in, and one of them stands up and steps to the counter to be the first in the queue. As a result the others feel that they, too, must stand in the queue, and a number of people end up standing when they could have been sitting.

Here is a numerical example to illustrate a payoff structure that might lead to this result. There are six people, and the gross payoff to each passenger depends on when that passenger is served, with gross payoffs as shown in the second column of Table 11.1. Order of service is listed in the first column.

The gross payoffs assume, however, that one does not stand in line. There is a two-point effort penalty for standing in line, so that for those who stand in line, the net payoff to being served is two less

---

1 10! is read "ten factorial," and is computed as follows: $10 \times 9 \times 8 \times 7 \times 6 \times 5 \times 4 \times 3 \times 2 \times 1$. The number of possible combinations in any game is $N!$, where N is the number of players.

that what is shown in the second column. These net payoffs are given in the third column of the table.

Those who do not stand in line are chosen for service at random, after those who stand in line have been served. (Assume that these six passengers are risk neutral.) If no one stands in line, then each person has an equal chance of being served first, second, . . . sixth, and an expected value payoff of $(1/6) \times 20 + (1/6) \times 17 + \ldots + (1/6) \times 5 = 12.5$. In such a case, the aggregate payoff is 75.

But this will not be the case. This game has a large family of Nash equilibria, depending on who stands and who sits, but we can show that there is no Nash equilibrium in which everybody sits, and in fact that a Nash equilibrium can occur only if four people are standing in line and two are sitting.

We will show this equilibrium by eliminating all other possibilities. First, "everyone sit" is not a Nash equilibrium, since an individual can improve his or her payoff by standing in line, provided that person is first in line. The net payoff to the person first in line is 18 > 12.5, so someone will get up and stand in line.

Heads Up!

Here are some concepts we will develop as this chapter goes along:

N-Person Game: A game with *N* players is an *N-person game*. *N* may be any number, 1, 2, 3, or more, but as the numbers increase we may need some simplifying assumptions to make the game analysis useful.

Representative Agent: In game theory we may sometimes make the simplifying assumption that every agent chooses from the same list of strategies and gets the same payoffs in given circumstances. This is called a *representative agent* model or theory.

State Variable: A *state variable* means a single number, or one of a small list of numbers, that together express the "state" of the game, so that a player who knows just the value of the state variable or variables has all the information needed to choose a best-response strategy.

Proportional Game: A game in which the state variable is the proportion of the population choosing one strategy rather than another is a *proportional game*.

This leaves the expected value of the payoff at 11 for those who remain. (You should verify this by computing the expected value for your notes. The probability for each payoff will now be 1/5.) But we can also eliminate the five-sit, one-stand possibilities. Since the second person in line gets a net payoff of 15, someone will be better off to get up and stand in the second place in line.

This leaves the expected value payoff at 9.5 for those who remain. We can also show that this possibility, two standing and four sitting, cannot be a Nash equilibrium. Since the third person in line gets a net payoff of 12, someone will be better off to get up and stand in the third place in line.

This leaves the expected value payoff at 8 for the three who remain. But this will not be a Nash equilibrium, either. Since the fourth person in line gets a net payoff of 9, someone will be better off to get up and stand in the fourth place in line.

This leaves the expected value payoff at 6.5 for those who remain. Since the fifth person in line would get a net payoff of only 6, no one else will join the queue. Moreover, if five or six people were standing in line, it would pay the fifth and sixth persons to sit down.

You should verify this by computing the expected values. (*Hint:* If there are six people in line, the last person in line can get a payoff of 5 with probability 1). Every assortment of strategies with four people in line (regardless of order) and two sitting is a Nash equilibrium, and no other assortment of strategies is. The total payoff is 67 (18 + 15 + 12 + 9 + 8 + 5), less than the 75 that would have been the total payoff if, somehow, the queue could have been prevented.

Two people are better off—the first two in line—with the first gaining an assured payoff of 5.5 above the uncertain expected value payoff that person would have had in the absence of queuing, and the second gaining 2.5. But the rest are worse off. The third person in line gets 12, losing 0.5; the fourth 9, losing 3.5, and the rest get average payoffs of 6.5, losing 6 each. Since the total gains from queuing are 8 and the losses are 16, we can say that, in one fairly clear sense, queuing is inefficient. The best solution, the one with the greatest total payoff, is for no one to stand in line, but that is not a noncooperative equilibrium.

Simplifying Assumptions for *N*-Person Games

The previous section presents an N-person game that extends the Prisoner's Dilemma in some important ways. The Prisoner's Dilemma is often offered as a paradigm for situations—*social dilemmas*—in which individual self-interested rationality leads to bad results, so that the participants may be made better off if an authority limits their freedom to choose their strategies independently. Powerful as the example is, there is much missing from it. Just to take one point: The Prisoner's Dilemma game is a two-person game, and many of the applications are many-person interactions. The game considered in this example extends the social dilemma to a group of more than two people.

Von Neumann and Morgenstern spent a good deal of time on games with three players, and some more recent authors follow their example. This serves to illustrate how even one more player can complicate things, but it does not help us much with realism. We need an analysis of games with N > 3 players, where N can be quite large. To get that, we will simply have to pay our way with some simplifying assumptions. The Queuing Game example illustrates two common simplifying assumptions in N-person games.

> **Definition**
>
> *Representative Agent*—In game theory we may some-
> times make the simplifying assumption that every agent
> chooses from the same list of strategies and gets the
> same payoffs in given circumstances. This is called a
> **representative agent** model or theory.

In the Queuing Game, all of the participants are assumed to be identical, to be **representative agents**. This illustrates one kind of simplifying assumption—the *representative agent model*. In this sort of model, we assume that all players are identical, have the same strategy options, and get symmetrical payoffs. This does not mean that they end up in the same situation! As we saw in the Queuing Game, only one ended up first in line; others were later in line, and some were still sitting. That's a key point of the representative agent model: Even though the agents have the same strategy options and the same payoffs in a given situation, they may do different things in equilibrium. The differences are a result of the Nash equilibrium in the game, *not* a result of any differences in the agents.

This representative agent approach should not be pushed too far. It is quite common in economic theory, and economists are sometimes criticized for overdoing it. But it is useful in many practical examples, and the next few sections will apply it.

There is another powerful simplifying assumption in the Queuing Game. Notice that no passenger has to know anything about the strategies the other passengers have chosen (e.g., who is first in line and who is second in line, and so on). All a passenger needs to know is the length of the line right now. If the line is short enough, the best-response strategy is to get in line; otherwise the best-response strategy is to continue to sit. Thus, we could say that the length of the line is a **state variable**.

A state variable is a single variable, or one of a small number of variables, that sum up the state of the game from the point of view of the representative agent. The state variable, or variables, are all that the agent needs to know in order to choose the best-response strategy.

> **Definition**
>
> *State Variable*—In this book, a **state variable** means a single number, or one of a small list of numbers, that together express the "state" of the game, so that a player who knows just the value of the state variable or variables has all the information she needs to choose a best-response strategy.

This terminology—a *state variable*—is usually used more narrowly in game theory. It is taken from the study of games that evolve continuously over time. Because these games are based on the mathematical study known as *differential equations*, they are called *differential games*. One example of such a game is a **pursuit game**, in which one agent, the pursuer, wants to catch the other agent, the quarry, in the shortest possible time. In many such games, all that the pursuer needs to know is the distance between the pursuer and the quarry. The pursuer's best response is the response that makes that distance as small as possible. Similarly, all the quarry needs to know is that same number—the distance from the pursuer. The quarry's best response is the response that makes that distance as large as possible. Thus, the distance serves as a state variable in a pursuit game of that

> **Terminology**
>
> *Pursuit Games, Differential Games, Differential Equations*—A **pursuit game** is a two-person game in which one of the players tries to capture the other or draw close enough to destroy the other. The objective of the player who is being pursued is to keep out of range as long as possible. In a typical pursuit game, each player's strategy is the rate and direction of travel. Since these can change continuously, pursuit games are expressed as differential equations. A **differential equation** is an equation in which the dependent variable is a rate of change. Games expressed in differential equations are called **differential games**.

kind. Of course, differential equations is a branch of calculus, and mathematics required to analyze pursuit games is beyond the limits of this book. Students who are interested in differential games will need to take a more advanced course in game theory, as well as intermediate-level mathematics. But the state variable idea itself requires little or no mathematics.

In the rest of this book, we will use the phrase *state variable* to refer to any variable defined as above—a variable that sums up the state of the game so that players need to know only that state variable, and nothing else, in order to choose their best-response strategy. I believe this terminology will be helpful, but do keep in mind that many other game theorists use it more narrowly.

The two assumptions, representative agents and a state variable, can complement one another as they do in the Queuing Game, and help us to think through complicated games with very large numbers of participants. They are powerful tools, and like all powerful tools, should be used carefully—a point we will return to at the end of the chapter.

Games with Many Participants
Proportional Games

The Queuing Game gives us one example of how the social dilemma can be generalized, and it provides some insights on some real human interactions. But there is another simple approach to multiperson, two-strategy games that is closer to textbook economics, using the representative agent and state variable assumptions, and it is important in its own right.

As an example, let us consider the choice of transportation modes—car or bus—by a large number of identical individual commuters. The basic idea here is that car commuting increases congestion and slows down traffic. The more commuters drive their cars to work, the longer it takes to get to work, and the lower the payoffs are for both car commuters and bus commuters. The commuters are representative agents—their payoffs vary in the same way with the number of cars on the road—and the state variable is the proportion of all commuters who drive cars rather than ride the bus. The larger the proportion who drive their cars, the slower the commute will be, regardless of which transport strategy a particular commuter chooses.

Figure 11.1 illustrates this. In the figure, the horizontal axis measures the proportion of commuters who drive their cars. Accordingly, the horizontal axis varies from a lower limit of 0 to a maximum of 1, or 100 percent. The vertical axis shows the payoffs for this game. The upper gray line shows the payoffs for car commuters. We see that it declines as the proportion of commuters in their cars increases. The lower black line shows the payoffs to bus commuters.[2] We see that, regardless of the proportion of commuters in cars, cars have a higher payoff than buses. In other words, commuting by car is a dominant strategy in this game. In a dominant strategy equilibrium, all drive their cars. The result is that they all have negative payoffs at −1.5, whereas, if all rode buses, all would have positive payoffs of 1. If all commuters choose their mode of transportation with self-interested rationality, all choose the strategy that makes them individually better off, but all are worse off as a result.

This is a social dilemma, in that there is a dominant strategy equilibrium, but the choice of dominant strategies makes everyone worse off. But it probably is not a very realistic model of choice of transportation modes. Some people do ride buses. So let's make it a little more realistic, as in Figure 11.2.

---

2 For the sake of the example, payoffs were scaled so that the best payoff to bus riders is 1. Payoffs to bus commuters were computed as $1 - 3q$, and to car commuters as $1.5 - 3q$, where q is the proportion of car commuters. These numbers are arbitrary ones meant to express the ideas in the discussion. The idea comes from Herve Moulin, *Game Theory for the Social Sciences* (New York: New York University Press, 1982), pp. 92–93.

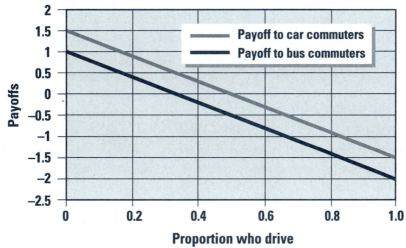

Figure 11.1 | Payoffs in a Commuter Game

The axes and lines in Figure 11.2 are defined as they were for Figure 11.1. In Figure 11.2, congestion slows the buses down somewhat, so that the payoff to bus commuting declines as congestion increases; but the payoff to car commuting drops even faster.[3]

When the proportion of people in their cars reaches q = 2/3, the payoff to bus riding overtakes the payoff to car commuting, and for larger proportions of car commuters (to the right of q), the payoff to car commuting is worse than to bus commuting.

3 For this diagram, the payoff to bus commuters is unchanged, but the payoff to car commuters is calculated as 1.5 – 3.75q.

Figure 11.2 | Payoffs in a More Complex Commuter Game

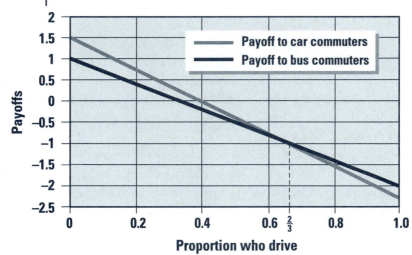

Thus, the game no longer has a dominant strategy equilibrium. However, it has a Nash equilibrium. When two-thirds of commuters drive cars, that is a Nash equilibrium. Here is the reasoning: Starting from two-thirds, if one bus commuter shifts to the car, that moves into the region to the right of two-thirds, where car commuters are worse off, so someone will switch from the car to the bus, taking us back to two-thirds. On the other hand, starting from two-thirds, if one car commuter switches to the bus, that moves into the region to the left of two-thirds, where bus commuters are worse off, so someone will switch from the bus to the car, taking us back to two-thirds. No one can be better off by individually switching from $q = 2/3$.

This again illustrates an important point: In a Nash equilibrium, identical people may choose different strategies to maximize their payoffs. This Nash equilibrium resembles some *supply-and-demand* type equilibria in economics, having been suggested by models of that type, but also differs in some important ways. In particular, it is inefficient, in the sense that if everyone were to ride the bus, moving back to the origin point in Figure 11.2 (as in Figure 11.1), everyone would be better off. The Nash equilibrium payoff is −1 (for both bus riders and car drivers) and the payoff to 100 percent bus riders is +1. As in a social dilemma, though, they will not do so when they act on the basis of individual self-interest without coordination.

> ### Definition
>
> ***Tragedy of the Commons***—The **tragedy of the commons** is an illustrative example in environmental policy and related areas. The example is based on the medieval practice of keeping a common pasture on which the residents of the village would be allowed to pasture their animals. According to the example, they would have no incentive to limit the number of animals put to pasture on the commons, so that the pasture would be overexploited and rendered unproductive. The conclusion is that common property resources in general tend to be overexploited.

This example is an instance of the **tragedy of the commons**. The highways are a common resource available to all car and bus commuters. However, car commuters make more intensive use of the common resource, causing the resource to be degraded (in this instance, congested). Yet the car commuters gain a private advantage by choosing more intensive use of the common resource, at least while the resource is relatively undegraded. The tragedy is that this intensive use leads to the degradation of the resource to the point that all are worse off.

In general, *the tragedy of the commons* is that all common property resources tend to be overexploited and thus degraded, unless their intensive use is restrained by legal, traditional, or (perhaps) philanthropic institutions. The classical instance is common pastures, on which, according to the theory, each farmer will increase his or her herd until the common pasture is overgrazed and all are impoverished. Most of the applications have been in environmental and resource issues. The recent collapse of fisheries in many parts of the world seems to be a clear instance of the tragedy of the commons.

All in all, it appears that the tragedy of the commons is correctly understood as a multi-person social dilemma along the lines suggested in Figures 11.1 and 11.2, and, conversely, that the social dilemma is a valuable tool in understanding the many tragedies of the commons that we face in the modern world.

Hawk vs. Dove, Revisited

In Chapter 5, we studied a classical two-by-two game called Hawk vs. Dove. The payoffs for that game are shown again, for convenience, in Table 11.2. This game is a biological application of game theory, but it might not seem quite right. After all, hawks and doves are different species, and birds don't decide to be hawks or doves as strategies that they can change if they think the other strategy will pay better. Also, hawks and doves are not interested in money payoffs, and we have no idea what subjective "costs and benefits" they might experience.

In fact, when game theory is applied in biology, it has to be interpreted a little differently. The perspective for biological applications of game theory is evolution and population biology. The payoffs are not in dollars or utility, but in reproductive fitness. That is, the payoffs to a hawk or a dove are the bird's chances of surviving and leaving young. The greater the **expected value** of the number of young, the greater the payoffs. On the other hand, since population biology is concerned with whole populations of animals, there are always many more than two players. For the Hawk vs. Dove Game, any play of the game is between just two birds, but the birds are matched at random from large populations.

Table 11.2 | Hawk vs. Dove

Repeats Table 5.9, Chapter 5

		Bird B	
		hawk	dove
Bird A	hawk	−25, −25	14, −9
	dove	−9, 14	5, 5

Definition

Expected value—(repeated from Chapter 7) Suppose an uncertain event can have several outcomes with numerical values that may be different. The **expected value** (also known as *mathematical expectation*) of the event is the weighted average of the numerical values, with the probabilities of the outcomes as the weights.

An individual bird—hawk or dove, as the case may be—is matched with another bird, who may be a hawk or a dove with probabilities that depend on the proportion of the population of hawks to the population of doves.

Suppose that hawks are more reproductively fit than doves. That means that, on the average, a hawk rears more baby birds to reproductive age than a dove does. That means that the population of hawks will grow faster than the population of doves, increasing the probability that a bird of either species will be matched with a hawk, and this might eventually tip the balance, making doves equally fit or more fit than hawks.

For a bird looking forward to her next match, we could think of the match as a game against nature, since nature determines, at random with given probabilities, which type of bird will be the match. Table 11.3 shows the Hawk vs. Dove Game from this perspective. We assume that the probability of being matched with a hawk is equal to the proportion of hawks in the whole population.

Thus, the payoff for each kind of bird depends on the probability of being matched with a hawk and thus on the proportion of hawks to doves in the population. This is shown by Figure 11.3. The probability of being matched with a hawk (the proportion of hawks) is shown on the horizontal axis, and the payoffs to hawks and doves on the vertical axis. The

Table 11.3 | Hawk vs. Dove as a Game Against Nature

		Matching Bird		Expected value payoff
		hawk	dove	
Bird to be matched	hawk	−25	14	$-25p + 14(1-p)$
	dove	−9	5	$-9p + 5(1-p)$
	probability	p	$1-p$	

payoff to hawks is shown by the solid dark line, while the payoff to doves is shown by the gray line. We see that, if there are fewer than 36 percent hawks in the population, populations of both species will grow, but the population of hawks will grow faster, so the probability of being matched with a hawk increases. This continues until the proportion of hawks reaches 36 percent. If the proportion of hawks goes beyond 36 percent, doves are more reproductively fit than hawks. Both populations decline, but that of hawks declines faster. Thus, the proportion of hawks declines, again until it reaches 36 percent.

In this game, the proportion of hawks is the state variable. "Hawk" is the best response strategy whenever it is less than 36 percent, and "dove" whenever it is more than 36 percent. Thus, 36 percent hawks gives a Nash equilibrium—the only proportion at which every player is playing a best-response strategy.

Figure 11.3 | Payoffs to Hawks and Doves

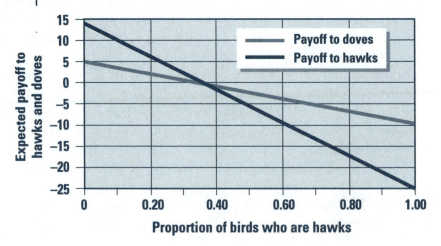

This example gives a better flavor of the application of game theory in biology than the examples in earlier chapters, since the applications are to population biology and thus to more than two players, even if only two are matched at any one time. (We will expand on that in the last chapter of the book.) It also gives us another example of the use of the simplifying assumptions, and particularly the state variable.

In addition, we have a good example of how probabilities and expected values can enter into games of many players, by random matching of players to play simpler, perhaps two-by-two games. Finally, we see that the representative agent model can be modified to allow for more than one **type of representative agent**. Agents predisposed to play "hawk" are of a different kind (in population biology) than those predisposed to play "dove." In games played by human beings, different types of agents may

> **Assumption**
>
> **_Types of Representative Agents_**—In some game analyses we may assume that there are a small number of different types of representative agents.

have different tastes, different information, different commands of resources, or even different kinds of rationality—though we will not get to that last one until a later chapter.

Supply, Demand, and Tattonement

The simplifying assumptions we have looked at in this chapter did not originate in game theory, but in economics. The theory of supply and demand in microeconomics, for example, can be expressed in terms of representative agents and state variables. There are two kinds of representative agents, buyers and sellers, and the market price is the state variable for each of them. Sellers want to maximize their profit, so profit is their payoff. Buyers want to maximize the subjective satisfaction, or utility, that they obtain from all of the goods that they consume, within their limited income. This subjective utility is the buyer's payoff.

In the game of Supply and Demand, the rules of the game are determined by a process called **tattonement**. *Tattonement* is a French word we owe to the Belgian-Swiss economist Leon Walras. It means "groping," and it refers to a trial-and-error process to

> **Definition**
>
> **_Tattonement_**—In economics, the French word **tattonement** refers to a process for the determination of a market price, as though a two-sided auction were conducted.

determine the price of a good or service. The tattonement begins when an auctioneer[4] calls out a price at random. All of the buyers respond by indicating the quantities that they would want to buy at that price, and all of the sellers respond by indicating the quantities that they would want to sell at that price. The auctioneer adds up the quantities that people want to buy and the quantities that people want to sell. If the total quantity demanded is greater than the quantity supplied, the auctioneer tries again with a somewhat higher price. If the total quantity

---

4 Since many markets have nothing quite like the auctioneer, this might not seem a very realistic model of some markets. This criticism is often made in economist's discussions of the tattonement concept. The optimistic response is that many markets work *as if* they had an auctioneer fixing the price by means of a tattonement. In future chapters we will look at some other, quite different game theoretic models of pricing.

demanded is less than the total quantity supplied, then the auctioneer tries a somewhat lower price. Once again, the buyers and sellers respond by indicating the quantities that they respectively want to buy and sell at that price. The auctioneer adds up the quantities demanded and supplied yet again, and again lowers or raises the price according to whether quantity supplied is greater than quantity demanded or less. This trial-and-error adjustment of the price continues until the quantity that people offer to buy is the same as the quantity the others offer to sell. At that point, everyone buys and sells quantities they have announced at the price that has been finally arrived at. This is the *equilibrium price*, in supply and demand theory. The key point about the tattonement process is that no one buys or sells anything until the auctioneer arrives at a price that balances the offers to buy against the offers to sell.

We assume that each of the buyers and sellers is a rational game player, aiming to maximize the benefits from buying or selling. So how will the buyers and sellers respond to the prices that the auctioneer cries out? Two familiar ideas from basic economics will help us answer that question. At least, they will be familiar to anyone who has studied the principles of economics. The two ideas are the demand curve (or demand function) and the supply curve (or supply function).

The supply function is a relationship between the price and the quantity of a good that a person is willing to sell. For each price, the corresponding quantity *on the supply curve* is the quantity that gives the greatest profit to the seller at that price. A higher price will justify more expensive methods of production, and so, generally, result in a larger quantity supplied.

The demand function is a relationship between the price and the quantity of a good that a person is willing to buy. For a given price, the corresponding quantity is the quantity that gives the buyer the greatest net benefit for his money spent at that price.

Now let's return to the tattonement process. When the auctioneer announces a price, how will a rational seller respond? Will he offer the quantity on his supply curve, corresponding to that price, or some other quantity? To decide how he will respond, the seller will have to think in terms of two contingencies, as shown in Table 11.4. Since he does not know what strategies the other buyers and sellers will adopt, he doesn't know whether the quantity offered will balance the quantity demanded at this price. Recall, the rules of the game say that buying and selling will take place only if the price balances the quantity offered against the quantity demanded. So those are the two contingencies: either the goods will be sold at the announced price, with no surplus or shortage, or nothing will be sold if the price does not balance quantity offered against quantity demanded.

If the price does not balance quantity supplied against quantity demanded, the seller has nothing to lose by announcing the quantity on his supply function. On the other hand, if the

Table 11.4 | Contingencies, Strategies, and Results for a Seller

		Strategy	
		announce quantity on supply curve	announce some other quantity
Contingency	quantities balance	maximum profit	less than maximum profit
	quantities unbalanced	nothing	nothing

price does balance quantity supplied against quantity demanded, then the seller has something to lose by announcing a quantity other than the one on his supply function. For either contingency, then, his best response is the quantity on his supply function.

This could be different if the rules of the game were different (see Figure 11.4). Suppose that the tattonement rules do not apply, and people sell what they offer to sell as long as the quantity demanded is either equal to or *greater than* quantity supplied. Then the amounts offered are sold when the price is either at or below the equilibrium price. But when the quantity demanded is greater than the quantity supplied, the price will continue to rise. As a result, sellers lose the chance to get the higher price. Because of that, offering the amount on the supply curve might not be the best response—the seller would have to balance the probabilities of the two contingencies and maximize the expected value of his payoffs. If the rules of the game allow sales at prices that do not balance supply and demand, they are called *nontattonement processes*.

It is similar for the rational buyer. He, too, must think in terms of two contingencies: trading at a price that balances quantity supplied against quantity demanded, or not trading at all if the price does not balance quantity supplied against quantity demanded. On one hand, if he does sell, he has something lose by selling any quantity of other than the quantity on his

Figure **11.4** | Rules of the Tattonement Game

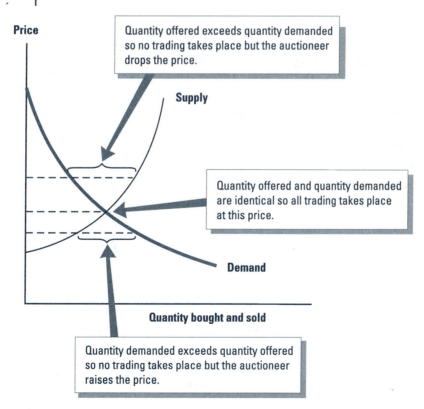

demand function. On the other hand, if the price does not balance supply and demand, he has nothing to lose by announcing the quantity on his demand function.

The supply and demand model in the Principles of Economics course[5] can be thought of as an N + M person tattonement game, with N buyers and M sellers, where N and M are both "large."

Keynesian Economics and Coordination Problems

Modern economics is divided between two great branches: microeconomics and macroeconomics. The theory of supply and demand plays a part in both. However, some macroeconomists, in the Keynesian tradition, say that the supply-and-demand approach misses some important difficulties in a market economic system, perhaps because many of the market games played in the real world are nontattonement processes. They say that there could be failures of coordination,[6] particularly between consumer/savers and producer/investors, that as a consequence the economy may not perform up to its potential, and they say that expectations may be important in determining whether it performs up to potential.

Coordination problems bring to mind coordination games. Table 11.5 shows a coordination game between two players, a "producer" and a "consumer." The game is designed to express these ideas insofar as they can be expressed in a two-by-two game.

There are six assumptions behind the game:

Table **11.5** | A Macroeconomic Coordination Game

		Consumer	
		save	spend
Producer	simple	5, 5	8, 8
	roundabout	10, 10	6, 6

1. The producer can choose "roundabout" or "simple" methods of production.[7] Examples of *roundabout* methods are mechanization, research and development, and major training programs. These methods are more productive, on the whole, but the producer can successfully put them into practice only if the producer can borrow money from the consumer, by selling the consumer bonds or stock.

2. The consumer's choices are to save or to spend on current production.

3. If the consumer saves and the producer chooses roundabout production, the producer is able to pay a good return on the consumer's investment, and this is best for both, ranking as 10 on a 10-point scale.

5 For example, see W. Baumol and A. Blinder, *Economics, Principles and Policy*, 8th ed. (New York: Harcourt, 1999), p. 77.

6 For example, see W. Baumol and A. Blinder, *Economics, Principles and Policy*, 8th ed. (New York: Harcourt, 1999), pp. 560–562, and note also J. Bradford DeLong, *Macroeconomics* (New York: McGraw-Hill, 2002), p. 471.

7 This idea—that investment corresponds to more roundabout production—comes from the first generation of the Austrian school of thought in economics: Karl Menger, Friedrich von Wieser, and Eugen von Bohm-Bawerk. See, for example, Karl Menger, *Principles of Economics* (Grove City, Penn.: Libertarian Press, 1994), pp. 149–165.

4. If the producer chooses simple methods and the consumer spends what he has on current production, that is not as good for either of them (since simple production is less productive), but each enjoys benefits at 8 on the 10-point scale.

5. If the consumer chooses "spend" and the producer chooses "roundabout." the attempt to finance the roundabout methods will fail, and production will not be proportionate to consumers' spending, resulting in moderate inflation and making both relatively worse off—6 on the 10-point scale.

6. If the consumer chooses "save" and the producer chooses "simple," spending is less than proportionate to production, so the producer must cut back on production. When that happens, the consumer loses some income from employment, and has a poor return on savings in addition. The result is that both are worse off still, at 5 out of a possible 10.

These payoffs are shown in a two-by-two game in normal form in Table 11.5. It is easy to see that the game has two Nash equilibria, and they correspond to assumptions 3 and 4. Thus, it is a coordination game, and as we recall, coordination games cause some special problems. Which equilibrium will be chosen? If the producer and the consumer come to the game without any past experience, the efficiency of the (save, roundabout) equilibrium may attract their attention, so it would become a Schelling point. That will be the maximum potential output of the economy in this case. But, we know, a Schelling point may also be a result of expectations based on past experience. Suppose that the producer expects that the consumer will spend rather than save, and the consumer expects that the producer will choose unproductive simple methods of production. These expectations also define a Schelling point—simple production and consumer spending.[8] Thus, as Keynesians say, expectations may determine whether the economy performs at its potential.

Items 5 and 6 on the list correspond to *coordination failures* in that each one is choosing a strategy that is inconsistent with the strategy chosen by the other one, and as a result, they are even worse off than in the below-potential equilibrium. The fear of such a coordination failure keeps the two at the below-potential equilibrium.

Of course, this example is oversimplified in three ways, one of which should be very familiar by now.

1. There are many more than two players—many consumers and many producers.

2. Each consumer can choose more than just two levels of spending. In fact, consumers can choose to save a fraction of their income, from nothing up to most of it. Similarly,

8 This is suggested by Paul Rosenstein-Rodan, "Problems of Industrialization of Eastern and South-Eastern Europe," *Economic Journal* 53 (June–Sept. 1943) pp. 202–211, although Rosenstein-Rodan speaks more directly of a coordination problem among producers in *N* distinct industries.

producers can choose among many different kinds of roundabout production, with different investment requirements and payoffs.

3.   There is a missing market, the market for loans and stocks. This market will solve at least a part of the coordination problem. If, for example, producers choose "roundabout" and consumers choose "spend," then the supply of capital for loans and stock purchases is less than the demand. Interest rates on loans, the price of loan capital, will rise,[9] and that will persuade producers to cut back on roundabout production until the supply and demand for capital for roundabout production are equal. Nevertheless, this equilibrium of the supply and demand for capital will depend on expectations—if consumers expect producers to choose "simple," then it is best for the consumers to choose "spend," and conversely, so that both the supply and demand for capital are low—and the result is that the equilibrium is less efficient than another, potential equilibrium, as in the upper left cell of Table 11.5.

Accordingly, the textbook Keynesian model[10] can be thought of as an N + M person coordination game, with N investors and M employee-consumer/savers. For the investors, the state variable is the interest rate (or the rate of return on stocks, or both). For the consumers, the state variable is income. The investors and the consumers each choose their best responses to the state variable, and the resulting income-expenditure equilibrium is a Nash equilibrium of the N + M person game.

Pros and Cons of the Simplifying Assumptions

Simplifying assumptions are tools of thought, and like all powerful tools they should be used with care. The assumptions of representative agents and one or a few state variables are taken from economics, and particularly from the theory of supply and demand. But the theory of supply and demand has been criticized for these assumptions, which seem to be more applicable to some markets than to others. One of the purposes of game theory at the start was to avoid those simplifying assumptions, allowing for the fact that (in some situations, such as industries with a small number of competitors) decision makers cannot rely on any state variable, such as market price, but have to consider the specific reactions of their individual rivals to their own choices of strategies. A critic might ask: "If we have to bring those simplifying assumptions back into the picture to deal with games with a large number of participants, what is the point?"

To answer the critic, we have seen that rival theories, such as supply/demand and Keynesian theories, can also be understood as Nash equilibria with representative agents and state variables. With these examples, we see that something has been gained. We may understand the theory

---

9 Also, the price of stocks will fall, which raises the rate of return on stocks. In macroeconomics it is traditional to focus mainly on the interest rate as the price of capital for roundabout production.

10 For example, see Baumol and Blinder, *Economics, Principles and Policy*, 8th ed. (New York: Harcourt, 1999), p. 556.

of supply and demand and the Keynesian model as different examples of a more fundamental concept, Nash equilibrium. By contrast, a prominent economist has suggested that economics be defined as *the study of the implications of maximization with clearing markets.* "Clearing markets" is another term for *equilibrium of supply and demand.* This definition would make it a basic principle that agents need to know only the price to decide what strategy to choose.

But suppose we observe the real world and find that some markets do not clear, such as labor markets (in macroeconomics) or markets with only a few sellers—*oligopolies,* as economists call them (in microeconomics). Then, the economist (by that definition) is helpless—if the basic principle is not true, then the economist has to start all over from scratch, perhaps as a sociologist! But when we see the supply and demand equilibrium as a particular example of a more fundamental kind of equilibrium, Nash equilibrium, we can apply the same principles to model equilibrium with a different state variable, as in a Keynesian model, or give up the simplifying assumptions and analyze the pricing strategies of individual firms in an oligopoly industry, as we did in the previous chapter.

Game theory is a kit of tools with different tools for different jobs. We should not make a principle of choosing a particular tool when it does not fit the job—and we should always use our tools with care!

Summary

Many important real-world games and strategic situations involve more than three agents, sometimes very large numbers of agents. If each agent tries to consider the strategies chosen by every other agent, as we have assumed in the previous chapters, the number of combinations of agents and strategies increases much more rapidly than the number of the agents. This is a problem for the agents, and an even bigger problem for the game theorist.

In order to understand and analyze these very complicated games, many game theorists have found it necessary to make some simplifying assumptions. One simplifying assumption is that there is a single variable, or a small number of variables, which sum up the condition of the game in such a way that each agent can choose the best response strategy if she or he knows the value of only that one variable or those few variables.

Using a word common in the study of games that evolve over time, we can refer to these variables that sum up the condition of the game as *state variables*, although we are using the term a little more broadly than it has usually been used in the past.

Another useful simplifying assumption is that all of the agents have the same payoff for the same strategy and the same value of the state variables. Then will we have to analyze only one decision for the whole population of agents. Even if this is not quite right, there may be only a *few* types of agents, with different information, preferences, or opportunities, and this is still much simpler than making a separate analysis for each of millions of different agents.

In this way, we can extend the analysis of social dilemmas to problems of congestion and the tragedy of the commons, in which millions of people may interact. We can analyze interactions in whole populations of people or hawks and doves, and we can even find that the equilibrium of supply and demand and the Keynesian expenditure equilibrium from basic economics textbooks are instances of Nash equilibria with state variables and one or more type of representative agent.

Exercises and Discussion Questions

11.1 Patenting Game. Firms A, B, C, D, E, and F are all considering undertaking a research project that will lead to a patent for just one firm. The first firm to complete the research project will receive the patent. For each firm that undertakes the project, the cost will be $210 million. Each firm that undertakes the research project will have an equal chance of finishing first and thus gaining a profit of $1 billion − $210 million = $790 million. Those who undertake the research but do not finish first lose the $210 million stake. Those that do not undertake a research project get payoffs of zero.

For this problem, the state variable is the number of firms that undertake a research project. Solve the problem along the lines of the Queuing Game, keeping in mind one important difference: In this game, those who "sit out" get a certain payoff of zero, while those who "jump in" get the uncertain payoff that has to be evaluated in expected value terms.

   a. Compute the expected value payoff for those who undertake research projects for all values of the state variable from 1 to 6.
   b. Determine how many firms undertake research projects at equilibrium.
   c. The net social value of the research is the $1 billion value of the patent minus the total expenditure of the research. Compute the net social value of the research at equilibrium. Determine how the net social value of the investment changes as the state variable goes from 1 to 6.
   d. Determine the number of firms doing research that corresponds to the maximum net social value. Defining an efficient situation as one in which net social value is maximized, comment on the efficiency of the equilibrium in this case.
   e. Economists Robert Frank and Philip Cook argue that "winner-take-all" competition, in which only the one agent ranked first gets a payoff, is inefficient in that it leads people to commit "too much" resources to the competition. Comment on that idea in the light of this example.

11.2 Public Goods with N Agents. Consider the following N-person public goods contribution game. Each of the N agents can decide whether to contribute. Assume $N > 10$. The state variable is the number, M, of agents who contribute. For an agent who does not contribute the payoff is $1,000 + 100M$. For those who contribute it is $800 + 100M$, since the cost of a contribution is 200. On a coordinate graph, draw the curve or line representing the payoff to a noncontributor as a function of the state variable M. (A spreadsheet XY graph utility will probably work for these purposes, but graph paper works, too). On the same graph, draw the curve or line representing the payoff to a contributor as a function of the state variable M. Determine whether the two curves intersect, and, if so, where; and draw conclusions with respect to the value of the state variable M at a Nash equilibrium. Compare the result to a Prisoner's Dilemma.

11.3 Gone Fishin'. Swellingham is a fishing port near the Fishy Banks. There are N fishermen and potential fishermen in Swellingham, and N is very large. On any given day M ≤ N fishermen take their boats out to Fishy Banks to fish. The catch per boat per day is 100/M tons of fish. The price of fish on the world market is $100 per ton. The cost to take a boat out on a particular day is $200. Each agent has two strategies on a particular day: fish or do not fish. They payoff to "do not fish" is always zero. Let M be the state variable for this problem. Determine how the profit (per day) of a representative fisherman varies as M changes. This is the payoff to the strategy "fish." On a coordinate graph, draw the curve or line representing the payoff to an agent who fishes as a function of the state variable M. On the same graph, draw the curve or line representing the payoff to a nonfisher. Determine whether the two curves intersect, and if so where; and draw conclusions with respect to the value of the state variable M at a Nash equilibrium. Compare the result to a Prisoner's Dilemma.

11.4 Medical Practice. Recall Problem 5 in Chapter 6.[11] Doctors are considering whether to practice as ob/gyns or to limit their practices to gyn. Let's extend that model to a market with N doctors qualified for ob and gyn practice. Assume M ≤ N practice both ob and gyn, while the rest practice only gyn.

The total revenue from gyn practice is Q, so the payoff to a doctor who practices only gyn is Q/N.

The revenue from ob practice is R, but those who practice ob pay a fixed overhead cost of S, which is the dollar equivalent of the subjective disutility of being on call 24/7, so the net payoff to a doctor with an ob/gyn practice is Q/N + R/M − S.

Let M be the state variable for this problem. Assume

Q = 10000000
R = 1000000
S = 50000
N = 50

11 Thanks to Dr. David Toub, a student in my course on game theory for MBA students, for this very nice example.

Determine how the revenue of a representative ob/gyn varies as M changes. This is the payoff to the strategy ob/gyn. On a coordinate graph, draw the curve or line representing the payoff to an agent who practices ob/gyn as a function of the state variable M. On the same graph, draw the curve or line representing the payoff to a doctor who practices gyn only. Determine whether the two curves intersect, and, if so, where. Draw conclusions with respect to the value of the state variable M at a Nash equilibrium. Compare the result to a Prisoner's Dilemma.

11.5 Internet Congestion. According to the *Philadelphia Inquirer*, July 25 1997 (p. C1), congestion of the Internet is an instance of the tragedy of the commons. They quote a study by Bernardo Huberman of the Xerox PARC laboratory that indicates that unpredictable periods of very slow service at or near peak use times correspond to a *tragedy of the commons* model of Internet use. Here is a small-scale example (five-person game) to illustrate the idea. The access time for users of Nibbienet depends on the number of users, as shown in Table 11.E1. For example, if three people use Nibbienet, each of the three has to wait 10 seconds to get online.

Table **11E.1** Payoffs to Using Nibbienet

Number of users	Access time
0	0
1	0
2	5
3	10
4	50
5	95

The payoff to each user is 100 minus the access time, if she uses Nibbienet. Any player can get a payoff of zero by not using the Nibbienet.

What are the strategies in this game? Are the players representative agents? Explain. Is there a state variable? Explain. Does this game have a dominant strategy equilibrium? If so, what is it? Why or why not? Does the game have a Nash equilibrium? If so, what is it? Why? If so, is it efficient? Why or why not? Explain the relationship of this game to the Prisoner's Dilemma.

11.6 Scaling Up. Rewrite the above game as a proportional game with a very large number of participants.

11.7 El Farol. Reread the El Farol Game information from Chapter 6. Rewrite it as a proportional game with a very large number of participants.

What are the strategies in this game? Are the players representative agents? Explain. Is there a state variable? Explain. Does this game have a dominant strategy equilibrium? If so, what is it? Why or why not? Does the game have a Nash equilibrium? If so, what is it? Why? If so, is it efficient? Why or why not?

11.8 More Proportional Games. Like Hawk vs. Dove, Heave-Ho (Chapter 4) and Drive On (Chapter 4, Exercise 4.3) can be rewritten as proportional games with very large numbers of participants.

For each of these games, indicate the state variable. Draw a diagram to represent the proportional game. Discuss the implications for application of the models.

11.9 Drive Right! In some countries, it is customary to drive on the right side of the road, while in others (Britain and Japan, particularly) it is customary to drive on the left side. Explain this in game theory terms, commenting on interpretation as a two-person game, the Schelling point of the game, and interpretation as a proportional game.

Part 3

Cooperative Solutions

12 Elements of Cooperative Games

To best understand this chapter 12

To best understand this chapter you need to have studied and understood the material from Chapters 1–4 and 6.

All of the examples so far have focused on non-cooperative solutions to games. We recall that there is, in general, no unique answer to the question, "What is the rational choice of strategies?" Instead, there are at least two possible answers—two possible kinds of "rational" strategies, in nonconstant sum games. Often, there are more than two rational solutions, based on different definitions of a *rational solution* to the game. But there are at least two: a *noncooperative solution* in which each person maximizes his or her own rewards regardless of the results for others, and a *cooperative* solution in which the strategies of the participants are coordinated so as to attain the best result for the whole group. Of course, "best for the whole group" is a tricky concept—that's one reason why there can be more than two solutions, corresponding to more than one concept of "best for the whole group."

Definition

Cooperative and Noncooperative Games and Solutions— If the participants in a game can make binding commitments to coordinate their strategies, then the game is cooperative, and otherwise it is noncooperative. The solution with coordinates strategies is a cooperative solution, and the solution without coordination of strategies is a noncooperative solution.

Games in which the participants cannot make commitments to coordinate their strategies are **noncooperative games**. The solution to a noncooperative game is a **noncooperative solution**. In a noncooperative game, the rational person's problem is to answer the question, "What is the rational choice of a strategy when other players will try to choose their best responses to my strategy?"

Conversely, games in which the participants can make commitments to coordinate their strategies are **cooperative games**, and the solution to a cooperative game is a **cooperative solution**. In a cooperative game, the rational person's problem is to answer the question, "What strategy choice will lead to the best outcome if we all choose a common, coordinated strategy?" Let's begin with an example in which this makes a very great difference.

Buy My Bike?

Adults experience cooperative games every day, since every purchase and sale is a cooperative game. Here is a two-person game of exchange. We suppose that Joey has a bicycle but Joey doesn't have any money. The money value Joey attaches to his bicycle is $80.[1] Mikey has $100 and no bicycle, and would value a bicycle at $100.[2] The strategies available to Joey and Mikey are to give or to keep. That is, Joey can give his bicycle to Mikey or keep it, and Mikey can give some of this money to Joey or keep it all. Suppose, for example, it is suggested that Mikey give Joey $90 and that Joey give Mikey the bicycle. Then the payoffs are as shown in Table 12.1.

By way of explanation, at the upper left, Mikey has a bicycle he values at $100, plus $10 extra, while Joey has a game machine he values at $80, plus an extra $10. At the lower left, Mikey has the bicycle he values at $100, plus $100 extra. At the upper right, Joey has a game machine and a bike, each of which he values at $80, plus $10 extra, and Mikey is left with only $10. At the lower right, they simply have what they begin with—Mikey $100 and Joey a bike.

If we think of this as a noncooperative game, it is much like a Prisoner's Dilemma. To "keep" is a dominant strategy and (keep, keep) is a dominant strategy equilibrium. However, (give, give) makes both better off. Children may distrust one another and fail to make the exchange that will make them better off. But market societies have a range of institutions that allow adults to commit themselves to mutually beneficial transactions. Thus, we would expect a cooperative solution, and we suspect that it would be the one in the upper left.

When Joey and Mikey agree on a sale, they are forming a coalition. They are committing themselves to coordinate their strategies and to adopt (give, give) as the joint strategy of the coalition. Thus, the game of Buy My Bike is a cooperative, not a noncooperative, game. The transfer of money from

Heads Up!

Here are some concepts we will develop as this chapter goes along:

Cooperative Games and Solutions: If the participants in a game can make binding commitments to coordinate their strategies, then the game is *cooperative*. The solution with coordinated strategies is a *cooperative solution*.

Coalition: A group of players who coordinate their strategies is called a *coalition*.

Side Payment: When part of the payoff is transferred from one member of a coalition to another in order that no member of the coalition is worse off as a result of adopting the coordinated strategy of the coalition, this transfer is called a *side payment*.

Solution Concepts: There are a number of solution concepts for cooperative games. Two are important for this book: the *solution set*, which includes all efficient solutions, and the *core*, which includes all those efficient solutions that cannot be destabilized by some coalition dropping out and coordinating its strategies for the advantage of its members.

Table 12.1 | Payoffs in a Game of Exchange

		Joey	
		give	keep
Mikey	give	110, 90	10, 170
	keep	200, 0	100, 80

1 How do we know this? In economics, money values are based on substitution. The sum of money Joey would accept in return for his bike is the amount just big enough to allow him to buy something he would rather have than a bike. So if Joey would rather have a game machine than a bicycle, and he could buy a game machine for $80, we express this by saying that Joey values his bicycle at $80.

2 Mikey would rather have a bicycle than anything else he can buy for $100. Reasoning in the same way as in footnote 1, we express this by saying that Mikey values a bicycle at $100.

Mikey to Joey makes it possible for both to be better off as a result of the shift of the bicycle from the boy who values it less to the boy who values it more.

In a world of noncooperative games, *there could be no buying and selling*, because buying and selling always requires an enforceable agreement.

Figure **12.1** | Payoffs to Joey and Mikey

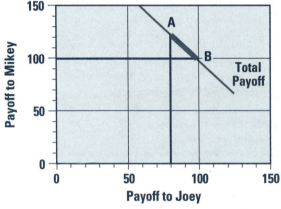

In cooperative games, however, the transfer payments cement the agreement, and these payments are called **side payments**. The terminology comes from gambling. In a poker game, if one player pays another to bluff or to fold, that would be cheating. The rules of poker do not allow payment outside the game (side payments). However, buying and selling is not poker, and side payments are very much part of games of exchange.

But Table 12.1 is not quite the whole story. The price of $90 was given only as an example, and the price could be higher or lower. How much higher or lower? There are some limits, as shown in Figure 12.1. In Figure 12.1, payoffs to Joey are shown on the horizontal axis and payoffs to Mikey are on the vertical axis. First, regardless of the side payments, the total payoff to both young traders cannot be more than $200, since that is the total value of Joey's bicycle (at the higher money value, which is Mikey's) and Mikey's $100. In Figure 12.1, this is shown by the downward-sloping diagonal line. But not all points on that line are acceptable to both players. Joey can get a payoff worth $80 to him by refusing to join the coalition (refusing to trade), since $80 is his payoff in the noncooperative equilibrium. This is shown in Figure 12.1 by the vertical line at 80. Joey will agree to payoffs only to the right of that line or on it. Similarly, Mikey gets a payoff of $100 in the noncooperative equilibrium (by keeping the $100 he has), and so he will not accept any deal that leaves him with less than $100 worth of payoffs. This is shown by the horizontal line at 100. Only payoffs above this line or on it are acceptable to Mikey. Thus, the payoffs to the two boys must be on the *thick segment* of the diagonal line between points A and B.

But any point on that thick line segment will satisfy the requirements above, adding up to 200 and giving each trader at least what he can get if he does not trade. In that sense, all the points on the line segment are possible solutions to the cooperative game. One kind of cooperative solution for a game such as this is what von Neumann and Morgenstern called the **solution set**. The solution set in a game with side payments consists of all coalitions that yield the maximum total payoffs and all payoff arrangements that make every player at least as well off as she or he would be in the noncooperative solution of the game. But this solution set covers a multitude of sins. How are we to narrow down the range of possible answers? There are several possibilities. The range of possible payments might be influenced, and narrowed, by any of these factors:

- Competitive pressures from other potential buyers and sellers

- Perceived fairness

- Bargaining

For the first of these we would have to consider the competitors as players in a larger, N-person cooperative game. That is a possibility we will explore further in this chapter.

Credible Commitment

Before continuing our exploration of cooperative games, we need to consider a preliminary question. Why do we study noncooperative games at all?

Without going into technical details, here is the problem: If people can arrive at a cooperative solution, any nonconstant sum game can, in principle, be converted to a win-win game. How, then, can a noncooperative outcome of a nonconstant sum game be rational? The obvious answer seems to be that it cannot be rational: Some game theorists have argued that the cooperative solution is the only truly rational outcome in a nonconstant sum game. Yet we do seem to observe noncooperative interactions every day, and the noncooperative solutions to nonconstant sum games often seem to be descriptive of real outcomes. Arms races, street congestion, environmental pollution, the overexploitation of fisheries, inflation, and many other social problems seem to be accurately described by the noncooperative solutions of rather simple nonconstant sum games. How can all this irrationality exist in a world of absolutely rational decision makers?

New Classical economics has a possible answer to that question. The answer has been made explicit mostly in the context of inflation. According to the New Classical theory, inflation happens when the central bank increases the quantity of money in circulation

> **Definition**
>
> **New Classical Economics**—The **New Classical economics** is a school of thought in macroeconomics that has restated and renewed traditional ideas of classical economics, especially on the role of money and efficient markets in the macroeconomy.

too fast. Then, the solution to inflation is to slow down or stop increasing the quantity of money. If the central bank were committed to stopping inflation, and businesspeople in general knew that the central bank was committed, then (according to New Classical economics) inflation could be stopped quickly and without disruption. But in a political world, it is difficult for a central bank to make this commitment, and businesspeople know this. Thus, the businesspeople have to be convinced that the central bank really is committed—and that might require a long period of unemployment, sky-high interest rates, recession, and business failures.

Therefore, the cost of eliminating inflation can be very high—which makes it all the more difficult for the central bank to make the commitment. The difficulty is that the central bank cannot make a *credible commitment* to a low-inflation strategy.

Evidently (as seen by New Classical economics), the interaction between the central bank and businesspeople is a nonconstant sum game, and recessions are a result of a *noncooperative solution to the game.* This can be extended to nonconstant sum games in general: Noncooperative solutions occur when participants in the game cannot make credible commitments to cooperative strategies. Evidently, this is a very common difficulty in many human interactions.

But sometimes people can make credible commitments, and then we apply the theory of cooperative games.

Buy My Bike is a two-person game. Most cooperative games with more than two players will have many **coalitions** of two or more players but not the whole group. Coalitions can also form in noncooperative games with three or more players, as we saw in Chapter 6. However, in the absence of some credible commitment, we will see only coalitions that correspond to Nash equilibria. In the rest of this chapter, we will assume that credible commitments can be made, and will see that there is a wider range of possibilities. Here is an example with three players and a fourth party, not a player in the game but an entrepreneur who wants to get some of the players together in a coalition.

A Real Estate Development

Table 12.2 | Payoffs in a Real Estate Coalition (Version 1)

	Coalitions	Payoffs
1	(KLM)	(10)
2	(KL) (M)	(6) (4)
3	(KM) (L)	(4) (4)
4	(LM) (K)	(4) (4)
5	(K) (L) (M)	(3) (3) (3)

Definition

Grand Coalition—A coalition of all the players in the game is called a **grand coalition**.

Jay, a real-estate developer, wants to put together two or more parcels of property in order to develop them jointly. He is considering properties owned by Kaye, Laura, and Mark. Jay wants to propose a deal that will be stable in the sense that none of the three property owners will want to renegotiate with some other property owners not included in the deal. Having studied game theory, Jay recognizes that the property consolidations are coalitions in a cooperative game, and that his offer needs to be in the solution set of the game. But is that good enough? To find out, Jay will look in detail at the various ways the property owners might combine (or be combined) in coalitions and what the payoffs will be. All of the possible coalitions, and the payoffs to each coalition, are shown in Table 12.2.

The first line of Table 12.2 shows a coalition of all three property owners. In game theory terms, this is called the **grand coalition**. On the second, third, and fourth lines we see the group divided into a coalition of two property owners, with the third property owner going it alone. A player who goes it alone is called a **singleton coalition**. On the fifth line of Table 12.2, we see each of the three property owners going it alone as a singleton coalition—in other words, there is no consolidation of the property at all. The payoffs to the singleton coalitions on this line are what an economist would call the *opportunity costs* of the property owners when they enter into any coalition. Each line of the table gives an alternative **coalition structure** for the game.

> **Definition**
>
> *Singleton Coalition*—A single player who goes it alone in a cooperative game is called a **singleton coalition**.

> **Definition**
>
> *Coalition Structure*—A division of the players in a game into coalitions (including singleton coalitions) is called a **coalition structure**.

We can see that there are two possible coalition structures in the solution set for this game. The grand coalition of all three property owners, (K, L, M), and the second line of coalitions, (K, L)(M), each have total payoffs of 10, while all the rest have lesser payoffs. Therefore, these two coalition structures are in the solution set. However, Jay believes that the grand coalition on line 1 will not be stable. Jay notices that Mark, by dropping out, shifts to the coalition structure on line 2, thereby getting a payoff of 4 for himself. Similarly, Laura can drop out, shifting to the coalitions on line 3, and in that way she can obtain a payoff of 4. Kaye, too, can get a payoff of 4 by dropping out of the grand coalition, shifting to the coalitions shown on line 4. Jay concludes that in order to keep all three property owners in the grand coalition, each one of them has to get a payoff of 4. But the total payoffs for that coalition are no more than 10. So it is impossible for the grand coalition to be stable.

However, the coalitions on line 2 can be stable, provided that the payoffs to Kaye and Laura are correctly adjusted by side payments. Line 5 tells us that if either Kaye or Laura drops out of the coalition, each of them will get a payment of 3. Thus, the payoff to the coalition of Kaye and Laura must give each of them no less than 3. Since payoffs of 3 + 3 = 6, the total payoff to that coalition, the coalition will be stable on the condition that Kaye gets 3, Laura gets 3, and Mark goes it alone to get 4.

Line 2, which divides the group into stable coalitions, is the **core** of this game. In general, the core of any cooperative game includes all of the different ways that the group can be divided into coalitions

> **Definition**
>
> *The Core of a Cooperative Game*—The **core of a cooperative game** consists of all coalition structures (if there are any) that are stable in the sense that there is no individual or group who can improve their payoffs (including side payments) by dropping out or reorganizing to form a new or separate coalition.

that are stable in the way we have seen here; that is, no group can benefit by withdrawing from the coalitions they are in, in order to form new coalitions (including singleton coalitions).

Let us see how the example changes if we make a small change in the payoffs. In a new real estate consolidation, Jay is now dealing with Noreen, Pete, and Quincy (N, P, and Q). The payoffs to coalitions among these three are shown in Table 12.3.

The first two coalition structures are in the solution set, as before, since both yield total payoffs of 11. Also as before, no one needs to settle for less than 3, and the coalition structure

Table **12.3** | Payoffs in a Real Estate Coalition (Version 2)

	Coalitions	Payoffs
1	(NPQ)	(11)
2	(NP) (Q)	(8) (3)
3	(NQ) (M)	(4) (3)
4	(PQ) (N)	(4) (3)
5	(N) (P) (Q)	(3) (3) (3)

at line 2 is stable, provided the side payments are appropriate. In this case, though, line 1 is a stable coalition structure as well. Suppose that the payoffs are (4, 4, 3) to N, P, and Q respectively. No one can improve her or his payoff by dropping out as a singleton coalition (since no singleton coalition pays more than 3). There are some limits as to how the payoffs can be allocated, though. Suppose the payoffs were (3.5, 3.5, 4). Then the grand coalition would not be stable, since N and P could withdraw from the grand coalition and form a new coalition of the two of them, and get a total of 8 to divide between them. Thus, N and P have to be paid a total of at least 8, and that means Q can be paid no more than 3. However, if Q is paid 3 and the payoffs to N and P are in the range from (3, 5) to (5, 3), then the grand coalition is stable. The coalition on line 2 is also stable, and the first two lines constitute the core of the version 2 game—the set of all stable coalition structures (provided the correct side payments are made).

These examples illustrate several points about the analysis of cooperative games.

First, we have not said very much about the specific strategies of the coalitions, once they get together: whether they are building a mall or new houses or an industrial park. We have limited our analysis in this game to the *coalitional form*, which associates a payoff with each coalition without saying just how the coalition coordinates strategies to get the payoffs. This is a common approach in cooperative game theory.

Second, the core is always contained within the solution set. In the second version of the Real Estate Game, the core is identical with the solution set, while in the first version, it is a proper subset of the solution set—that is, a part but not the whole of it.

Rule

The Core and the Solution Set—In any cooperative game, the core is a subset of the solution set; that is, either the core and the solution set are identical, or the core is contained within the solution set, or the core is empty.

Definition

Transferable Utility—A game is said to have **transferable utility** if the subjective payoffs are closely enough correlated with money payoffs so that transfers of money can be used to adjust the payoffs within a coalition. Side payments will always be possible in a game of transferable utility but may not be possible in a game without transferable utility.

Third, in this example and in the previous one, the payoffs are valued in money, and transfers of money are used to compensate the players for giving up the alternatives they might obtain in singleton coalitions (or in other multiperson coalitions). These money payments are called the side payments. In a world of noncooperative games, there could be no buying and selling—because buying and selling always means that an enforceable agreement is made, and on the basis of the agreement, a payment changes hands

There are two major kinds of cooperative games: those with transferable utility and those without. **Transferable utility** means that the subjective benefits are closely correlated with money payoffs, so that transfers of money can be used to adjust the payoffs among the participants.[3] The next example will be one without transferable utility. First, however, we need to review the terminology for cooperative games in a systematic way.

Solution Set

At the beginning of game theory, von Neumann and Morgenstern argued that (at the very least) the solution to a cooperative game must be **efficient**. They took the concept of efficiency from neoclassical economics.

In neoclassical economics, the concept of efficiency is applied to an allocation of resources, including details of income, consumption, work assignments and pay as well as natural resources. In game theory, what the members of the various coalitions get, after all the bribes, side payments, and quids pro quo have cleared, is called an *allocation*. The allocation has two aspects: the coalition structure and the payoffs the members of the coalitions get. An allocation is said to be *efficient* if there is no way to reallocate resources and incomes so that at least one person is made better off,

In games with side payments, the solution set consists of all coordinated strategies that give the highest total payoff. This means the payoffs can be distributed in such a way that someone is better off, and no one worse off, than he would be if other strategies were chosen. It follows that the other strategy choices would not be efficient, and the solution set is the set of all efficient (Pareto optimal) coalitions and payoffs that make every player at least as well off as he would be in a noncooperative solution. This is the more general definition, applicable to all cooperative games whether they allow for side payments or not.

The idea behind all this is that rational, self-interested players would never settle for an inefficient choice of their strategies. If they could rearrange their agreement so that some were better off, and none worse off, they would do it.

> **Definition**
>
> **Efficient (Pareto Optimum)**—In neoclassical economics, the allocation of resources is said to be **efficient**, or **Pareto optimal**, if no one can be made better off without making someone else worse off.

while no one is made worse off. If this is a little hard to follow, think of it this way: Whenever one person can be made better off without making anyone else worse off, this is an *unrealized potential*. The allocation is not efficient unless *all* of its potential is realized. An efficient allocation is an allocation that realizes all of the potential of the game: no unrealized potential means no one can be made better off without making someone else worse off. In economics, this is called **Pareto optimum**.

In many cases, there is more than one efficient allocation. That should not be surprising. Suppose the only way we can make Paul better off is to "rob Peter to pay Paul." There are two allocations—one in which Paul gets paid, and one in which Peter keeps what he has. Shifting from one to the other always makes somebody worse off. (That's the point of the saying, "robbing Peter to pay Paul," after all.) But for that very reason, both are "efficient."[4] Because there are usually two or more efficient allocations, the set of all efficient allocations is called the **solution set** in game theory. We saw that, in the game of "Buy My Bike," every division of payoffs

---

3 The terminology comes from *The Theory of Games and Economic Behavior* by von Neumann and Morgenstern.

4 The saying also illustrates another point about economic efficiency: The situation can be efficient but not satisfactory. An efficient allocation may be a case of making the best of a bad—unsatisfactory—situation.

A Closer Look

In these examples, we have not treated Jay, the property developer, as a player in the game. Of course, it would be more complete to treat it as a four-person game, with Jay as one of the players, but because Jay's objective is to put together a stable coalition, we wouldn't gain much beside completeness by treating this as a four-person game. Indeed, one way to think about cooperative solution concepts is to think of them as blueprints for arbitrators, facilitators, and deal makers. That is particularly clear with the solution set—since efficiency is its defining property, and it surely could not make sense for a deal maker to propose a deal that is not efficient for the people who form the coalition. There are other solution concepts for cooperative games, with more emphasis on fairness, that lend themselves especially to being thought of as arbitration schemes.

Terminology

Coalition Dominance—In coalition structure A, suppose there is a group of people who can withdraw from their coalitions and form a new coalition, and be better off as a consequence. This results in a new coalition structure, structure B. We then say that structure B *dominates* structure A. Note that, if the game has transferrable utility, then side payments may be made to assure that everyone in the new coalition is better off. If there is no coalition that dominates coalition C, then we say that coalition C is *undominated*.

Definition

The Core of a Cooperative Game—The **core of a cooperative game** consists of all undominated coalitions in the game, if there are any. If there are none, we say that the core is empty.

between (100, 100) and (80, 120) is in the solution set. All are "efficient," since the only way to make one little boy better off is to increase his side payment, reducing the side payment to the other little boy and making him worse off. In the Real Estate Development Game, Version 1, the noncooperative payoffs are 3 each. Both the Grand Coalition and (KL)(M) pay 10, which is one more than the total necessary to make each landowner as well off as she or he is in the noncooperative solution. Thus, for example, (4, 3, 3), (3.3, 3.3, 3.4), and (3.8, 3.1, 3.1) are all in the solution set. Indeed, every allocation of payoffs that gives each landowner at least 3 but that adds up to 10 is in the solution set. (But, as we have seen, most of them are not in the core.)

The Core

The idea behind the solution set is something like this: If one person can be made better off, but no one worse off, then the group as a whole must not yet be coordinating its strategies effectively. In that case, a grand coalition can form that can improve the situation, moving to an efficient solution. But what if a smaller coalition can take unilateral action to make itself better off? In the real estate game, version 2, NP can assure themselves of a total payoff of 8 by forming a two-person coalition among themselves. Notice also that in the second version, (NQ)(M) and (PQ)(N) can be improved by drawing the third person into the coalition, shifting to (NPQ). We would say, therefore, that (NPQ) **dominates** (NQ)(M) and (PQ)(N). Further, (NPQ) dominates (N)(P)(Q). Similarly, (NP)(Q) dominates any coalition (NPQ) in which Noreen and Pete, together, get less than 8. Looking back at version 1, (KLM) dominates (KM)(L), (LM)(K), and (K)(L)(M), but in turn (KLM) is dominated by (KL)(M).

In general, the **core of a cooperative game** includes all allocations that have the property that no group can form a new coalition so that all members of the new coalition are better off. That is, the core includes all allocations that are not dominated, supposing that there are any.

Now, two very important limitations should be mentioned. The core of a cooperative game may be of any size—it may have only one coalition structure, or there may be many coalition structures in the core (corresponding either to one or many coalitions), and it is also possible that there may not be any coalition structures in the core at all. What does it mean to say that there are no coalition structures in the core? It means that there are no stable coalitions—whatever coalition may be formed, there is some subgroup that can benefit by deserting it. A game with no coalition structures in the core is called an **empty-core game**. We will see an example of an empty-core game at the end of this chapter.

Carpool

Anna, Bob, Carole, and Don are all employed at the University of West Philadelphia (UWP) and commute by car from their homes in the western suburbs of Philadelphia to

UWP. They are interested in forming one or more carpools to commute together. The advantages of a carpool include some saving of gasoline and upkeep costs on their cars, the possibility of riding rather than driving some days, and having company while driving. However, carpooling also has a downside. The four commuters live some miles apart in various locations around the suburbs, and it would usually be necessary for the driver in the carpool to go some miles out of the way to pick up other members of the carpool. It is less of a problem for Carole to pick up Don, for example, since he lives on her shortest route, but Carole doesn't want to drive all the time, and when Don takes a turn driving he would have to double back to pick up Carole, increasing his drive time by the round trip to Carole's place. Similarly, if Don, Bob, and Anna were in the carpool, the extra pick-up mileage is even greater, since (even by the shortcut down Bridle Road) Don and Bob live six miles apart and Bob would have to add on a round trip to pick up Anna. Thus, these various routing problems imply that the different carpools have different advantages for their members.

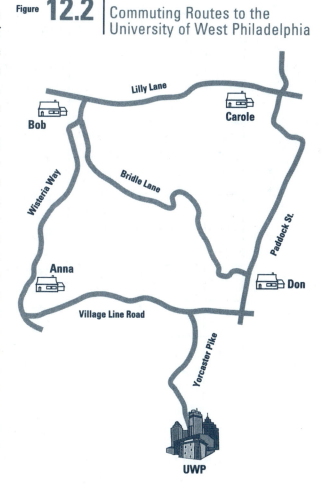

Figure 12.2 | Commuting Routes to the University of West Philadelphia

Table **12.4** | Carpooling Coalitions and Individual Payoffs Expressed in Units of Mile-Equivalent Inconvenience

Line	Coalition structure	Payoffs
1	(ABCD)	(7, 7, 7, 7)
2	(ABC) (D)	(6, 6.5, 9) (12)
3	(ABD) (C)	(6.5, 7, 6.5) (16)
4	(ACD) (B)	(8, 8, 7) (13)
5	(A) (BCD)	(7, 6.5, 6) (11)
6	(AB) (CD)	(8, 7) (7, 8)
7	(AC) (BD)	(9, 7) (8, 9)
8	(AD) (BC)	(7, 9) (8, 7)
9	(AB) (C) (D)	(8, 7) (16) (12)
10	(AC) (B) (D)	(9, 7) (13) (12)
11	(AD) (B) (C)	(7, 9) (13) (16)
12	(A) (B) (CD)	(11) (13) (7, 8)
13	(A) (C) (BD)	(11) (16) (8, 9)
14	(A) (D) (BC)	(11) (12) (8, 7)
15	(A) (B) (C) (D)	(11) (13) (16) (12)

We will treat the carpools as coalitions in a cooperative game. The possible coalition structures and their payoffs are shown in Table 12.4. The coalition structures are shown in the second column, much as in Tables 12.2 and 12.3, so that, for example, on line 3 we have a coalition of Anna, Bob, and Don with Carole commuting solo as a singleton coalition. The numbers in the third column are *negative* payoffs, or commuting penalties, to the individuals. The commuting penalties would be increased by (a) more miles total, (b) more miles driving alone, (c) more miles driving rather than riding, and (d) more gasoline cost and wear and tear on the car. The penalties are expressed in units of equivalent miles commuting alone. For example, on line 3, Anna's subjective penalty for commuting with the carpool is the same as it would be for driving 6.5 miles alone; Bob's is the same as he would experience commuting 7 miles alone, Don's is the same as he would experience commuting 6 miles alone. Since Carole is commuting alone as a singleton coalition, her commuting penalty is the miles she must drive on her commute: 16. Thus, individuals are better off when they have lower numbers in the third column of Table 12.4. Given a choice, each person will prefer a coalition that gives her or him a lower number. However, there are no money side payments in this game, for two reasons. First, some of the benefits are subjective, and it is not clear that money payments would be proportional to the subjective benefits. Second, "it just isn't done." Transferring money payments among these friendly coworkers would destroy the friendly atmosphere that is one of the benefits of the carpool. Notice that the penalties to individuals in a coalition are listed in the same order as the individuals are listed in the second column. Since there are no side payments, the total payoff of the coalition is not meaningful, and we have to consider the payoffs to individuals separately. Thus, this is a nontransferable utility (NTU) game.

How are we to compare coalitions in an NTU game such as this? Compare, for example, line 4 and line 1. A shift from line 4 to line 1 means that the carpool is expanded to include

Bob, who had been out of the carpool before. This lowers the penalties for three of the four participants in the new (grand) coalition, and leaves Don no worse off. Thus, we say that the coalition structure on line 1 **weakly dominates** the coalition structure on line 4, and that means that the coalition structure in line 4 will be unstable, and will not be in the solution set nor in the core. On the other hand, compare line 2 and line 1. A shift from line 2 to line 1 (taking Don into the coalition) will make Anna and Bob worse off, raising their penalties from 6 and 6.5 miles, respectively, to 7. Thus, they will not want to make the shift, and the coalition structure on line 2 is (tentatively) stable.

How do we define the solution set, then? Remember that the solution set consists of all coalition structures (1) that are efficient, and (2) in which no one does worse than she or he would do in a singleton coalition. To judge efficiency, we use the Pareto criterion: the coalition structure is "efficient" if no one can be made better off (by shifting to a different coalition structure) without making someone else worse off. For example, compare line 13 with line 1. Everyone is better off (with lower penalty miles) on line 1 than on line 13. Thus, we say that the grand coalition **strongly dominates** the coalition structure on line 13 and conclude that the coalition structure on line 13 is not efficient. Consequently, it is not in the solution set. If a coalition structure is either weakly or strongly dominated, we can rule it out of the solution set.

This is how we have to deal with an NTU cooperative game. The advantages of each coalition to each individual in that coalition have to be separately considered. The Pareto principle is a good example of that.

So, what is the solution set for this game? First, we can rule out everything from line 6 on. All of these coalition structures are at least weakly dominated by the grand coalition. For the same reason, line 4 can be ruled out. However, a careful analysis shows that lines 1 to 3 and 5 are efficient in the Pareto sense. Therefore, those four lines are in the solution set for this game.

NOW IT'S YOUR TURN. Verify this by listing the possible shifts from one line to another, among the four lines 1–3 and 4, and writing next to each shift the name of at least one person who is made worse off.

What about the core? We will use the criterion of coalition dominance, again, but with the difference that we have to allow for the payoffs to individual members of coalitions. The application is a bit like the Pareto principle. A coalition structure X is said to be dominated if there are a group of people who can drop out of the coalitions they are members of in X, and join together to form a new coalition in coalition structure Y, in such a way that everyone in the new coalition is either better off or no worse off. In that case we say that structure Y dominates structure X. The core consists of all nondominated coalition structures, if any. For example, consider line 7. A has a penalty of 9 and B of 8. By getting together, they shift to line 9, reducing their penalties to 8 and 7, respectively. Thus, line 9 dominates line 8, and line 8 is unstable. Notice that the fact that C and D are made worse off does not affect the conclusion—they are not members of the new coalition. In fact, though, line 9 is not stable, either. It is dominated by line 6, and also by lines 1 to 3.

Reasoning in this way, we find that the core of the carpool game consists of the coalition structures on lines 2 and 5—meaning that either Anna or Don is out of luck! In fact, the grand coalition, despite its overall advantages, is not in the core. It is dominated both by line 3, which makes A and C better off while B is no worse off, and by line 5, which makes CD better off, and B no worse off.

This example illustrates several points about the analysis of cooperative games.

- Once again, we have not said very much about the specific strategies of the coalitions—which routes they drive and how they rotate the driver's role, for example. We have limited our analysis in this game to the "coalitional form," which associates payoffs with each coalition without saying just how the coalition coordinates strategies to get the payoffs.

- In this case the payoffs are partly subjective. In general, the payoff to each person is the rank in her or his preference listing. In this case, we have summarized that by giving the equivalent number of miles the person would drive alone. The "penalty miles" are equivalent in this sense: Given the choice (for example) of commuting alone for nine miles or participating in the coalition on line 2, Carole would have no net preference one way or the other. She would be indifferent between the two choices. This "indifference relation" is a standard method of handling subjective preferences in economics.

- That is part of the reason there are no side payments. To say there is "transferable utility" is to say that the subjective benefits are closely correlated with money payoffs, so that transfers of money can be used to adjust the payoffs among the participants. We have seen "side payments" in other games where the payoffs are monetary.

- A coalition structure can be ruled out of the core by another coalition structure that is itself not stable and therefore not in the core. In this case, remember, line 3 dominates line 1, but is, in turn, dominated by line 2.

Some Political Coalitions

The concept of coalitions came into game theory from parliamentary politics, so here is an example in parliamentary politics. Britain, Canada, and Germany are examples of countries with parliamentary governments. In a parliamentary system, the government cannot be formed or continue for long unless it has a majority in the legislature (i.e., Parliament). There are often three or more parties with representation in Parliament. That means that in order to form a government, parties in the Parliament who together constitute a majority of the votes have to form a coalition and agree on a common program. If there is no coalition, no

Table 12.5 | Parties in the Parliament of Mitteleuropa

Party	Vote	Position
Christian Conservative	40%	This party is strongly conservative on moral and family issues but moderate on economic issues, supporting measures favorable to small business and farmers.
Socialist Labor	40%	This party supports measures favorable to labor, and, in practice, generally supports central control of the economic system, but is neutral on moral and family value issues.
Radical	20%	This party favors free markets and limited government, but is extremely libertarian on family values and moral issues.

measures can be passed, and a new election has to be called. These are the rules common to countries with parliamentary government.

For our example, the Republic of Mitteleuropa has a parliamentary government. In Mitteleuropa, there are three parties that are strong enough to be represented in Parliament. The three parties are as shown in Table 12.5.

The formation of a government in the Parliament of Mitteleuropa is a cooperative game, but side payments are not allowed, since they would be considered corrupt. Thus, the parties in the coalition can be rewarded only to the extent that measures they favor are passed. Each party favors some measures more than the others, and opposes still others. In Table 12.6, the four measures expected to come before the next government are shown in the second column, and the relative strength of each party's support for each one of these measures is indicated by

Table 12.6 | Issues and Party Points in Mitteleuropa

	Issue	Party and Points		
		CC	SL	R
1	Free trade	+1	−3	+10
2	Same-sex partner benefits under social security	−10	0	+9
3	Tax and medical benefit cuts	+3	−10	+8
4	Subsidies[5] to farmers and businesses that compete with imports	+6	+3	−10

5 In case the word is unfamiliar, a *subsidy* is a direct payment from the government to a person or business, not in payment for any service the person or business delivers to the government, but simply to support that person or business. Subsidies to agriculture and to businesses that export or that compete with imports are quite common worldwide.

certain number of points—positive if the party supports the measure, negative if it opposes the measure, and zero if the party is neutral on that measure. A party's total payoff is the total number of points it associates with the measures that actually are passed.

The rules of the game are that a coalition will pass any measure on which it has a clear position—that is, any measure that no party in the coalition actively opposes. This means that payoffs to each party in the coalition are either positive or zero. Thus, for example, the coalition of the Christian Conservatives and the Radicals will pass measures one and three: free trade and cuts in medical benefits and taxes. Thus, if the government is formed by a coalition of the Christian Conservatives and the Radicals, the Christian Conservatives will score 4 points, the Radicals 18 points, and the Socialist Labor Party −13 points.

All of the possible coalitions and their payoffs, as well as the issues passed, are shown in Table 12.7. As we examine this table we can see, first, that all possible coalition structures are in the solution set for this game. Even line 5, which says that no government is formed so a new election has to be called, is in the solution set, since every shift from one arrangement to another—that makes one party better off—also makes some other party worse off. That should not be surprising, since a change in the balance of political power will usually make the people who have been pushed out of power worse off.

However, only line 4 is in the core. We see that, beginning from any other line, the Christian Conservatives and the Socialist Labor Party can both improve their payoffs by shifting to form a coalition with one another and excluding the Radicals from power. In common-sense terms, the Socialists and the Conservatives can work together because each is willing to

Table 12.7 | Coalitions and Payoffs in the Parliament of Mitteleuropa

	Coalitions	Issues Passed	Party and Total Points		
			CC	SL	R
1	(CC, SL, R)	0	0	0	0
2	(CC, R) (SL)	1, 3	4	−13	18
3	(SL, R) (CC)	2	−10	0	9
4	(CC, SL) (R)	4	6	3	−10
5	(CC) (SL) (R)	0	0	0	0

give the other a veto on the key issue the other wants to kill. (In real parliamentary governments, coalitions of traditionalist conservatives and socialists have not been very common, but they have occurred more than once.)

Even though there are no side payments, the solution set and the core can still be defined. The solution set is defined to include all coalition structures that are efficient, in that no player can be made better off by shifting to a different coalition structure without making some other player worse off. Without transferable utility and side payments, the solution set is likely to be even bigger, since there is no way for one player to compensate another if the first is made better off at the expense of the second. The core, as always, is the set of all undominated coalitions, but we must consider the payoff to each player individually rather than the total payoff to the coalition.

Now let us look at a game of international politics.

Another Look at the International Alliance Game

In Chapter 6, the idea of coalitions in games was introduced in the context of international alliances, and the numerical example made reference to three imaginary countries with shores on the same bay. The strategies and payoffs for the three countries are shown in Table 12.8.

Should we treat this as a transferable utility game, with side payments, or an NTU game without side payments? Side payments between countries are not very common, but they have been paid in history—allies have sometimes subsidized their allies to keep them in the alliance. Thus, we will treat this game as a TU game.

What is the solution set for this game? Since the grand coalition of all three countries generates the largest total payoff—18—by choosing strategies north, west, and onshore, that is the only coalition in the solution set.

What is the core? Since the grand coalition is the only coalition structure in the solution set, and the core is always contained within the solution set,

Table 12.8 Countries on Overflowing Bay

Repeats Table 6.1, Chapter 6

		Wetland			
		onshore		offshore	
		Soggia		Soggia	
		west	east	west	east
Runnistan	north	6, 6, 6	7, 7, 1	7, 1, 7	0, 0, 0
	south	0, 0, 0	4, 4, 4	4, 4, 4	1, 7, 7

the grand coalition is the only possibility. But is it stable? By dropping out of the grand coalition and allying between themselves (for example), Runnistan and Soggia can get 14 between them by choosing north and east. Thus, Runnistan and Soggia have to be paid 14 between them to keep them in the grand coalition. But, similarly, Runnistan and Wetland can get 14 between them by choosing north and offshore, and Wetland and Soggia can get

14 between them by choosing offshore and east. Indicate the payoffs to Runnistan, Soggia, and Wetland by R, S, and W, respectively. We have

$$R + S \geq 14$$
$$R + W \geq 14$$
$$S + W \geq 14$$

Adding them up, we have

$$R + S + R + W + S + W = 2(R + S + W) \geq 3 \times 14 = 42$$

that is,

$$R + S + W \geq 21$$

But this is impossible, since there are only payoffs of 18 to the grand coalition to make these side payments. We conclude that *there is no coalition structure in the core of this game.*

The game of international alliances, then, is an empty-core game. Perhaps this example explains why—although treaties of alliance have been common enough in history—general disarmament or *grand coalition* alliances among all potential adversaries have been much more rare.

As we saw in the second version of the Real Estate Development Game, there may be more than one coalition structure and allocation in the core of a game. In this example, we find that there may be no coalition structures or allocations in the core. These are unfortunate limits of the core concepts, but as we have seen, most game theoretic solution concepts have similar shortcomings. The fact that the core is empty may be an important diagnostic point, because it tells us that competition among coalitions may have no stable outcomes whatever.

Summary

A cooperative game is a game in which the participants can make credible or binding commitments to coordinate their choices of strategies. This can make a great difference in nonconstant sum games—and indeed, every act of market exchange is an example of a cooperative game. In a contract between a seller and a buyer, the coordinated strategies are that the seller bears the cost of the good supplied, and the demander gets the use of it—with a side payment from the buyer to the seller to cover the costs and assure that both are better off as a result of the deal.

There are several concepts of the solution of a cooperative game. Two are considered in this chapter. One, the solution set, consists of all efficient combinations of strategies and side payments that leave all parties no worse off than they would be in the absence of a deal. For many games, however, there are more than one and perhaps many outcomes in the solution set. The second concept of solution, the core, consists of all arrangements of participants in coalitions in which the coalition structures are undominated—meaning that there are no possibilities for people to make themselves better off by leaving the coalitions they are in and associating with some other coalition. This requirement limits both the coalitions and the range of side payments in the core. Thus, the core will be encompassed in the solution set—will be all or part of the solution set or may be empty. Although the core provides a reasonable answer, for many games, to the question of how the players will sort themselves into coalitions, there may be no solutions at all in the core.

Even though neither the core nor the solution set provides a final answer for all cooperative games, they are important additions to our kit of tools for all games in which players can make commitments and coordinate their strategies.

Exercises and Discussion Questions

12.1 A Prehistoric Game. Gung, Mog, and Pok are prehistoric tribesmen planning a hunting expedition. They have different skills: Gung is very strong, Mog is quick and agile, and Pok has great stamina. They have to decide which of them will collaborate and which (if any) are to be left to hunt independently, and how the catch is to be divided among those who collaborate. The payoffs to coalitions are shown in Table 12.E1, with the payoffs measured by the expected value of the number of antelope they can catch. Assume this is a TU game with portions of antelope serving for side payments.

Which coalition structures are in the solution set? Which coalition structures, if any, are in the core? Would a division of the catch in the proportions 3, 1, 1 (in the order GMP) be a stable side-payment schedule? Why or why not? Would a division of the catch in the proportions 2, 2, 1 (in the order GMP) be a stable side-payment schedule? Why or why not?

Table 12.E1 | Prehistoric Coalitions

Coalition	Payoff
(GMP)	(5)
(GM) (P)	(4) (0)
(GP) (M)	(3) (1)
(PM) (G)	(3) (0)
(G) (M) (P)	(2) (1) (1)

12.2 Choosing Information Systems. Here is a two-person game with a technological twist: choosing an information system. For this example, the players will be a company considering the choice of a new internal e-mail or intranet system, and a supplier who is

Table 12.E2 | Payoffs in the IT Game

		User		
		advanced	proven	no deal
Supplier	advanced	−50, 90	0, 0	0, 0
	proven	0, 0	−30, 40	0, 0
	no deal	0, 0	0, 0	0, 0

considering producing it. The two choices are to install a technically advanced system or a more proven system with less functionality. We'll assume that the more advanced system really does supply a lot more functionality, so that the total payoffs to the two players are as shown in Table 12.E2. This is a TU game.

What will be the total payoffs in the solution set of this game? Why? Describe the payoffs to both players, after side payments have been made, in the solution set of this game. Does the core of this game differ from its solution set? Why or why not?

12.3   A John Bates Clark Game. As (especially) Japanese economists have pointed out, the business firm can be analyzed as a cooperative game. We will borrow John Bates Clark's idea and assume there are two kinds of players: workers and entrepreneurs. (Clark would also have included capitalists, but we will leave them out for simplicity.) Assume that there are five workers and two entrepreneurs. Workers can work independently as craftsmen, but only entrepreneurs can organize firms. A firm can benefit from division of labor, which leads to increasing returns to the scale of the firm's employment, but also face decreasing returns to the fixed factor of entrepreneurship. (According to Clark, entrepreneurs provide the service of coordination among the workers in the firm. If there is only one worker there is no need for coordination, but also no scope for division of labor). We think of a firm as a coalition and a worker working independently as a singleton coalition. Thus

Table 12.E3 | JBC Game

Number of workers	Product
1	11
2	33
3	45
4	50
5	50

- A singleton coalition of one worker gets a payoff of 10 (from craft production).

- A singleton coalition of one entrepreneur gets nothing (he has nothing to coordinate).

- A coalition of one or more entrepreneurs and one or more workers gets a payoff that depends on the number of workers (but not on the number of entrepreneurs) according to Table 12.E3.

Since workers and entrepreneurs are alike and substitutable, we need not look at all coalition structures, but only at those that differ in the number of workers in a coalition. Moreover, since a second entrepreneur can add nothing to a coalition we will ignore coalitions of more than one entrepreneur.

1. List all distinct coalition structures for this game.
2. Describe the core of the game.
3. Suppose that instead of two entrepreneurs there were three. Repeat steps 1 and 2.

12.4 **The Make Room Game.** Consider the following three-person game in normal form. The three players are Al, Bob, and Carl (A, B, and C). Payoff order is Bob, Carl, Al. The payoffs are shown in Table 12.E4.

Analyze this game as both a noncooperative game and a cooperative TU game.

Table **12.E4** | A Crowding Game

		Al			
		up		down	
		Carl		Carl	
		up	down	up	down
Bob	up	3, 3, 3	5, 0, 5	5, 5, 0	12, 0, 0
	down	0, 5, 5	0, 0, 12	0, 12, 0	1, 1, 1

12.5 **A Business Partnership.** Gina, Harry, and Laura are interested in starting a small firm in some field related to Web site design. Gina is a skilled computer technician, Harry a talented graphic artist, and Laura a dynamite salesperson.

The payoffs to coalitions among these three players are shown in Table 12.E5. Initials grouped in parentheses represent a coalition, so that (HL) means a coalition of Harry and Laura (that is, Harry and Laura form the new firm and Gina goes it alone), and the payoffs to coalitions are shown in parentheses in the same order in the second column.

What coalition structures are in the core of this game? What are the payoffs to Gina, Harry, and Laura in the core? Why?

Table **12.E5** | Payoffs for Partners

(GHL)	(55)
(G) (HL)	(5) (35)
(H) (GL)	(5) (35)
(L) (GH)	(15) (30)
(G) (H) (L)	(20) (20) (5)

12.6 **The Band Game.** According to a song recorded by the country music diva Emmylou Harris, "If you're going to play in Texas, you gotta have a fiddle in the band." A band is a coalition, and it has to choose a strategy—a musical style and venues in which to play—that suits the talents and the instruments played by the musicians who form the coalition. What Emmylou is telling us is that the "rules of the game" are such that a band without a fiddle is unwise to choose to play (country music) in a Texas venue.

Table 12.E6 | Musicians in Bands in Three Towns

Number of players	Instruments	Symbol
2	guitar	G
2	drums	D
1	banjo	Bj
1	bass	Bs
1	mandolin	M
1	fiddle	F
1	accordion	A
1	horn	H

Table 12.E7 | Styles, Towns, Payoffs, and Instruments Required

Style	Instruments	Towns and Payoffs		
		San Marcos	Lafayette	Branson
Bluegrass	BjMGF	1	1	1
Old-Time Country	BGF	3	1	1
Contemporary Country	GGFD	2	1	3
Rock	GGBsD	0	1	2
Cajun	GAFD	0	3	2
Jazz	GBsDH	0	2	0
Request	GGFDBjBsMAH	4	4	4

Here is an example based on that insight: We have a 10-person cooperative game in which the 10 players are 10 musicians who play 8 instruments. The instruments, number of players of each instrument, and the symbols we will use for each instrument are shown in Table 12.E6. The bands can play in one of three towns with different regional tastes: San Marcos, Texas; Lafayette, Louisiana; and Branson, Missouri. They can also choose among three country styles and three noncountry styles. The grand coalition of all ten musicians could choose to form a Request band, since they can play in any of the styles at request. Since tastes differ from town to town, the choice of a town and a style together constitute the coordinated strategy for a coalition. Assume that a coalition will always choose the strategy that gives it the greatest payoff, and that more than one band can play in any town. The styles and payoffs and instruments required for each style are shown in Table 12.E7.

Table 12.E7, for example, tells us that a Bluegrass Band cannot be formed by a coalition that does not include at least one banjo, mandolin, guitar, and fiddle (BjMGF), and that a band playing in that style will earn 1 unit payoff in any of the three towns. The limitations on what instruments are required for a style are the "rules of the game" that limit the coalitions that can be formed.

Treating this as a TU game, list all possible coalition structures and the payoffs to all coalitions in each coalition structure. Describe the solution set for this game. Explain. Describe the core of this game. Explain.

Applications of the Core to Economics

A lthough the concept of the core of a cooperative game can be applied to applications in any field, it was inspired by the work of the nineteenth-century economist F. Y. Edgeworth, and has been conceived mainly with applications in economics in mind. This

To best understand this chapter 13

To best understand this chapter you need to have studied and understood the material from Chapters 1–4, 6, 11, and 12. A background in the principles of economics will also be helpful.

chapter considers some applications in economics. As usual, we will avoid any mathematical treatment, instead making a few extra simplifying assumptions.

A Market Game

Economists often claim that *increasing competition* (an increasing number of participants on both sides of the market, demanders and suppliers) limits monopoly power. Our market game is designed to bring out that idea.

The concept of the core, and the effect of increasing competition on the core, can be illustrated by a fairly simple numerical example. We will assume that there are just two goods: "widgets" and "money." We will also assume that the subjective payoff (*utility*) is proportional to money. In other words, we assume that the subjective benefits a person obtains from her or his possessions can be expressed in money terms, as is done in cost-benefit analysis. In a model of this kind, *money* is a stand-in for "all other goods and services." Thus, people derive utility from holding money—that is, from spending on "all other goods and services," so that we can use equivalent amounts of "money" or "all other goods and services" as a measure of the utility of widgets. Since money is transferable, in effect we have *transferable utility*.

Some terminology from microeconomic principles will be helpful, here. (Students who have studied microeconomic principles will find it familiar.) In microeconomics, we think of **utility** as a measure of the overall benefits a person gets from consuming goods and services, and define the **marginal utility** or **marginal benefit** of a particular good or service as the additional utility the person derives from one more unit of the good or service. Thus, for

Definition

Marginal Utility—The additional utility a person obtains as a result of increasing the consumption of a good or service by one is called the **marginal utility** of the good or service. If measured in monetary units, it is called the **marginal benefit**.

example, the marginal utility of widgets is the additional utility the person derives from possessing and enjoying one more widget. In Table 13.1, for example, Jeff derives $15 worth of utility from two widgets and $18 worth from three. Thus, his marginal utility or benefit from the third widget is $18 - 15 = 3$. If Jeff then acquires two more widgets, increasing his consumption to five, his utility is increased to 22. We can approximate his marginal utility of the fourth and fifth widgets by $MU = \Delta U/\Delta \text{widgets} = (22 - 18)/2 = 2$. When we assume that utility is proportional to money payoffs, we are assuming that the marginal utility of "all other goods and services" is (near enough) constant. We can then measure utility in monetary units, and conventionally we then use the term *marginal benefit* interchangeably with *marginal utility.*

The Core of a Two-Person Exchange Game

We will begin with an example in which there are just two persons, Jeff and Adam. At the beginning of the game, Jeff has five widgets but no money, and Adam has $22 but no widgets. The benefits functions are shown in Table 13.1.

As we learn in microeconomic principles, Adam's demand curve for widgets will be his marginal benefit curve, while Jeff's supply curve will be his marginal cost curve. In this case Jeff's cost is an **opportunity cost:** the benefit he has to give up when he sells a widget. Thus, it is shown as the reverse of his marginal benefit curve. These are shown in Figure 13.1. **Market equilibrium** comes where $p = 3$, $Q = 2$, (i.e., Jeff sells Adam two widgets for a total payment of $6). The two transactors then have total benefits as shown in Table 13.2. The total benefit divided between the two persons is $24 + $29 = $53.

Now we want to look at this from the point of view of the core. The strategies that Jeff and Adam can choose are unilateral transfers—Jeff can give up 0, 1, 2, 3, 4, or 5 widgets, and Adam can give up from 0 to 22 dollars.

Table 13.1 | Payoffs in a Bilateral Trade Game

Jeff			Adam		
widgets	benefits		widgets	benefits	
	total	marginal		total	marginal
1	10	10	1	9	9
2	15	5	2	13	4
3	18	3	3	15	2
4	21	3	4	16	1
5	22	1	5	16	0

Figure 13.1 | Adam's Demand and Jeff's Supply of Widgets

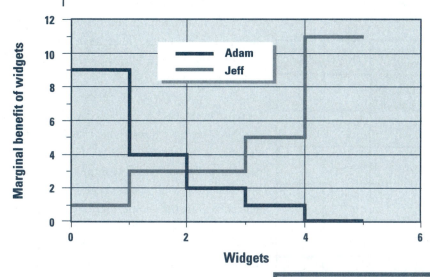

Presumably, both would choose "zero" in a noncooperative game. The possible coalitions are (1) a grand coalition of both persons, or (2) two singleton coalitions in which each person goes it alone. In this case, a cooperative solution might involve a grand coalition of the two players. In fact, a cooperative solution to this game is a coordinated pair of strategies in which Jeff gives up some widgets to Adam and Adam gives up some money to Jeff. (In more ordinary terms, that is, of course, a market transaction.) The core will consist of all such coordinated strategies such that (1) neither person (singleton coalition) can do better by going it alone, and (2) the coalition of the two cannot do better by a different coordination of their strategies. In this game, the core will be a set of transactions, each of which fulfills both of those conditions.

Let us illustrate both conditions: First, suppose Jeff offers to sell Adam one widget for $10. But Adam's marginal benefit is only nine—Adam can do better by going it alone and not buying anything. Thus, "one widget for $10" is not in the core. Second, suppose Jeff proposes to sell Adam one widget for $5. Adam's total benefit would then be 22 − 5 + 9 = 26, Jeff's 5 + 21 = 26. Both are better off, with a total benefit of 52. However,

> ## Definition
>
> **Cost and Supply**—The **opportunity cost** of any good or service consists of the other goods or services we have to give up in order to obtain it. The money cost is the money measure of the opportunity cost. The **marginal cost** is the additional cost of selling one more unit. Generally, the marginal cost is the price on the supply curve.

> ## Definition
>
> **Market Equilibrium**—The price high enough so that the quantity offered by suppliers is equal to the quantity demanded is the **market equilibrium price**, and the quantity traded at that price is the **market equilibrium quantity**.

Table 13.2 | Total Benefits to Jeff and Adam

	Jeff	Adam
widgets	18	13
money	6	16
total	24	29

Table 13.3 | Benefits to Jeff and Adam Depending on the Number of Widgets Sold

quantity sold	benefit of widgets		money	total
	to Jeff	to Adam		
0	22	0	22	44
1	21	9	22	52
2	18	13	22	53
3	15	15	22	52
4	10	16	22	48
5	0	16	22	38

Table 13.4 | Some Prices for the Trade between Jeff and Adam, and the Distribution of Benefits

quantity sold	total payment	total benefits	
		Jeff's	Adam's
2	12	18 + 12 = 30	22 − 12 + 13 = 23
2	5	18 + 5 = 23	22 − 5 + 13 = 30
2	8	18 + 8 = 26	22 − 8 + 13 = 27

they can do better, if Jeff now sells Adam a second widget for $3.50. Adam now has benefits of 13 + 22 − 8.50 = 26.50, and Jeff has benefits of 18 + 8.50 = 26.50, for a total benefit of 53. Thus, a sale of just one widget is not in the core. In fact, the core will include only transactions in which exactly two widgets are sold.

We can check for this in the following way. We recall that the core is contained within the solution set. Since we have transferable utility, the only transactions in the solution set will be transactions that maximize the total benefits for the two persons. When the two persons shift from a transaction that does not maximize benefits to one that does, they can divide the increase in benefits among themselves in the form of money, and both be better off—so a transaction that does not maximize benefits cannot satisfy condition (2) above. From Table 13.3, we see that a trade of 2 maximizes total benefits.

But we have not figured out the price at which the two units will be sold. This is not necessarily the competitive supply-and-demand price, since the two traders are both monopolists and one may successfully hold out for a better-than-competitive price. Table 13.4 shows some possible transactions and side payments.

What all of these transactions have in common is that the total benefits are maximized—at 53—but the benefits are distributed in very different ways between the two traders. All the same, each trader does no worse than the 22 of benefits he can have without trading at all. Thus, each of these transactions is in the core.

It will be clear, then, that there are a wide range of transactions in the core of this two-person game. We may visualize the core in a diagram with the benefits to Jeff on the horizontal axis and benefits to Adam on the vertical axis. It is shown as Figure 13.2. The core then is the line segment $\overline{ab}$. Algebraically, it is the line BA = 53 − BJ, where BA means "Adam's benefits" and BJ means "Jeff's benefits," and the line is bounded by BA ≥ 22 and BJ ≥ 22. The competitive equilibrium is at C.

The large size of the core is something of a problem. The cooperative solution must be one of the transactions in the core, but which one? In the two-person game, there is just no answer. The supply-and-demand approach does give a definite answer, shown as point C in Figure 13.2. According to the supply-and-demand story, this equilibrium comes about because there are many buyers and many sellers. In our example, instead, we have just one of each, a bilateral monopoly. That would seem to be the problem: The core is large because the number of buyers and sellers is small.

The Core with More than Two Pairs of Traders

So what happens if we allow the number of buyers and sellers to increase until it is very large? To keep things simple, we will continue to suppose that there are just two kinds of people—jeffs and adams—and we will assume that every jeff begins the game with 5 widgets, and every adam with $22. Each jeff and each adam has just the same endowment and benefit function as before. However, we will consider a sequence of games with 2, 3, . . . , 10, . . . , 100, . . . adams and an equal number of jeffs and see what happens to the core of these games as the number of traders gets large.

First, suppose that there are just two jeffs and two adams. What coalitions are possible in this larger economy? There could be two one-to-one coalitions of a jeff and an adam. Two jeffs or two adams could, in principle, form a coalition; but since they would have nothing to exchange, there would be little point in it. There could also be coalitions of two jeffs and an adam, two adams and a jeff, or a grand coalition of both jeffs and both adams.

We want to show that this bigger game has a smaller core. There are some transactions in the core of the first game that are not in this one. Here is an example: In the two-person game, an exchange of $12 dollars for two widgets is in the core. But it is not in the core of this game. At an exchange of $12 for 2, each adam gets total benefits of 23, each jeff 30. Suppose, then, that a jeff forms a coalition with two adams, so that the jeff sells each adam

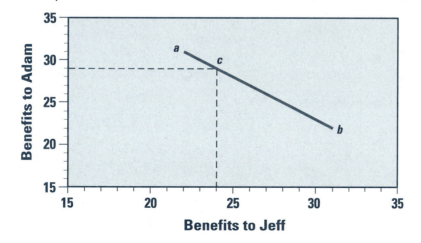

Figure 13.2 | Limit to the Net Benefits to Jeff and Adam

one widget for $7. The jeff gets total benefits of 18 + 7 + 7 = 32, and so is better off. Each adam gets benefits of 15 + 9 = 24, and so is better off. This three-person coalition—which could not have been formed in the two-person game—"dominates" the 12-for-2 coalition structure, and so the 12-for-2 coalition structure is not in the core of the four-person game. Of course, the other jeff is out in the cold, but that's his problem—the three-person coalition is better off. But, in fact, we are not saying that the three-person coalition is in the core, either. It probably isn't, since the odd jeff out is likely to make an offer that would dominate this one.

This is illustrated by the diagram in Figure 13.3. Line segment $\overline{de}$ shows the trade-off between benefits to the jeffs and the adams in a three-person, two adam, coalition. It means that, from any point on line segment $\overline{fb}$, a shift to a three-person coalition makes it possible to move to the northwest—making all members of the coalition better off—to a point on $\overline{fe}$. Thus, all of the coalition structures on $\overline{fb}$ are dominated, and not in the core of the four-person game.

Here is another example. In the two-person game, an exchange of two widgets for five dollars is in the core. Again, it will not be in the core of a four-person game. Each jeff gets benefits of 23 and each adam of 30. Now, suppose an adam proposes a coalition with both jeffs. The adam will pay each jeff $2.40 for one widget. The adam then has 30.20 of benefits and so is better off. Each jeff gets 23.40 of benefits and is also better off. Thus the one-adam-and-two-jeffs coalition dominates the 2-for-5 coalition, which is no longer in the core. Figure 13.4 illustrates the situation we now have. The benefit trade-off for a two-jeff-one-adam coalition is shown by line $\overline{gj}$. Every coalition structure on $\overline{ab}$ to the left of h is dominated. Putting everything together, we see that coalition structures on $\overline{ab}$ to the left of h and to the right of f are dominated by three-person coalitions, but the three-person coalitions are dominated by the two-person coalitions between h and f. (Four-person coalitions function like pairs of two-person coalitions, adding nothing to the game.)

Figure 13.3 | Limits to the Payoffs to an Adam or a Jeff in a Four-Person Game

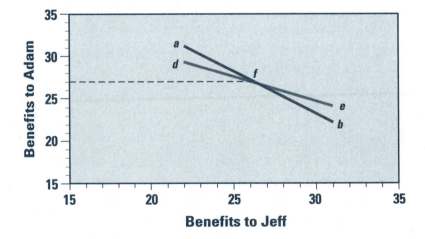

Figure 13.4 | More Limits in the Four-Person Game

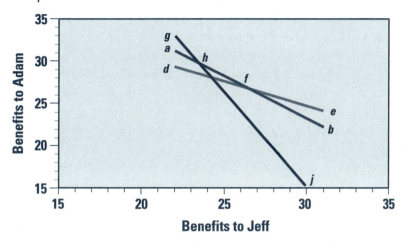

We can now see the core of the four-person game in Figure 13.4. It is shown by the line segment $\overline{hf}$. It is limited by BA ≥ 27, BJ ≥ 24. The core of the four-person game is part of the core of the two-person game, but it is a smaller part, because the four-person game allows for coalitions that cannot be formed in the two-person game. Some of these coalitions dominate some of the coalitions in the core of the smaller game. This illustrates an important point about the core. The bigger the game, the greater the variety of coalitions that can be formed. The more coalitions there are, often, the smaller the core.

Let us pursue this line of reasoning one more step, considering a six-person game with three jeffs and three adams. We notice that a trade of two widgets for $8 is in the core of the four-person game and we will see that it is not in the core of the six-person game. Beginning from the 2-for-8 coalition structure, a coalition of two jeffs and three adams is proposed,[1] such that each jeff gives up three widgets and each adam buys two, at a price of 3.80 each. The results are shown in Table 13.5.

Table 13.5 | A Shift to a 2-Jeff, 3-Adam Coalition

Type	Old coalition structure			New coalition structure		
	widgets	money	total benefits	widgets	money	total benefits
Jeff	4	8	26	3	11.4	26.4
Adam	2	14	27	2	14.4	27.4

1 Larger coalitions play a key role in this model. In more general versions of the model, we allow for fractional trades, smooth marginal benefit curves, or for barter trade without transferable utility. In these cases, the size of the coalitions can increase without limit, and the core of every game with a finite number of players can include allocations other than the competitive equilibrium, although the core becomes smaller and smaller around the competitive equilibrium. This brings to the fore another important assumption of the model: There are no limits on the size of coalitions, and no cost of coalition formation. If there were such limits or costs, the results might be different.

We see that both the adams and the jeffs within the coalition are better off, so the 2-and-3 coalition dominates the 2-for-8 bilateral trade. Thus, the 2-for-8 trade is not in the core of the six-person game.

What is in it? This is shown by Figure 13.5. As before, the line segment $\overline{ab}$ is the core of the two-person game and line segment $\overline{gj}$ is the benefits trade-off for the coalition of two jeffs and one adam. Segment $\overline{kl}$ is the benefits trade-off for the coalition of two jeffs and three adams. We see that every point on $\overline{ab}$ except point h is dominated, either by a 2-jeff, 1-adam coalition or by a 2-jeff, 3-adam coalition. The core of a six-player game is exactly one coalition structure: the one at point h. And this is the competitive equilibrium! No stable coalition can do better than it.

If we were to look at games with 8, 10, 100, 1,000, or 1,000,000 players, we would find the same core. This series of examples illustrates a key point about the core of an exchange game: As the number of participants (of each type) increases without limit, the core of the game shrinks down to the competitive equilibrium. This result can be generalized in various ways. First, we should observe that in some types of games, any game with a finite number of players has more than one coalition structure in the core. This game has been simplified by allowing players to trade in only whole numbers of widgets. That is one reason why the core shrinks to the competitive equilibrium so soon in our example. We may also eliminate the assumption of transferable utility, assuming instead that utility is nontransferable and not proportional to money. We can also allow for more than two kinds of players, and get rid of the "types" assumption completely, at the cost of much greater mathematical complexity. But the general idea is simple enough.

With more participants, more kinds of coalitions can form, and some of those coalitions dominate coalitions that could form in smaller games. Thus, a bigger game will have a smaller

Figure 13.5 | Limits to Payoffs in a Six-Person Exchange Game

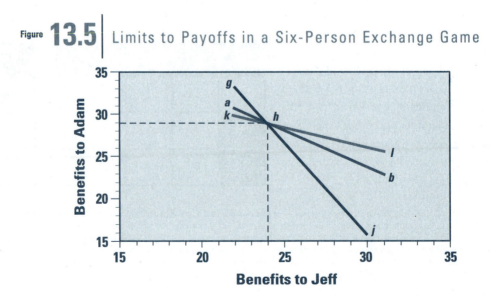

A Closer Look

Cooperation and Competition

Is the competitive supply and demand model a cooperative or a noncooperative model? In chapters 10 and 11 we have seen the supply-and-demand equilibrium as a noncooperative equilibrium. A traditional view in microeconomic theory is based on the idea of a *tattonement*, or auction market. In an ideal auction market, the rules of the game are such that the buyers and sellers can bid noncooperatively, and all trades take place at the price that makes the quantity supplied equal to the quantity demanded. Some markets (such as stock markets) have literal auctions, but it is argued that many other markets function "as if" they were auction markets. In any case, interactions in an auction market are noncooperative. What is interesting and important is that these noncooperative interactions can do the work of a potentially complex cooperative process of coalition formation. If markets in general really do function "as if" they were auction markets, then the noncooperative auction market equilibrium and the ideal cooperative coalition system with an unlimited number of players have the same outcomes.

Why then study the core of a market game? For two reasons. First, multilateral deals—coalitions—can be important in some real markets, as we saw in the last chapter. Second, the cooperative model of market games helps us to understand the importance of having many participants on both sides of the market. That is a traditional assumption of the "competitive model," but does not play a leading role in the noncooperative models of markets. It seems that both the cooperative and noncooperative models can help us to understand real competitive markets.

core; in that sense, "more competition limits monopoly power." But (in a market game) the supply and demand is the one coalition structure that is always in the core. And this provides us with a new understanding of the unique role of the market equilibrium.

The Core of a Public Goods Contribution Game

For another example of the core of a cooperative game, let us look at a social dilemma—specifically, the three-person Public Goods Contribution Game from Chapter 6. We know that noncooperative solutions are particularly unsatisfactory in social dilemmas—that is what makes them social dilemmas! Suppose, then, that the players in the Public Goods Contribution Game can find a way to make binding and therefore credible commitments to coordinate their strategies. How will the contribution game go in that case? The payoffs for the contribution game are shown again as Table 13.6.

We recall that the game has a dominant strategy equilibrium: don't contribute. Suppose that the three players form the grand coalition.

Table 13.6 | A Contribution Game

Repeats Table 6.5, Chapter 6

		Larry			
		contribute		don't contribute	
		Karl		Karl	
		contribute	don't contribute	contribute	don't contribute
Jack	contribute	1.5, 1.5, 1.5	0.5, 2, 0.5	0.5, 0.5, 2	−0.5, 1, 1
Jack	don't contribute	2, 0.5, 0.5	1, 1, −0.5	1, −0.5, 1	0, 0, 0

By coordinating their strategies and playing (contribute, contribute, contribute), they can generate 4.5 of total benefits. If they were to shift from (don't contribute, contribute, contribute) to (contribute, contribute, contribute), Karl and Larry could each make a side payment of 0.5 to Jack and so everyone would be better off; therefore (don't contribute, contribute, contribute) is not efficient. Indeed, since no other coalition structure can pay a total greater than 3, a shift to (contribute, contribute, contribute) from any other coalition structure can, with appropriate side payments, make everyone better off. (Verify this by listing other possible shifts and indicating whether side payments are needed to make everyone better off, and what they are.) We conclude that the grand coalition and (contribute, contribute, contribute) are the solution set for the game.

But what about the core? Is the grand coalition stable against defection? By dropping out and forming a singleton coalition, Jack can increase his payoff to 2, provided that the coalition of Karl and Larry continue to contribute. And, in fact (contribute, contribute) is the best response of the (Karl, Larry) coalition to a no-contribute strategy by Jack. Eliminating both their contributions would reduce the (Karl, Larry) coalition's total payoff to 0 from 1. Karl and Larry cannot do any better than 1 by any other coordinated strategy. Thus, when Jack chooses (don't contribute) and the Karl-Larry coalition chooses (contribute, contribute), we have a *Nash equilibrium between the coalitions*, and so the payoffs for this coalition structure are (2, 0.5, 0.5). On the other hand, if either Karl or Larry were to drop out of their coalition, the new Nash equilibrium among the coalitions would be (don't contribute, don't contribute, don't contribute), making them both worse off, so the (Karl, Larry) coalition would remain. This, in turn, means Jack's total payoff (game payoff plus side payments) has to be at least 2 in order to keep him in the grand coalition.

But Karl and Larry can both make the same shift, with the same results. So each of them has to have a total payoff of 2 as well. That could happen only if the total payout were 6, but in fact it is only 4.5. We conclude that the grand coalition is not stable. Since the grand coalition is the only coalition in the solution set, and the core is either encompassed in the solution set or is empty, we find that the core of this game is empty.

It seems that we are back where we started. Without binding commitments, there is no satisfactory solution to the contribution game. With binding commitments, there is no solution at all, because no coalition is stable against defection that increases the payoffs of those who defect. We have moved from individual egoism to coalitional egoism—and it doesn't help!

It seems that, to get the solution set for a social dilemma, we need some limit on the coalitions that can be formed. In this case, the "rules of the game" would have to outlaw singleton coalitions. Suppose, for example, the rules said "You must choose a strategy that you would want everyone else to choose." Then everyone would choose "contribute." But with these rules, we have entered the world of ethical theory. "Choose according to a rule that you could wish to have everyone adopt" is the Kantian categorical imperative from ethical theory.

Another possibility would be to require that each player choose the strategy designated by a majority vote. Everyone would then vote for "contribute," and the public good would be provided by government and paid for by taxation. This takes us into the world of social contract theory and social mechanism design.

In short, when we think of social dilemmas in terms of cooperative games, we find ourselves drawn to the common ground of game theory and social or moral philosophy, because of the conflict of results between two major concepts of cooperative-game solution: the (efficient) solution set and the core.

Monopoly and Regulation

The previous examples give two contrasting applications of the concept of the core in economics. On the one hand, the shifting of coalitions can progressively limit the price in a market to the unique supply-and-demand equilibrium price. On the other hand, the shifting of coalitions can lead to an empty core, and this implies that public goods will not be supplied, even in a cooperative game, without some further restriction or commitment on the part of the players. The University of Chicago economist Lester Telser has argued that empty-core games provide a rationale for government regulation of markets.[2] Let us see how that works.

We will begin with a "natural" monopoly in a very small economy. The game has six players: Monopocorp, which has the capacity to produce monopostuff, and five consumers, Ann, Bob, Carole, Don, and Elaine, each of whom would like to consume some monopostuff, provided the price is right.

Monopocorp's costs depend on how much monopostuff it produces. The cost function rule is

$$cost = \begin{cases} 0 \text{ if } q=0 \\ 7+5q \text{ if } q>0 \end{cases}$$

where q is Monopocorp's production of monopostuff.

The five consumers have no capacity to produce monopostuff, but each would like to buy just one unit. They differ in how much they are willing to pay. Each has a different reservation price. The reservation price is the highest price the person will pay, and the consumer's payoff in the game is the reservation price minus the price actually paid. The reservation prices for the five customers are shown in Table 13.7.

Table 13.7 Reservation Prices for Buyers of Monopostuff

Ann	10
Bob	9
Carole	8
Don	7
Elaine	6

2 Lester Telser, *Economic Theory and the Core* (Chicago: University of Chicago Press, 1978). See also L.G. Telser, "Competition and the Core," *Journal of Political Economy* 104, 1 (February 1996), pp. 85–107.

Table 13.8 | Determinants of Profits for Monocorp

q	Price	Total revenue	Marginal revenue	Marginal cost	Profit
1	10	10	10	5	−2
2	9	18	8	5	1
3	8	24	6	5	2
4	7	28	4	5	1
5	6	30	2	5	−2

> **Definition**
>
> *Marginal Revenue*—A monopoly's **marginal revenue** is the additional revenue it will realize by cutting its price (without price discrimination).

> **Rule**
>
> *Monopoly Profit Maximization*—Without price discrimination, a monopoly maximizes its profits by increasing its output so long as its marginal revenue is greater than its marginal cost.

Knowing the reservation prices, and knowing that no consumer will buy more than one unit at any price, makes it easy to construct the demand relationship. It is shown in Table 13.8.

Students who have studied the principles of microeconomics will recognize some of the terminology in Table 13.8. The **marginal revenue** is the monopoly's additional revenue from selling one more unit of monopostuff, assuming the monopoly charges the same price for every unit it sells. To sell a third unit of monopostuff (to Carole), the monopoly must cut its price to 8 (since Carole will not pay any higher price) so that Monopocorp finds itself selling three units at 8 for a revenue of 24 rather than two units at 9 for a revenue of 18. The difference, 24 − 18 = 6, is the marginal revenue on the third unit. The marginal cost is the additional cost of producing one more unit of monopostuff. In this case it is a constant, 5. The microeconomic principles textbook teaches us that the monopoly will **maximize its profits** by increasing its sales so long as the marginal revenue is greater than the marginal cost. Thus, the textbook discussion of monopoly leads us to expect that Monopocorp will sell to Ann, Bob, and Carole at a price of 8, and Don and Elaine will not buy any monopostuff. That is, the coalition structure will consist of (Monopocorp, Ann, Bob, Carole) and (Don) and (Elaine) as singletons.

This is inefficient. The monopoly price results in a *consumers' surplus* of 3. That is, Ann gets something she values at 10 for a price of 8, retaining a surplus of 10 − 8 = 2, and Bob gets a similar surplus of 1. The monopoly gets a profit of 2, so the total benefits to this coalition structure are 5, the sum of the consumers' surplus and the monopolist's profits. Suppose, instead, that the grand coalition were formed and monopostuff were sold at a price of 5. Monopocorp would lose its fixed cost of 7, but the consumers' surplus would be 5 (for Ann) + 4 (for Bob) + 3 (for Carole) + 2 (for Don) + 1 (for Elaine) = 15. Thus, the solution set for this problem includes only coalition structures that yield net payoffs of 15 − 7 = 8.

Indeed, the monopoly policy of selling only three units to keep the price up is not in the core. Monopocorp can produce one more unit at a cost of 5, and Don would be willing to pay up to 7 for it. If Monopocorp were to offer one unit to Don at a price of 6, its profits would increase to 3, while Don would also be better off with a payoff of 1 rather than 0. Thus, (Monopocorp, Ann,

Bob, Carole, Don) dominates (Monopocorp, Ann, Bob, Carole). Similarly, if Monopocorp produces a fifth unit and offers it to Elaine for 5.5, Monopocorp's profits are increased to 3.5, while Elaine is better off with 0.5 than she would be with 0 as a singleton. Thus, (Monopocorp, Ann, Bob, Carole, Don, Elaine) dominates (Monopocorp, Ann, Bob, Carole, Don). In fact, the only coalition structure in the core is the grand coalition of all six players. This is efficient—the maximum net payoffs of 8 are realized—but notice that it can be accomplished only with price discrimination. A nondiscriminatory price strategy cannot be in the core of this game.

The monopoly game *does* have a nonempty core, but it is not the kind of equilibrium we study in the microeconomic principles textbooks! The core approach tells us to look for **price discrimination**, while the microeconomic textbook approach tells us to look for restric-

tion of output as a means of pushing up the price. No doubt there are some monopolies that operate primarily as the microeconomic textbook describes. It may not always be possible to practice price discrimination. Sellers of tickets to concerts and athletic events, for example, may try to practice price discrimination, only to be undercut by scalpers. This is a noncooperative equilibrium. On the other side, a broad study of real-world monopolies will give many examples of price discrimination.

Now we change the game by adding a second potential producer of monopostuff, Newcorp. Newcorp has a different cost relationship than Monopocorp. For Newcorp,

$$cost = \left\{ \begin{array}{l} 6q \text{ if } q < 4 \\ 18 + 8\,(q-3)\text{ if } q > 3 \end{array} \right\}$$

that is, Newcorp's marginal cost is 6 for the first three units and 8 for all additional units. Now, (Monopocorp, Ann, Bob, Carole, Don, Elaine) is no longer in the core of this game. Suppose, as before, that Monopocorp sells to Ann, Bob, and Carole at 8, to Don at 6, and to Elaine at 5.5, for a total revenue of 35.5, cost of 32, and profit of 3.5. Newcorp can sell to Ann, Bob, and Carole at 6.25 and make a profit. The coalition of Newcorp, Ann, Bob, and Carole dominates the original, price-discriminatory coalition. If Monopocorp offers those three lower prices to bring them back, it cannot get more than 18.75 of revenue from them. In fact, since Newcorp will sell to any three at any price greater than 6, the greatest revenue Monopocorp can get from the five customers is now 6 × 5 = 30, and so Monocorp cannot avoid losing money.

Monopocorp will not join a coalition on terms that would cause it to take a loss—it can break even by staying out of business entirely. To cover its cost in the grand coalition, Monopocorp has to get an average price of at least 6.4 = 5 + 7/5. (The fixed cost of 7 is divided over 5 customers.) Since Elaine will pay no more than 6, some of the other customers have to pay more than 6.4. But competition with Newcorp will not allow this to happen. No matter how Monopocorp assesses its fixed costs over Ann, Bob, Carole, and Don, some of them will join a coalition with Newcorp that dominates the coalition of five customers and Monopocorp.

Table 13.9 Costs and Total Payoffs Depending on How Customers are Served

Monopocorp customers	Newcorp customers	Total cost	Total payoffs
5	0	32	8
4	1	33	7
3	2	34	6
2	3	35	5
1	4	38	2
0	5	34	6

The truth is that no matter how the five customers are distributed between the two suppliers, there is no stable coalition structure. To see that, we first ask what coalition structures can be in the solution set. To be in the solution set, the coalition structure has to yield the highest possible total payoffs. Table 13.9 shows the total payoffs resulting from different numbers of customers associating with the two sellers. (Since Monopocorp can always sell more cheaply when it has more customers, we can rule out any coalition structures in which some customers are not served).

What we see in Table 13.9 is that any coalition structure other than {(Monopocorp, Ann, Bob, Carole, Don, Elaine)(Newcorp)} leads to higher costs and therefore to lower total payoffs. It follows that only {(Monopocorp, Ann, Bob, Carole, Don, Elaine)(Newcorp)} is in the solution set. But any coalition structure in the core must be in the solution set, and since the only coalition structure in the solution set—{(Monopocorp, Ann, Bob, Carole, Don, Elaine) (Newcorp)} is not in the core, the core must be empty.

In more ordinary economic terms, here is the story. Monopocorp is using a technology with economies of scale, with two results. First, Monopocorp can serve the entire population cheaply, and second, the more customers Monopocorp serves, the more efficient it can be. Newcorp is using a different technology. Newcorp's technology has decreasing returns to scale, perhaps because it uses some natural resource that is in very limited supply. Because of that, Newcorp can serve a few customers fairly cheaply, although it costs more for Newcorp to serve all five than for Monopocorp to do so. By taking a few customers away from Monopocorp, however, Newcorp can prevent Monopocorp from making effective use of its large-scale technology, and because of that possibility, there is no coalition structure that cannot be improved on by some new coalition.

However, regulation might stabilize the game. Suppose, for example, that a law were to be passed that prohibits dealing with customers individually or in smaller groups, but instead requires that competitors in this market make joint offers to all five customers. Since the cost to Newcorp of serving all five customers is 34, Newcorp will have to charge a total of 34 in some combination. Monopocorp, however, can beat that with a total charge of 33 and still make a profit of 1. Thus, the regulation will lead to a stable and efficient coalition structure. Traditional rate-of-return regulation is much more complex, of course (as it deals with more complex real-world industries) but typically requires the regulated public utility to serve an entire region, and to propose a schedule of prices and charges, with limited price discrimination and a limited rate of profit, on the basis of which it offers to sell to anyone in the service area. At the same time competitors are prohibited from chipping away customers from the public utility.

In this example, the core is empty because efficient coalition structures are dominated—people can defect to coalitions that can promise them more than they can get from an efficient coalition structure. What government regulation does in such a case is to prohibit some of the coalitions. Ruling out some coalitions by means of regulation may allow an efficient coalition to form and to remain stable—the coalitions through which it might be dominated are prohibited by regulation.

Summary

It is generally agreed that the solution of a nonconstant sum game must be in the solution set, that is, must be efficient in traditional economic terms. However, in many economic (and other) applications, there are very many coalition structures and strategies that may be in the solution set. The core narrows the possibilities by considering only those coalition structures and side payments that are stable in the face of defections by new coalitions. The idea is that—although it is possible for a coalition to make a binding commitment to a common strategy with side payments—a group will not make that commitment when they have the possibility of forming a coalition among themselves and doing better still.

The core narrows the possibilities by ruling out those coalition structures that are not stable. The more possible coalitions there are, the narrower these limits are likely to become, since more coalitions can rule out more possibilities. When we apply this idea to games of exchange, we find a new way of interpreting the traditional idea that the supply and demand equilibrium is realized when there are many buyers and many sellers. In an exchange game with relatively few participants, the core may be quite large, but as the number of participants grows, the core is narrowed. But it is narrowed in a very specific way. No matter how large the population becomes, the supply-and-demand equilibrium is always in the core. As the game gets larger, every other coalition and side payment structure is eliminated.

On the other hand, monopoly is a deep problem for cooperative game theory. The traditional model of profit maximizing monopoly is not in the core, and (at least for natural monopoly) the core may require price discrimination. Moreover, when a natural monopoly is open to competition, the core may be empty. Regulations, by limiting the coalitions that may be formed, can stabilize an efficient coalition structure in the core. The trend to deregulation in recent decades, based on the idea that market competition always promotes efficiency, may be based on a false premise.

When we apply the core to public goods, we get even worse news. Even for quite small public goods games, the core is empty. Thus, although we look to enforceable agreements—probably through a political mechanism—for a supply of public goods, there is the possibility that continued conflict among coalitions may make the supply of public goods even more difficult than we had supposed.

Exercises and Discussion Questions

13.1 **Collusive Pricing.** Collusive pricing is a cooperative agreement among a few firms selling the same product (an *oligopoly*) to restrain production and keep the price up in order to divide profits among themselves. Many economists hold that profitable collusive pricing is unstable. Suppose that three firms collusively charge the same high price. What is the coalition structure implied by this description?

13.2 **Production.** The supply-and-demand model in this chapter considers only exchange, but there is no production. How would it change if jeffs could produce widgets? How would it change if adams could produce widgets?

13.3 **Public Goods with *N* Players.** What difference would it make to the core of the public goods contribution game if there were more than three players?

13.4 **The Queuing Game.** In Chapter 11, we looked at a game that has an inefficient non-cooperative equilibrium: the Queuing Game. Analyze that game as a cooperative game. Describe the core of the Queuing Game and explain your description. Compare the Queuing Game with the games discussed in this chapter.

13.5 **Dividing a Dollar.** Tom, Dick, and Harry have inherited a large sum of money on the condition that they decide for themselves how to divide it. The terms of the will say that they must decide by majority rule what proportion of the bequest is to go to each of the three heirs. Analyze the core of this game.

14 Sequential Games

To best understand this chapter 14

To best understand this chapter you need to have studied and understood the material from Chapters 1–4. Review Chapter 2 particularly.

Thus far, we have dealt mostly with games presented in *normal* or tabular form. While all games can be treated in normal form, as von Neumann observed, the normal form is particularly useful for games in which all agents choose their strategies more or less simultaneously, such as the Prisoner's Dilemma. Many real human interactions are like that, as we have seen. But there are other important interactions in which the agents have to choose their strategies in some particular order, and in which commitments can be made only under limited circumstances or after some time has passed. These are *sequential games*, and we may say that such games have a *commitment structure*. The extensive form of the game can help us to understand the commitment structure and its implications, and so it has become customary to study sequential games in terms of their extensive form. Here is an example and a business case.

Strategic Investment to Deter Entry

In the business case in Chapter 2, we saw that the entry of new competition can reduce the profits of established firms. (A great deal of economic theory says the same.) Accordingly, we would expect that companies might try to find some way to prevent or deter the entry of new competition into the market, even if it is costly to do so. Here is an example of that kind.

Spizella Corp. produces specialized computer processing chips for workstations. A plant to fabricate these chips (a "fab") will produce three million chips per year at a cost of $1 billion per year and so at an average cost of $333.33 per chip. Table 14.1 shows the relationship between the number of chips on the market and the prices buyers are willing to pay (or, as economists call it, the demand relationship).

Spizella's management has learned that Passer, Ltd., is considering building a "fab" to enter this market in competition with Spizella. As things are, selling 3 million chips at $700, Spizella obtains an annual profit of $1.1 billion (ignoring the cost of wear and tear and amortization of the fab). But if a second fab comes on line, output will increase to 6 million chips, the price per chip will drop to $400, and revenue per fab will be $1.2 billion, for

Table 14.1 | Demand for Chips

Q	Price per chip
3,000,000	700
6,000,000	400
9,000,000	200

a profit of $200 million per year for each fab. Worse still, if two new plants come on line, output will be 9 million chips and the price will drop to $200, for a loss of $400 million per plant.

Nevertheless, Spizella is considering investing in a second fab. Its reasoning is as follows:

1. If Spizella builds before Passer makes its decision, Passer will realize that its plant would be the third one, and that if it builds the plant everyone will lose $400 million per plant per year. So Passer will not build, and Spizella will retain $400 million a year of profit, which is nothing to sneeze at.

2. If Spizella doesn't build the second plant, Passer will, and Spizella will be left with only $200 million of profits on its one present fab.

In building the new plant to keep Passer out, Spizella would be engaging in "strategic investment to deter entry." By building first, Spizella commits itself to retaining dominance of the market and to driving any potential competitor out of the market—since the two plants, plus the third for a new competitor, could not all produce at their capacity without depressing the price below the costs of all competitors.

Let's look at this game in extensive form. In Figure 14.1 each black oval represents a decision by one player or the other, a "node" of the game. Each arrow represents one way the player may decide. The node labeled S is Spizella's decision to build the new fab or not, and the nodes at PA and PB are Passer's decision to build its new fab or not, depending on whether Spizella has built its. The payoffs on the far right show the payoff to Spizella first and to Passer second.

In analyzing games in **extensive form**, a useful concept is the **subgame**. A subgame includes all branches that originate from a single, well-defined choice point and also from the branches that originate from all choice points that follow from it. Thus, in Figure 14.1, each of the gray ovals defines a subgame—one, in the lighter gray, originating from choice point PA, and the other, in the darker gray,

Heads Up!

Here are some concepts we will develop as this chapter goes along:

Extensive Form: A game is represented in extensive form when it is shown as a sequence of decisions. The game in *extensive form* is commonly shown as a tree diagram.

Subgame: A *subgame* of any game consists of all nodes and payoffs that follow a complete information node. If the subgame is only part (not the whole) of the game it is called a "proper subgame."

Subgame Perfect Equilibrium: A Nash equilibrium in a game in extensive form is *subgame perfect* if it is an equilibrium for every subgame.

Basic Subgame: A subgame in a game in extensive form is *basic* if it contains no other proper subgames. Otherwise, it is a complex subgame.

Backward Induction is a method of finding subgame perfect equilibria by solving the basic subgames, substituting the payoffs back into the complex ones, solving those, and working back to the beginning of the game.

Definition

Extensive Form—A game is represented in **extensive form** when it is shown as a sequence of decisions. The game in extensive form is commonly shown as a tree diagram.

Definition

Subgame—A **subgame** of any game consists of all nodes and payoffs that follow a complete information node.

Figure **14.1** | Extensive Form of "Strategic Investment to Deter Entry"

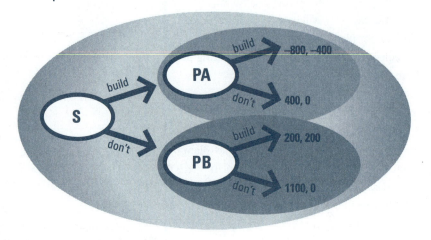

> **Definition**
>
> ***Proper Subgame***—A **proper subgame** is a subgame that includes only part of the complete game.

> **Definition**
>
> ***Commitment Structure***—The set of proper subgames in a sequential game is the game's **commitment structure**.

originating from choice point PB. In addition, the whole game is a subgame! After all, it includes the branches from choice point S and, since PA and PB follow from S, the subgame beginning from choice point S includes those branches, too. In general, every game has at least one subgame, namely itself. The other subgames, the ones that are not identical to the game as a whole, are called **proper subgames**.

When I said before that sequential games have a **commitment structure**, I meant that typically sequential games have one or more proper subgames.

   Recall, at the beginning of the example, that Spizella "reasoned out" what Passer would do. Spizella's reasoning is based on subgames. In reasoning that "If we don't build the second plant, Passer will," Spizella is observing that the bottom branch with the payoff (1100, 0) is not an equilibrium in the lower subgame. Similarly, "If we build before Passer makes its decision, Passer will realize that its plant would be the third one, and that if it builds the plant everyone will lose $400 million per plant per year. So Passer will not build," says that the top branch, in which both companies build, is not an equilibrium in the top subgame. Anticipating that each of the subgames will be in equilibrium, Spizella can anticipate the results and make its decision accordingly. Thus, Spizella will choose its strategy on the assumption that every subgame would be in equilibrium. This sort of equilibrium in the game as a whole is called a **subgame perfect equilibrium**—an equilibrium in which the players always, consistently, anticipate their rivals' decisions in this way.

> **Definition**
>
> ***Subgame Perfect Equilibrium***—A game is a **subgame perfect equilibrium** if and only if every subgame is in a Nash equilibrium.

Here is a principle that game theorists agree upon: In order for a game with one or more proper subgames to be in equilibrium, every subgame must be in equilibrium. This sort of equilibrium we call a *subgame perfect equilibrium*.

To find a subgame perfect equilibrium, we may use *backward induction*. We start with the last decision in each sequence, determine the equilibrium for that decision, and then move back, determining the equilibrium at each step, until we arrive at the first decision. Thus, in the game of strategic investment, decision PA or PB is last, depending on the decision at S. At PA, Passer will decide not to build, since it is better to lose nothing than to lose $400 million! At PB, Passer will decide to build, since a profit of $200 million is better than nothing. Now we move back to stage 1. Spizella knows that, if it chooses "build," its payoff will be $400 million, while if it chooses "don't," its payoff will be $200 million. It knows this because it knows Passer's decision makers are rational and self-interested, and Spizella can figure out what Passer's decisions will be in these cases just as we can. So Spizella chooses "build," and the sequence (build, don't build) is the subgame perfect equilibrium for this game.[1]

Both competitors have reasons for regrets. Passer would rather have the profit of $200 million from splitting the market if it built and Spizella did not. Spizella would rather have the profit of $1.1 billion if nobody built. But these outcomes are not available. Each is doing the best it can, making its *best response* to the other's strategy choice. That is what we mean by *equilibrium* in general. But in this case, the equilibrium must also take into account the fact that Spizella has to commit itself first—the commitment structure. Thus, the subgame perfect equilibrium is the best-response equilibrium.

Concepts for Sequential Games

This example illustrates the key concepts for sequential games. First, let's take a little closer look at the concept of a subgame. As a contrast to Figure 14.1, we can take another look at the Prisoner's Dilemma in extensive form. For convenience, Figure 14.2 repeats Figure 2.3. We suppose that Al makes his decision to confess or not confess at 1, and Bob makes his decision at 2. Notice one difference from Figure 14.1. Bob's decision, in the two different cases, is enclosed in a single oval. That tells us that when Bob makes his decision, he doesn't know what decision Al has made. Bob has to make his decision without knowing Al's decision. Graphically, Bob doesn't know whether he is at the top of the oval or the bottom. This uncertainty means that the branches to the right of 2 in this figure are NOT subgames. In Figure 14.1, the fact that PA and PB are in separate ovals tells us, in game theory code, that Passer knows Spizella's decision before Passer makes its decision. For the purposes of the game, Passer has *complete information* (i.e., Passer knows all previous decisions).

Recall that the whole game is at the same time one of its own subgames, and a subgame that is only a part of the whole is called a proper subgame. Contrast Figure 14.2 with Figure 14.1.

---

1 Strictly speaking, Passer's subgame perfect strategy is the contingent strategy, "*If Spizella builds*, don't build; *otherwise* build." However, we will ignore the contingencies where (we hope) it will not cause confusion.

Figure 14.2 | The Prisoner's Dilemma in Extensive Form

Repeats Figure 2.3, Chapter 2

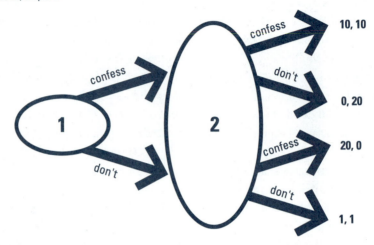

A node like PA or PB is a *complete information node*. Each complete information node is the beginning of a subgame, and each subgame begins with a complete information node. The decision branches enclosed in the gray ovals are proper subgames in the game of Strategic Investment to Deter Entry, as we have observed. They also illustrate another important prop-

erty that a subgame may have. *Neither of them contains any other proper subgames within them.* Instead, the branches at PA and PB lead directly to payoffs. Thus, they are **basic subgames**. By contrast, the subgame beginning at node S in Figure 14.1 (which is the entire game) is a **complex subgame**.

A subgame cannot begin with an information set. That is why the branches to the right of node 2 in Figure 14.2 are not subgames. The Prisoner's Dilemma has no proper subgames. However, node 1 is a complete information node—there are no previous decisions Al needs to know anything about—so node 1, together with the nodes to its right, constitute a subgame. The Prisoner's Dilemma has only one subgame, a trivial subgame consisting of the entire game, and has no commitment structure.

For games like Figure 14.1 that do have proper subgames, however, our equilibrium concept is subgame perfect equilibrium, as we have seen. For a subgame perfect equilibrium, we require that every subgame is at a Nash equilibrium. This is illustrated by the sequence (build, don't enter) in the game of Strategic Investment to Deter Entry.

But we can determine the Nash equilibrium directly only for the basic subgame, that is, the last subgame in any sequence. In Figure 14.1 at S, for example, we cannot determine the Nash equilibrium because the payoffs depend on Passer's decision, and Spizella cannot make a best response to a strategy that will be chosen later. Accordingly, we start with the basic proper subgames in each sequence—PA and PB. At those nodes, there is no commitment that any later decision can exploit, since there are no later decisions. Accordingly, we can calculate the Nash equilibrium and payoffs for those two nodes. That tells us the payoffs for node S. By solving the games at PA and PB we have reduced the entry-deterrence game in Figure 14.1 to the smaller game shown in Figure 14.3.

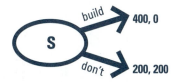

Figure 14.3 | Reduced Game of Strategic Investment to Deter Entry

This game can immediately be solved. The solution is "build for 400 rather than 200." This illustrates the general method for solving games with commitment structures: Solve the subgames at the last stage in each branch, and in this way "reduce" the game to a smaller one, and then repeat until all subgames have been solved. This gives the subgame perfect equilibrium. In the words of a management consultant's slogan: "Think forward, reason backward."[2] That is, think forward to determine what the proper subgames are, and reason backward to solve them for the best-response strategies and equilibrium.

Backward induction and subgame perfect equilibrium are important principles of rational strategy in sequential games. Strategists should indeed "think forward and reason backward." This is no less true in other fields than in business, and applies to military strategy, public policy, and personal life, as we will see in examples to follow in this chapter.

> **Method**
>
> *Backward Induction*—To find the subgame perfect equilibrium of a sequential game, first determine the Nash equilibria of all basic subgames. Next, reduce the game by substituting the equilibrium payoffs for the basic subgames. Repeat this procedure until there are no proper subgames, and solve the resulting game for its Nash equilibrium. The sequence of Nash equilibria for the proper subgames of the original game constitutes the subgame perfect equilibrium of the whole game.

The Spanish Rebellion, Again

Let's take one more look at the game with which the book began: the rebellion in Roman Spain. The contestants, as we recall, are Hirtuleius and Metellus Pius. Hirtuleius' strategies are to go to New Carthage or to remain at Laminium until Pius marches, and then cut Pius off at the River Baetis. Pius' strategies are to march directly for Laminium and fight through Hirtuleius' forces, or to march to Gades and go on to New Carthage by ship. The extensive form of this game is shown in Figure 14.4, with numerical payoffs.

In Figure 14.4, the subgames are shown as lightly shaded gray ovals. As usual, the game as a whole is considered a subgame. There are two proper subgames, and both of them are basic. In Colleen McCollough's novel, she says that Hirtuleius' only reasonable choice is to cut Pius off at the River Baetis. Let's see whether this is the subgame perfect solution of the game.

To solve this game for its subgame perfect equilibrium we will, of course, "think forward and reason backward." That is, we will solve the basic subgames, and work back from that to solve the game as a whole. Looking at the two basic subgames, we first solve the upper subgame. In this subgame, Pius can get 5 by going to Laminium, but loses 3 if he

2 Hugh Courtney, "Games Managers Should Play," *World Economic Affairs* 2, no. 1 (Autumn 1997), p. 48.

Figure **14.4** | The Spanish Rebellion with Subgames

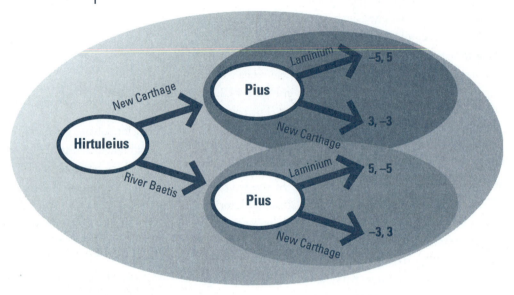

Figure **14.5** | Reduced Spanish Rebellion

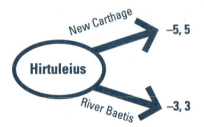

goes to New Carthage. Thus, Laminium is the solution to this subgame. In the lower basic subgame, Pius wins 3 by going to New Carthage but loses 5 if he goes to Laminium. Thus, New Carthage is the solution to this subgame. Using this information, we can reduce the Spanish Rebellion to the game shown in Figure 14.5. In that game, Hirtuleius loses 5 by going to New Carthage but only 3 by going to the River Baetis.

Thus, the River Baetis is the solution to the reduced game, and the sequence in which Hirtuleius cuts off Pius at the River Baetis as Pius is going to New Carthage is the subgame perfect solution. It seems that Colleen McCollough got the game equilibrium right when she said that the River Baetis strategy was the only one Hirtuleius could reasonably choose.

So Hirtuleius is in a bad situation—because he is between Pius and Pius' objectives in Eastern Spain, he has to commit himself first either to go or not to go to New Carthage. As a result, he has to choose between bad and worse. But what if it were reversed? What if Pius had to choose first? The answer is that if Pius had to choose first, Pius would have to choose between bad and worse—in this game, whoever chooses first gets the worst of it.

NOW IT'S YOUR TURN. Draw the game in extensive form with the difference that Pius chooses his strategy first, verifying that Hirtuleius does better, by solving this game for its subgame perfect equilibrium.

Nash and Subgame Perfect Equilibrium

We have seen that the subgame perfect equilibrium, like the Nash equilibrium, is a best-response equilibrium. In finding the subgame perfect equilibrium, we first determine the Nash equilibrium in the basic subgames. Clearly the two equilibrium concepts are closely related. To better understand the relationship between the two, let's look at another example from Chapter 2, the entry game between Goldfinch and Bluebird. This game in extensive form is repeated in Figure 14.6. Table 14.2 shows the game in normal form, repeating Table 2.1 in Chapter 2 except that the Nash equilibria of the game are shaded.

The two Nash equilibria of this market entry game are not equal, though. Notice what happens when we apply backward induction to this game. At node 2, we notice that Goldfinch is better off to choose "no war," rather than war, for 5 rather than 2. This puts us in the left column of the normal form table for the game, and shows that the darker shaded Nash equilibrium is the only subgame perfect equilibrium for this game. The lighter shaded Nash equilibrium at the lower right is not subgame perfect. Why is that? It is a Nash equilibrium, since no unilateral deviation from it can make either player better off. But this is less meaningful, since Bluebird chooses first and can commit itself to the "enter" strategy in such a way that Goldfinch will also shift to the "no war" strategy. To put it in another way, Goldfinch's threat of a price war is not credible, since it is not an equilibrium in the basic subgame.

In this case, there are two Nash equilibria, but only one is subgame perfect. The other corresponds to an "incredible threat." This illustrates the relationship of subgame perfect equilibrium to Nash equilibrium in general. Every subgame perfect equilibrium is a Nash equilibrium, but not every Nash equilibrium is subgame perfect. Game theorists express this by saying that subgame perfect equilibrium is a refinement of Nash equilibrium. A refinement,

Table 14.2 | The Market Entry Game in Normal Form

Approximately repeats Table 2.1, Chapter 2

		Goldfinch	
		If Bluebird enters, then accommodate; if Bluebird does not enter, then do business as usual.	If Bluebird enters, then initiate price war; if Bluebird does not enter, then do business as usual.
Bluebird	enter	3, 5	−5, 2
	don't enter	0, 10	0, 10

Approximately repeats Figure 2.1, Chapter 2

Figure 14.6 | The Game of Market Entry in Extensive Form

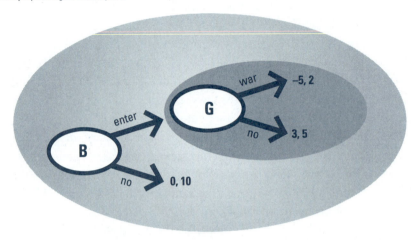

in general, is a class of Nash equilibria that also fits some more demanding standard for a solution, such as the criterion of subgame perfection.

The Centipede Game

The analysis of games in extensive form has been influential in recent game theory and experimental research. One example of this is called "the Centipede Game" or just "the Centipede." (That strange name will be explained a few paragraphs further on.) Here is the simplest of Centipede Games.

The two participants will be Anna and Barb. At the first stage player A—Anna, of course—can either take or pass a money payment. If she takes it, Barb gets a smaller payment. If Anna passes at the first stage, the total payoff grows and Barb has an opportunity to take a share of the payment, leaving Anna the smaller share. However, if Barb passes at the second stage, they divide the pot. Figure 14.7 shows the game in extensive form. The first node is a decision by player A (Anna), as shown by the letter in the oval; the second by player B (Barb). The payoffs are at the ends of the arrows, with the number to the left representing the payoff to Anna while the number to the right is the payoff to Barb. Thus, for example, if Anna passes on the first stage, and Barb takes the pot, Anna gets $2 and Barb gets $6. This Centipede game is simple in that it has just the two stages, but it can be extended to three, four, six, hundreds, or even

Figure 14.7 | A Centipede Game

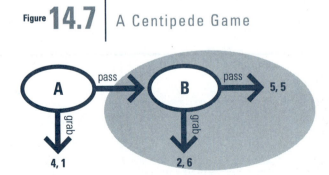

more stages. If you can visualize Figure 14.7 extended for 100 steps, you might understand why it is called "the Centipede Game."

To solve the game, we think forward and reason backward. The two-stage Centipede Game has just one proper subgame, shown by the gray oval in Figure 14.7, and it is basic. In that subgame, Barb will choose "grab," and the payoff will be 2 for Anna and 6 for Barb. With this solution we reduce the Centipede Game to the game shown in Figure 14.8. In this game Anna chooses "grab" for 4 rather than "pass" for 2, and that is the subgame perfect solution to the game. If the game were extended to any number of stages, 100 or even more, we would analyze it in the same

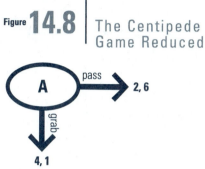

Figure 14.8 | The Centipede Game Reduced

way and come to the same conclusion—lopping off one step at a time until we are left with Figure 14.8 and find that the subgame perfect equilibrium is for Anna to "take the money and run." The next section will illustrate with a four-stage Centipede.

The Centipede Game is a parallel to the Prisoner's Dilemma. Just as the Prisoner's Dilemma has become a standard illustration for the possibility that noncooperative games in normal form may have inefficient outcomes, the Centipede Game illustrates how that can happen with the subgame perfect equilibrium of a game in extensive form. We will return to the Centipede Game more than once in this book. There are many illustrations. Here is a four-stage example and an application to economic theory.

Going Coconutty

There are many applications of sequential games in economics, politics and public policy. Economists of the Austrian school of thought like to use examples having to do with Robinson Crusoe. Here is a story about Robinson and his American pal, Joe Friday, which draws on sequential games and Austrian economics.

Robinson and Joe were on an ocean cruise when the ship sank and they were cast away. They possessed nothing but a rowboat and a small kit of tools. After rowing all night and part of the morning they have arrived at a lagoon with a number of islands. The island nearest them is a tiny islet with just four coconut trees. Just visible, on the other side of the lagoon, is a larger island with enough resources so that the two men can survive until they are rescued. But they are very hungry and thirsty right now, so they agree to land on the tiny islet and harvest the coconuts. The coconut milk and meat will restore their energy so they can row the rest of the way.

Their plan is to take turns climbing up to the top of the coconut trees and throwing down the coconuts. Robinson will climb the first tree, Joe the second, and so on. The one at the bottom will collect the coconuts and store them in the boat. (If no one collects them they will roll down into the surf, wash away, and so go to waste.) Then they will divide the coconuts equally. There are exactly five coconuts per tree, so they can collect 20 coconuts before rowing on to

The Austrian School

A distinctive school of thought in economics that originated in Vienna, Austria, the "Austrian School," share some things with neoclassical economics but differ in some important ways. The "older Austrian School" contributed such ideas as opportunity cost and a version of marginal utility theory to economics, and originated the interpretation of capital and investment in terms of "roundabout production." The "younger Austrian school" focused more on defending market capitalism in controversies with socialism, the importance of private information in resource allocation, and business cycle research. All Austrian economists share the idea that the ultimate determinants of economic activity are subjective and that economics is concerned with rational action, but real human beings make errors.

the larger island. (Of course, things are only that exact in textbook examples.) The problem is that there is no enforcement to keep the one at the bottom from cheating. At any stage, the castaway at the bottom of the tree could take all the coconuts accumulated so far and get away in the boat with them. Then he could enjoy them all, rather than splitting them with his companion. That may seem pretty underhanded, but these castaways are rational game players. Each one aims to maximize his coconuts, and each one assumes that the other one will maximize his coconuts, too.

The extensive form of this game is shown in Figure 14.9. At each step the two castaways have to choose between two strategies—collecting the coconuts and taking the next turn to climb the tree (or dividing equally at the end) or cheating and running away with the hoard so

Figure 14.9 | The Coconutty Game

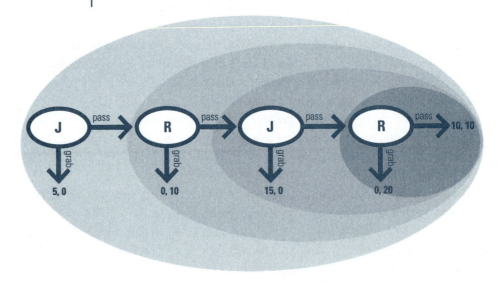

far. We will call these two strategies "pass" and "grab," respectively. Joe makes the choice at the first node, Robinson at the second, and so on. The payoffs are shown with Joe's payoff first and Robinson's second. The subgames are shown by the gray ovals, and we notice that in this game all of the subgames are nested. This simplifies the solution. Only the last subgame is basic. We solve it first. Clearly, Robinson is better off to grab the 20 coconuts than to pass and split them evenly. Therefore, at the third node, Joe can expect 0 if he passes and is better off to grab 15 coconuts. But that means, at the second node, Robinson can expect 0 if he passes and is better off to grab the 10 coconuts accumulated by then. But, taking the last step, that means Joe can expect 0 if he passes at the first node, and is better off to grab the first 5 coconuts. The game stops there—that is the subgame perfect equilibrium—and it is a very unsatisfactory, noncooperative equilibrium in which only a quarter of the coconuts are harvested and Robinson gets nothing. Probably Robinson will refuse to agree to this plan in any case.

This game is a parable for some aspects of production in industrialized countries that the Austrian school of thought and their predecessors thought were important: division of labor and roundabout production. Adam Smith had put great emphasis on the division of labor, claiming that the division of labor is the major source of increasing labor productivity and the resulting high standards of living in industrializing countries. The Austrian school felt that roundabout production—producing intermediate goods, such as machines, which are then used to produce final goods for consumption—had a greater impact on productivity. (They conceded that division of labor could play a role too.) In practice, roundabout production and division of labor go together, as they do in this example. The harvesting of the coconuts is roundabout—one of the castaways has to "invest" his energy in climbing up before anything can be produced, and a coconut on the ground is an *intermediate product* on the way to being a consumable coconut—and no coconuts can be harvested unless there are two people to divide the labor and do the two jobs, climbing and collecting.

The point of the example is that roundabout production and division of labor create opportunities for underhanded opportunism, which, in turn, can make high-productivity roundabout production impossible. How is it that some societies industrialize anyway? The key point is that they have institutions of contracts with legal enforcement. People engaged in roundabout production sign contracts for their performance, and if they take the coconuts and run they can be sued. The problem for Robinson and Joe, in the example, is that they have no outside authority to enforce a contract. In the real world, less-developed countries with very corrupt governments, and little effective enforcement of contracts, often do indeed fall further behind in economic development.

The Coconutty Game is a particular example of the Centipede Game. As this example suggests, the Centipede tells us something about the importance of being able to make a commitment, for example by signing a contract. The chapter will conclude with an application of the Centipede to U.S. military and political strategy in the Cold War.

Counterattack

During the Cold War, roughly 1949 to 1989, the United States was allied with several European powers, including the German Federal Republic (West Germany) against the Soviet Union. The Soviet Union had superior numbers of ground troops in Europe and it was generally believed that if it chose to attack, it would have been able to overrun West Germany very rapidly. To prevent this, U.S. troops were stationed on German soil. But the American troops were not strong enough to defeat an all-out Soviet attack. That would have required a much larger infantry force than the United States was willing to commit to Germany. Thus, the United States stationed in West Germany a force that the Soviets could surely defeat if they wished—a force who, in the words of a great Iroquois leader of a war two centuries earlier, were too few to fight and too many to die.[3]

It was not the troops in West Germany, but the threat of a massive counterattack by the United States, possibly even using nuclear weapons, that deterred a Soviet attack. And yet threats, as we have seen in this chapter, are not always credible.

Figure 14.10 | The Cold War on the European Frontier without Troops in Germany

Figure 14.10 shows a game somewhat like the situation the United States believed it was in without any troops in West Germany. If the Soviet Union (SU) attacks, the United States (US) may either counterattack or it may not. If it does counterattack, both countries are worse off, indicated by the payoffs, (−2, −2). If the United States does not counterattack, it is worse off than before the attack on West Germany—with a payoff of 1 rather than 3 if the Soviet Union did not attack—but not as badly off as it would be if it should counterattack. In technical terms, the U.S. decision is the only basic subgame in this game, and the Nash equilibrium in the subgame is not to counterattack; therefore, (attack, don't counterattack) is the subgame perfect equilibrium. Thus, the threat of a counterattack was not credible.

However, the United States was able to change the rules by stationing troops in West Germany. A phrase that was often used at the time provides a hint. The American troops were spoken of as a *tripwire*. The implication was that the destruction of the American troops in West Germany, while within the Soviet Union's means, would inevitably result in a counterattack sufficient to deter the Soviet Union from attacking in the first place. With a contingent of troops in West Germany, the United States would see them overwhelmed and lost if it should not mount a counterattack to rescue them. The payoffs

3 The Mohawk chief Tiyanoga, known in English as King Hendrick, is recorded as saying (with respect to a proposed expedition during King Philip's War), "If my warriors are to fight, they are too few. If they are to die, they are too many." The phrase is also sometimes attributed to a later Mohawk leader, Thayendanega, known as Joseph Brant. Thayendanega might have quoted or paraphrased his predecessor, but the attribution to Thayendanega may have originated as fiction.

would then be more like those shown in Figure 14.11.

Placing the troops in West Germany improves the Soviet Union's payoff if they attack and there is no counterattack—they are able to destroy more of their enemy's forces—but it reduces the payoffs to the United States in every possible case. Even if there is no attack, the United States has the cost of maintaining the troops. If it counterattacks, there

Figure 14.11 | The Cold War on the European Frontier with Troops in Germany

will be troops lost before they can be rescued. But the biggest change is in case the Soviet Union attacks and there is no counterattack. The entire force stationed in West Germany is lost. (It was also said that there would be a political cost—no government that would allow the destruction of the U.S. troops in West Germany would remain in power for very long. Accordingly, we might think of the payoffs in Figure 14.10 as being political rather than just military payoffs.) Since the payoffs to the United States are reduced in every case, it might seem, on the face of it, that the U.S. deployment of troops was irrational.

Nevertheless, the outcome is better for the United States. The solution of the basic subgame is changed, and now "counterattack" becomes the best response. The threat of counterattack is credible, and the subgame perfect equilibrium is for the Soviet Union not to attack. And that is what happened.

Of course, the numerical payoffs are guesswork. No one can ever know (thank Heaven!) what the payoffs would have been in the case of an all-out war between the nuclear powers of that time. But the relative orders of magnitude will serve to illustrate the U.S. strategic thinking at the time—thinking that was, on the whole, successful.

Summary

In this chapter on sequential games, we have studied games in which one or more players make a commitment to which the other player can then respond. In analyzing these games, we make use of the concept of subgame perfect equilibrium. This is expressed intuitively in the slogan "think forward and reason backward." First, the game is analyzed into its subgames, "thinking forward." The condition for a subgame perfect equilibrium is that each subgame of the game is itself in a Nash equilibrium. A subgame is proper if it does not include the entire game, and is basic if it has no proper subgames within it. The basic proper subgames are those at the end of the game tree. To find the subgame perfect equilibrium, we use backward induction, "reasoning backward." We first solve all of the basic proper subgames, and reduce the game by replacing the basic proper subgames with their equilibrium payoffs. We then analyze the reduced game in the same way, continuing step by step until we arrive at a game that has no proper subgames. The solution to that game, followed successively by the solutions of the subgames, gives us the subgame perfect equilibrium.

We have seen that the existence of a sequence of play makes a difference in the outcome of the game. It may be that the one who takes the first move has the advantage, as in the entry game between Spizella and Passer; or as in the Spanish Rebellion, the first mover may be at a disadvantage. As in many noncooperative games, both players may have reasons to regret the outcome.

Games of threat and retaliation (including price wars) are an important category of sequential games. In such games, threats are credible only if they are subgame perfect. This principle has wide application, extending to the deployment of military forces, and many other threat and retaliation games. The Centipede games are another important category of sequential games. These games have application in economics and public policy, but are also important for a large volume of recent experimental work on them, which we shall explore in a later chapter.

Exercises and Discussion Questions

14.1 Road Rage. Consider the following simple game, which we may call the Road Rage Game. There are two players, Al and Bob. Bob has two choices: to aggress (perhaps by cutting Al off in traffic) or not to aggress. If Bob chooses "do not aggress," then there is no choice of strategies for Al, but if Bob aggresses, Al can choose between strategies "retaliate" (perhaps by dangerous driving or by taking a shot at Bob's car with a firearm) or "not retaliate." An example in tabular normal form is shown in Table 14.E1.

Table 14.E1 | The Road Rage Game

		Bob	
		aggress	don't aggress
Al	if Bob aggresses then retaliate; if not, do nothing	−50, −100	5, 4
	if Bob aggresses then don't retaliate; if not, do nothing	4, 5	5, 4

As usual, the payoff to the left is the payoff to Al, while the payoff to the right is the payoff to Bob. Draw the tree diagram for the game. What are the subgames of this game? Which subgames are basic? Determine the subgame perfect equilibrium of this game. Does it seem that the subgame perfect equilibrium is what occurs in the real world? Explain your answer. Although many governments have tried to discourage road rage by penalizing retaliation, the Washington State Police adopted a policy to discourage road rage by increasing the penalty for aggressive driving. Does this make sense in terms of game theory?

14.2 Omnicorp. Omnicorp is the established monopoly seller of Omniscanners, which are widely used in business. Newcorp, however, has obtained a monopoly on a process to produce Omniscanners more cheaply. Newcorp has not yet begun selling Omniscanners, and Omnicorp has let it be known that, if the new company does enter the market, Omnicorp is prepared to cut price below their own cost in order to bankrupt the new competitor. If Newcorp enters the market, both companies have the option of pricing at p_1 or p_2, where c_1 is the cost per Omniscanner using the old technology (the technology Omnicorp would have to use) and c_2 is the cost using the new technology, and $p_1 > c_1 > p_2 > c_2$. If the two firms compete and charge the same price, assume that they split the market, each selling $Q/2$ units, while if one charges a lower price, that one firm will sell the entire Q units and the other will sell nothing.

Omnicorp has threatened to retaliate with a price war if Newcorp enters the omniscanner market. Is this threat credible? Why or why not?

14.3   Teabags. (From a student's e-mail). Sometimes new entering firms face retaliation from the established firms in their markets. One such example was Tetley Tea versus Lipton in the "round tea bag war." The first round tea bags were introduced by Tetley in the United Kingdom. Consumers went wild for it, and Tetley's market share jumped by 40 percent and remained there. Following this success, Tetley introduced the round tea bag in Canada with the same response. As Tetley was preparing to introduce the round teabag in the United States, Lipton resolved that Tetley would not take its 40 percent market share from Lipton. Therefore, Lipton dropped the price of its tea to below cost. Tetley introduced the round bag and gained its 40 percent market share, though not at Lipton's expense. (Smaller labels, such as Red Rose, were the losers.) Lipton, however, realized that Tetley had expended significant resources bringing the round tea bag to these three markets and so deduced (correctly) that Tetley's financial resources were thin. Lipton chose to maintain the low price (continuing to take a loss). Tetley did not have the financial resources to compete at below-breakeven prices and ended up being sold and having its upper management replaced.

What are the strategies of the two firms in this game? What commitments are involved? Draw a tree diagram for this game in extensive form. Express the strategies in normal form. How does the slogan "Think forward and reason backward" apply to this game?

14.4   Divorce. Mrs. Jones is seeking a divorce from Mr. Jones. Under the terms of her prenuptial agreement, her settlement will be $100,000 if she can prove that Mr. Jones has had an affair, but $50,000 otherwise. Her lawyer, acting as her agent, can prove the affair only if he hires a private detective for $10,000, which will come out of the lawyer's fee. Mrs. Jones has the option of paying her lawyer a flat fee of $20,000 regardless of the outcome of the case or one-third of the settlement. The lawyer will hire the private detective only if it is profitable for him to do so.

Whose is the first move? Draw a tree diagram for this game in extensive form. Express the strategies in normal form. Which payment method will enable Mrs. Jones to win her case? (Use backward induction). Can you think of any other way (besides the flat fee and the one-third share) that Mrs. Jones might compensate the lawyer so as to get the best outcome for herself?

14.5 Gambling the Night Away. This is a true story, according to my informant. The names are changed to protect the innocent, if any. The game is based on the gambling and entertainment industries in Atlantic City, New Jersey. A Nevada gambling millionaire, whom we shall call NM, wants to buy one of the largest and most prestigious properties in Atlantic City, a property now owned by the Biggernyou Corporation, BC. BC owns two major properties, one at the middle of the Boardwalk and one on the beach at the south end. The property on the south end is almost a square block, except for the small Dunecreep Casino, which faces the beach and occupies the middle of the block. The property at the middle of the boardwalk is the swank and famous Biltwell Hotel.

NM wants the Biltwell, but BC doesn't want to sell. The Dunecreep, owned by a third party, is available but too small for NM's plans. BC has two strategies—offer to sell the Biltwell or don't offer—and so far its strategy has been "don't offer." NM has three strategies. He can wait until a better offer comes along (wait), or he can buy the Dunecreep and operate it as a luxury casino (luxury), or he can buy the Dunecreep and operate it as a cheap slot machine hall (slots).

Market research says that the Dunecreep will make more money as a luxury casino, but NM intends to run it as a slots hall. Here is his reasoning: "The slot machines draw a lower class of customers, and the wealthy customers of the Biggernyou Corporation will not want to share the beach with them, so the Biggernyou Corporation will lose customers and money as a result of having a slots hall in the middle of their block. To keep their clientele, they will need to get the Dunecreep away from me, and to do that they will have to give me a chance to buy the Biltwell, which is what I really want."

Figure 14.E1 shows this game in extensive form. NM has the first decision node and BC the second. The first payoff is to NM and the second to BC. Will NM's strategy work? Explain in terms of subgame perfect equilibrium.

Figure 14.E1 | Payoffs in a Game of Casinos

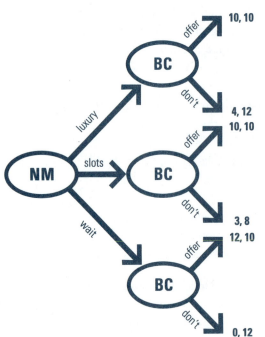

14.6 War of Attrition. In a war of attrition, there are two or more stages (and there may be an unlimited number of stages) but the game ends when one player drops out. The first player to surrender or withdraw from the game loses, and the other player wins; but the longer the game continues the less is won and the more is lost. The idea of it is that the continuing conflict uses up or destroys resources that the victor might otherwise use to increase her rewards and the loser might otherwise use to repair her position. We will consider a simplified two-stage war of attrition.

At each stage, each player has the choice of fighting or withdrawing from the game. The decisions at each stage are made simultaneously. At the first stage, if both withdraw, they split 150 evenly as 75 each, while if one fights and the other withdraws, the fighter gets 100 and the player who withdraws gets 50. If both fight, then the game goes to a second stage, in which the total payoff is at most 90 because of the resources wasted in the conflict at the first stage. If both fight at the second stage, the further conflict reduces the payoff to 10 each. If one fights and the other withdraws, the fighter gets 55 and the withdrawn player 15.

a. Draw the tree diagram for the game in extensive form.
b. Write a list of all strategies in the game for each player, allowing for different responses to the other player's first round play.
c. Using information from part (b), write the table for the game in normal form.
d. Has this game any Nash equilibria? What?
e. Use backward induction to solve the game.

14.7 Strike! A union and the employer expect that there may be a strike. Before the decision to strike, the union can either build up its strike fund, or not, and the employer can either build up its inventories to continue service to customers during a strike, or not. Those decisions are made simultaneously. Thereafter, the union decides whether or not to strike.

a. Using the payoff table, Table 14.E2, and ignoring the sequence of commitments, would there be a Nash equilibrium in pure strategies? If so, what?

Table 14.E2 | Strike

		Union			
		build		don't build	
		strike	don't strike	strike	don't strike
Employer	build	−5, −5	−2, −2	−2, −10	−2, 0
	don't build	−10, 10	0, −2	−5, 5	0, 0

b. Draw the tree diagram for the game.
c. What are the subgames of this game?
d. Which subgames are basic?
e. Reduce the game by solving the basic subgames, write the payoff table for the reduced game, and use it to determine the subgame perfect equilibrium of this game.
f. Compare the answers to Questions (a) and (e). Explain the differences or similarities.

14.8 Cricket. In Cricket, as in Baseball, each play begins as a confrontation between two individuals: in Cricket, the bowler who throws a ball, and the batsman who tries to hit it.[4] But from that point on there are very many differences. One important difference is that, in

4 I am indebted to Dr. Vibhas Madan, a fast bowler, colleague, and friend, for most of the little I know about Cricket.

Cricket, the batsman has to try to protect the "wicket" at his base, and is out if the bowler can knock part of the wicket down. There are only 10 outs allowed in a Cricket game. Another difference is that the ball may strike the ground in front of the batsman, who can attempt to hit it on the first bounce. Depending on its spin, the ball can bounce either to the batsman's right ("leg-break") or his left ("off-break"). Naturally, a good batsman will watch the bowler's throwing motion for clues as to which way the ball will bounce. He will adjust his swing accordingly. But some bowlers can throw a *googly*—that is, a ball thrown off the heel of the hand with what looks like a right-bouncing motion, but which then actually bounces to the left. Thus, the bowler has three strategies: right breaking, left breaking, and googly. The batsman can adjust for a leg-break or an off-break, but if he adjusts for a leg-break, he might be taken off-balance by a googly. Another possibility is to adjust his stance. Before the bowler makes a move, he can back up closer to the wicket so that he can better see how the ball is thrown and how it bounces. If he does this, he might be better able to spot a googly, or the other two breaks, but it is risky, since it will make it easier for the bowler to knock the wicket down if the batsman misses with his swing. Also, if the ball hits the batsman when it would otherwise hit the wicket—so that in effect the batsman has shielded the wicket with his body—the batsman is called out for "leg before wicket," and this is more likely when he is nearer the wicket.

Compose a game-theoretic analysis of bowling and batting in Cricket, awarding the batsman payoffs of −1 when it seems most likely he will be out, +1 if it seems most likely he will hit the ball and score some runs, and 0 otherwise. Show the game in extensive form. Are there proper subgames? Are there information sets?

14.9 Another Centipede. Figure 14.E2 shows the extensive form diagram for a variant of the Centipede Game. The players are Al and Bob, and the first payment is to Al, the second to Bob. At each stage, the players' strategies are "pass" or "grab."
(a) Suppose the payoffs (Y, Z) are (5, 5). What is the subgame perfect equilibrium? Why?
(b) Suppose the payoffs (Y, Z) are (8, 8). What is the subgame perfect equilibrium? Why?

Figure 14.E2 | Variant Centipede

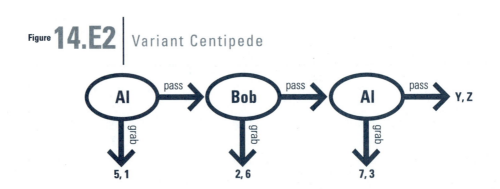

Imbedded Games 15

Sequential games have a wide range of applications in many fields of human action. They are also being applied in experimental research with implications for evolutionary psychology and may reveal important facts about basic human nature. This chapter offers some further examples of applications of sequential games in extensive form, illustrating backward induction and related methods.

Game theory begins from the assumption of rationality, and rationality in sequential games is identified with subgame perfect equilibrium. We know from experience that people do not always act rationally, and as we will see in a later chapter, there is experimental evidence also for that. Nevertheless, it is good procedure to explore every possibility for an explanation in terms of rationality before concluding that agents are acting irrationally—if only because that will help us to choose our own best response. For example, it often seems that people are acting irrationally in some games they play, but the action is understood as rational when we realize that the game is really part of a bigger game. The game in which people seem to act irrationally is **imbedded** or **nested** in a larger game, and to choose the best response in the larger game means choosing something that would not be a best response if the smaller game were isolated from other players and other interactions. In particular, the smaller game may be imbedded as a subgame in a larger sequential game. This chapter will illustrate that idea with several examples, beginning with an example of a student's curriculum plan.

Planning Doctoral Study

Aspiring Anna is considering doctoral study. If she can study software engineering under Nobel Nora, who is famous for research in that field and also in information retrieval, Anna can expect an excellent position. However, her prospects in information retrieval are not so bright, for personal reasons, and in any case Anna has a good job now that she will have to give up to prepare for doctoral work. As for Nora, she can benefit from working with an able graduate student like Anna, and there is no other equally good graduate student coming into the program. However, Nora's recent work is in information retrieval, and in order to guide a cutting-edge project in software engineering she would have to do some updating on the topic. In any case, Nora is on sabbatical in Paris, so it is impossible for Anna and Nora to confer before Anna chooses

Heads Up!

Here are some concepts we will develop as this chapter goes along:

Nested Games: If a game is part of a larger game, then equilibrium strategies in the smaller game may depend on the larger game. The smaller game is said to be *nested* within the larger.

Imbedded Games: If a nested game is a proper subgame of the larger game, then the nested game must be in equilibrium for the larger game to be in a subgame perfect equilibrium. Then the smaller game is said to be *imbedded* in the larger.

Forward Induction: In some games, a player may be able to infer something from earlier decisions made by other players, because the game is nested or imbedded in a larger one. This is called *forward induction*.

Changing the Rules: When a game has an unsatisfactory outcome, the outcome may be changed, for example, by signing a contract to enforce an agreement. Thus, the original game is nested or imbedded in a larger game, so that the outcome is changed from the original game.

Table 15.1 | Payoffs at the Second Stage of the Doctoral Study Game

		Nora	
		IR	SE
Anna	IR	3, 7	0, 0
	SE	0, 0	7, 3

her preliminary coursework. If Nora and Anna choose different lines of research, then Anna will work under the direction of a less-distinguished scholar, which will leave her with mediocre prospects, while Nora will work without a first-rate graduate assistant, reducing her productivity. This game in extensive form is shown in Figure 15.1.

Anna's strategies are to keep her day job ("job") or quit to study ("study"), and if she studies, strategies for both players are the choice of research fields SE or IR. This is a two-stage game, and the second-stage subgame is a game of incomplete information. The second-stage game is shown in Table 15.1.

Figure 15.1 | Aspiring Anna Plans for Doctoral Study

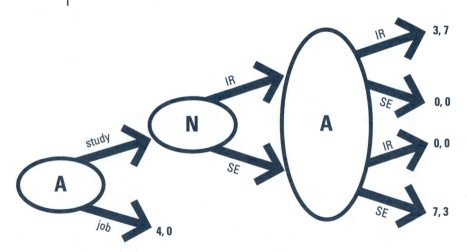

The second stage game is a coordination game of a familiar, somewhat puzzling type. The Nash equilibria are at the upper-left and lower-right corners where the two researchers choose the same field. However, coming into the game without prior information, there is uncertainty as to which Nash equilibrium will occur and some probability that an impasse, with payoffs of (0, 0), could occur if the two make opposite guesses.

In this case, however, Nora has some information. Even though she does not know which research track Anna will choose, she does know that Anna has given up her job to enter the program. Since Anna's payoff continuing with the job was 4, Nora can reason that Anna would not have entered the program had she not expected a payoff greater than 4. Nora reasons, "She must be assuming I will work in software engineering, so that her payoff would be 7 > 4, since she would not have entered the program with the assumption that I would work in information retrieval and her best payoff would be 3 < 4. Therefore, she will prepare for research in software engineering, and if I want a payoff of 3 rather than 0, I had best have a good project in software engineering for her."

This is an example of **forward induction**. The idea is that Nora can infer something from a choice that her partner has made in the past, and this inference can solve the uncertainty in the coordination problem. What Nora can infer is that Anna has high expectations for her doctoral study, expectations that can only be realized if they coordinate on research in software engineering.

There is no conflict between backward induction and forward induction, and, indeed, they complement one another. This is a problem that cannot be solved by backward induction alone—the basic subgame, shown in Table 15.1, may have payoffs for Anna either better or worse than the 4 she can get by keeping her day job. Thus, the reduced game is as shown in Figure 15.2. This gives Anna no unequivocal basis on which to make her choice. But when Anna takes into account what Nora can infer from her choice, and the influence that inference can have on Nora's choice—that is, when Anna uses forward induction—the reduced game looks like Figure 15.3. Thus, on the basis of both forward and backward induction, the subgame perfect equilibrium for this game is for Anna to quit her job and

Figure 15.2 | The Reduced Doctoral Study Game with Backward but not Forward Induction

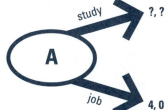

Figure 15.3 | The Reduced Doctoral Study Game with both Backward and Forward Induction

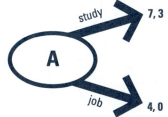

Nested and Imbedded Games

Although the terms *nested* and *imbedded games* have been used in some research, there seems to be no standard terminology. This book will use the terms in the following ways.

Suppose we have a group of players and some of their strategy options, which, if isolated, might be treated as a game either in normal or extensive form. Suppose, however, that this group of players and strategies is only part of a larger game. Then the smaller "game" is said to be "nested" within the larger game, and the larger game is the "nesting" game. In general, the only valid equilibria are equilibria of the nesting game, and proposed equilibria based on analysis of the nested game in isolation are likely to be misleading.

Suppose, however, that a nested game is a proper subgame of a nesting game. Then we say that the subgame is imbedded in the larger game, and the larger game is the imbedding game. In such a case, subgame perfect equilibrium in the imbedding game will require that the imbedded game is in equilibrium. However, analysis of the imbedded game in isolation may still be incomplete, since agents may be able to use information from the imbedding game (as in forward induction) or the equilibrium in the imbedded game may not be part of a subgame perfect sequence of strategy choices.

Nora to restart her research on software engineering. Another way to put the same point is to observe that the coordination game between Anna and Nora is imbedded in a larger game. In this case, information from the larger game allows Nora to anticipate what Anna will do, by forward induction.

Here is another example of an imbedded game,[1] derived from a classic motion picture. John Huston was the director, and Humphrey Bogart, Peter Lorre, Sidney Greenstreet, and Mary Astor led the cast. It doesn't come much better than that.

The Maltese Falcon

In the movie *The Maltese Falcon*, the plot turns on attempts to steal a statuette of a bird, which is believed to be very valuable. (If you haven't seen the movie, stop reading now and skip the rest of this example until you have seen it. I'm going to give away the ending.) The statuette was gold and jewel-encrusted. However, it was disguised by a thick coat of paint that hid the jewels and gold. Before the movie began, a gang of crooks led by Caspar Gutman (played by Sidney Greenstreet) had stolen the bird from General Kemidov in Istanbul. Gutman's confederates—Joel Cairo (Peter Lorre) and a woman named O'Shaunessy (Mary Astor)—double-crossed both Gutman and one another, and O'Shaunessy got away with the bird, but, with Gutman and Cairo in pursuit, she was unable to dispose of it at a profit.

Once Gutman and Cairo join forces again and recover the bird in San Francisco, with some help from detective Sam Spade (Bogart), they scrape off some paint and discover that what they have stolen is a lead fake, not the real statuette at all. "No wonder we had such an easy time stealing it," Cairo laments. Cairo doesn't say just what he means—how they had an easy time stealing it. But here is a reconstruction. Perhaps General Kemidov, whom we will call GK, could have chosen two strategies: either hire a guard or don't hire a guard. The Gutman Gang (GG) could go after the statue either armed or unarmed. Going armed involves costs and risks, but it means that they have a chance of getting the bird even if it is

---

1 George Tsebelis' book *Nested Games: Rational Choice in Comparative Politics* (Berkeley: University of California Press, 1990) argues that many political interactions are best understood as nested games. Many of the nested games he describes are not imbedded, and the point is that the actions observed reflect equilibria of the nesting game but may not appear rational if the nested game were considered in isolation.

Figure 15.4 | A Theft Game

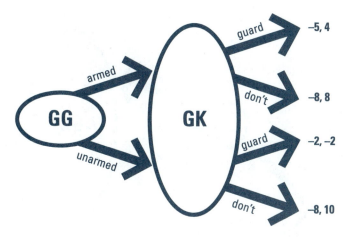

guarded. If it is not guarded, they can steal the bird even if they go unarmed. Thus, the Gutman Gang thought they were playing the game shown in Figure 15.4. The first payoff is to General Kemidov and the second is to the Gutman Gang.

The theft game is a game of incomplete information. It is shown in normal form in Table 15.2. The first payoff is to GK, the second to the GG. For this game, "guard" is a dominant strategy for GK. The crooks in the Gutman Gang, GG, thus know that their best response is to go armed. In fact, though, they discover that the statuette is unguarded, and thus their payoff is (so they believe) 8.

However, GK has another option, a strategy he can choose before the Theft Game takes place, and the Gutman Gang have overlooked it. His option is to fake the statuette and leave it where it will be easy for the crooks to steal. As a result, the crooks are really playing in a larger game shown in Figure 15.5. This game has two basic subgames, both of which are games of incomplete information. We have already solved the upper game, noting that its Nash equilibrium is (guard, armed) for a payoff of (-5, 4). The lower game is shown in Table 15.3.

For GK, "fake and don't guard" is a dominant strategy combination with a payoff of −1. In the lower subgame, (don't, unarmed) is the dominant strategy equilibrium. Thus,

Table 15.2 | The Theft Game

		GG	
		armed	unarmed
GK	guard	−5, 4	−2, −2
	don't guard	−8, 8	−8, 10

Table 15.3 | The Theft Game with a Fake Statuette

		GG	
		armed	unarmed
GK	guard	−3, −2	−3, 0
	don't guard	−1, −2	−1, 0

Figure 15.5 | Theft Game with Fakery

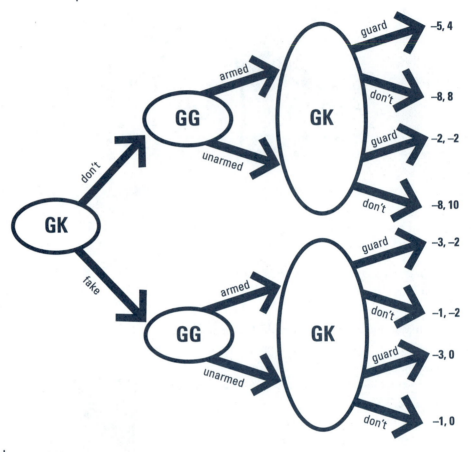

Figure 15.6 | The Theft Game with Fakery, Reduced

we can reduce the game in Figure 15.5 to the one shown in Figure 15.6. Clearly, the subgame perfect equilibrium is for the general to fake the statue and not guard the fake, allowing the Gutman Gang to steal the fake.

It had seemed to Joel Cairo that General Kemidov acted irrationally—blundered—in leaving the statuette so easy to steal. But Cairo and the Gutman Gang did not realize (until later) that their theft game was nested in a larger game. In that larger game, the general had acted rationally. Had they realized they were playing in the larger game, rather than the nested game, they could probably have seen as easily as we do that fakery would be General Kemidov's dominant strategy. They would have acted differently—not gone armed to steal the statuette, or not tried to steal it at all.

This idea—that action may be rational in the larger game, even though it seems irrational if we look only at a smaller imbedded game—has many applications. It brings with it another kind of possibility: People may find ways to change the games they are in by imbedding them in larger games. To illustrate this possibility, we return to the Centipede Game from the last chapter.

The Centipede Solved

Figure 15.7 shows the Centipede Game, repeated from the last chapter. We recall that the subgame perfect equilibrium is to grab immediately, which is inefficient. The problem is that there is no commitment. But there is a simple and fairly familiar solution to the problem. Suppose that Barb could engage a third party and post a bond of $2, with the understanding that whenever she might fail to pass the pot, Barb would forfeit the bond, but that the bond

Figure 15.7 | A Centipede Game

Repeats Figure 14.7, Chapter 14

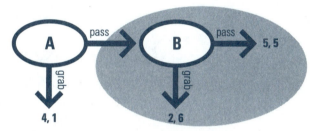

would be returned at the end if the pot were passed. This introduces a new strategy at the beginning of the game: Barb can choose, or not, to give up her freedom and flexibility, binding herself to (pass) at each stage of the game. Even though Barb posts the bond unilaterally, she will be better off to choose to do so. Unilateral initial commitment is subgame perfect and leads to the efficient cooperative outcome.

The game with payoffs **net** of the bond forfeit is shown in Figure 15.8. Once again, we solve it by starting at the end and working backward: Barb's decision is now between payoffs of 4 and 5 and since 5 is better, so she will pass at the last stage. Anticipating this, Anna is choosing (also) between 4 and 5 and chooses to pass to get the 5. Thus, the bond changes the subgame perfect equilibrium into the cooperative one.

Figure 15.8 | The Centipede after Posting a Bond

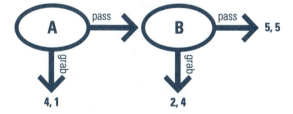

But strictly speaking, this is not a complete picture of the game with the option to post a bond. We now have a three-stage game. The first stage is Barb's decision of whether or not to post a bond. Accordingly, this larger and more complicated game is represented in extensive form in Figure 15.9.

This is a bit complicated, but we have already done most of the work. Using the method of reasoning backward, we will start at the end and work backward to Barb's decision at the beginning, reducing the tree diagram. Having solved the subgames at both of the main

Figure 15.9 | A Centipede Game with the Option to Post a Bond

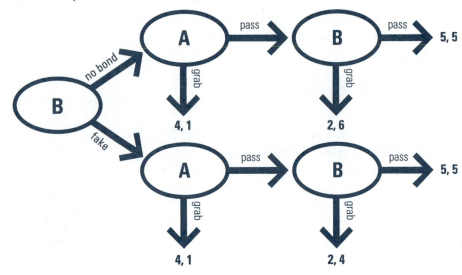

Figure 15.10 | Reduced Version of the Centipede Game with Bond

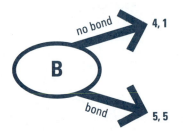

branches, we know that the game in Figure 15.9 is equivalent to the one shown in Figure 15.10.

Barb's choice is now a no-brainer. A payoff of 5 is better than 1 and Barb chooses to post the bond. But notice that Barb's rational self-interest has led her to give up one of her options, to unilaterally limit her future freedom of action. This is one surprising result in the Centipede model. Moreover, even if the bond is paid Anna does not get it. Nobody does. The bond (if paid) is lost to both players—a deadweight loss with no compensating gain. Thus, the bond, if it should be paid, would be inefficient (from the viewpoint of the two participants in the game), and it is this inefficiency[2] that makes the efficient cooperative outcome possible!

The Centipede Game is one of several examples in the theory of games in extensive form in which unilateral commitment to limit flexibility can improve the payoff both to the player who makes the commitment as well as to other players. For another example, let us revisit the Cold War—that is, the example about the Cold War that was given in the previous chapter.

---

2 If Anna did get the bond, the cooperative outcome would still be subgame perfect, and there would be no inefficiency. But that is not what we have assumed in this model. What the model shows is that *even* when the commitment is inefficient, it may nevertheless result in an efficient equilibrium—a conclusion that seems even more surprising.

Counterattack Revisited

We recall that the United States had deployed troops to West Germany as a "tripwire." Without troops in West Germany, the U.S. threat of counterattack on the Soviets was not credible. By deploying troops to West Germany, the United States in effect changed the rules of the game. The force was not strong enough to defeat a Soviet attack, but it was sufficient to make a counterattack "subgame perfect," and thus to make the threat of a counterattack credible and to deter the Soviets from attacking.

The United States was able to **change the rules** because its game of counterattack was imbedded in a larger game, in which its decision to deploy troops was one of the moves. This game is shown in Figure 15.11

In the Cold War Game, the first move is the U.S. decision either to deploy troops or not. The subgame perfect equilibrium is (deploy, don't attack) for payoffs of 3 to the Soviet Union (SU) and 2 to the United States (US)—an uneasy peace, not the best outcome we could envision, but the best available in the circumstances. The United States was able to change the rules by imbedding its game in a larger game. Labor unions can do that, too.

Why Are There Strikes?

Strikes were a common occurrence in labor-management relations in the twentieth century, and there is no reason to think that they will soon go away in the twenty-first. It is sometimes

Figure 15.11 | The Cold War with Counterattack Subgames Imbedded

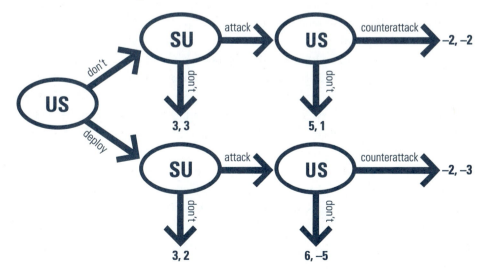

said (especially by employers) that strikes do nobody any good, and thus are irrational. Common sense says that strikes are the threat the employees use to get better wages and conditions, but, as we have seen, that doesn't really answer the question, since some threats are not credible when everyone behaves rationally and everyone knows that they do.

Table 15.4 | Strike Game

		Employees	
		strike	don't strike
Employer	don't concede	1, 1	4, 2
	concede	2, 3	3, 4

The reasoning that says that strikes are irrational goes something like this: Suppose that employees have two strategies, strike or do not strike, and employers have two strategies, concede (higher wages or better conditions) or do not concede. The employers will be less hurt by making a concession than by a strike, but the strike hurts both sides. Suppose the employer-employee game is a game of incomplete information, and the payoffs are like those shown in Table 15.4. These payoffs are meant to indicate the order of payoffs—worst, second worst, . . . best—rather than the absolute magnitudes.

Thus, the employer is always best off if there is no strike, but if there is a strike, the employer is better off to make a concession to end it quickly, whereas if there is no strike then the employer has nothing to gain by making a concession, and can only lose by doing so. This seems to express the common-sense idea that the threat of the strike is necessary for employees to get concessions. But it also agrees with the idea that the workers will never strike, if they are rational, since "don't strike" is a dominant strategy for the employees.

But strikes do happen. How so?

This game, too, is imbedded in a bigger game. The employees would like to make the threat of a strike effective, and there is a way they can do it: They can affiliate with a tough international union that is not afraid of conflict. Let's see how that works out. By affiliating, the employees give up their freedom to decide whether to strike. Instead, the strike decision will be made by a professional union tough guy (UTG) who has little to lose if there is a strike. The UTG's payoff is proportional to his reputation for toughness. Indeed, we will assume that the UTG gets a payoff of 1 if he leads a strike when the employer does not concede, or when the employer concedes without a strike. Those results enhance his reputation for toughness. If the employer does not concede and there is no strike, the UTG loses a point. That would erode his reputation for toughness. If there is a strike leading to a concession, the UTG neither gains nor loses—that's what anyone would expect from an average UTG, so it has no effect on his reputation for toughness.

This is now a sequential game and it is shown in extensive form in Figure 15.12, with E for employeEs, R for employeRs, and G for the UTG. The payoffs are shown with employer first, then employees, then UTG. The employees' payoffs do not allow for union dues. We will take care of that later.

In the first stage, the employees decide whether to affiliate with the international union. If they decide not to, then we have the game we looked at before, and it is the upper basic subgame in the diagram. If they do affiliate, we have the lower basic subgame, which is not a game between the employees and the employer but rather between the employer and the UTG.

This game is shown in normal form in Table 15.5. The table shows the payoffs in the same order as Figure 15.12.

The employer's payoffs are the same as before, but the tough guy's payoffs are quite different from those of the employees, and this game has no equilibrium in pure strategies. But, like any noncooperative game, it has an equilibrium, and since the equilibrium is not in pure strategies it must be an equilibrium in mixed strategies. Doing

Table 15.5 | Strike Game with Union

		UTG	
		strike	don't strike
Employer	don't concede	1, 1, 1	4, 2, −1
	concede	2, 3, 0	3, 4, 1

Figure 15.12 | Union Affiliation Game

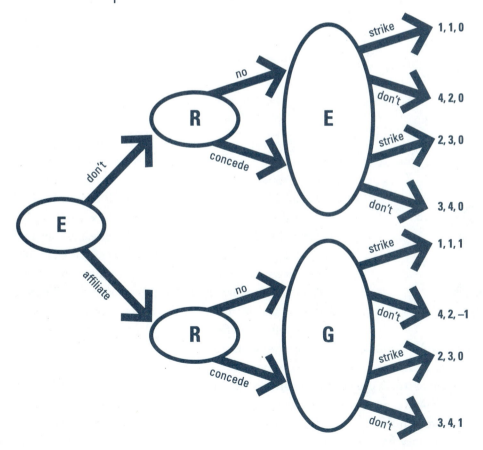

the algebra, we find that there is an equilibrium when the tough guy calls a strike with probability 1/2, and the employers make concessions with probability 2/3.

How does this work out for the employees? Since there are positive probabilities for all four outcomes, we have to compute the expected value of their payoffs (assuming they are not very risk averse). The expected value is

$$EV(Employees) = \left(\frac{1}{3}\right)\left(\frac{1}{2}\right)(1) + \left(\frac{1}{3}\right)\left(\frac{1}{2}\right)(2) + \left(\frac{2}{3}\right)\left(\frac{1}{2}\right)(3) + \left(\frac{2}{3}\right)\left(\frac{1}{2}\right)(4)$$

$$= \frac{1}{6} + \frac{2}{6} + \frac{6}{6} + \frac{8}{6} = 2\frac{5}{6}$$

But this does not allow for the union dues. We have to deduct the payoff to the UTG. (Since the UTG's payoff is partly in reputation, and the future payoffs he may get from other groups of employees, the employees in this game may not have to pay it all. But we will assume they do, since we want to see how much the workers end up with, in the worst case.) His payoff, too, is calculated in expected value terms, and it is

$$EV(UTG) = \left(\frac{1}{3}\right)\left(\frac{1}{2}\right)(1) + \left(\frac{1}{3}\right)\left(\frac{1}{2}\right)(-1) + \left(\frac{2}{3}\right)\left(\frac{1}{2}\right)(0) + \left(\frac{2}{3}\right)\left(\frac{1}{2}\right)(1)$$

$$= \frac{1}{6} - \frac{1}{6} + 0 + \frac{2}{6} = \frac{2}{6}$$

Thus, deducting the UTG payoff from that of the employees, we have

$$2\frac{5}{6} - \frac{2}{6} = 2\frac{1}{2}$$

Figure 15.13 | Reduced Union Affiliation Game

don't → 4, 2, 0

E

affiliate → 2.5, 2.5, 0.33

Since we have solved both of the basic subgames, we can now reduce the game shown in extensive form in Figure 15.12 to the one shown in Figure 15.13. This reduced game is just the employees' decision whether to affiliate with the international union. If they do affiliate, their expected value payoff is 2.5, whereas if they do not, the payoff is 2. Of course, the unionized payoff of 2.5 is risky, and if the employees are sufficiently risk-averse, this increase in their average payoff may not be enough for them. However, if they are less risk averse, they will choose to affiliate, and in that case, the international union leader, whose payoffs are different, will call strikes often enough to increase the probability of an employer concession to 2/3 from 0.

We have an answer to the question "why are there strikes?" There are strikes because a credible threat of strikes can obtain enough concessions from the employers to make it worth their while. However, in a two-person game between the employers and the employees, the employees cannot make the strike threat credible, because their dominant strategy is not to strike. Instead, they find a way to make the strike threat credible by imbedding their game with the employers in a larger game, in which the international union leader is also a player. Union officials are sometimes called *union goons*—a derogatory term, of course, but it makes a point. It is the leader's reputation for toughness and readiness for conflict, the goonishness of his reputation, that makes him useful to the employees. In the larger game, they do better than they would in the two-person game, with enough left over to pay union dues—and no one is acting irrationally or supposes that anyone else does so.

Summary

When games are nested—that is, when players make choices of strategies but those choices are incorporated within a larger game—this challenges both the game theorist and the players in the game. For the game theorist, the challenge is that the nested game cannot be analyzed in isolation, as if it were a whole game in itself. An isolated analysis along those lines is likely to be misleading, or incomplete at best. If the nested game is a proper subgame of a game in extensive form, we say that it is an imbedded game The analysis of an imbedded game in isolation is only one step in determining the subgame perfect equilibrium of the imbedding game. In the real world, in which people's activities are always "nested" in a broader context, the game theorist's challenge is to draw boundaries between games and analyze them in a way that minimizes the misunderstanding, allowing, for example, for the fact that players in an imbedded game may use information from the imbedding game, in forward induction, or may "change the rules" by choosing a different move at an earlier stage in the imbedded game. Since the equilibrium strategies in the nesting game may seem irrational in the context of the nested game, part of the challenge to the game theorist is to apply the rationality assumption correctly—in the context of the nesting game.

The challenge to the players is to understand just what game they are playing. If the players believe they are playing only in the subgame, in isolation, they may fail to choose best-response strategies (as the characters in *The Maltese Falcon* did), fail to use available information (as Nobel Nora would) or fail to assure a mutually profitable cooperative solution (as in the Centipede example) or fail to prevent an enemy from attacking (as in the confrontation between the United States and the Soviet Union in the Cold War).

Nested and imbedded games are always a challenge to the imagination. Once we have understood the game we think we are playing, or that we think we are studying, are we really finished? Or is it part of a bigger game that would give a better explanation of the decisions people make, or better decisions to accomplish their purposes?

Exercises and Discussion Questions

15.1   It's Good to Be the Dean? A few years ago, Pixel University was negotiating with a candidate for a position as dean of the College of Neat Stuff. The negotiation went on for months, with the candidate insisting that a new building should be built for the college as a condition for him to take the position. Finally the university floated a bond issue for the building, and the candidate signed the contract.

The diagram in Figure 15.E1 represents this negotiation as a game in extensive form. P stands for Pixel and D stands for Dean. At the last stage, if it has not floated a bond issue, (strategy "don't") but the candidate accepts the offer anyway (strategy "sign"), then Pixel has the options of promising the Dean that the building will be built, hiring him, and then refusing to build the new building but renovating Old Main anyway (strategy "hire"), hiring him and building the college building (strategy "college"), and declining to hire him but proceeding with the renovation of Old Main (strategy "main") The diagram is based on the assumption that once the university floated the loan, it could no longer refuse to build the college building, since the bond issue could not be used for other purposes. Therefore, if the university chooses "float"

Figure 15.E1 | The Dean's Negotiation

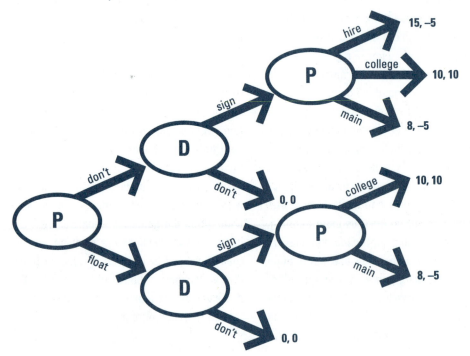

and the candidate chooses "sign," the university has only the choices of building the college building or refusing to hire the candidate.

What is the subgame perfect equilibrium of this game, and why did the dean sign the contract? Who changed the rules in this game? How were they able to do that? *Hint:* Think of the negotiation game as being imbedded in a larger game.

15.2 Corporate Partners. Transport Equipment Corp. (TECORP) sells buses primarily to urban bus services and wants to convert its buses to fuel-cell power since its customers are concerned about air pollution. Queen Hill Power (QHP) has perfected the technology for the buses and TECORP has approached QHP to produce power plants for its buses. However, this will require QHP to construct a costly, specialized facility for which TECORP will be the only buyer. QHP is concerned that TECORP will then demand a renegotiated price, which QHP will be forced to grant, and thus be a loser. Assume:

- If there is no agreement, payoffs are 0, 0.

- If there is an agreement and no renegotiation, payoffs are 100, 100.

- If there is a demand for renegotiation and QHP refuses, payoffs are 0, –100.

- If there is a demand for renegotiation and QHP gives in, payoffs are 200, –50.

- Payoffs are in millions, and the first payoff is to TECORP, second to QHP.

Construct the tree diagram for this game in extensive form. Use backward induction to determine the equilibrium. The primary stockholder in QHP proposes a merger of the two companies. How would the merger change the equilibrium and analysis? Explain in terms of imbedded games.

15.3 Free Samples. Acme Cartoon Equipment (ACE) Corp. relies on other companies to supply the semifinished parts it assembles into cartoon equipment, under contract. There are, however, two types of suppliers: Type R (reliable) and Type U (unreliable). When ACE interviews a potential supplier, ACE has two strategies: buy or not buy. Some suppliers give free samples and others do not. With a type R supplier, the game in extensive form is as shown in Figure 15.E2, in which the first payoff is to ACE and the second is to the supplier.

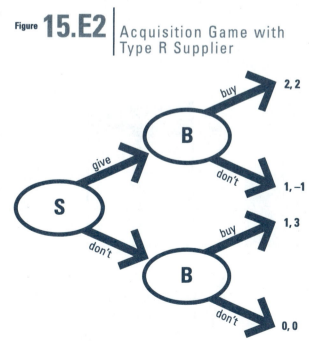

Figure 15.E2 | Acquisition Game with Type R Supplier

Figure 15.E3 | Acquisition Game with Type U Supplier

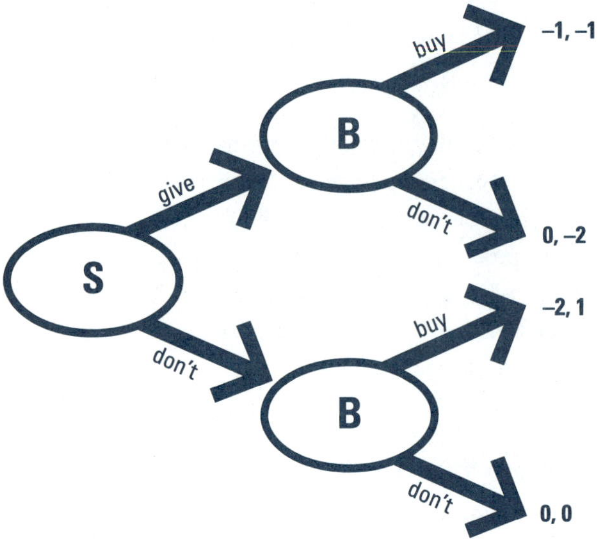

-1, -1
0, -2
-2, 1
0, 0

Node S is the decision node for the supplier, to give free samples or not, while node B is the node for the buyer, to buy or not. When the supplier is Type U, however, the payoffs are as shown in Figure 15.E3.

ACE does not know which suppliers are R and U. Suppose that the probability that the supplier is type R is 0.5.

What are the subgame perfect equilibria in the two games taken separately? Given the probabilities of 0.5 that the supplier is R or U, what is the optimum strategy for the buyer and what is the payoff from it? Suppose that ACE were to adopt the strategy of buying only from suppliers who give free samples, and suppliers know this. What would the results be? Explain this in terms of imbedded games.

15.4 Sam Spade. In *The Maltese Falcon*, detective Sam Spade advises Miss O'Shaunessy that she should not believe he is as crooked as his reputation says he is. He says that the reputation brings in high-priced business and helps in dealing with the enemy. Discuss that reasoning, drawing on the idea of imbedded games.

Table 15.E1 | Payoffs to Hot Dog Vendors

		Frank	
		$1.50	$2.00
Ernest	$1.50	10, 10	18, 5
	$2.00	5, 18	12, 12

15.5 Getcha Hot Dog. Frank and Ernest sell hot dogs from neighboring vending trucks. Each week they choose between the strategies of pricing their dogs at $1.50 or $2.00, and the payoffs are as shown in Table 15.E1. The payoff to Ernest is first.

What is the noncooperative equilibrium of this game? Frank approaches Ernest and proposes an agreement on pricing. What Frank suggests is that they both post bond of $9 and if one cuts price and the other does not, the cutter forfeits the bond, which is then paid to the other person. Will this bring about a "cooperative" solution to their pricing game? Explain your answer in terms of imbedded games.

15.6 Accreditation. College accreditation agencies often impose conditions for accreditation that universities and colleges find it costly and inconvenient to make. For example, the AACSB (which accredits business schools) requires that at least a certain proportion of course credits be taught by faculty who are full time, hold doctoral degrees, and such, and that evening courses as a group meet the same standards as the day courses as a group. This deprives the deans of business colleges of the flexibility to hire cheap part-time faculty to staff evening classes, a strategy that could be highly profitable for the schools. Yet the policies of AACSB are determined by a committee comprised of deans of business schools.

Explain why the deans of the business schools are willing to deprive themselves of flexibility and opportunities for profit in this way, using the concepts of imbedded games and games in extensive form. Here are some incidental facts that you might draw on for your analysis. (a) Deans often have to negotiate with higher administrators, presidents, and vice presidents, for increased resources for their schools. (b) If people in general were to come to believe that most evening business degree programs are staffed by less-qualified faculty, they might be less willing to enroll in those programs. (c) Large, rich business programs might benefit by using high standards to limit entry in the business school market by lesser universities that would be unable to meet those standards.

15.7 Agency. *Agency models* are used in a large literature of applied game theory in economics. For example, a corporate executive is the agent of the shareholders. Critics of corporations, such as Adam Smith, focus on this point. Adam Smith wrote, "The directors of such companies, however, being the managers rather of other people's money than of their own, it cannot well be expected that they should watch over it with the same anxious vigilance with which the partners in a private copartnery frequently watch over their own. . . . Negligence and profusion, therefore, must always prevail, more or less, in the management of the affairs of such a company. . . . To establish a joint stock company [corporation] . . . would certainly not be reasonable. . . ."[3] However, many modern corporations encourage the executives to "watch over" the assets of the company by offering them stock options in lieu of part of their salary.

For a very simple example, suppose a corporate chief executive can choose either high or low effort (H or L) and the share value of the company will be 20 (million?) if he chooses H and 10 if he chooses L; except that his compensation is deducted from the share value. Thus, for example, if he is paid a salary of 3 and chooses L the payoff to the shareholders is $10 - 3 = 7$. The executive's game payoff is his pay if he chooses L and his pay minus 2 if he chooses H. Thus, for example, if the executive is paid a salary of 3 and chooses H, his payoff is $3 - 2 = 1$. The shareholders can choose between paying him a salary of 3 or stock options worth a fraction q of the gross stock value. Thus,

---

3 Adam Smith, *An Inquiry into the Nature and Causes of the Wealth of Nations* (Oxford: Clarendon Press, 1976), Bicentenary Edition edited by R. H. Campbell, A. S. Skinner, and W. B. Todd, v. 2, pp. 741, 757. Also available online from the McMaster University Archive for the History of Economic Thought at *http://www.socsci.mcmaster.ca/~econ/ugcm/3113/smith/wealth/wealbk05* as of June 9, 2003. These passages, along with a great deal of tedious historical detail, are left out of some editions.

for example, if the executive is paid with stock options and chooses H, his game payoff is $20q - 2$, and the shareholders get $20(1 - q)$. The shareholders choose their strategy first and commit to it by signing an employment contract.

Draw the tree diagram for this problem. What is the minimum value of q that will give the executive an incentive to choose H? What is the maximum q that will make it subgame perfect for the stockholders to offer a stock option? What is the upper limit on the payoff to the stockholders? Can they get as much as they would if they paid the salary and the executive chose H? Since the corporate accounting scandals of 2001–2002, there has been much discussion of the large amounts paid to corporate CEOs in the form of stock options. What determines the maximum compensation that a CEO could get in the form of stock options in this model?

Repeated Play

All of the games we have investigated so far in this book are played just once, as if the players would never interact again in the future. In some applications that seems clearly appropriate. In political games, for example, an old saying tells us that there is no tomorrow

To best understand this chapter 16

To best understand this chapter you need to have studied and understood the material from Chapters 1–4, 6–8, and 14.

after the next election. When two cars meet at an intersection, matched at random to play the Drive-On Game, the chances that they will meet again are slight enough to overlook. But if the two drivers live on the same block, they are not matched at random, and are likely to meet one another again and again, so that they can become accustomed to one another's habits. When we look at a social dilemma like the Advertising Game, the supposition that the game is played just once with no future interaction seems quite wrong. The same firms will continue to compete in the same market year after year.

Game theorists suspected very early in the development of the field that repeated play could make a difference, especially in social dilemmas. The suspicion was so strong that it seemed as if someone must have already proved the case. Today, game theorists speak of the **folk theorem**—and we are using the word *folk* as it is used in the phrase *folk tale*. The folk theorem was supposed to say that when social dilemmas were played repeatedly, cooperative outcomes would be rather common. In fact, there was no theorem and no proof: only a folk tale. And repeated play in social dilemmas has proved to be more complex than the folk theorem suggests. Nevertheless, there is an element of truth in the folk theorem. This chapter will explore the complexities of repeated play in simple two-person games. The next chapter will try to discover the nugget of truth. Here is an example of repeated play in a social dilemma of public goods provision.

The Campers' Dilemma

Amanda and Buffy are camp counselors for the summer, and they are sharing a room with a TV and DVD player. DVDs can be rented from the camp store for the weekend for $5. Amanda and Buffy would each get $4 worth of enjoyment from a weekend movie DVD, so if each of them rents a DVD on a particular weekend they can each get $8 worth of enjoyment at a cost of a $5 rental. Their strategies are rent or don't rent, and the payoffs for the DVD rental game are shown in Table 16.1.

Heads Up!

Here are some concepts we will develop as this chapter goes along:

Repeated Games: When a game is played repeatedly, we must analyze the sequence as a whole, and the subgame perfect equilibrium of the sequence is the equilibrium of the game.

Folk Theorem: The widely held intuition that noncooperative games played repeatedly may often have cooperative equilibria is called the *folk theorem* of game theory.

Games Played a Limited Number of Times: If a game with a Nash equilibrium in pure strategies is played repeatedly, the repeated play of the Nash equilibrium is always subgame perfect. If the game is a social dilemma and is repeated a definite number of times, repeated play of the dominant strategy equilibrium is the only subgame perfect equilibrium—contrary to the folk theorem.

Table 16.1 | The Campers' Dilemma

		Buffy	
		rent	don't
Amanda	rent	3, 3	−1, 4
	don't	4, −1	0, 0

We see that this is yet another social dilemma, very much like the Public Goods Contribution Game. In fact, the DVD movies are indeed a public good to the two campers. The game in extensive form is shown in Figure 16.1.

In a social dilemma there are basically two kinds of strategies: cooperate (in this case, rent) and defect (in this case, don't rent). The idea behind the term *defect* is that the player who chooses a non-cooperative strategy is "defecting" from a (potential) agreement to cooperate.

A social dilemma is a problem! But perhaps it is not so much of a problem as all that. After all, the summer is just beginning, and there are 10 weekends ahead of them before they return to their colleges in different states for the fall term. It seems likely that they will choose "cooperate," at least for the first few weeks. After all, if (for example) Amanda chooses to "rent" this

Figure 16.1 | The Campers' Dilemma

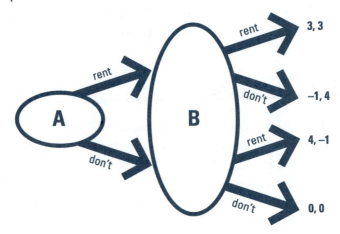

week, Buffy can reward her by continuing to choose "rent" next week, whereas if Amanda chooses the noncooperative "don't rent" strategy, Buffy can penalize or "sanction" her by turning noncooperative with a "don't rent" strategy next week and perhaps for several future weeks.

But are those rational best-response strategies? To answer that question, we have to use the theory of games in extensive form, and subgame perfect equilibrium. Surprisingly, they are not best-response strategies. To get the flavor of the reasoning, let's suppose that the DVD game is played for just two stages. The two-stage game is shown in extensive form in Figure 16.2.

The two-stage Campers' Dilemma has four basic proper subgames, shown by the gray ovals. Applying backward induction, we first solve these subgames. If we express them in normal form, we find that each of them is a social dilemma with a dominant strategy equilibrium at (don't, don't). When we substitute the equilibrium payoffs for the four subgames, we have the game shown in Figure 16.1 and Table 16.1. Since the second-round equilibrium payoffs are (0, 0), it simply reproduces the original social dilemma! The conclusion is that the repeated play in this game makes no difference: the subgame perfect equilibrium is (don't rent, don't rent) at both stages.

We can extend this reasoning to the whole 10 weeks of camp. No matter how many weeks camp continues, the method to use is backward induction. As we have seen, whatever may happen in the earlier weeks, the best-response strategy in the last week is the noncooperative "don't rent" strategy. There cannot be any rewards or sanctions on the next round because there will not be a next round. Now we proceed to the ninth week.

We already know that there will be no rewards or sanctions in the tenth week, since only noncooperative strategies will be played in the tenth. That being so, there is no reason to play anything other than the noncooperative strategy in the ninth. Now we proceed to the eighth week. Since we already know that there will be no rewards nor sanctions in the last two weeks, there is no reason to play anything other than a noncooperative strategy. And so on. . . . Reasoning in this way, we induce the result all the way to the first round of play, when there is no reason to choose the noncooperative strategy. The conclusion is that no cooperative strategy will ever be played.

"So Amanda was like, I am so out of here next week, why am I thinking of spending my money renting a DVD, and Buffy was like, it's nice to be nice, but that person is not renting a video and I'm not either. It's not like I was ever going to see her again . . ."

The intuitive folk theorem suggests that in a **repeated social dilemma** such as this one, cooperation can occur even though it is dominated in the corresponding **one-off game**. It seems that the folk theorem, however true it may be in some other cases, is not applicable to this particular game. Here is another example.

> **Rule**
>
> **Repeated Social Dilemmas**—When a social dilemma is repeated for a definite number of times, the subgame perfect play is always for both players to defect, just as in the original social dilemma.

> **Definition**
>
> **One-off Game**—When a game is played just once—and not repeated—we describe it as a **one-off game**.

Figure **16.2** | The Repeated Campers' Dilemma

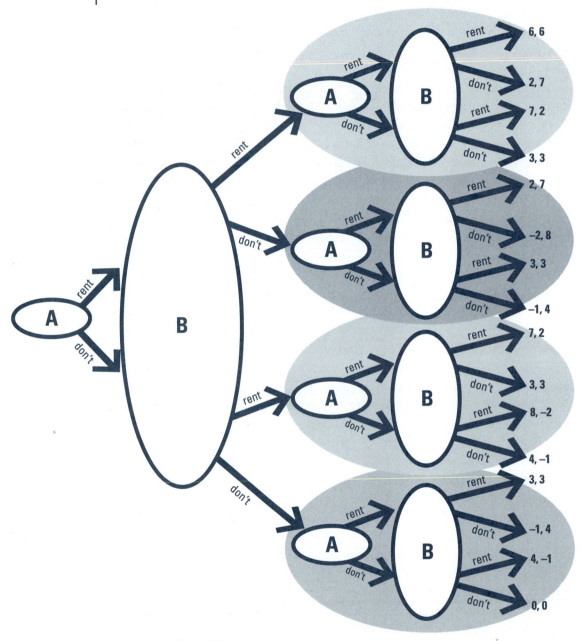

Pressing the Shirts

Nicholas Neatnik likes to have his shirts pressed every week. He can do them himself or take them to the Neighborhood Cleaners, just down the street. However, Nicholas is concerned that Neighborhood Cleaners will not take enough care, and will spoil some of his shirts.

Nicholas' strategies are to have his shirts pressed by the cleaners ("press") or not ("no"), and the cleaner's strategy is to take care ("care") or not ("no"). This game is shown in extensive form, with its payoffs, in Figure 16.3. Nicholas is A, Neighborhood Cleaners is B, and the first payoff is to Nicholas, the second to Neighborhood Cleaners.

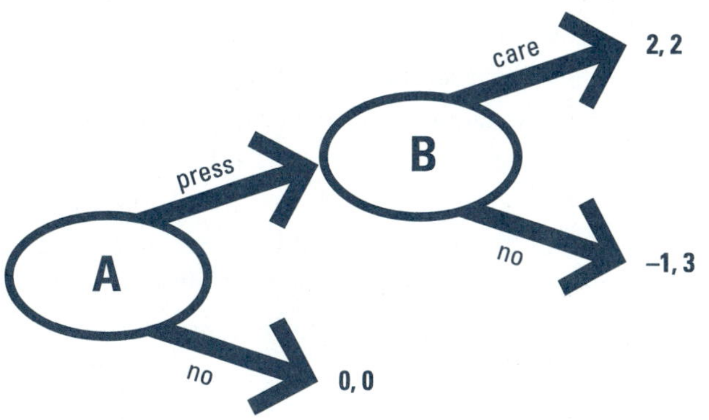

This game has a basic proper subgame in which the cleaner decides whether or not to take care, and the rational decision is not to take care, for a payoff of 3 rather than 2. That means Nicholas can anticipate a payoff of –1 if he takes his shirts to the cleaner. The payoff of 0 (doing his own pressing) is better than –1, so the subgame perfect equilibrium is that Nicholas does his own pressing.

Let's pause and look at this game in normal form. Remember, for a game like this, it is important to keep in mind that the strategies are contingent. In particular, Neighborhood Cleaners will have a choice of strategies only if Nicholas brings his shirts in for cleaning. The payoff table is shown in Table 16.2, and the equilibrium is in the lower right.

However, this is a repeated game. Nicholas will want to get his shirts done every week for the next five years. At the end of five years, he plans to retire and never wear a pressed shirt again. Thus, the Pressing Game will be played for 5 × 52 = 260 times in succession. Intuition suggests that Nicholas might be able to persuade the cleaners to take care by threatening to retaliate. Nicholas might—for example—respond to a "no care" strategy by doing his own pressing the following week. This would give the cleaner something to lose by taking no care. Could this policy of retaliation bring about a cooperative solution—(press, care)—in the pressing game?

This policy is called a **Tit-for-Tat** strategy rule. In general, when one player defects from the cooperative solution on one round, and the other player responds by defecting from the cooperative solution on the next round, the second player is said to be playing Tit-for-Tat. Strategies for a game that is

Figure 16.3 | Pressing the Shirts

Table 16.2 | Payoffs for Pressing the Shirts

		Nicholas	
		press	no
Neighborhood Cleaner	if Nicholas chooses press, then take care; otherwise, do nothing	2, 2	0, 0
	if Nicholas chooses press, then take no care; otherwise, do nothing	3, –1	0, 0

> **Definition**
>
> **Tit-for-Tat**—In game theory, **Tit-for-Tat** refers to a rule for choosing strategies of play in a repeated social dilemma or similar game. The rule is to play "cooperate" until the opponent plays "defect," and then to retaliate by playing "defect" on the following round.

repeated many times, like this one, are highly complicated contingent strategies, and there can be a huge number of them. Consider Nicholas's choice to take his shirts in to be pressed, or not, on the 201st week of his five years. This choice may depend on the choices made in each of the previous 200 rounds of play. On the first round, there are three possible patterns of play— (press, take care), (press, take no care), and (don't press, do nothing). Thus, Nicholas's choice on the second round is based on those three contingencies.[1] In the third round, his choice is based on $3 \times 3 = 3^2 = 9$ contingencies: three for the first, each of them followed by three for the second. In the fourth round, his choice is based on $3 \times 9 = 3^3 = 27$ contingencies. For the 201st round, his choice is based on 3^{200} possible sequences of play that may have gone before. If he plays according to a Tit-for-Tat rule on round 201, however, the first 199 rounds do not matter. The Tit-for-Tat rule groups together 3^{199} sequences of play that might have taken place before. It says, "*If you played press and Neighborhood Cleaners took no care on the last play*, then play no; *otherwise*, play press."[2] This rule gives the same result for all of the 3^{199} sequences of play on the first 199 rounds. Grouping together this huge family of contingent strategies by using a simple rule simplifies repeated games enormously. But does it work?

To explore that, Figure 16.4 shows a tree diagram for two successive rounds of the game. The payoffs shown are the sum of the payoffs in two rounds, with the payoff to A first and B second, as before.[3] If Nicholas plays according to a Tit-for-Tat rule, there is an implicit threat and an implicit promise. The implicit threat is this: If Neighborhood Cleaners takes no care, Nicholas will retaliate by not bringing it any business next week. The promise is this: If Neighborhood Cleaners takes care, he will reward it by bringing his business next week. What we must ask is this: Assuming Neighborhood Cleaners is rational, will it find either the threat or the promise credible?

In game theory, remember, credibility is associated with subgame perfection. So we rephrase the question, asking whether the Tit-for-Tat rule with its threat and promise leads to subgame perfect play. The key to the threat is the sequence of moves in the lighter gray oval in Figure 16.4. It is a subgame, equivalent to the single-stage game in Figure 16.3, and as we have already noticed, a play of "no" by Nicholas (player A) is a subgame perfect Nash equilibrium in this subgame. So it is subgame perfect to carry out the threat—the threat is credible.

If the promise is credible, then the threat and the promise together *are* enough to persuade Neighborhood Cleaners (player B) to use care in stage 1. If it does not use care, it ends up at the bottom of the light gray oval with a payoff of 3. If it uses care, then it is in the darker gray, upper oval (which is not a complete subgame). Within the dark gray oval, if Nicholas carries out the "promise" and brings in his shirts, then Neighborhood Cleaners can do no

---

1 Neighborhood Cleaners' strategy choice is based on six contingencies—those three if Nicholas does bring his shirts on round two and the same three if he does not—though only four of those six leave Neighborhood Cleaners with a choice to make.

2 This means Nicholas plays "press" even if he played "no" last time, so that Neighborhood Cleaners had no opportunity to ruin his shirts. In a Tit-for-Tat strategy the player who defects always gets another chance after only one round of defection by the victim.

3 Since the payoffs are only one week apart, we are ignoring the fact that the future payment is worth less than a payoff today. An economist would not approve—it is important to get this right and to discount future values to the corresponding present value! We will revisit that point in the next chapter and find that we gain more than just the satisfaction of getting the economics right. For now, we will leave it inexact for the sake of simplicity.

Figure **16.4** | Two Stages in the Pressing Game

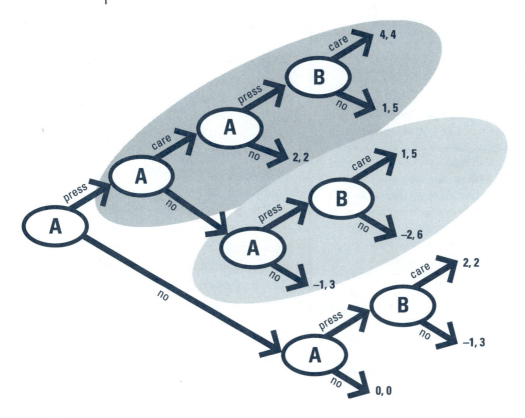

worse than a payoff of 4, better than the 3 it gets in the lower, light gray oval. However, Nicholas will bring in his shirts only if he can get the (4, 4) payoff at the upper right. If Neighborhood Cleaners plays "no care" at this step, Nicholas will be better off to renege on the promise and not bring his shirts to be pressed. Will Neighborhood Cleaners repeat its choice of "take care" on this second round? It will if Nicholas continues to play Tit-for-Tat on the 201st and 202nd plays. Thus, it is rational for Nicholas to continue to play "press" and for Neighborhood Cleaners to continue to play "take care." We have a subgame perfect Nash equilibrium with a continuing play of Tit-for-Tat on every round of play, by Nicholas, coupled with an unbroken sequence of "take cares" by Neighborhood Cleaners.

This sounds pretty promising, but unfortunately (again) it breaks down at the last round. Nicholas cannot play Tit-for-Tat on the 260th round because there is no 261st on which he can reward or punish good performance by Neighborhood Cleaners. But, remember, Nicholas' promise of reward is credible only if Nicholas is continuing his unbroken sequence of Tit-for-Tat plays. Instead, on that last round, Neighborhood Cleaners will choose no care (upper right in dark gray oval) and since Nicholas can anticipate that, he will choose "no pressing" on round 260. However, since we now know that Nicholas will choose "no pressing" on round 260,

A Closer Look

Reinhard Selten 1930 –

Born in 1930 in Breslau, Germany, which is now the Polish city of Wroclaw, Selten was of partly Jewish descent and thus suffered hardship as a youth. While a high school student, he read a *Fortune* magazine article about game theory and studied *The Theory of Games and Economic Behavior* by von Neumann and Morgenstern. While a research assistant at the University of Frankfurt am Main, he earned a Ph.D. in mathematics. Though a mathematician, he has worked on experimental studies and applications to economics; and by working on games in extensive form, then an unpopular field, he was able to do path-breaking work that led to his sharing the Nobel Memorial Prize in 1994. He lives in Bonn, Germany, where he directs the Laboratorium für experimentelle Wirtschaftsforschung, is active in the movement for the international language Esperanto, and has a Siamese cat named Chui Jr.

regardless of what happens on round 259, Nicholas cannot play a Tit-for-Tat rule on round 259. His promise to reward good behavior on round 259 with his business on round 260 is no longer credible to Neighborhood Cleaners, so it will take no care on round 259; and because he can anticipate that, Nicholas will definitely choose no pressing on round 259. But since Nicholas will definitely choose no pressing on round 259, that means he cannot credibly play a Tit-for-Tat rule on round 258, either, for the same reasons—and we can continue this sequence all the way back to round 1.

The answer to the question we started with—can the threat and the promise be credible?—is no, because there can be no unbroken sequence of play into the future. The sequence breaks at round 260, and unravels back from round 260 to round 1. Once again, we see that the folk theorem is not applicable to noncooperative games that are repeated a definite, limited number of times. And that is a general rule: In a social dilemma, consistent play of the dominant strategy equilibrium is the only subgame perfect equilibrium.

If only the sequence of repeated play could go on forever, Tit-for-Tat could work—but, of course, nothing goes on forever, right? In Chapter 17, we will revisit this and other examples and see what happens when the social dilemma is not repeated a definite number of times.

I'm going to break one of the textbook-writer's taboos, here, and speak for myself, not even putting it in a footnote. I use something approximating a Tit-for-Tat strategy in dealing with merchants myself. It's a little more complicated and probably less predictable, but if I get service that I am not happy with, I will skip doing business with that merchant for a while, and then give it another chance—and as with Tit-for-Tat, I'm relying on the implicit threat and promise. Am I irrational? Well, maybe, but . . . .

We could think of this result as a puzzle. Strategies like Tit-for-Tat seem very promising in repeated games, but in the examples we focus on in this chapter, in which the repetition comes to an end, Tit-for-Tat won't work. Is there something wrong with the Tit-for-Tat rule, or something missing from the examples? That is a question we will return to in the next chapter.

Threat of retaliation plays a part in other important games, and the next example played an important part in the development of the concept of subgame perfect Nash equilibrium—and in Reinhard Selten's share of the Nobel Memorial prize.

The Chain Store Paradox

Here is another example of repeated game reasoning. A large chain store we shall call Chainco has stores in 20 American communities. There are local companies preparing to enter those 20 markets one after another in the future. Thus, Chainco expects to play 20 market-entry games over the next few years. Intuition suggests that Chainco should retaliate in the early games, even if it takes losses doing so, in order to create a reputation as a retaliator and thus deter future entrants. But is this a subgame perfect strategy? It is not!

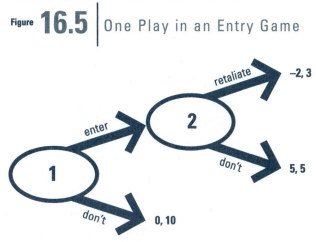

Figure 16.5 | One Play in an Entry Game

A single play in the Chain Store Game is shown in Figure 16.5. At node 1 the new company decides whether to enter or not. If it does not, then the Chain Store earns profits of 10 (on a scale of 1 to 10) in that market. If none of the local companies enters their markets, Chainco will earn 10 in each market and $10 \times 20 = 200$ in all. If the local company does enter, then at 2 Chainco decides whether to retaliate by engaging in a price war. If it does, Chainco will make only 3 of profits in this market, but the new entrant will take a loss of 2, indicated by –2. If Chainco decides not to retaliate, the market is divided and both firms earn profits of 5.

Consider the last in the series of 20 repetitions of the game. Clearly there is nothing to be gained in this case by retaliating: there are no further threats of entry. We notice then that (enter, don't retaliate) is the subgame perfect solution for the single play. Now consider the nineteenth repetition. Since retaliation is not subgame perfect on the last play, any threat to retaliate, either verbal or implicit in action, will not be credible. Therefore, there is no purpose in retaliating in the nineteenth repetition either. The same reasoning applies to the eighteenth, the seventeenth, and so on. We conclude that retaliation to create a reputation is not a best-response strategy in this game, and a rational chain store will never retaliate.

Terrorism

This section will take up a difficult and troubling topic: terrorism, and the responses of governments to terrorism. The model in the previous section will be applied. If you "just don't want to think about that today," you can skip this section without missing any new concepts of game theory.

A popular view of terrorism is that terrorists must be irrational, motivated by religious ideas that are beyond reasonable understanding or unable to reason clearly about the consequences of their actions. However comforting this view may be, it is probably *unhelpful* in thinking through responses to terrorism. One may make the judgment that the objectives of terrorists are, in some sense, irrational objectives.[4] But the term *irrational objectives* has no very clear meaning in game theory (or in neoclassical economics). In game theory, we take the objectives as given, and analyze the best-response strategies in terms of those objectives. In this section, it will be assumed that terrorists are rational *in this narrow and limited sense*.

Terrorism has a history that extends before the twentieth century. During the French Revolution, the revolutionary government of one period adopted "the terror" as a policy, and the term is traced to that period. However, governments and military forces and other armed bands, such as pirates, had terrorized people before that—probably thousands of years before—and in the twenty-first century, we usually use the word *terrorism* to refer to political violence carried out by people who are neither governments nor military forces. In the mid-nineteenth century, opponents of absolute monarchy in eastern and central Europe—constitutionalists, democrats, agrarians, and, most notoriously, anarchists—formed the "terrorist party," which resorted to bombing and assassination as part of its political strategy. This is probably the beginning of terrorism in the modern sense. This strategy has been used by groups from all points on the political spectrum, from anarchists and Marxist-Leninists to Nazis and other nationalists.

Terrorists differ in the details of their objectives and strategies, so there is no reason to think that one game-theoretic analysis applies to all cases. This section will point out one important difference. We begin, however, with a pattern that was common from about 1960 to 1995, political hostage taking. On a number of occasions during this period, hostages were taken—often by hijacking an aircraft—and the hostage takers made demands, threatening to kill the hostages if the demands were not met. There were often negotiations, and while some demands might not be met, the terrorists gained some publicity for their cause, and in some cases most hostages were released. However, some governments took the position that they would not negotiate, and, if given the opportunity, would attack hijackers despite the risk to the hostages. One reason for this policy is that negotiation gives the terrorists something they want, while a policy of consistently attacking hijackers would deter terrorist hijackings. But is that a subgame perfect strategy? It is not.

The reasoning behind this policy seems to be captured by Figure 16.6. In this hostage-taking game, the first decision is made by the terrorists, T, who decide either to take hostages or to pursue their objectives by other means. If they take hostages, then the government, G, can decide to attack or to negotiate. As usual, the payoffs are shown at the branches of the tree, with the payoff to the terrorists first and to the government second.

Notice the resemblance to the Chain Store Game (Figure 16.5). Treating it as a one-off game, we solve the game by reasoning backward. The government minimizes its losses by negotiating, which means that if the terrorists take hostages, they will gain 5, and 5 (publicity?)

4 Certainly they are objectives with which I personally disagree utterly. However, this is not quite the same thing as saying that they are irrational. Consider, for example, the objectives of a financial swindler who attempts to fleece investors of their wealth through some scheme of stock fraud. His objectives—to increase his wealth without concern about whether the means are legal or moral—would generally be considered rational. Nevertheless, I believe most people in developed modern societies would (as I do) disagree with and disapprove of the objective to increase one's wealth regardless of violations of law. What is rational might not be morally acceptable, and that applies equally to fraud and terrorism.

is better than 0, so the subgame perfect path is take (hostages), negotiate.

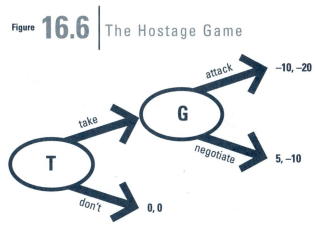

Figure 16.6 The Hostage Game

How can the policy of never negotiating with terrorists be justified? During the late twentieth century, hostage taking was not a unique event, and deterring hostage takers was a game played repeatedly. Thus, if a country could acquire a reputation as a hostage attacker, so that the terrorists would expect a negative payoff from taking hostages, this would deter terrorism. In a unique incident, the threat to attack is not credible, because it is not subgame perfect. But in repeated play, an attacker might gain in future repetitions by the deterrence effect of a reputation as an attacker.

But, so far, that is just the same as the case of the Chain Store, and as we have seen, the threat of a price war is not credible, because backward induction from the last threat tells us that it is never subgame perfect to retaliate. Is this reasoning applicable to terrorism? Can we think of a last terrorist incident, beyond which there would be no benefit from a reputation for attacking terrorists? Certainly the government hopes that terrorism will be eliminated, so there will no longer be any need for a reputation, and the terrorists probably hope to win, and become a government, so that they will no longer engage in terrorism. That doesn't quite answer the question, but suppose that the Chain Store reasoning does apply. It would tell us that even with repeated play, attacking is not subgame perfect, and so the threat to attack will never be credible. This seems to be consistent with what we observe: Terrorism was not deterred in the twentieth century. Evidently the terrorists did not find the threat of attack credible.

Of course, this analysis depends on a guess about the motivation of the terrorists—that their payoffs are negative if there is an attack, and that there is some chance that they will release hostages in order to get it. If that guess is wrong, the analysis would have to be revised. The terrorism of the late 1990s and 2001 does seem to have reflected different motives. There were no demands. The objective of the terrorists was, it appears, simply to kill and hurt—in the words of executed terrorist Timothy McVeigh, they wanted "body count."

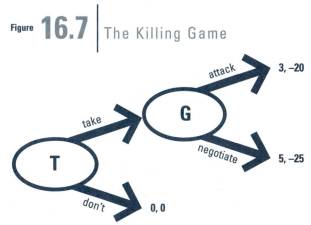

Figure 16.7 The Killing Game

That means that the terrorists get a positive payoff from hostage taking even if they are attacked. However, it might also mean that the government has something to gain by attacking the terrorists, since by doing that the government (or citizens) may disrupt the terrorists' intentions to do even greater harm. This leads to a game more like the one shown in Figure 16.7. Notice

If the chain store example is applicable, then there is no point in trying to build a reputation for "toughness." Yet, in fact, some governments did adopt the policy of not negotiating with terrorists. Were they irrational?

One assumption of this example is that all victims of terrorism are of the same type—they have the same strategies and the same payoffs. But that may not be so. John L. Scott argues* that there may be more than one type. Suppose that some victims of hijacking simply do not have the possibility of negotiating, and suppose that the terrorists do not know which potential victims are of this type. There is no point in attacking a victim who is unable to concede—that just means a certain loss of 10 for the hijackers. Not knowing which victims can and cannot negotiate, the terrorists would have to judge the likelihood of negotiations from the victim's past behavior. But that means that a victim who could negotiate might gain something by refusing—building a reputation as one of the type who cannot negotiate, and thus deterring future attacks.

But why would a victim be unable to negotiate? In this case, the victims are governments. It might be that the interactions with the terrorists are nested in a bigger game in which the ruling party interacts with opposition parties and the voters. If negotiation would be unpopular enough to cause the ruling party to lose its majority or be voted out in the next election, then, for practical purposes, negotiation would not be an option.

Some governments that took no-negotiation positions may have been in just that nested-game situation, while others may have wanted to build a reputation for being limited even though they were not.

*John L. Scott, "Deterring Terrorism Through Reputation Building," in *Defense Spending and Economic Growth*, edited by James Payne and Anandi Sahu (Boulder, CO: Westview Press, 1993) pages 257–268.

that, in this case, the terrorists get a positive payoff if they are attacked, but an even bigger payoff if they are not.

In this game, on the one hand, attacking terrorists will not deter terrorism, because the terrorists get a positive payoff even if they are attacked. On the other hand, attacking terrorists is a credible threat, because it is subgame perfect.

In the twentieth century, many countries and other authorities adopted a policy of not fighting hijackers but negotiating with them. When hijackers were motivated as shown in Figure 16.6, that was a subgame perfect strategy. However, if terrorists are motivated as shown in Figure 16.7, attacking them is subgame perfect.

We see that game theory can give two different answers, depending on the motivations of the terrorists. That should not be surprising. The message for antiterrorism policy is that we need to know the motivation of the terrorists. If we assume that they are irrational, we are not likely to ask the questions that would enable us to find out.

Summary

When social dilemmas are played "one-off," noncooperative play leads to bad results all around. However, a strong intuition suggests that repeated play changes all this, since cooperative behavior can be rewarded, and noncooperative play sanctioned, in future rounds of play. This intuition has been expressed as a *folk theorem*.

Such sequences of repeated play can be analyzed by methods from the theory of sequential games, such as subgame perfect equilibrium. This allows us to test the intuition behind the folk theorem. However, if the repetition continues only for a definite number of rounds, repeated play does not, in fact, lead to cooperation, since the only subgame perfect Nash equilibrium is a sequence of noncooperative plays. This paradoxical result extends beyond social dilemmas to other kinds of games, such as market entry games, in which the subgame perfect equilibrium is one in which an established monopolist is unable to prevent entry, a profitable noncooperative outcome.

This is a surprising result of backward induction. In every case, we begin the analysis with the last repetition of play. In this case, the play is exactly like play in the one-off game, and so the equilibrium must be the same. Any cooperative rule for retaliation or reward, such as the Tit-for-Tat strategy rule, is inapplicable on that last round. Reasoning backward, we extend that result to each repetition of the play. The strategy rule unravels from the end right back to the beginning of the game. Thus, so long as there is an end point, cooperative play cannot be an equilibrium in a repeated social dilemma. Something similar happens in a threat game like the Chain Store Game. Retaliation is not subgame perfect in the last round, and any reputation the chain store may have gained does not change that. Once again, the motivation to build a reputation as a retaliator unravels back to the first round. Intuition can be very misleading when repeated play has an end point.

Exercises and Discussion Questions

16.1 Repeated Battle of the Sexes. Sylvester and his Tweetie Pie want to get together after work either for a baseball game or an opera, but they can't get in touch with one another to decide which, because Sylvester's e-mail isn't working and Tweetie's cellphone battery is dead. (They have season tickets together at both the opera and the baseball park.) Their strategies are "game" and "opera" and the payoffs are as shown in Table 16.E1.

Table **16.E1** | Battle of the Sexes

		Tweetie	
		game	opera
Sylvester	game	5, 3	2, 2
	opera	1, 1	3, 5

Sylvester and Tweetie expect to be out together for two dates in succession. Thus, they will be playing a repeated game.

For this repeated game in normal form, enumerate the strategies of each person. How many are there? Draw the game tree. Find four different subgame perfect solutions to this repeated game. Is there any reason to think that one of these solutions might be more likely than another? Noted Unitarian-Universalist minister Robert Fulghum wrote "All I Really Need to Know I Learned in Kindergarten," and said that one of the most important things he learned in kindergarten was "taking turns." From a commonsense point of view, does this example tell us anything about the advantages or disadvantages of taking turns? What?

Table 16.E2 | Payoffs to Hot Dog Vendors

Repeats table 15.E1, Exercise 5, Chapter 15

		Frank	
		$1.50	$2.00
Ernest	$1.50	10, 10	18, 5
	$2.00	5, 18	12, 12

16.2 Getcha Hot Dog for Five More Weeks. Refer to Exercise 15.5. Frank and Ernest sell hot dogs from neighboring vending trucks. They compete against one another every week, but after five more weeks Frank is retiring and selling his truck. Each week they choose between the strategies of pricing their dogs at $1.50 or $2.00. And the payoffs are as shown in Table 16.E2.

What is the unique subgame perfect equilibrium of this repeated game? Why?

16.3 Congressional Gridlock. Gridlock has been a common problem in U.S. congressional politics in recent years. Gridlock occurs when neither party has a strong majority in Congress so that each is able to block initiatives by the other. If they do not act cooperatively, and in fact do block initiatives by the other party, nothing gets done—nothing moves, and we have *gridlock*. Analyze this in the terms of this chapter. *Hint:* Remember the old saying: "There is no tomorrow after the next election."

16.4. Whiskey and Gin. Recall the Advertising Game from Chapter 1. In that example, we observed that advertising could be a social dilemma, in that when both firms advertise, the profits for both are less than they would be if neither were to advertise. The distilled alcoholic beverage industry faced a similar dilemma in the period of the 1960s to the 1990s. In the 1990s, an unspoken agreement not to advertise on television broke down when one of the major distilled beverage companies was in danger of bankruptcy.

Suppose that Table 16.E3 gives the payoffs (on a 10-point scale) for Ginco and Whisco. Assume, also, that Whisco is in financial trouble and it is clear that Whisco will be bankrupt after three more years. What will happen in the meantime? Will one or the other of the companies advertise this year, next year, and the year after? Which? Why?

Table 16.E3 | Another Advertising Game

		Whisco	
		don't advertise	advertise
Ginco	don't advertise	8, 8	2, 10
	advertise	10, 2	4, 4

16.5 Joe Deadbeat. Joe Cool is a student at Nearby College. Joe runs short of money from time to time, and would like to borrow from his fellow dorm residents to get by, and would pay a reasonable rate of interest. However, his classmates are reluctant to lend to him, since they don't know whether he is a good risk to pay back the loan. This is a repeated game of moneylending, and each loan is a subgame like the one shown in extensive form in Figure 16.E1. In the figure, Joe's classmate, C, makes the first decision and the first payoff is to the classmate, and Joe makes the second decision and gets the second payoff.

Joe might not have much money, but he is an excellent student and is sure to graduate on schedule in four years. Joe would like to create a reputation as a good risk by paying promptly if someone will lend him money this term, but no one will take the chance. Using the theory of repeated play, explain why Joe cannot get a loan.

Figure 16.E1 | Loaning Money to Joe Cool

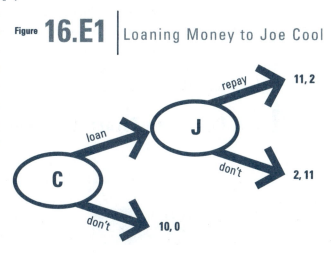

Indefinitely Repeated Play

As we think back over the examples in the previous chapter, there is a common factor that causes all the trouble—a common factor that causes both the difficulty in reaching cooperative arrangements and the counterintuitive results. The common factor is that the interactions have an end point. In the Campers' Dilemma, camp is over after 10 weeks, so the girls will not be seeing one another again. Therefore, there is no reward for cooperative behavior in that last week. The motive for cooperative behavior unravels from that last week to the first. Similarly, in the Pressing the Shirts example, the relationship ends at Nicholas' retirement after 260 weeks, and in the Chain Store example, there is a last entry threat when all other markets have been entered. There is no motive for retaliation in that last market, and the motivation for retaliation unravels from there to the first entry threat. If there were no end point—if the game were to continue indefinitely—this particular problem would not arise. We now consider an example of that kind.

A Repeated Effort Dilemma

Table 17.1 | An Effort Dilemma

		Bill	
		work	shirk
Andy	work	10, 10	2, 15
	shirk	15, 2	5, 5

Effort dilemmas are social dilemmas based on the contribution of effort to a common enterprise. Like other social dilemmas, they are likely to be played repeatedly. Table 17.1 shows an effort dilemma played by two working teammates, Andy and Bill. We can see that it is a social dilemma, since the dominant strategy is "shirk." Andy and Bill don't know how many times they will play the game, but they will play for some time and then quit. How does this work?

The idea is that there is always a 10 percent probability that this play will be the last one—and conversely, a 90 percent probability that there will be another round of play. And that will be true in the same way on every future round of play: There is always a 10 percent probability that there will be no further round of play. How likely is it that there will be at least two further rounds of play? To find that out, we have to compound the probability of two events:

with a 90 percent probability that there will be one more round of play and a 90 percent probability that (if there is a new round) there will be another new round after that. The probability that both things will happen is the product of the probabilities, 90 percent times 90 percent, or 81 percent. The general rule is that the probability that two things in succession will both happen is the product of their probabilities. The probability that n things happen in succession is the product of their n probabilities. Thus, the probability that there will be at least n more rounds of play is the power $(0.9)^n$. Table 17.2 shows the probabilities of 1, 2, . . . 20 further rounds of play for this example.

Suppose that Andy and Bill play "always shirk," so that payoffs are always 5 on every round, so long as they play at all. If they do not play, of course, payoffs are 0. Since it is uncertain what (if anything) the payoffs will be after the present round, the total payoff has to be calculated as an expected value. Thus the expected value payoff is the sum $5 + (0.9 \times 5) + (0.9^2 \times 5) + (0.9^3 \times 5) + (0.9^4 \times 5) + \ldots = 5(1 + 0.9 + 0.9^2 + 0.9^3 + 0.9^4 + \ldots)$

We can simplify this by relying on a useful fact from algebra. The useful fact[1] is that for any sequence $y, y^2, y^3, \ldots$, provided $0 < y < 1$,

$$1 + y + y^2 + y^3 + \ldots = \frac{1}{1 - y}$$

In particular, since

$$0 < 0.9 < 1, (1 + 0.9 + 0.9^2 + 0.9^3 + 0.9^4 + \ldots) = \frac{1}{1 - 0.9} = \frac{1}{0.1} = 10$$

Therefore, $5 + (0.9 \times 5) + (0.9^2 \times 5) + (0.9^3 \times 5) + (0.9^4 \times 5) + \ldots = 5 \times 10 = 50$. If Andy and Bill play (always shirk, always shirk) the expected value of their payoffs on all future play is 50.

Bill might consider playing Tit-for-Tat as a means of deterring Andy from playing "shirk." Will that work? Andy's expected value payoff if he shirks is

$$V_1 = 15 + 2\delta + 10\delta^2 + 10\delta^3 + \ldots$$

where δ is the probability of another round of play.

---

1 If you have taken macroeconomic principles, this may seem somewhat familiar—in that it resembles the multiplier formula in Keynesian economics. This is because the multiplier formula uses the same useful fact from algebra.

Heads Up!

Here are some concepts we will develop as this chapter goes along:

Indefinitely Repeated Games: When a game is played repeatedly, but with no definite end point, we treat the game as if it were repeated infinitely many times, and the subgame perfect equilibrium of the sequence is the equilibrium of the game.

Discount Factor: In future plays of the game, payoffs are *discounted* both for the passage of time and the probability that the game will not be played so many times. The discount factor for the next play is

$$\delta = p\left(\frac{1}{1 + r}\right)$$

where p is the probability that the game will be played again and r the rate of discount for time passed between plays.

Trigger Strategy: A rule for choosing strategies in individual repetitions in an indefinitely repeated game is called a *trigger strategy* if the rule is that noncooperative play triggers one or more rounds of noncooperative play by the victim in retaliation.

Tit-for-Tat: A trigger strategy that responds to a defection by a single defection on the next round.

Grim Trigger: A trigger strategy that responds to a defection by defection from that time on. Other trigger strategies are called *forgiving triggers*.

Table **17.2** | Probabilities of More Rounds of Play

Round	Probability
present	1
1	0.90
2	0.81
3	0.73
4	0.66
5	0.59
6	0.53
7	0.48
8	0.43
9	0.39
10	0.35
11	0.31
12	0.28
13	0.25
14	0.23
15	0.21
16	0.19
17	0.17
18	0.15
19	0.14
20	0.12

However, if he works it is

$$V_2 = 10 + 10\delta + 10\delta^2 + 10\delta^3 + \ldots$$

Andy is deterred if $V_1 < V_2$, that is, $15 + 2\delta < 10 + 10\delta$, that is, $5 < 8\delta$, or $\delta > 5/8$. Since the shirk strategy is a dominant strategy in the subgame, and since $\delta = 0.9$, Bill's threat is credible.

Suppose the two players choose among three strategy rules: "always defect," a cooperative "always work" strategy, and a Tit-for-Tat strategy rule. These are shown in Table 17.3. For "always shirk" and "always work" cells, we just multiply the entries from Table 17.1 by

$$\frac{1}{1 - 0.9} = 10$$

Where one person chooses Tit-for-Tat and the other chooses either Tit-for-Tat or "always work," payoffs are (10, 10) on each play, so the expected value payoffs are (100, 100). To get the payoffs when (for example) Andy chooses "always shirk" and Bill chooses "Tit-for-Tat," we observe that the payoffs in the first round will be (15, 2) and they will be (5, 5) on every subsequent round. Thus, the sequence for Andy is $15 + (0.9 \times 5) + (0.9^2 \times 5) + (0.9^3 \times 5) + (0.9^4 \times 5) + \ldots = 15 + 0.9 \times (5 + (0.9 \times 5) + (0.9^2 \times 5) + (0.9^3 \times 5) + \ldots) = 15 + (0.9 \times 5 \times 10) = 60$. For Bill the expected value payoff is $2 + (0.9 \times 5 \times 10) = 47$.

The game in Table 17.3 has two Nash equilibria: one where Andy and Bill play "always shirk" and one where both

Table **17.3** | Strategy Rules and Payoffs in a Repeated Effort Dilemma

		Bill		
		always work	always shirk	Tit-for-Tat
Andy	always work	100, 100	20, 150	100, 100
	always shirk	150, 20	50, 50	60, 47
	Tit-for-Tat	100, 100	47, 60	100, 100

play Tit-for-Tat. Moreover, the equilibrium where both play Tit-for-Tat is better for both players than the payoffs for "always shirk." Thus, it may attract the attention of the players as a Schelling point equilibrium, and we can expect that there is a good chance that it will be the equilibrium chosen out of these possibilities.

It seems we have found the kernel of truth in the folk theorem. When a social dilemma is repeated with some definite probability, but without any predictable end, there is at least the possibility that the cooperative outcome may be an equilibrium. In the real world, people work together over unpredictable but extended periods, so it is likely that many effort dilemmas are **indefinitely repeated** with some high probability.

> ### Definition
>
> **Indefinitely Repeated Games**—When a "game" is played repeatedly, but with no definite end point, we treat the game as if it were repeated infinitely many times. Such games may also be said to be **infinitely repeated**.

The Discount Factor

When we talk about infinitely repeated games, we seem to be talking about a world in which nobody ever dies, retires, or moves away! But not necessarily. The point is that there is no *definite* end to the repetition. If there is a definite end, then retaliation and reward strategies will unravel. But suppose, as in the repeated effort dilemma, there is no definite ending time, but there is some probability that the play will end on any particular round. Then we have a different situation. As we have seen, the expected value of future payoffs is finite.

The role of the probability is very much like discounting future values of payoffs that only come after some time has passed. This is a familiar idea from finance and economics. Taking it for granted that people prefer payoffs now to payoffs in the future, financial economists define a discount factor, δ, which answers the question "How much would a person pay today to get a payoff of one dollar a year from today?" The answer is, the person would pay δ today for a dollar one year from today. In general, since payoffs now are preferred to payoffs in the future, $\delta < 1$. If we then ask, "How much would a person pay today to get a payoff of one dollar two years from today?" the answer is δ^2; for three years, δ^3; and so on.

The discount factor is, of course, related to the interest rate (*discount rate*) on loans and investments. Let's say that Y is the payoff next year, and V the discounted value of the payoff on the next round. If I lend money at a rate of r, I get $1 + r$ dollars at the end of the year for every dollar I lend at the beginning of the year. Therefore, a dollar now is worth $1 + r$ dollars at the end of the year, and conversely, a dollar at the end of the year is $1/(1 + r)$ now. Therefore,

$$V = \frac{1}{1+r}Y \text{ and } \delta = \frac{1}{1+r}$$

Instead, as in the effort dilemma, we might assume that the next payoff comes so soon that the discounting to present value can be ignored, but the probability of a new round of play is $p < 1$, Y the payoff if there is a next round, and V the expected value of the payoff on the next round. Then $V = p(Y) + (1 - p)(0) = pY$. Therefore, $\delta = p$.

Suppose, for example, that the discount rate is 5 percent. We want to know the value of a $10,000 payment three years from today. Booting up the trusty spreadsheet, we find that every dollar we invest today at a 5 percent interest rate will be worth $1.05 at the end of one year and worth $1.158 at the end of three years. We divide the $10,000 by 1.158 to find that $8,638.38, invested at 5 percent for three years, would give us the same $10,000 after three years. Accordingly, $8,638.38 is the discounted present value of $10,000 three years in the future, at a discount rate of 5 percent.

Putting both ideas together, let p < 1 be the probability of another round of play, but the next round will not come until next year, and let r be the rate of time discount for one year. Then the expected value of the payoff is

$$V = p\frac{1}{1+r}Y + (1-p)\left(\frac{1}{1+r}\right)(0) = p\frac{1}{1+r}Y$$

and

$$\delta = p\frac{1}{1+r}$$

In the Chain Store Game, for example, suppose that the entry threats occur once per year, so that the twentieth entry threat is twenty years in the future. Suppose Chainco can invest its money in risk-free bonds at a rate of return of 5 percent. Therefore, a dollar invested this year, with compound interest, is worth 1.05 to the twentieth power, or $2.65 twenty years in the future. Conversely, a dollar to be received in twenty years is worth only 1/2.65 = 38 cents today. Thus, 0.38 is the discount factor for a dollar twenty years in the future at a discount rate of 0.05. But suppose also that, instead of certain entry threats for the next 20 years, there is always a 75 percent probability of yet another entry threat. Then the discount factor for the chain store game is 0.75(1/1.05) = 0.714.

The Campers' Dilemma Solved

Let's return to the Campers' Dilemma for a further example. Suppose that on the first day of camp, Amanda and Buffy start talking and discover that they have both enrolled in the same college for fall term. Not only that, they have been assigned as college roommates. Not only that, but they are both going with boys from the same town. "Is this just too incredibly incredible?" Suddenly, it seems quite probable that Amanda and Buffy will be seeing one another and playing dilemmas with one another for the rest of their lives. It isn't certain, of course—one of them might flunk out or transfer to MIT; one of them might break up with her boyfriend; one of the boyfriends, safely married, might be elected president and have to move to Washington—and, come to that, one of the girls might get sick and have to go home from camp. So there is some probability that each play could be the last. But the probability is fairly small.

Suppose the probability that this is the last play is 5 percent. A player might think: "Then the probability that cooperation on this round will be rewarded on the next round is at most 95 percent, and that means that the reward has to be at least 1/0.95 of what I give up by cooperating on this round—otherwise it will not be worth my while to cooperate on this round. I will get back, on the average, only 95 percent of the reward, so the reward has to be large enough to compensate for that."

So—supposing that Amanda and Buffy have discovered that they are (probably) going to see one another for the rest of their lives, and suppose the time discount *rate* for one week is 0.00094 and the probability that this is the last interaction is 0.05. Thus, δ is 0.95(1/1.00094) = 0.949. Suppose, also, that Amanda plays Tit-for-Tat. On the first play Amanda plays "rent (cooperate)." Buffy can reason that, if she (Buffy) plays "don't rent (defect)" this weekend, she will get a payoff of 4, but that means at most 0 on the next round, as Amanda retaliates by playing "don't rent (defect)." Her sequence of payoffs will be[2]

| Play "rent" | $3, 3, X_3, X_4, \ldots$ |
| Play "don't rent" | $4, 0, X_3, X_4, \ldots$ |

For the Tit-for-Tat strategy, the play and payoffs after the second play are not influenced directly by play on the first, so we don't need to know the value of $X_3, X_4, \ldots$. The value will be the same in either case. Thus, Buffy's choice is between payoffs of $3 + 3\delta$ and 4. "Rent" is the best choice if $3 + 3\delta = (1 + \delta)3 > 4$, that is, if

$$4 < 3(1+\delta)$$
$$\delta > \frac{4}{3} - 1 = \frac{1}{3}$$

and since 0.949 is greater than one-third, Tit-for-Tat will lead to the cooperative outcome, (rent, rent).

The payoffs to "always rent," "never rent" and "Tit-for-Tat" are shown in Table 17.4. We can see that, with $(1 + \delta)3 > 4$, (Tit-for-Tat, Tit-for-Tat) is a Nash equilibrium. However, (never rent, never rent) is also a Nash equilibrium. Perhaps the fact that (Tit-for-Tat, Tit-for-Tat) makes both players better off will make it a Schelling point in the game among these three strategies.

[2] This may seem to apply only if the noncooperation takes place on the first round, but that is *not* correct because an infinite series always has infinitely many rounds remaining to be played, and every play is the first round of such an infinite series. As the saying goes, "This is the first day of the rest of your life."

Table 17.4 Payoffs to the Infinitely Repeated Campers' Dilemma with Three Strategies

		Buffy		
		always rent	never rent	Tit-for-Tat
Amanda	always rent	$3\left(\frac{1}{1-\delta}\right), 3\left(\frac{1}{1-\delta}\right)$	$-\left(\frac{1}{1-\delta}\right), 4\left(\frac{1}{1-\delta}\right)$	$3\left(\frac{1}{1-\delta}\right), 3\left(\frac{1}{1-\delta}\right)$
	never rent	$4\left(\frac{1}{1-\delta}\right), -\left(\frac{1}{1-\delta}\right)$	0, 0	4, −1
	Tit-for-Tat	$3\left(\frac{1}{1-\delta}\right), 3\left(\frac{1}{1-\delta}\right)$	−1, 4	$3\left(\frac{1}{1-\delta}\right), 3\left(\frac{1}{1-\delta}\right)$

> ## Definition
>
> **Trigger Strategy**—A rule for choosing strategies in individual repetitions in an indefinitely repeated game is called a **trigger strategy** if the rule is that noncooperative play triggers one or more rounds of noncooperative play by the victim in retaliation.

However, this is still not the whole story. There are other rules for choice of strategies. Tit-for-Tat is one instance of what are called **trigger strategies**. (A noncooperative strategy on one play *triggers* a sanction on the next.) We could also consider a number of other trigger strategies, for example:

- *The Grim Trigger*, which means that a single, noncooperative strategy from one player triggers a switch to "never cooperate" so the retaliator chooses noncooperative strategies from that time on.

By contrast, Tit-for-Tat is known as a "forgiving trigger." The "Grim Trigger" is grim because it means no further cooperation whatever. In the Campers' Dilemma, the Grim Trigger will secure cooperation provided

$$4 + \delta\left(\frac{1}{1-\delta}\right)0 < 3\left(\frac{1}{1-\delta}\right)$$

Here is the reasoning: If Amanda plays the Grim Trigger and Buffy doesn't rent on this round, then Buffy gets a payoff of 4 on this round and 0 on all subsequent rounds, and

$$4 + \delta\left(\frac{1}{1-\delta}\right)0$$

is the discounted expected value of that stream of payoffs. If Buffy rents on this and every other subsequent round, the discounted expected value of her payoff is

$$3\left(\frac{1}{1-\delta}\right)$$

With a little algebra, Buffy will be better off always to rent if

$$4 < \left(\frac{1}{1-\delta}\right)3, \text{ that is, } 1-\delta < \frac{3}{4}, \text{ or further, } \delta > 1 - \frac{3}{4} = \frac{1}{4}$$

We see that in this case the Grim Trigger can be effective when Tit-for-Tat is not, since Tit-for-Tat is effective only with $\delta > 1/3$. For δ between 1/4 and 1/3, the Grim Trigger is effective but Tit-for-Tat is not. This is true in general: The Grim Trigger can enforce cooperation where forgiving triggers do not.

Other forgiving trigger strategies include the following:

- *A Tit for Two Tats*, meaning that the player retaliates with one round of noncooperation only after two rounds of noncooperation. Notice that this strategy rule can be "beaten" by a counterstrategy of alternating cooperation and noncooperation, since in that case the aggressor gets the benefits of acting noncooperatively on alternative rounds without ever suffering retaliation. Thus A Tit for Two Tats is likely to be weakly dominated by Tit-for-Tat.

- *Two Tits for a Tat*, which means that the player retaliates with two rounds of noncooperation for every noncooperative play by the other player. In the Campers' Dilemma, Two

Tits for a Tat will lead to cooperation whenever δ is greater than 0.2637. Notice that this is slightly more than the 0.25, which is the limit for the Grim Trigger, but less than the 0.33 needed for Tit-for-Tat. This makes sense, since the threat of two rounds of noncooperation is intermediate between one round and every future round.

It must be clear that there could be an infinite family of variations on these themes for an infinite game, and many of them will be equilibria. Not all of the equilibria will be efficient cooperative play, either. In fact, in many games there are equilibria with average payoffs at all levels between purely noncooperative and purely cooperative play.

From a mathematical point of view, this range of possible equilibria is an embarrassment of riches. The mathematician wants one solution, and wants the solution to have given properties, such as efficiency. But from a pragmatic point of view, the glass is half full. Using the Schelling point concept, it is likely that among all these equilibria, the ones that bring forth efficient cooperative play will attract attention, so that players of dilemmas that will probably be repeated will often find ways to enforce cooperative play.

Poison Gas

Poison gas was used as a weapon by both sides in World War I, but was not used in World War II. Of course, World War II was not a picnic in the park. Weapons even more terrible than gas were used, and horrors that some would find more terrible than any weapon took place. Yet gas was not used.

Table 17.5 is an example based on the experience of the use of poison gas. The two countries are Allemand and Angleterre. If one uses gas and the other does not, then the country that uses gas gains a slight advantage, indicated by a payoff of 3 rather than 0. The country that is the victim of gas suffers great loss, indicated by a payoff of −10. If both use gas, both suffer losses nearly as great, indicated by payoffs of −8 for

Table 17.5 | Gas

Repeats Table 3.E3, Exercise 4, Chapter 3

		Angleterre	
		gas	no
Allemand	gas	−8, −8	3, −10
	no	−10, 3	0, 0

both. Looking at the table, we see that this is a social dilemma. Table 17.5 repeats the table from the exercise in Chapter 3, where it was used as an example of a social dilemma.

Played as a one-off game, the Gas Game has a dominant strategy in which both sides use gas—as did happen in World War I. But it is not necessarily a one-off game. In a long war, there may be many occasions in which gas may be used by one side or another or both, and there is also some probability that the war will continue until a future occasion for the possible use of gas. Thus, we can apply the theory of indefinitely repeated games.

If neither side uses gas, the payoffs in this repeated game are a string of zeros. Suppose, then, that Allemand plays Tit-for-Tat and Angleterre "cheats" just once on this round by using gas. Then the payoffs for Angleterre are as follows:

Play "gas"   3, –10, X$_3$, X$_4$,…
Play "no"   4, 0, X$_3$, X$_4$,…

The cooperative strategy "no" is better if

$$3 + \delta(-10) < 0 + \delta 0 = 0$$

that is

$$\delta > \frac{3}{10}$$

The conclusion is that the Tit-for-Tat strategy can lead to a cooperative outcome in which nobody uses gas, provided the chances of the war continuing until an occasion of retaliation are no less than 3 in 10.

What about the Grim Trigger? The Grim Trigger may be realistic in this case, as the issue is often put this way: "If we use gas, that will open the door, and gas will be used from that point on." So, suppose that Allemand plays the Grim Trigger and Angleterre uses gas on this round. Then the payoffs for Angleterre are

Play "gas"   3, –8, –8, –8,…
Play "no"   0, 0, 0, 0,…

The cooperative strategy is better if

$$3 + \delta \frac{1}{1-\delta}(-8) < \frac{1}{1-\delta}0$$

that is

$$\delta > \frac{3}{11}$$

so the Grim Trigger can maintain the nonuse of gas so long as the probability of the war continuing to at least one more occasion for retaliatory use of gas is at least 3/11.[3] We see, as always, that the Grim Trigger, with its more complete retaliation, can maintain cooperation when Tit-For-Tat cannot, that is, when

$$\frac{3}{10} > \delta > \frac{3}{11}$$

So we may be able to understand how it is that gas was not used in World War II. But gas was used in World War I, and nuclear weapons were used in World War II. How are these contrasts explained?

The payoffs to the use of gas may have been greater in World War I than in World War II. In World War I, gas was used in trench warfare, as one part of a coordinated attack to overcome the enemy's trenches. Trench warfare was not as important in World War II, so the payoffs to using gas could have been even less. But, in fact, even if the payoffs were the same, the different outcomes in different cases should not be surprising. Remember, the repeated game has more

---

3 The probability would have to be more than 3/11 to allow for time discounting, but, since the timing is uncertain, it is not quite clear how much to allow for discounting.

than one equilibrium, and "always defect" is always one of the equilibria in a repeated social dilemma. It may be that we simply observed one equilibrium ("always defect") in World War I and another equilibrium (symmetrical Tit-for-Tat) in World War II.

As to nuclear weapons, they were used in World War II in these circumstances: (1) the enemy did not possess nuclear weapons with which to retaliate, and (2) it was expected that the use of the weapon would end the war, so that there would be no further occasions for the use of nuclear weapons between the United States and Japan. Thus it was not a repeated game.

All in all, it seems that gas in World War II was nearly an ideal case for cooperative strategies via a trigger strategy. There are many other instances of self-restraint in war that fit the same reasoning. All the same, we should not lose sight that there is nothing inevitable about the cooperative equilibria, and unrestrained use of all weapons and tactics, however dreadful, is a possibility whenever nations go to war.

Collusive Pricing

The most important applications of trigger strategy reasoning in economics are probably to collusive pricing. In an oligopoly (i.e., an industry with only a few sellers), the sellers may be able to maintain the monopoly price, and so maximize the profits for the group as a whole. This creates an incentive to "cheat" by offering a cheaper price and thus taking business away from the rival firms that continue to charge the monopoly price. For an example, consider the pricing dilemma shown in Table 17.6. The duopolists, Magnacorp and Grossco, can each benefit by maintaining prices, but each can gain an even bigger advantage by cutting price when the other does not. Thus, cutting is a dominant strategy.

However, pricing games are played repeatedly. Thus, the duopolists might consider using trigger strategies to elicit cooperation. For example, a Tit-for-Tat strategy will work if $\delta > 3/5$. The Grim Trigger strategy will work if $\delta > 3/7$.

There is evidence that thinking in terms of trigger strategies played at least some role in the decision not to use gas in World War II. According to Robert Harris and Jeremy Paxman,* an early British proposal to use gas was rejected on the grounds that "British use of gas would 'immediately invite retaliation against our industry and civil population.'"(p. 112) Winston Churchill, the British prime minister, advocated use of gas in some circumstances but the circumstances never arose, and Churchill attributed concern about British retaliation to the Germans. He said, "But the only reason they have not used it against us is that they fear retaliation." (p. 130) Under interrogation, German government figure Hermann Göring confirmed this (p. 138). American President Franklin Roosevelt explicitly threatened retaliation amounting to a Grim Trigger if the Japanese were to use gas against the Chinese (p. 120). Other motives, including treaty obligations and moral restraint, clearly played some role, too, but underlying it all was the fear of retaliation.

*_A Higher Form of Killing_ (New York: Random House Trade Paperback Edition, 2002). I am indebted to my student Ying Zhang for bringing this book to my attention.

Table **17.6** | Payoffs in the Pricing Dilemma

		Grossco	
		maintain price	cut
Magnacorp	maintain price	5, 5	0, 8
	cut	8, 0	1, 1

Here is the reasoning. Suppose Magnacorp is considering a Tit-for-Tat strategy rule. The question is whether retaliation will deter a single round of defection by Grossco. If Grossco cuts price just once and then returns to the maintain price strategy, its payoffs are

$$8, 0, X_3, X_4, \ldots$$

whereas if they continue to maintain price, the payoffs are

$$5, 5, X_3, X_4, \ldots$$

So Grossco will be deterred if

$$5 + \delta 5 > 8$$
$$(1 + \delta)5 > 8$$
$$(1 + \delta) > \frac{8}{5}$$
$$\delta > \frac{8}{5} - 1 = \frac{3}{5}$$

For the Grim Trigger, both companies know that a single defection will lead to mutual defection on every subsequent play. Therefore, the payoffs for a "cut" strategy are

$$8, 1, 1, 1, \ldots$$

and for "maintain" they are

$$5, 5, 5, 5, \ldots$$

so the discounted value payoffs are

$$\text{cut} \qquad 8 + \frac{\delta}{1 - \delta}$$

$$\text{maintain} \qquad 5\frac{1}{1 - \delta}$$

Grossco will be deterred from cutting if

$$5\frac{1}{1 - \delta} > 8 + \frac{\delta}{1 - \delta}$$
$$5\frac{1}{1 - \delta} - \delta\frac{1}{1 - \delta} > 8$$
$$(5 - \delta)\left(\frac{1}{1 - \delta}\right) > 8$$
$$5 - \delta > 8(1 - \delta) = 8 - 8\delta$$
$$7\delta > 3$$
$$\delta > \frac{3}{7}$$

Thus, again, we see that the Grim Trigger may deter noncooperative behavior where Tit-for-Tat fails.

Thus, it should not be difficult for the members of a stable duopoly to collude to keep prices up. What is modestly good news in many other situations is modestly bad news for price competition and antitrust policy, since cooperative behavior by duopolists in pricing dilemmas corresponds to prices that exploit monopoly power vis-a-vis consumers. When the members of an oligopoly keep their price high without making an explicit agreement to do so, this is called **tacit collusion**. What the example suggests is that in duopolies, tacit collusion may be common and difficult for public policy to prevent.

> **Definition**
>
> *Tacit Collusion*—When sellers of a particular good or substitutable goods keep their prices up to obtain a monopoly profit, they are said to *collude*. If they are able to do this without an explicit agreement to maintain their prices, their collusion is *tacit*, that is, unspoken. We then describe it as **tacit collusion**.

However, oligopolies may have more than two firms—three, certainly, perhaps four or more. The upper limit for oligopoly is vague and probably depends on the circumstances. All of our examples on repeated games have been two-person games, including this oligopoly example. There has been little research (if any!) on trigger strategies with more than two players, and, indeed, it is hard to know what a Tit-for-Tat strategy would mean in a three-firm industry or a three- or more-person game in general. Does the retaliator cut price if just one of his rivals have cut in the previous round, or only if both of them have cut?

Errors

The Grim Trigger strategy seems rather, well, grim, since it shuts off all possibility of cooperation in the future, to the disadvantage of both parties. But it is not really that bad, in theory. The Grim Trigger will never be adopted unless it is sufficient to induce both parties to cooperate, so when it is adopted, we will see cooperative behavior, and the sanction of cutting off cooperation will never be invoked. But this runs into some difficulties if we allow for any irrationality at all. Suppose that the players sometimes have *trembling hands*: they always know the best-response strategy but sometimes, by accident, choose the wrong one. Then a single error could lead to a Grim Trigger sanction, and no further cooperation between the players. That really is pretty grim.

Forgiving trigger strategies may be more tolerant of error, but even so, errors could have serious consequences. Suppose that both players are playing Tit-for-Tat. One chooses noncooperation in error, the other retaliates on the following round, and the first retaliates for that on the next round, and so on, with no further mutual cooperation. However, application of the Tit-for-Tat strategy needs not be quite that mechanical. Expected play on rounds $n + 2$ and so on does not influence play on round n, with the Tit-for-Tat strategy, whereas the Grim Trigger gets its power from the expectation of noncooperation on all future rounds. Thus, a Tit-for-Tat strategy could be modified by some error-correction routines. We might have a

"Tit-for-Tat but Pardon Me" strategy: "retaliate on round n + 2 for a noncooperative play on round n + 1 except when I myself have played noncooperatively by error on round n." (An apology might help, too.) The victim might apply a "Tit-for-Tat with Pacific Overtures," along the lines of "Retaliate on round n + 1 for a noncooperative play on round n, but skip the retaliation after four rounds of alternating noncooperative play." These more complex routines could allow recovery from errors, but might be open to exploitation by a shrewd opponent.

Trigger strategies with errors have not been much studied, however, so there remains a good deal to learn.

Summary

As we have seen, repeated play in itself does not solve the problem of social dilemmas. The answer to the paradox seems to be in the fact that people often don't know just how long their relationships will last. When we allow for the fact that there is some probability of continuing the relationship for another play—but the probability is usually less than 1—we can introduce *trigger strategies*, such as Tit-for-Tat and the Grim Trigger. These trigger strategies can often support cooperative equilibria. (As a dividend, we also give a correct treatment of discounting payoffs to present value in games that continue over time.) When we see cooperation in repeated social dilemmas, it is probably because the game does not have a definite end, but, rather, there is always some probability of another round of play.

Thus, repeated play does make a difference, but does so primarily when the game continues for an indefinite, not a definite, period. Even then, there may be many equilibria. After all, there are infinitely many trigger strategies, and generally there will be equilibria with average payoffs at the cooperative level, the noncooperative level, and every possibility in between. So even in indefinitely repeated games, cooperative play is not a certainty. But it is a possibility.

Exercises and Discussion Questions

17.1 Pressing the Shirts. Reanalyze the "Pressing the Shirts" example from Chapter 16 on the assumptions that the probability of Nicholas retiring and not having any more shirts pressed is .02 on any round of play and that a dollar today is worth 1.00094 dollars a week from today (which corresponds to a 5 percent rate of discount for a year). Does the Tit-for-Tat rule work in this case? Explain.

17.2 Tourist Trap. Stores in tourist resorts have a reputation for being untrustworthy, offering poor-quality merchandise at excessive prices, which leads to the stereotype of the "tourist trap." Assume that there is some truth to the stereotype—that stores in tourist resorts are at least somewhat more likely to victimize their customers than other stores—and explain why this might be, using concepts from this chapter.

17.3 Getcha Hot Dog from Now On. Refer to Exercise 15.5 and Exercise 16.2. Frank and Ernest sell hot dogs from neighboring vending trucks. Each week they choose between the strategies of pricing their dogs at $1.50 or $2.00, and the payoffs are as shown in Table 17.E1. Suppose (although there is no bond) Frank changes his mind and decides to continue in the business as long as his health permits. What difference would this make?

Table 17.E1 | Payoffs to Hot Dog Vendors

Repeats Table 15.E1, Exercise 15.5, Chapter 15

		Frank	
		$1.50	$2.00
Ernest	$1.50	10, 10	18, 5
	$2.00	5, 18	12, 12

17.4 Why Gridlock? Refer to Chapter 16, Exercise 3. In recent years, "gridlock" between the two parties has been a problem. During the administrations of Dwight Eisenhower, John Kennedy, and Lyndon Johnson, Congress was very divided but nevertheless the two parties cooperated fairly well on routine business. However, after President Nixon had to give up the office of president over the burglary of the Democratic party office in the Watergate Hotel, "gridlock" resulting from a failure of the two parties to cooperate on routine business has been more common. In retrospect, it seems likely that President Nixon made an "error," (i.e., the Watergate burglary was not a best-response strategy). Discuss this experience, before and after Watergate, using the concepts of trigger strategies.

17.5 The CEO Game. The CEO of Enrob Corp. is very powerful. He administers the employees' pension fund and could convert it for his own profit if he wished. This strategy is "grab" and the CEO's other strategy is "don't grab." The employees' strategies are "work" and "shirk." The payoffs are as shown in Table 17.E2.

Table 17.E2 | The CEO Game

		Employees	
		work	shirk
CEO	grab	7, 0	1, 1
	don't grab	5, 3	0, 4

a. Treat this game as a one-off game and determine its Nash equilibrium or equilibria. Contrast the Nash equilibrium in this analysis with the cooperative solution.

b. Observers note that the employees of Enrob are very loyal and hardworking and the employees' pension fund is very generous and stable. (It is all invested in Enrob stock, but that stock has been rising consistently.) Explain this, using concepts from this chapter and assuming that $\delta = 1/2$.

c. The CEO is notified by the CFO that some innovative investment strategies have failed, losing a great deal of money, so that the CEO is certain to be fired at the next meeting of the board of directors. How is this likely to change the equilibrium of the CEO game?

Table **17.E3** | The Advertising Game

Repeats Table 1.3, Chapter 1

		Fumco	
		don't advertise	advertise
Tabacs	don't advertise	8, 8	2, 10
	advertise	10, 2	4, 4

17.6 **"Cigareets and Whiskey and Wild, Wild Women."** Recall the Advertising Game from Chapter 1. In that example, we observed that advertising could be a social dilemma, in that when both firms advertise the profits for both are less than they would be if neither were to advertise. In fact, the tobacco companies were able to restrain themselves from advertising on TV. Suppose that Table 17.E3 gives the payoffs (on a 10-point scale) for Fumco and Tabacs, as shown in Chapter 1. Using the theory of indefinitely repeated games, explain why the tobacco companies were able to maintain the cooperative solution in this game.

As we noted in Exercise 16.4, the distilled alcoholic beverage industry faced a similar dilemma in the period of the 1960s to the 1990s. They, too, were able to continue a cooperative solution without advertising. However, in the early 1990s, one of the major distilled beverage companies was in danger of bankruptcy. At that point, the agreement broke down, but a threat of government enforcement restored the status quo without TV advertising. What might have changed to cause the breakdown of an agreement that had been maintained for decades?

Selected Applications

18 Game Theory, Law, and Social Mechanism Design

To best understand this chapter 18

To best understand this chapter you need to have studied and understood the material from Chapters 1–9, 12, 14, and 15.

Games such as poker, golf, and soccer are defined by their rules, and, in many cases, there are international commissions or associations to define and sometimes revise the rules. Many of the metaphorical games we have considered in this book, such as economic competition and environmental pollution, have "rules" more or less defined by law or public policy. Those who make the laws and policy rules—legislators, judges, citizens—should be concerned that the rules have good results. But the results will depend on how people respond and interact with one another once the rules are in place. Some kinds of rules may lead to unanticipated bad results if people act noncooperatively, choosing a best response to the actions of others without efficiently coordinating the action of a whole group. Since there is evidence that people often (though perhaps not always) behave noncooperatively, it seems reasonable to try to design rules that can achieve their objectives even when people do indeed act noncooperatively. Rules with that property are said, in the jargon of economic game theory, to be *incentive compatible*, meaning that no rational self-interested person has an incentive to act against the objectives of the rules.

We can approach the design of incentive-compatible rules in this way:

1. Start with a candidate set of rules.

2. Consider the rules as a game and determine the Nash equilibrium as a prediction of the results of the rules, supposing people act noncooperatively.

3. If the results are not satisfactory, change the candidate rules and try again. The game-theoretic analysis may give important clues as to how the rules can be changed to make them more effective.

4. If this process leads to a set of rules with a satisfactory Nash equilibrium, propose them as the rules to be adopted. Since the rules can be thought of as defining a social mechanism, this process is called *social mechanism design*.[1]

---

1 Of course, this program has deep and distinguished roots in the tradition of social philosophy. Without returning to ideal societies in classical Greek philosophy, we see in social mechanism design strong echoes of Jeremy Bentham's "utilitarian" philosophy of law and of the rule-utilitarianism of the great philosopher of liberty, John Stuart Mill. However, the application of game theory contributes both a more precise conception of rational self-interest and the contrast of cooperative and noncooperative solutions.

Liability

One familiar role of law is to define liability or responsibility for accidents. Consider, for example, a game between a motorist and a pedestrian. Each participant can choose between two strategies: take "due care" to avoid an accident, or take no care.[2] Exercising due care requires effort, and the money equivalent of the effort cost is $10. If there is an accident, the pedestrian bears the cost, assumed to be $100. If either participant fails to exercise due care, there will be an accident with certainty. Thus, for example, if neither participant exercises due care, the payoff to the pedestrian is −100 and the payoff to the motorist is 0. Even if both parties exercise due care, there is still a 10 percent probability of an accident, so that, even if due care is exercised by both, the pedestrian faces an expected value of −10 accident cost. As a result, the payoff to the pedestrian, even if both participants exercise due care, is −20, the total of −10 effort cost and −10 expected accident cost. (Of course these numbers are arbitrary and are chosen for purposes of illustration.) The payoff table for this game is shown as Table 18.1, assuming that the law does not define any liability for the accident. The first payoff in each cell is the payoff to the pedestrian.

This game can be solved by eliminating dominated strategies. The dominated strategy is shaded in Table 18.1. For the motorist, we see, no care dominates due care. Taking that into account, the pedestrian chooses his best (least bad!) response, which is to exercise no care. Thus, (no care, no care) is the Nash equilibrium for this game.[3]

This does not seem satisfactory. With *transferable utility*, the cooperative solution is that both participants exercise due care, for the maximum total payoff of −30. As such, it is efficient. The law is also

Heads Up!

Here are some concepts we will develop as this chapter goes along:

Mechanism Design: When we treat the desired outcome of the game as a given and try to discover what rules will give that outcome as a Nash equilibrium, we are engaging in *mechanism design*.

Liability: In law, liability rules determine who is responsible for accidents or for the consequences of insufficient care. Different liability rules may lead to different Nash equilibria in some applications.

Revelation: Successful mechanism design may require that people be given incentives to reveal information they have that the designer and authority lack.

Rules Rather than Discretion: Many economists and game theorists believe that it is best to design a monetary authority that acts according to rules, rather than acting with discretion.

Table **18.1** | No Liability

		Motorist	
		no care	due care
Pedestrian	no care	−100, 0	−100, −10
	due care	−110, 0	−20, −10

Definition

Transferable Utility—A game is said to have **transferable utility** if the subjective payoffs are closely enough correlated with money payoffs so that transfers of money can be used to adjust the payoffs within a coalition. Side payments will always be possible in a game with transferable utility but may not be possible in a game without transferable utility.

2 Legal routines have evolved to give precise enough meanings to terms like *due care* and *great care* so that they can be verified in court proceedings, vague as the terms may seem to laypersons.

3 The examples in this section have been influenced by Douglas Baird, Robert Gertner, and Randall Picker, *Game Theory and the Law* (Cambridge, Mass.: Harvard University Press, 1994), Ch. 1.

Table 18.2 | Strict Liabilty

		Motorist	
		no care	due care
Pedestrian	no care	0, −100	0, −110
	due care	−10, −100	−10, −20

concerned with equity, and since the lower-right cell is the only one in which the vulnerable pedestrian does not suffer the full loss of an accident, it appears that (in this instance!) the cooperative outcome is also relatively equitable. It seems pretty clear that the bilateral due care outcome is the one we would want to see in equilibrium. Thus, we might want to consider a *legal mechanism* with a liability law that assigns some or all responsibility to the motorist, who is less vulnerable. Although legal scholars do not use the term **mechanism design**, which comes from economics, this is an instance of (legal) mechanism design.

In a legal system with *pure strict liability*, the motorist would be held responsible (liable) for any accident. Thus, if an accident were to occur, the pedestrian could go to court and sue the motorist, and the court would "make the pedestrian whole" by awarding him the $100 cost of the accident.[4] The payoffs for this case are shown in Table 18.2.

This game, too, can be solved by elimination of dominated strategies. In this game, the pedestrian has a dominated strategy. "No care" dominates "due care." Knowing this, the motorist minimizes his losses by exercising no care, and we are back at the same outcome as before, although for a different reason. Apparently, strict liability is not the answer. We want a legal rule that creates an incentive for each of the two participants to take due care.

A legal standard with wide application in Anglo-American law of torts[5] would allow the

Table 18.3 | Negligence and Contributory Negligence

		Motorist	
		no care	due care
Pedestrian	no care	−100, 0	−100, −10
	due care	−10, −100	−20, −10

pedestrian to recover his costs only if the motorist has been negligent (failed to exercise due care) and the pedestrian has not been negligent (has exercised due care). If the pedestrian has not exercised due care, he is said to have contributed to the danger of the accident by his negligence, and because of this *contributory negligence* the motorist is not held responsible. The payoffs for this game are shown in Table 18.3. This game, too, can be solved by elimination of dominated strategies. For the pedestrian, "no care" is now a dominated strategy, as shown by the shaded cells. Once we eliminate those cells, "no care" becomes a dominated strategy for the motorist, and we are left with the cell at the lower right in Table 18.3. Both the motorist, knowing that he will be

---

4 It is a truism that all lawsuits are about money, so the victim can only be "made whole" in monetary terms. Thus, the game theoretic assumption that money is equivalent to transferable utility fits well in legal applications. At the same time, when we use game theory analyses as predictions of human behavior, as these applications do, we should use "due care" by keeping in mind that real human beings may be motivated by subjective considerations, including risk aversion, that are not easy to reduce to monetary terms. These issues lead to models that are too complicated for this introductory text, of course.

5 The word *tort* in legal language means an unintentional violation of the rights of another. By contrast, a crime would be intentional. Although the word *tort* is not often used in everyday language, words like *torture* and *torturous* are derived from the same root, and the common meaning is to hurt.

responsible if there is an accident, and the pedestrian make the rational, self-interested choice of exercising due care. With negligence and contributory negligence, the noncooperative equilibrium is the same as the cooperative equilibrium. Thus, the rules of negligence and contributory negligence together define a game with an efficient outcome. This is probably one reason why these rules have been used so widely in Anglo-American law.

The law is concerned with equity as well as efficiency. In mechanism design, this depends on the designer. The designer determines what kind of outcome is desired. Efficiency is almost always one of the criteria, but equity (in some sense) may also be a criterion. In the legal system of negligence and contributory negligence, the pedestrian still bears the cost of accidents that occur with a 10 percent probability, even when both parties take due care. It might be said that it is inequitable for this cost to fall on the more vulnerable party, the pedestrian, when the pedestrian has done all he can to reduce the risk. (This is a personal judgment on which individuals may differ, but we adopt it tentatively for the sake of the example.) Thus, the legal rule of strict liability would be seen as being more equitable (although inefficient) in that it always places responsibility on the less vulnerable motorist. Do we have to choose between equity and efficiency?

Perhaps not. Strict liability can be combined with contributory negligence. This means that the motorist is responsible *unless* the pedestrian has contributed to the danger by failing to take due care. Thus, if both parties take due care, and an accident happens anyway, the motorist, who is less vulnerable, bears the cost. The payoffs for this game are shown in Table 18.4.

The equilibrium in this game is the same—both players take due care—but the payoffs in the equilibrium are different, in that the vulnerable pedestrian does not bear the cost of accidents that occur, despite the fact that he has done all he can to avoid the accident.

Thus, game theory helps us to choose among legal rules to find the one that leads to the outcomes we think of as desirable. This example illustrates several points that are common to mechanism design and applications of game theory in the law. First, we consider the noncooperative equilibrium as our prediction of the outcome of the game. Second, some equilibria are preferable to others. In each of these examples the equilibrium is unique and can be determined by eliminating dominated strategies. We recall that some games have multiple Nash equilibria, and in that case the prediction (and therefore the outcome of the design) may not be conclusive. On the one hand, several of these are not dominant strategy equilibria, since only one party has a dominant strategy. It would be ideal if the mechanism were to define a cooperative dominant game—one in which the cooperative strategy is also a dominant strategy equilibrium—since in that case we would have

Table 18.4 | Strict Liability and Contributory Negligence

		Motorist	
		no care	due care
Pedestrian	no care	−100, 0	−100, −10
	due care	−10, −100	−10, −20

the greatest possible confidence in our prediction that the game equilibrium really would occur. On the other hand, the chosen design will depend on the objectives adopted by the designer. If efficiency is good enough, we might have more than one possible set of rules to achieve it; whereas if equity in some sense is among our objectives (or there are other objectives still), our satisfactory alternatives may be more restricted.

We can think of mechanism design as a kind of imbedded game. In this case, the game between the pedestrian and the motorist is imbedded in a larger game, in which the designer is also a player. The payoff to the designer depends on the extent to which the Nash equilibrium under a particular set of rules realizes the objectives the designer has imposed. We might say that the payoff is 1 for an outcome that is either efficient or equitable, but not both, and 2 for an outcome that is both. Thus, no liability pays 0, strict liability and negligence with contributory negligence 1, and strict liability with contributory negligence 2, to a designer who is equally concerned with efficiency and equity (in the sense used here). To maximize her payoff, the designer chooses strict liability with contributory negligence.

In some ways, however, this legal example is relatively simple. Another example will point up some possible complications.

Grading Team Projects

Dr. Schönsinn requires the students in his Game Theory class to do projects as teams, with three students in each team.[6] As a game theorist, Dr. Schönsinn worries that his students may face an effort dilemma, especially if they all get the same grade for the project. Consider, for example, Team Technology, a group of three freshman engineering majors who took the class thinking that it would be about videogames.[7] They now know that it isn't, but they think it is pretty cool, anyway. These three students, Augusta, Bill, and Cecilia, each can choose to make a big effort (work) or a slight effort (shirk) on the team project. Their common grade will depend on the average effort. A student's payoff is the grade minus the subjective cost of effort if she or he chooses "work." The payoffs are as shown in Table 18.5. Grades are shown on a numerical scale of D = 0, C− = 1, C = 2, C+ = 3, B = 4, A = 5. (Dr. Schönsinn's university gives only plus or minus

Table 18.5 | A Student Effort Dilemma

Augusta		Cecilia			
		work		shirk	
		Bill		Bill	
		work	shirk	work	shirk
work		4, 4, 4	3, 5, 3	3, 3, 5	0, 4, 4
shirk		5, 3, 3	4, 4, 0	4, 0, 4	1, 1, 1

6 This example was suggested by Pablo Amoros, Luis C. Corchon, and Bernardo Moreno, "The Scholarship Assignment Problem," *Games and Economic Behavior* v. 38, no. 1 (January 2002) pp. 1–18.

7 Yes, this has happened in one of my classes. After we got things sorted out, the student did a project on competition in computer-game industries and made an A.

grades for Cs). This game has a dominant strategy equilibrium in which everybody shirks and the group get a C–.

Dr. Schönsinn wants to set up grading rules for his class that will lead them to choose the cooperative solution at the upper left, where everyone works. There are two difficulties. First, effort is unobservable. All that anyone can observe is the results of the effort—how great a contribution each student makes to the project. Dr. Schönsinn assumes that a student who works will always make a bigger contribution than a student who shirks. Thus, if he can rank the students in the team by their contributions to the project, and give extra points to those who make the bigger contributions, that will create an incentive for the students to work rather than shirk. The second problem, though, is that Dr. Schönsinn doesn't know which students make the bigger contribution in any given team. Only the students in the team know that. But we will set the second problem aside, for now, and focus on the first. The students are ranked according to their contributions, and the student who is first in the ranking gets three points, while the student ranked second gets two. The student ranked last gets nothing. Now suppose that all of them choose "work." Then each one has a 1/3 chance at the three-point bonus and a 1/3 chance at a two-point bonus, so the expected value payoff is $4 + (1/3)3 + (1/3)2 = 5\ 2/3$. For another example, suppose Bill shirks, but Augusta and Cecilia work. Bill gets only the 5-point payoff in the original payoff table, but Augusta and Cecilia both get 3 plus a 1/2 chance at a 3-point bonus plus a 1/2 chance at a 2-point bonus, that is $3 + 3/2 + 2/2 = 5\ 1/2$. The payoffs with the bonus system are shown in Table 18.6.

We see that in the revised game, "work" is a dominant strategy. The game is now cooperative dominant—just what we want for a mechanism to lead to efficient results!

But now we have to deal with the second problem: Dr. Schönsinn doesn't even know which student makes the bigger contribution to the project. He gets only their completed paper. The students themselves know who has made the bigger contributions, so that means Dr. Schönsinn has to get the information from them. The problem is that each student has an incentive to distort the

Table **18.6** | The Student Effort Dilemma with Bonus Points

		Cecilia			
		work		shirk	
		Bill		Bill	
		work	shirk	work	shirk
Augusta	work	$5\frac{2}{3}, 5\frac{2}{3}, 5\frac{2}{3}$	$5\frac{1}{2}, 5, 5\frac{1}{2}$	$5\frac{1}{2}, 5\frac{1}{2}, 5$	$3, 5, 5$
	shirk	$5, 5\frac{1}{2}, 5\frac{1}{2}$	$5, 5, 3$	$5, 3, 5$	$2\frac{2}{3}, 2\frac{2}{3}, 2\frac{2}{3}$

report. Each could rank him- or herself best, regardless of contribution, for a better chance of getting the bonus points anyway. Dr. Schönsinn will have to design a mechanism that can solve that problem.

Here is his plan. Each student will rate the other two students. Dr. Schönsinn believes that his students agree that the person who makes the biggest contributions should get the biggest rewards, if their own rewards are not affected.[8] So each student will honestly rate the other two students on their relative contribution: greater or less. As a first approximation, Dr. Schönsinn assigns each student the minimum of the rankings the other two students have given. But there may be ties at this stage. If there is a tie between two of the students, then Dr. Schönsinn rates them as they are rated by the third student not involved in the tie.

In Team Technology, Augusta and Bill worked, but Cecilia shirked.[9] Augusta and Bill drew lots, and Augusta got to write the more important section of the paper, so hers was the biggest contribution, while Bill's was second and, because of her shirking, Cecilia's was least. Thus, their rankings are as shown in Table 18.7, where the students doing the ranking are listed vertically on the left and the students being ranked are listed horizontally across the top. Thus, for example, student B (Bill) ranks student A (Augusta) first and student C (Cecilia) second, not counting himself. The diagonal cells are blank because nobody is allowed to rank herself or himself. At the bottom row are the minimum rankings for each student, the column minimum, and as a first step, Dr. Schönsinn applies those rankings. That means Augusta will get the 3-point bonus—as she should. But Bill and Cecilia are tied. Dr. Schönsinn breaks the tie by looking at the rating by the third student, the one not in the tie, Augusta. Since Augusta ranked Bill first (relative to Cecilia) Dr. Schönsinn demotes Cecilia to third ranking, and Bill gets the two point bonus—as he should.

Thus, Dr. Schönsinn has succeeded in his objective. He has designed a grading system that (1) eliminates the effort dilemma and makes "work" a dominant strategy, and (2) elicits from the students information that they have in order to do this, and (3) does not give students any opportunity to enhance their own grades by falsifying the information they give. The grading system gave the students an incentive to **reveal** the information they have to the authorities.

As this example illustrates, information is often a key to successful mechanism design. Agents have information that may be needed to direct the mechanism—but their decisions to

Table 18.7 | Rankings of Students by Students on Team Technology

		Ratings of student		
		A	B	C
Ratings by student	A		first	second
	B	first		second
	C	first	second	
	minimum	first	second	second

8 This could be upset by collusion, if two students were to agree to get the third to do all the work, and then rank one another as first. This would be a cooperative arrangement between the two, and Dr. Schönsinn is following the standard practice in social mechanism design: relying on noncooperative equilibria to predict the actions of the people in the game. However, in this case and in some others, it might be helpful to allow also for collusion and irrationality. Perhaps future research will push in this direction.

9 She must not have understood the unit on dominant strategies! Remember, this is just an illustration, for the sake of the example, to make the rules clear.

reveal that information, and to reveal it truthfully, are strategic decisions! If lying or withholding information is a best response, then some people (if not all) will lie or withhold information. A successful mechanism needs to have safeguards against this tendency.

In the next example, we return to politics. In a very general sense, what sort of authorities do we want? If we must have authorities in charge of decisions that affect us all, we want them to be benevolent—don't we? Perhaps not.

The Paradox of Benevolent Authority

Results from game theoretic analyses are often *counterintuitive*. That means they go against our intuition, our "common sense." This is a *good thing*, since it makes us rethink and look for the loopholes in our intuition—or in the game theory. Either way, we learn more when game theory challenges our intuition than when it follows common sense.

Much of this book has dealt with social dilemmas. In a social dilemma, rational self-interest leads people to make decisions that make them all worse off. Many social scientists, philosophers and mathematicians have used social dilemmas as a justification for interventions by governments and other authorities to limit individual choice. A difficulty with this sort of reasoning is that it treats the authority as a *deus ex machina*—a sort of predictable, benevolent robot who steps in and makes everything right. That's not true, and to remedy this problem we need to treat the authority as a player in the game. Intuition tells some of us that the authority in these cases ought to be benevolent.[10] She (or he) should "feel the pain"[11] of the people over whom her authority is exercised, and do her best to make the decisions that make them better off. But is that intuition reliable? That's what we will investigate.

The authority aims to regulate the behavior of players in a social dilemma. To keep to the simplest case, we will consider a two-person social dilemma. The two persons who play the dilemma have no regulator powers, so we shall call them commoners. The Commoner's Dilemma, without regulation, is shown in Table 18.8.

> As a rule, any social mechanism or authority will need information, and the information may have to come from the players in the imbedded game. The players could have incentives to "game the system" by lying or withholding information. In the grading example, the students could benefit by ranking themselves first, if they were allowed to do so. To make the mechanism successful, the designer must take care that players have incentives not to lie or withhold information but do have incentives truthfully to reveal the information they have. This is an important principle of mechanism design.

Table 18.8 | The Commoner's Dilemma

		Commoner 1	
		cooperate	defect
Commoner 2	cooperate	10, 10	0, 15
	defect	15, 0	5, 5

---

10 Of course, intuition may tell different people different things, so your intuition may be different.

11 American president (1993-2001) William Jefferson Clinton often assured voters that he felt the pain they felt, according to news reports at that time.

The third player in this game is the *authority*, and she is a very strange sort of player. She can change the payoffs to the commoners. The authority has two strategies, "penalize" or "don't penalize." If she chooses "penalize," the payoffs to the two commoners are reduced by 7. If she chooses "don't penalize," there is no change in the payoffs to the two commoners.[12]

The authority also has two other peculiar characteristics:

- *She is benevolent:* The payoff to the authority is the sum of the payoffs to the commoners.

- *She is flexible:* The authority chooses her strategy only after the commoners have chosen theirs.

Table **18.9** | Payoffs with Penalty

		Commoner 1	
		cooperate	defect
Commoner 2	cooperate	10, 10	−7, 8
	defect	8, −7	−2, −2

Now suppose that the authority chooses the strategy "penalize" if, and only if, one or both of the commoners chooses the strategy "defect." The payoffs to the commoners would then be as shown in Table 18.9. This would lead both commoners to choose "cooperate," the dominant strategy equilibrium, which is the authority's purpose.

But the difficulty is that this does not allow for the authority's flexibility and benevolence. Is that indeed the strategy the authority will choose? Is it the authority's subgame perfect choice? The strategy choices are shown as a tree in Figure 18.1. In the diagram, we assume that Commoner 1 chooses first and Commoner 2 second. In a Prisoner's Dilemma, it doesn't matter which participant chooses first, or they both choose at the same time. What is important is that the authority chooses last. The payoffs shown are for the authority only.

NOW IT'S YOUR TURN. What are the subgames for this game? Which are proper subgames?[13.]

Let's try "reducing" this game by solving it backward. Begin at the authority's decision at A1. The authority will not penalize because penalizing gives her a payoff (the total of the commoners' payoffs) of 6, while not penalizing gives 20. But the analysis is just the same at A2, A3, and A4. At each step, the payoff to the authority for "don't penalize" is greater than the payoff for "penalize." What we see in the figure is that the authority has a dominant strategy: not to penalize. But this reduces the game to Figure 18.2.

In Figure 18.2, the payoffs to the two commoners are shown. This is just the original Prisoner's Dilemma! Indeed, penalties are never subgame perfect. No matter what the two commoners choose, imposing a penalty will make them worse off, and since the authority is benevolent—she "feels their pain," her payoffs being the sum total of theirs—she will always

12 It may seem strange that the authority penalizes either both or neither. In the next section, we will apply this analysis to a monetary authority. The only way the monetary authority can restrain inflationary price increases is by restricting the money supply and causing unemployment, which penalizes everyone whether they have raised their prices or not. This is the reason for the assumption.

13 See the end of the chapter for answers to this exercise.

Figure 18.1 | An Authority Game

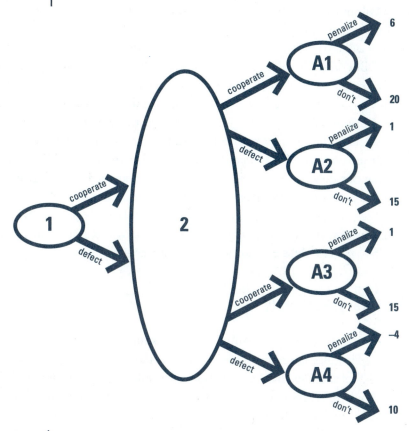

Figure 18.2 | A Reduced Authority Game

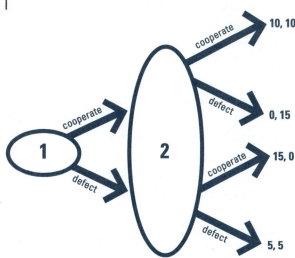

have an incentive to let them off, not to penalize. Thus, the result is that she cannot change the Prisoner's Dilemma. Both commoners will choose "defect," and the payoffs will be (5, 5) for the commoners, and 10 for the authority.

Perhaps the authority will announce that she intends to punish the commoners if they choose "defect." But they will not be fooled, because they know that, whatever they do, punishment will reduce the payoff to the authority herself, and that she will not choose a strategy that reduces her payoffs. Her announcement that she intends to punish will not be credible. As we know, a threat is credible only if it is subgame perfect to carry out the threat.

The benevolent authority is, paradoxically, unable to do any good for the commoners. Because she is benevolent and flexible, her threats to penalize are not credible, and the commoners, knowing that they will not actually be penalized, act out the Prisoner's Dilemma that the authority had hoped to protect them from. She cannot do it, unless she can somehow commit herself to penalize the commoners if one of them defects, despite the pain it causes her to do so. Benevolent and flexible authority may be ineffective precisely because it is benevolent and flexible, and this is the paradox of benevolent authority.

Application
Monetary Authority

Modern monetary systems are managed by monetary authorities such as the U.S. Federal Reserve System. The rules according to which the monetary authority conducts its management are a social mechanism that has great importance for the well being of millions of people. How should those rules work? Common sense tells us (or anyway, it tells some of us) that such an authority ought to respond to the needs of ordinary people by increasing the money supply to reduce unemployment and promote prosperity. The danger is that, if the monetary authority does this, inflation will result. This leads many economists and some other people to argue that the monetary authority ought to be independent of democratic politics and committed to inflexible rules designed to restrain inflation. The Federal Reserve and other monetary authorities in leading countries have increasingly been given this independence.

We have seen in an earlier example that a system of rewards can make cooperative behavior a dominant strategy. However, a monetary authority cannot reward good behavior. If prices go up, all the monetary authority can do is hold the line, with the result that unemployment increases. This "punishment" falls not only on those who have acted noncooperatively (by raising their prices), but often on others as well.

Monetary economists may not use game theory, but the game theoretic argument is there in the background! The key point is that the authority is a player in the game, and that makes a difference.

We have seen here two principles that play an important part in modern macroeconomics. Many modern economists apply these principles to the central banks that control the money supply in modern economies. They are the principle of **rules rather than discretion** and the principle of **credibility**.

- *The principle of rules rather than discretion.* The authority should act according to rules chosen in advance, rather than responding flexibly to events as they occur. In the case of the central banks, they should control the money supply or the interest rate on public debt (there is controversy about which) according to some simple rule, such as increasing the money supply at a steady rate or raising the interest rate when production is close to capacity, to prevent inflation. If some groups in the economy push their prices up, the monetary authority might be tempted to print money, which would cause inflation and help other groups to catch up with their prices, and perhaps reduce unemployment. But this must be avoided, since the groups will come to anticipate it and just push their prices up all the faster.

- *The principle of credibility.* It is not enough for the authority to be committed to the simple rule. The commitment must be credible if the rule is to have its best effect.

These two principles may have an effect on the way we want our institutions to function, at the most basic, more or less constitutional, level. For example, in countries with strong currencies, like Germany and the United States, the central bank or monetary authority is strongly insulated from democratic politics. This means that the pressures for a more "flexible" policy expressed by voters are not transmitted to the monetary authority—or, anyway, they are not as strong as they might otherwise be—so the monetary authority is more likely to commit itself to a simple rule and the commitment will be more credible. Insulating the monetary authority from democratic politics means that the monetary authority does not "feel the pain" of the voters. This brings us to a third, equally important, principle for monetary authorities: The monetary authority ought to be largely independent of democratic politics.

Summary

Games are defined by their rules, which, in turn, influence the noncooperative equilibria of rational players of the game. In mechanism design, we turn this around, first identifying the target noncooperative equilibrium, and then adjusting the rules (so far as possible!) to achieve this equilibrium. We can think of a problem as a mechanism design as an imbedded game, in which the game to be designed is imbedded within a larger game, so that the rules of the imbedded game are the strategies of the designer in the larger imbedding game. Applications of game theory to the law and to the creation of monetary institutions fit this pattern, although the terminology *mechanism design* has not always been used in these areas. In the law, liability rules, for example, may be adjusted so that in equilibrium all agents have incentives to take necessary care to prevent accidents. We can infer, from concepts of mechanism design, that monetary authorities should be independent of democratic politics and should base their policies on rules rather than discretion. But mechanism design is also limited by information, and when some of the players in the imbedded game have information necessary to make the mechanism work, the mechanism must be designed so as to give them incentives to reveal that information or put it to work.

Exercises and Discussion Questions

18.1 Building a Levee. Landowners Victoria and Wanda own adjacent plots along Winding River, and the plots may sometimes be flooded. Each can choose to build or not to build a levee, and if they both build a levee (at a cost of 1) both of their plots will be protected from floods. If either of them fails to build, they will both suffer flood losses of 5. The payoffs are shown in Table 18.E1.

This game has two equilibria, and one of them is inefficient. We want a social mechanism that assures efficient provision against floods. Now suppose the public authority proposes a flood insurance program that will pay all flood losses. The charge for the insurance is 1 if the landowner builds, 3 if a landowner does not build but the other landowner builds, and 4 each if neither landowner builds.

Draw the payoff table if both are insured. Draw a tree diagram for the imbedding game in which the two landowners have the option to insure or not. Determine a sub-game perfect equilibrium of the imbedding game using both backward and forward induction. Will the equilibrium be efficient? Will the insurance fund cover its costs?

Table 18.E1 Floodplain Payoffs

		Wanda	Wanda
		build	don't
Victoria	build	−1, −1	−6, −5
Victoria	don't	−5, −6	−5, −5

18.2 Laissez Faire. A market system can be thought of as a mechanism for the allocation of scarce resources to their most productive uses. According to economist Friedrich von Hayek, information about the availability of resources is widely distributed in the population, with no central group having any large proportion of that information. Hayek argues that market systems are superior to other systems for allocation of resources. Interpret Hayek's claim in terms of the ideas of this chapter.

18.3 Other Authorities. In the Paradox of Benevolent Authority example, a punishment must fall on both commoners, even if only one defects. This is reasonable for an analysis of a monetary authority—anti-inflationary "medicine" tends to be unpleasant for everyone. But other authorities can discriminate and penalize only some agents and not others. Does this make a difference for the result? Assume instead that the authority can impose a penalty on one and not the other, so that the authority has 4 strategies: penalize both, penalize commoner 1, penalize commoner 2, no penalty. What are the payoffs to the authority in the 16 possible outcomes that we now have? Under what circumstances will a benevolent authority penalize? What are the equilibrium outcomes in this more complicated game? What if, instead of simply imposing a penalty, the authority could fine one commoner and transfer the amount of the fine to the other?

18.4 Preservation. Mrs. Farmbody, a wealthy, elderly lady who has lived all her life on the family farm, wants to have the land continued as a farm indefinitely; but it is in an area that is suburbanizing and would be much more profitable if it were developed into houses. Now that she has retired, she can sell the farm to Piers Plowman, a for-profit farmer in the next county, or to the Farrow Creek Conservancy, a nonprofit corporation pledged to retain all of the land it possesses as farmland. Express Mrs. Farmbody's choice as a game in extensive form, with the operations of Piers Plowman and Farrow Creek Conservancy as imbedded games. Determine the subgame perfect equilibrium; Which buyer will Mrs. Farmbody choose? *Hint: Piers Plowman might choose to resell the property to a housing developer, but Farrow Creek Conservancy, because of its charter, cannot.*

18.5 Other Nonprofits. Many private universities, churches, and other institutions reliant on endowments or contributions are organized as nonprofit corporations. Drawing on your reasoning from the previous example, propose an explanation of this fact.

18.6 Patents. A patent grants an inventor the right to a monopoly on his invention for a limited period of time. The purpose of this protection is to make inventions more profitable since, in the absence of patent protection, every successful patent would promptly be imitated, and the inventor would be likely to lose his investment in developing the invention. Thus, there would be fewer inventions, and many inventions that would be beneficial to society on net might be delayed or might not occur at all. Patents may be granted for longer or shorter periods of time. A longer patent term will make inventions more profitable, and so lead to more inventions, but might also lead to waste as monopoly power continues longer than necessary to make invention profitable in many cases. Most economists believe that there is an optimal patent term, so that the patent lasts for just enough years to balance the benefits from more invention against the disadvantages of monopoly. Unfortunately, we have very little evidence as to what the optimum patent length is. Discuss the problem of patent policy as a problem of social mechanism design. What games are imbedded in this large game of public policy? Are there alternatives to patent protection that might achieve the same objective?

Answer to exercise on page 294. There are five subgames—A1, A2, A3, and A4 and the game as a whole. The first four are proper subgames.

Voting Games

To best understand this chapter 19

To best understand this chapter you need to have studied and understood the material from Chapters 1–9, 11, 14, and 15.

In an election, a group of people decide some issue by counting votes. Elections lend themselves to the scientific metaphor of game theory: like games, elections have known rules, and there is usually a definite winner and loser or losers. The strategy in an election game includes a decision of how to cast one's vote, although it might be more complex than that. In this chapter we sketch some basic ideas in the game-theoretic analysis of voting. We begin, as usual, with an example: The executive committee of a sorority has to decide how much to spend on a party.

Party! Party! Party!

Signa Phi Naught sorority is planning a big party, and the executive committee has to decide how much to spend from the sorority treasury. The members of the executive committee are Anna, Barbara, and Carole—A, B, and C, as usual. They can spend $100, $150, $200, $250, or $300. The three committee members' preferences are shown in Table 19.1. For example, Anna's top preference is to spend $150, while $100 is her least preferred alternative—fifth out of five. The preferences are shown in a diagram in Figure 19.1. Since first preference is highest, it is shown at the top of the diagram.

Table 19.1 Preferences for the Three Members of the Executive Committee

	$100	$150	$200	$250	$300
A	fifth	first	second	third	fourth
B	third	second	first	fourth	fifth
C	fifth	fourth	third	first	second

Anna moves that funds for the party be appropriated in the amount of $150. Barbara and Carole each propose an amendment to the motion. Barbara's amendment is that the amount be increased to $200. Barbara and Carole both vote for it, since they both prefer $200 to $150. ($200 is Barbara's first preference and Carole's third, but $150 is Barbara's second preference and Carole's fourth.) Carole's amendment is to increase the amount still further, to $250. Anna and Barbara both vote against it, since they both prefer $200 to $250. ($200 is Anna's second preference. $250 is Anna's third preference and Barbara's fourth). Thus, the final decision is for a $200 expenditure on the party.

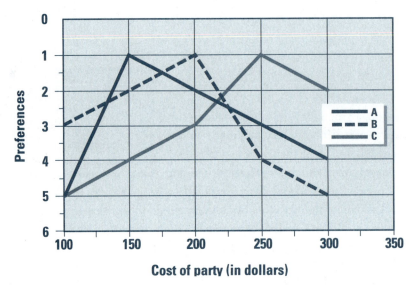

Cost of party (in dollars)

Barbara has gotten her way in this vote. Why? There are two interrelated reasons. First, if we start from the left, the preference level for each person rises (not necessarily at a steady rate, but without reversals) until the top preference is reached, and then the preference level declines, again without any reversals. When preferences have this property they are said to be **single-peaked**. For a contrast, look at Yolanda's preferences in Figure 19.2. Yolanda is not on the executive committee, so she doesn't have a vote, but she prefers a cheap party. At the same time, she feels that if more than $100 is spent, then the sorority might as well go all the way

Figure 19.2 | Yolanda's Preferences

and spend the maximum of $300, which is her second preference. Thus, Yolanda's peak preference is ambiguous: $100 is a peak, but the second preference of $300 is a sort of a peak, too—at least relative to the fourth and fifth preferences, $250 and $200. It is a *local peak*.

Because the members of the executive committee all have single-peaked preferences, we can pick out each person's peak preference without any ambiguity, and this also means that any movement toward a person's peak preference will make that person better off, in preference terms.[1]

Here is the second reason why Barbara gets her way: When we list the peak preferences, shown in Table 19.2, we see that Barbara's peak preference is at the middle. Barbara is the **median person** in this vote. She prefers spending more than Anna, so any movement toward her first preference, $200, from above will also be supported by Anna, and together they have a **majority**. She prefers spending less than Carole, so any movement toward $200, from below, will be supported also by Carole, and, again, together they have a majority. Taking both sides together, any movement toward Barbara's peak preference will have majority support. That's the advantage of being the median person.

In general, the median person is the person who prefers a quantity higher than half-minus-one of the voters, and also lower than half-minus-one of the voters. Thus, any movement toward the median person's first preference from below will be supported by all the voters whose first preference is greater than hers; so, with her vote as well, it will be supported by a majority. Similarly, any movements toward the median person's peak preference from above will be supported by all of those whose first preference is less than hers, so with her vote (once

Heads Up!

Here are some concepts we will develop as this chapter goes along:

Majority: More than half of the votes cast.

Plurality: More votes than any other candidate or alternative.

Single-Peaked Preferences: If there is some dimension on which each voter's preference ranking first increases to a "best" and then decreases, the voter's preferences are said to be *single-peaked*.

Median Voter: If one voter's peak preference lies between one-half of the voters who prefer more and one-half who prefer less, that person is the median voter and that vote can be decisive.

Strategic Voting: Voting for something other than one's first preference, in the hope of improving the outcome of the voting from one's own point of view, is *strategic voting*.

Naïve Voting: Voting for one's first choice, regardless of the consequences, is *naïve voting*.

The Condorcet Rule: The Marquise de Condorcet proposed that a candidate who would win a two-way naïve vote against every other candidate should be the candidate selected.

Preference Voting: Voters vote for more than one candidate or alternative, with each voter ranking them in order of preference.

Table **19.2** | Peak Preferences

Person	Peak preference
Anna	$150
Barbara	$200
Carole	$250

1 This discussion owes a great deal to Howard Bowen, "The Interpretation of Voting in the Allocation of Economic Resources," *Quarterly Journal of Economics* v. 58 (1943): pp. 27–48.

again!) it will have majority support. In general, so long as all voters have single-peaked preferences, a move toward the median person's peak preference will be preferred by a majority of the voters. Thus, the median person's preferences are decisive, under majority rule.

This example illustrates some important aspects of the game-theoretic analysis of voting. First, votes can be thought of as strategies in a game, and majority rule (or some alternative voting scheme) defines the rules of the game. Second, the sorority party example includes some important simplifying assumptions. The simplifying assumptions are that preferences are single-peaked and that the issues are laid out along a single dimension from less to more. We have also assumed that each member of the executive committee simply votes for the alternative she prefers. But that isn't always the rational choice of strategies, as we will see in a later section.

The Theme for the Party

The executive committee of Signa Phi Naught were unable to decide among three possible themes for decoration and costumes at the party. The three themes they were considering are Roaring Twenties (R), Swiss Alps (S), or Tropical Island (T). The executive committee has decided to put the issue before the whole membership of the sorority for a vote. There are three types of voters among the sorority membership, with different preferences among the three alternatives. We shall call the types X, Y, and Z. The preferences of the three types, and the proportion of the votes cast by each, are shown in Table 19.3.

Now, suppose each type votes for its first preference. The Tropical Island alternative has the **plurality** (it got the most votes), but for 60 percent of the voters, this is the worst of the three alternatives. This is a fundamental problem of plurality voting—it can, and often does, conflict with majority rule, in that the winning alternative is opposed by a majority of the voters. If the executive committee of Signa Phi Naught wants to have a majority decision, it will have to choose election rules that are a little more complex than plurality voting. One possibility is that it could have a runoff election—that is, hold two rounds of voting, with the alternatives in the second round of voting being the two that got the most votes in the first round. If there is a majority for one of the alternatives in the first stage, the second stage is cancelled. In this case—still assuming that

Table **19.3** | Preferences for Themes for the Party

Voter type	Themes			Voter percentages
	R	S	T	
X	first	second	third	31
Y	second	first	third	29
Z	third	second	first	40

the voters just vote for their first preferences—the first round will eliminate S, and R will win in a runoff election between R and T.

From this example we can see that the results of voting can depend on "the rules of the game." Without any change in the preferences of the voters, a switch from plurality rule to majority rule with a runoff election can change the outcome of the election. So far, we have assumed that the voters always vote for their first preference. But is that a best response? Could it be that in some circumstances, it might be strategically wise to vote for one's second preference to avoid an even worse alternative? This is the question we need to address next.

Strategic Voting

If the voters are rational game players, they might not vote for their first preferences. Suppose—for example—that the election is held in a single stage and the alternative with the plurality is adopted (plurality rule). Suppose also that types Y and Z vote for their first preferences. Then, by voting for their *second* preference, type X voters can improve their outcome from their third to their second preference. This is an example of **strategic voting**. Whenever a voter votes for something other than his or her first preference in order to get a better overall outcome, we say that the voter is voting *strategically*. When the voters simply vote for their first preference in each round, we would say that they vote *naïvely*.

> ### Definition
> ***Strategic and Naïve Voting*—Strategic voting** is voting for something other than one's first preference in the hope of improving the outcome of the voting from one's own point of view. **Naïve voting** is voting for one's first preference regardless of the outcome.

In fact, type Y could also benefit by voting strategically, in some circumstances. Let us look at the game of plurality voting as a game in normal form. The strategies will be to vote for the first or the second preference. We will ignore the possibility of voting for the last preference because it will be a weakly dominated strategy. Payoffs are listed as X, Y, Z.

For example, suppose all three types vote their first choice. Tropical Island wins with 40 percent of the vote, so type Z voters get their first choice, but types X and Y each get their third, so that the payoffs are (third, third, first). However, if type X voters shift to their second preference, Swiss Alps, while others continue to vote their first preferences, Swiss Alps wins 60–40. This is the second preference for types X and Z and first preference for type Y, so the payoffs are (second, first, second). The other payoffs are obtained in the same way.

Remember that, since the payoffs are preferences, smaller numbers are better in this game. Examining Table 19.4, we observe that there are three Nash equilibria. They are shaded in gray in Table 19.4. However, voting the second preference is a weakly dominated strategy for type Z voters, and if they choose the fail-safe approach—assuming that the other players might "tremble" and choose a non-best response—then we can rule out the right panel of the table and concentrate on the left part. What we have in the left panel is a coordination game

Table **19.4** | Plurality Voting in the Party Theme Game

		Type Z					
		first			second		
		Type Y			Type Y		
		first	second		first	second	
Type X	first	3rd, 3rd, 1st	1st, 2nd, 3rd		2nd, 1st, 2nd	1st, 2nd, 3rd	
	second	2nd, 1st, 2nd	3rd, 3rd, 1st		2nd, 1st, 2nd	2nd, 1st, 2nd	

of a type we already know is difficult. Both of the two lightly shaded cells are equilibria, but which will occur? There is some possibility that the type X and Y voters will guess wrong and choose (first, first), or indeed (second, second), and end up with their third preferences, anyway! (And it follows that type Z voters have good reason to stay away from their weakly dominated strategy.)

Nor is that the end of the story. Another possibility is that types X and Y might form a coalition, caucus, and take a vote among themselves, and coordinate their strategies on the alternative that gets a majority in their caucus. That will be alternative R, Roaring Twenties. Since it is a Nash equilibrium and the caucus vote makes it a Schelling point, the coalition will not need any enforcement to make this the outcome.

Notice that the runoff election is not immune to strategic voting, either. By voting for their second preference at the first stage, type Z voters can ensure that they get their second preference, Swiss Alps, instead of the third, Roaring Twenties.

Voting Problems and Criteria

The Party Theme Game illustrates the wide range of problems and possibilities in real elections. On the one hand, plurality voting is not very satisfactory. It can leave the majority very dissatisfied, and the outcome can be very unpredictable. In the Party Theme Game, any outcome is possible, depending on who votes strategically. Coalitions and caucus votes are also common in real elections. On the other hand, to get a majority decision will require some more complicated voting scheme, such as a runoff election. But runoff elections, too, may be influenced by strategic voting. Worse still, it is not obvious what outcome is the "correct" one. When there is no majority in naïve voting, which outcome represents majority rule?

This is not a new question! In the mid-1700s, the Marquis de Condorcet proposed a partial answer to the question. The **Condorcet Rule** says that electoral schemes ought to be set up in such a way that an alternative that would win a two-way naïve vote against every other alternative should be the one chosen. In the Party Theme Game, for example, S defeats R 69–31 and S defeats T 60–40. Thus, S is the Condorcet alternative. But not all voting games have a Condorcet alternative.

The Marquis de Condorcet 1743–1794

Marie-Jean-Antoine-Nicolas de Caritat, Marquis de Condorcet, was a major figure of the Enlightenment, a mathematician who made important contributions to integral calculus and probability as well as originating the mathematical study of elections. Although a supporter of the French Revolution, he opposed the Jacobins, was imprisoned by the Jacobin government in France, and died while in custody, from unknown causes.

Kenneth Arrow 1921–

A native New Yorker, Kenneth Arrow did his undergraduate work at the City College of New York, receiving a degree of Bachelor of Science in Social Science but a major in Mathematics. His graduate work was at Columbia. After obtaining an M.A. in Mathematics, he switched to economics, but his dissertation research was delayed by the war and other concerns. Completed in 1951, his dissertation, *Social Choice and Individual Values*, had immediate and lasting impact. His pathbreaking work on competitive equilibrium under uncertainty has had equal impact on economics and on innovation in financial markets. He shared the Nobel Memorial prize in 1972 with John Hicks for his "pioneering contributions to general economic equilibrium theory and welfare theory." Arrow is Joan Kenney Professor of Economics (Emeritus) at Stanford University.

In the mid-twentieth century, Nobel Laureate economist Kenneth Arrow proposed a more complete list of criteria for a good election scheme—and proved that no election scheme can possibly realize all of them.[2] In order to understand the point, we need to look at the list in detail; and indeed the list is of interest in itself:

1. *Efficient.* There should be no alternative that every voter prefers to the winning alternative.

2. *Complete.* The voting scheme leads to a complete and consistent ranking of all alternatives.

3. *Neutral.* The ranking of any two alternatives depends only on the preferences of the voters between those two alternatives (as with Condorcet's criterion).

4. *Nondictatorial.* There is *no one person* whose preferences decide the election regardless of the preferences of others.[3]

Arrow's *general impossibility theorem*, which states that there is no way of voting or more generally of deciding issues that satisfies all these criteria, has had a great influence on systematic thinking about elections, including game theoretic thinking. The third assumption,

---

2 In fact, Arrow's proposition is even broader. It applies to all mechanisms for social choice—including, for example, market mechanisms.

3 Recall that, in section 1, Barbara got her way in the election to determine how much to spend, because she was the median person—but if the preferences of Anna and Carole had been different, the outcome could have been different!

also known as the *independence of irrelevant alternatives*, has been the most controversial. It essentially rules out strategic voting. As we have seen, strategic voting will be common, but there is no reason to think that makes things any more predictable—quite the contrary.

Much of the controversy on the Arrow theorem has focused on the possibility that a small sacrifice on one of Arrow's criteria—for example, a less than complete or less than neutral scheme—might give us satisfactory overall results.[4]

We should observe that Arrow's result does not say that all four criteria can never be satisfied in any election. It says that there are some cases, in which people have certain preferences, for which one or more of the four conditions will fail. Some schemes might satisfy all those criteria for some, or even for very many, distributions of preferences. For example, we have seen that a runoff election with strategic voting results in a win by the Condorcet candidate in the Party Theme Game. However, as we will see in the next section, the results can also be the opposite. We might settle for an election scheme that would satisfy Arrow's criteria for a very large proportion of the preferences that we are likely to find in practice, but that is a deep and unsolved mathematical and psychopolitical problem!

Alternative Voting Schemes

Many alternative electoral schemes have been proposed. Here are a few.

1. *Plurality rule.* Although it is problematic, many elections are conducted according to plurality rule, including British Parliamentary elections, where it is known as the "first past the post" system.

2. *Runoff elections.* As we have seen, a runoff can produce a majority for one candidate, but runoff elections are highly strategic and can be unpredictable.

3. *Preference voting via a Borda rule.* One possible problem with conventional voting is that it provides information only on the first preference. **Preference voting** schemes are designed to obtain more information from voters. Proposed by another French Enlightenment figure, the Chevalier de Borda, the Borda rule is one such. The **Borda rule** has the voter assign points to each alternative in inverse proportion to their preference ranking. Thus, in a three-way election, the first preference gets 3 points, the second preference 2, and so on. The alternative with the greatest sum of points wins. In the Party Theme Game, alternative T gets 5 points, R 6, and S 7; so S, the Condorcet alternative, wins. But this will not always be so!

---

4 *Robert's Rules of Order*, a guide to parliamentary procedure used by many American voluntary organizations, prescribes that, if there is no majority, the ballot be repeated time and again until there is one. Presumably this relies on strategic voting in later rounds to produce a majority. But *Robert's Rules* do not define a neutral scheme, since the agenda order of presentation of issues can definitely influence the outcome.

The Enlightenment

In European history, the eighteenth century has sometimes been called the Age of Enlightenment. The mindset of the Enlightenment combined beliefs in the autonomy of reason, perfectibility of man and society and progress, an order of nature that could be discovered by reason and science, anti-authoritarianism, and anti-nationalism. Major enlightenment figures include Descartes, Pascal, Montesquieu, Hume, Voltaire, Rousseau, Adam Smith, and Condorcet.

De Borda and the Borda Count

In 1770 the French mathematician Chevalier Jean-Charles de Borda (1733–1799) proposed a new method of counting votes: The voter would rank the candidates or alternatives according to her order of preference. If there were N alternatives, the first preference would get N points, the second preference N − 1, and so on. The alternative with the most points would win.

Born in Dax, France, de Borda was a military engineer and inventor who perfected instruments of navigation, waterwheels, and pumps and, in between, found time to participate in the American War of Independence. He was among the creators of the metric system of measurements.

4. *Preference voting via an instant runoff.* Each voter ranks all the alternatives from most to least preferred. If the first preferences produce a majority, then it is adopted. If not, then the alternative getting the fewest first preference votes is eliminated and its supporters' votes transferred to their second preference listing. If (with more than two alternatives) this does not produce a majority, then the procedure is repeated until a majority is obtained. In the Party Theme Game, the "instant runoff" produces the same result as a two-stage runoff, but that will not always be true.

5. *Approval voting.* In this case there is no ranking of one alternative against another, but each voter simply votes yes or no for each alternative. The alternative that gets the largest number of yes votes wins. Approval voting is highly strategic, since there is no obvious (naïve) answer to the question of how many alternatives to approve. In the Party Theme Game, for example, suppose type Z approves its first and second choice, while type Y approves only its first choice. This is a Nash equilibrium, regardless of what X does. (See Table 19.5, which ignores some weakly dominated strategy choices.) Theme S is chosen. Thus, in this game, strategic approval voting yields the Condorcet alternative. But that will not always be true.

While there is much to be learned about these and other alternative voting schemes, it seems clear that there is no one scheme that is clearly best, or even satisfactory, in all circumstances.

But all of our examples so far have been made up. Do these difficulties arise in the real world? We will look at some cases, and find that they do indeed.

Table **19.5** | Approval Voting in the Party Theme Game

		Type Z			
		approve first		approve first and second	
		Type Y		Type Y	
		approve first	approve first and second	approve first	approve first and second
Type X	approve first	3rd, 3rd, 1st	1st, 2nd, 3rd	2nd, 1st, 2nd	2nd, 1st, 2nd
	approve first and second	2nd, 1st, 2nd	tie*	2nd, 1st, 2nd	2nd, 1st, 2nd

* The tie is between R and S, first and second for X and Y and second and third for Z. But either X or Y can assure the first preference by shifting unilaterally to "first," and Z can assure second preference by shifting unilaterally to "first, second." Therefore, the tie is not a best response for anybody and cannot be a Nash equilibrium.

Case
The Finnish Presidential Election[5]

The Republic of Finland is located in northern Europe on one of the Scandinavian peninsulas, sharing its main common border with the Russian Republic and sharing borders also, in the far north, with Sweden and Norway. Urho Kekkonen was president of Finland for 25 years, beginning in 1956. In Finland, in 1956, presidential elections were conducted by a 300-member electoral college.[6] The Finnish Electoral College was unlike the electoral college in the United States (among other ways) in that there could be a runoff if there were no majority in the first round of voting.

In 1956, four parties participated in the Finnish presidential election: the Agrarian (Farmers') Party, the Communists, the Conservatives, and the Socialists. The Communists, as the smallest of the four, did not propose a candidate, but the other three parties did. Kekkonen was the candidate of the Agrarians, J. K. Paasikivi, the incumbent, was the candidate of the Conservatives, and K. -A. Fagerholm was the candidate of the Socialists. Table 19.6 shows the preferences of the four parties, as reconstructed from the evidence, and the votes each party could cast in the Electoral College. We see that the Communists, without a candidate of their

5 This example is from George Tsebelis, *Nested Games: Rational Choice in Comparative Politics*, (Berkeley: University of California Press, 1990), pp. 2–4.

6 Finnish presidential elections are now conducted by popular vote, with a second "runoff" round in case there is no majority on the first round.

Table 19.6 | Parties and Preferences in the Finnish Presidential Election

Party	Kekkonen	Paasikivi	Fagerholm	Votes
Agrarian	first	second	third	88
Communist	first	third	second	56
Conservative (major faction)	third	first	second	77
Conservative (minor faction)	second	first	third	7
Socialist	third	second	first	72

own, favored Kekkonen,[7] and that the Conservatives were somewhat divided on their second preference, with a minority preferring the Agrarian Kekkonen over the Socialist Fagerholm.

Now let us see what happens if each party votes naïvely in each round. In the first round, Kekkonen gets 56 + 88 = 144; Paasikivi 84; and Fagerholm 72. The runoff would then be between Kekkonen and Paasikivi, and Kekkonen would get the same 144 votes, while Paasikivi would get 156. Thus, Paasikivi wins—the worst outcome from the point of view of the Communist party.

But the Communists did not vote naïvely. Instead, on the first round, 42 of the 56 Communist electors voted for Fagerholm. This could not have been a matter of different individual preferences. Communist parties at that time worked on the basis of "democratic centralism," meaning that individual members obeyed the party decision once it was made. In any case, the result was to swing the election to Kekkonen. In the first round Fagerholm got 114 votes, more than Paasikivi's 84, eliminating Paasikivi. Thus, the runoff election was between Kekkonen and Fagerholm. In the runoff, the Communists voted unanimously for Kekkonen and Kekkonen won, 151 to 149.

We see that a small party was able to manipulate the runoff electoral scheme by strategic voting. What about the other criteria and schemes?

1. *Condorcet.* Paasikivi defeats Kekkonen 156–144 and Fagerholm 162–128, so Paasikivi is the Condorcet candidate.

2. *Borda rule.* Paasikivi wins with 628 points to 595 for Kekkonnen and 577 for Fagerholm.

7 At that time, the Russian Republic was part of the Soviet Union, and relations with Finland's huge neighbor were the major problem for the Finnish government. Finland had been invaded by the Soviet Union 15 years before. Finland had successfully defended its independence, although it had lost some territory. It seems likely that the Communists saw Kekkonen as being more likely to maintain friendly relations with the Soviet Union than Fagerholm would have been.

3. *Instant runoff.* In the two-round runoff, the Communists were able to manipulate the system by changing the preferences they expressed between the first and second rounds. With an instant runoff they cannot do that. In order to get Fagerholm into the runoff, at least 13 Communists have to list him as their first preference rather than Kekkonen, but those preferences mean that they are counted as voting for Fagerholm after Paasikivi is eliminated, and Fagerholm wins 162 (72 Socialist, 77 Conservative, and 13 Communist votes) to 138. Since the Communists preferred Fagerholm somewhat to Paasikivi, they probably would have done this. Notice that Fagerholm would lose in a two-person race with either of the two other candidates.[8]

4. *Approval voting.* There are plural Nash equilibria, so the outcome is unpredictable.

Case
An American Presidential Election

As the Finnish example illustrates, strategic voting is especially likely where there are more than two alternatives and complicated voting rules. The United States, too, has an Electoral College that decides presidential elections, and it is part of a quite complex electoral routine that takes place every fourth year. The authors of the U.S. Constitution had hoped that this Electoral College would keep political parties out of presidential elections, but, in fact, political parties have dominated the Electoral College since the election of John Adams in 1796. Despite that, when there have been only two major candidates, so that one has gotten a majority of the popular vote, the Electoral College has usually given the same result as the popular vote.[9] When there were three or more significant candidates, however, the results have been less predictable. The election of William Clinton in 1992 provides an important example. In a three-way race with the incumbent George H. W. Bush and billionaire Ross Perot, Clinton received the plurality with 43 percent of the popular vote. Bush obtained 37 percent and Perot 20 percent. In Table 19.7, we see an example based loosely on this 1992 election. It is only loosely based

Table **19.7** | Preferences in a Simplification of the 1992 U.S. Presidential Election

	Ranking for			Percentage of Electorate
	Clinton	Bush	Perot	
Democrats	1st	2nd	3rd	.43
Republicans	3rd	1st	2nd	.37
Reformers	2nd	3rd	1st	.20

8 The Socialists could have prevented this by strategically voting for Paasikivi over Fagerholm, as indeed they could have in the actual election but did not. It seems that they did not vote strategically because they were responsible to their party members, who would not have tolerated it. That is, their electoral game was imbedded in a larger game of party politics in which a strategic vote was not a best response. Clearly, it is very difficult for a party to vote against its own nominee.

9 The exceptions were the elections of 1876, 1888, and 2000. In 1876 some states sent more than one delegation to the Electoral College, so that the result was really decided by the Congress. In 1888 the popular vote was extremely close. The 2000 election will be discussed later in this chapter.

because we are making the simplifying assumption that there were only three types of voters, and that each voter of a particular type had the same preferences as every other of the same type, especially for second and third preferences. We don't know that—in this case, we have little evidence on second and third preferences—and reality was probably more complicated. But the example is consistent with what we do know about the 1992 election and, as we will see, it is complicated enough!

The fifth column gives the assumed proportion of the electorate who is of each of the three types. These are the proportions in the actual popular vote, rounded off to percentages. We have assumed that the Reformers favored Clinton before Bush—some important leaders of the movement made that fairly clear—and that the Republicans preferred Perot to Clinton, as being less liberal, while the Democrats would have chosen Bush over Perot, perhaps seeing Perot as unpredictable. These last two are guesses for the sake of the example.

In this election, as in the Finnish one, no one of the candidates gets a majority. If everyone votes naïvely, then Clinton wins the plurality (as, in fact, he did). A question is this: Why did the Republicans not vote strategically? Had they voted for Perot rather than Bush, Perot could have been elected, and the Republicans would have had their second preference rather than their third. But perhaps they had the longer-term strength of their party in mind. That is, it might be that for the Republicans, the 1992 election game was nested in a larger game, in such a way that a win for Perot would have made it much more unlikely that the Republicans would come back, perhaps with another Bush in 2000.

This election differs from the Finnish one in that there was no provision for a runoff election. In fact, of course, the popular vote does not decide the issue, but the Electoral College does, and Clinton got a 370–168 majority in the Electoral College. This can happen because a candidate who gets the plurality in a state (or in a congressional district, in the case of two states) gets all the electoral votes for that state (congressional district). Thus, a candidate who gets 50.01 percent of the vote in every state (district) would get 100 percent of the electoral vote.

What about the other schemes and criteria?

1. *Condorcet.* Clinton defeats Bush, 63–37; Bush defeats Perot, 80–20; and Perot defeats Clinton, 57–43. This cycle means that there is no Condorcet candidate in this race. Cycles like this play an important part in recent analytical thinking about elections, especially the Arrow Impossibility Theorem. The cycle in this example reflects the assumption that all Republicans would vote for Perot over Clinton. This might not have been true in the real world. If as many as 25 percent of Republicans would have gone for Clinton in a Clinton-Perot race, then Clinton becomes the Condorcet candidate, but the extreme assumptions were chosen to illustrate the important possibility of a cycle, and the fact that there might not be a Condorcet candidate in some elections.

2. *Borda rule.* With naïve voting, Bush wins 36–34–30, in percentages, with Perot last; but if 50 percent of Democrats strategically (or sincerely!) shift their second-place listing to Perot, then Clinton wins 34–33–33.

3. *Two-round runoff.* With naïve voting, Clinton wins 63–37 in the runoff, but Republicans can shift it to their second preference, Perot, by strategically voting for him on the first round.

4. *Instant runoff.* Same as two-round runoff.

5. *Approval voting.* The Nash equilibrium is that the Republicans approve both Bush and Perot, Democrats and Reformers approve only their own candidates, and Perot wins with 57 percent of the population approving against 43 percent for Clinton and 37 percent for Bush.

Case

The American Presidential Election of 2000

Table 19.8 | Preferences in a Simplification of the 2000 U.S. Presidential Election

	Ranking for			Percentage of Electorate
	Gore	Bush	Nader	
Democrats	1st	2nd	3rd	.49
Republicans	2nd	1st	3rd	.48
Greens	2nd	3rd	1st	.03

In the antemillenial year 2000, as in 1876, the presidential decision from the Electoral College went to a candidate (Bush) who had fewer popular votes than another (Gore). As in 1876, this happened because the composition of the Electoral College was influenced by a federal body—in 1876, Congress; in 2000, the Supreme Court. In both cases, Florida electoral votes were at issue (though in 1876 there were other states at issue as well). The votes, and a reconstruction of the preferences, for the 2000 election are shown in Table 19.8. Since this election gave new impetus to the call for changes in the Electoral College,[10] it might be of interest to try the various criteria and schemes on this election as well, but we will leave that for the exercises.

The more interesting issue is, Why did the Greens not vote strategically for their second choice, Gore? Some Democrats have been quite bitter about this, writing as if it were immoral to refuse an opportunity to "game the system."[11] So why didn't the Greens vote strategically? And come to that, why were the Democrats so certain that they ought to, and would?

10 TRUTH IN AUTHORSHIP DISCLOSURE: For what it is worth, the author of this book favors the substitution of a popular vote with an instant runoff over the existing Electoral College.

11 In the words of Harold Meyerson, "There's something so very pure about the Greens' destructiveness. . . . What could possibly explain this idiocy?" This was written in "Greens to Liberals: Drop Dead," *The American Prospect*, v. 13, no. 12 (July 1, 2002), pp. 2–3. *The American Prospect* is a magazine committed to a liberal and progressive editorial policy.

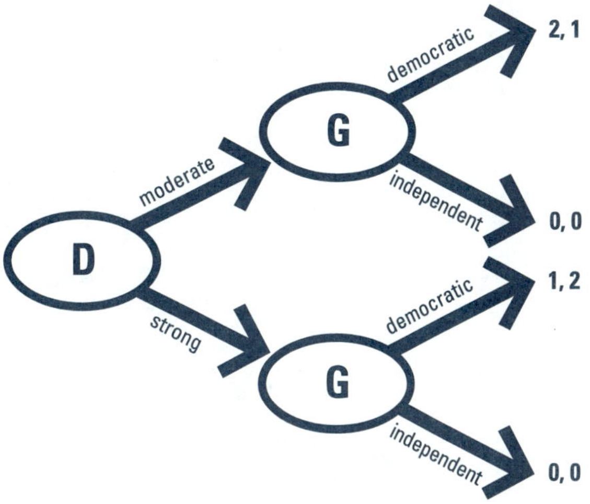

The answer can be found if we think in terms of imbedded games. For years, strong environmentalists have expressed dissatisfaction that the Democratic programs and candidates were not strong enough on environmental issues, although the strong environmentalists (believed they) provided the margin of victory for the Democrats in many elections. The frustrated environmentalists would have liked to persuade the Democratic Party to take a stronger position on the environment by threatening to withdraw their votes, but they found themselves in the situation illustrated by Figure 19.3.

Figure 19.3 shows a two-stage threat game in extensive form. The first payoff is to the Democrats, the second to the environmentalists. At

Figure 19.3 | An Incredible Threat by Greens

the first stage, the Democrats (D) decide whether to nominate a candidate who is moderate or strong on environmental issues. At the second stage, the environmentalists choose either to vote for the democratic candidate or for an independent candidate. In the latter case, both Democrats and independent environmentalist candidates lose, so the payoffs are (0, 0). If the environmentalists vote Democratic, the Democrats win,[12] so there are positive payoffs for both groups. However, if the candidate is a moderate, she is more satisfactory to mainstream Democrats, who are at least as concerned with other issues as with environmental issues, but less satisfactory to voters for whom environmental issues are of special concern. Thus, with a moderate candidate, the payoff is 2 (best) for the mainstream Democrats and 1 (second best) for Greens, whereas with a strong candidate, the payoff is 1 for mainstream Democrats and 2 for Greens.

But the Greens' threat is not credible, because voting for an independent candidate is never a subgame perfect equilibrium. The Greens are very much in the position of the labor union in Chapter 15. The labor union was able to make its threat credible by imbedding the strike game in a larger game and, in the larger game, choosing the strategy of affiliating with a tough union and turning the strike decision over to a union official who has nothing to lose by calling a strike. The Greens seem to have found a similar way to make their threat credible. They formed a Green Party and recruited a leader (Ralph Nader) more known for his willingness to fight than for his special commitment to environmental issues. In so doing, the Greens were able to divert enough environmentalist votes to threaten the Democrats successfully, and therefore, we must presume, credibly! The larger game in which Figure 19.3 was imbedded is shown as Figure 19.4.

---

12 The threat makes sense only in races the Democrats can win with environmentalist support. If the Democrats lose in either case, the payoffs are always 0 for both sides—both decisions are irrelevant.

Figure **19.4** | A Credible Green Threat

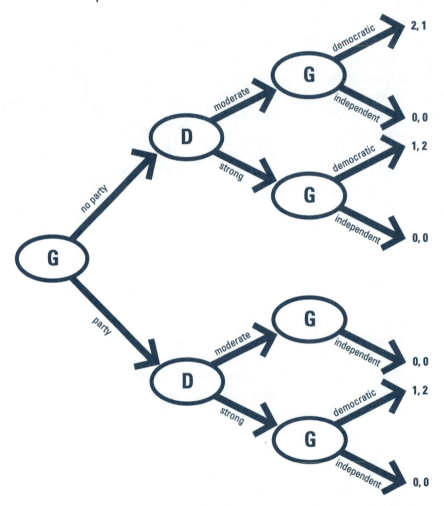

This is not new in American politics. Third-party movements in U.S. history have often been aimed at threatening to take the votes of a minority group away from a major party, at least partly in the hope of persuading the major party to adopt a position more acceptable to the minority. When George Wallace (candidate of the American Independent Party in 1968 and 1972) said, "There's not a dime's worth of difference" between the Democrats and Republicans, he was justifying a candidacy that primarily threatened the Democratic Party.

Summary

Elections can be predictable if (1) there are only two alternatives under consideration, or the alternatives can all be ordered as more and less, and (2) all voters have single-peaked preferences over the alternatives. In that case, naïve voting will make the median voter's preferences decisive, and there is little scope for strategic voting. With three or more alternatives that cannot be ordered as more or less, the possibilities emerge that no one alternative can get a majority, and that strategic voting can influence the results. In some cases, strategic voting with multiple Nash equilibria may give a majority to any of the alternatives, depending on which equilibrium is realized. There are a variety of schemes for finding a majority in such cases, but no one of them clearly works better than the others in every case.

There could even be controversy about what the "right" outcome of the election would be. If there is one candidate who will get a majority against all the rest in two-way elections, a *Condorcet candidate*, then it seems we might want that candidate to win the election—but there might not be a Condorcet candidate, and even if there is, election procedures simpler than holding all two-way elections will sometimes miss the Condorcet candidate. The more extensive (but still reasonable) list of criteria proposed by Kenneth Arrow can also be shown to be impossible. There is no mechanism that always satisfies all of the Arrow conditions. All in all, election procedures present trade-offs between different disadvantages, and there is no universal answer to what is the best election procedure.

Exercises and Discussion Questions

19.1 **Impasse in the Faculty Senate.** (This is a true story, with the names changed to protect the more or less innocent). At a Faculty Senate meeting, Prof. Gadfly brought a complex motion that was mostly supported by a large majority, but that had two controversial paragraphs. Some senators proposed amendments that would delete one or the other, and some proposed an amendment that would eliminate both. The chair, Prof. Marian from the Library School, put the three amendments to a vote together. The vote was 5–5–5. Prof. Marian then cast the tie-breaking vote for the amendment that would have eliminated both paragraphs, but Prof. Mugwump, the parliamentarian, pointed out that a majority vote would be necessary to amend the motion, and six votes is not a majority. Analyze Prof. Marian's problem using concepts from this chapter. What would you advise Prof. Marian to do?

19.2 **Analysis of the 2000 Election.** Using the methods and concepts of this chapter and the assumptions in Table 19.8, verify the following points about the year 2000 U.S. presidential election.

1. Gore was the Condorcet candidate.

2. Under the Borda rule, Gore wins with either naïve or strategic voting.

3. With a two-round runoff, or with an instant runoff, with naïve voting, Gore wins 52–48 in the runoff. There is no incentive for strategic voting

4. With approval voting, Gore wins, so long as all parties play their best responses.

19.3 Analysis of the 1968 Election. Obtain information on the 1968 U.S. presidential election, and analyze that election using the methods of this chapter.

19.4 The Pork Game. Pork-barrel politics seems to be a part of the American mainstream. *Pork-barrel politics* means that the legislators collude to provide federal money to their own districts, regardless of the public interest, and it is widely felt that the public expenditures that result are inefficient. We also observe that legislators with many years' seniority are more successful in getting the pork for their districts, and that is one reason why the same representatives keep getting elected. Who wants to vote against a senator or house member with the power to get the pork for our district, especially if the pork will just go to some other district instead? Americans keep saying that they would like to have term limits, so that members of Congress would serve only two terms, but Americans keep voting for incumbents who have served far more than two terms. Is this inconsistency or hypocrisy?

No. It is a social dilemma. For simplicity, let's limit the game to three districts, A-town, B-opolis, and C-land. Table 19.E1 shows a three-person game table in normal form with the payoffs in alphabetical order—A-town first, then B-opolis, then C-land. The strategies are "vote incumbent" or "vote challenger."

Payoff order is A, B, C. Determine what equilibria, if any, this game has. Explain why Americans continue to vote for incumbents even though they would prefer to have term limits.

Now suppose that a referendum is held for a proposed constitutional amendment to establish term limits. If the referendum is passed, no one will be able to vote for the incumbent. Now

Table 19.E2 | Payoffs in the Pork Game

		C-land			
		vote incumbent		vote challenger	
		B-opolis		**B-opolis**	
		vote incumbent	vote challenger	vote incumbent	vote challenger
A-town	vote incumbent	2, 2, 2	5, 1, 5	5, 5, 1	6, 3, 3
	vote challenger	1, 5, 5	3, 3, 6	3, 6, 3	5, 5, 5

we have a two-stage game. The first stage is a voting game, and the strategies are "vote for the referendum" and "vote against the referendum." If at least two of the districts vote for the referendum, it passes, and all three are required to vote for a challenger in subsequent elections (since the incumbents will not be allowed to run).

Analyze the referendum in terms of games in extensive form and embedded games. Draw the imbedding game in extensive form. Solving the imbedded games, reduce the game in extensive form and write a payoff table for the first stage, the referendum game. Does the referendum game have a Nash equilibrium in pure strategies? If so, what? Discuss the relationship between imbedded games and constitutional limits in democratic political systems. Why do you suppose Americans have never had an opportunity to vote on a term limits amendment to the constitution?

20 Games and Experiments

To best understand this chapter 20

To best understand this chapter you need to have
studied and understood the material from Chapters
1–9, 14, and 16–17.

Game theory and the experimental method both begin from an assumption of uniformity. In the experimental method, the assumption is that nature is uniform, so that the regularities observed in the experimental laboratory will also be applicable in other times and places. Throughout the twentieth century, experimental methods were increasingly applied to human behavior. When experimental methods are applied to human behavior, the assumption of uniformity becomes an assumption about human behavior: the assumption that what we observe of human behavior in the laboratory will also be observed outside the laboratory. This is not as compelling an idea as the idea that inanimate nature is uniform. Context does matter for human behavior, and the laboratory context may modify behavior in important ways. Nevertheless, the experimental method has been a powerful source of insights across the human behavioral sciences.

In game theory, the assumption is again about the uniformity of human behavior, so that what we learn from human behavior in games can be extended to other kinds of interactions. This is closely related to the assumption of uniformity in experimental work: Indeed, we could think of a game like Nim as a laboratory for a certain kind of human behavior. Here again, context counts for human behavior, and we need to be a bit cautious with this assumption of uniformity; but at the same time the parallel between games and experiments is important, and a foundation of game theory.

It should be no surprise, then, that there has been experimental work in game theory from very early days. Indeed, **experimental game theory** began in 1950.

A Prisoner's Dilemma Experiment

An experiment with a modified Prisoner's Dilemma was almost certainly the first experiment in game theory, and in the first few decades of the development of game theory, the Prisoner's Dilemma attracted much of the attention of the experimenters. In that first experiment, in January of 1950, Merrill Flood and Melvin Dresher of the RAND Corporation were the experimenters. A version the Flood-Dresher experimental game is shown in Table 20.1. (The table used in the experiment was different, and was designed to be a little confusing, since part of the purpose of the experiment was to find out if the subjects could figure out what the equilibrium strategies would be). The experimental subjects were Armen Alchian, an economics professor at UCLA, and John Williams, head of the mathematics department of the RAND Corporation. As Table 20.1 shows, the game is modified from the Prisoner's Dilemmas we have studied in earlier chapters in that it is unsymmetrical—Williams does better than Alchian in three of the four strategy combinations, including those in which both cooperate or both defect. This proved to be a complication in the experiment.

In the Flood-Dresher experiment, Alchian and Williams played the game 100 times in succession. A record was kept not only of their strategies but also of their comments—a "talking through" experimental protocol that has been widely used in experiments by cognitive scientists in more recent decades and that gives some insights on their thought processes.[1] It is clear that they started out with different expectations, and to some extent retained quite different expectations. Alchian expected Williams to defect, while Williams tried to bring about a cooperative solution by starting cooperatively and playing a trigger strategy. Alchian initially didn't get it and assumed that Williams was playing a mixed strategy. (Williams commented that Alchian was a dope.)

Eventually Alchian got the idea that Williams was signaling for cooperative play. As the victim of an unsymmetrical payoff table, however, Alchian thought Williams ought to equalize the payoffs somewhat by allowing him, Alchian, to defect now and then. At the end of 100 rounds of play, Alchian worried that there would be no cooperation on the last play (since there would be no next play to retaliate on) and considered defecting earlier in order to gain an advantage. In fact, both cooperated on plays 83–98 and both defected on play 100.

William Poundstone writes "Alchian talks of Williams' unwillingness to 'share.' It is unclear what he meant by that."[2] Let's pause to try to understand what Alchian had in mind. He seems to have continued to think in terms of mixed strategies and to have had in mind

Heads Up!

Here are some concepts we will develop as this chapter goes along:

Games as Experiments: We can often check ideas from game theory by having real people play the game, and observing the strategies they choose.

Bounded Rationality: If people do not always succeed in choosing the best response or in maximizing their payoffs, but do try to come close they are said to be *boundedly rational.*

Reciprocity: When people deviate from self-interested rationality to return favors or wrongs, they act with reciprocity.

Ultimatum Game: A game in which one player offers to divide an amount in proportions the player chooses, and both get the payoffs only if the other player agrees. This game has been widely played in experiments.

Centipede Game: A game in which one player can claim the bigger share of the benefits, but get an even bigger share if neither player takes this opportunity. This game, too, has played an important role in experiments.

Table 20.1 | A Modified Prisoner's Dilemma

		John Williams	
		cooperate	defect
Armen Alchian	cooperate	½, 1	−1, 2
	defect	1, −1	0, ½

1 These are reported in William Poundstone, *Prisoner's Dilemma* (New York: Doubleday, 1992), pp. 108–116.
2 Poundstone, p. 107.

something like the following "correlated" mixed strategy: If there could be an enforceable agreement, the two might have agreed to a joint mixed strategy in which they jointly play a mixture of (C, C) and (D, C)[3] with probability p for (C, C) and (1 − p) for (D, C). The plays of (D, C) would enable Alchian to get some of his own back, at some cost in terms of total payoff. The total payoff per play is 1.5p, but Alchian's payoff is 1 − 0.5p, so a reduction in p helps him out. Williams' payoff is 2p − 1, and the expected value payoffs are equal when p = 4/5.[4] Alchian expected Williams to purchase his (Alchian's) cooperation with some reduction of p toward 4/5, although perhaps not all the way. The correlated strategy should be relatively easy for Williams to play—he always plays C, after all—but that puts Alchian in control of p, and Williams would have to observe Alchian's play for several rounds to estimate the probability that Alchian was playing, and only then retaliate. Alchian noted, however, that Williams always retaliated, and interpreted that as a selfish unwillingness to share the benefits of cooperation.

Despite all this confusion, the two players managed to cooperate on 60 of the 100 games. Mutual defection, the Nash equilibrium, occurred only 14 times. Flood and Dresher showed their result to John Nash, and Nash pointed out that it was not really a test of the one-off Prisoner's Dilemma, since the repeated play changes the analysis considerably. Nash was right, of course, but we have since learned that the subgame perfect Nash equilibrium in a game like this (with a definite end-point) is to defect on every round. Neither player did that. Alchian started out expecting the game to go that way, but revised his expectation and learned a quite different—and equally nonequilibrium—approach! Williams knowingly played a nonequilibrium strategy in the hope of getting the benefits of mutual cooperation.

Prisoner's Dilemma Results

The results of this original experiment exemplify the results of many experiments on the Prisoner's Dilemma. In general, experimental subjects do not always play the dominant strategy equilibrium, and often they do play the cooperative strategy pair. This lends itself to two interpretations, and there has been controversy over which is the better interpretation:

1. People are not really as rational as game theory assumes, and fail to play the dominant strategy equilibrium because they do not understand the game.

2. People are better at solving social dilemmas than game theorists suppose, perhaps because they do not always base their actions on self-interest.

---

3 Alchian's strategy is listed first. C means cooperate and D means defect.

4 This correlated mixed strategy is not an equilibrium, since the probabilities are not best responses. The fact that it does not maximize the total payoff suggests that it is not efficient, and therefore not a cooperative solution either, but that is not quite right. Since there is no *transferable utility*, side payments cannot be made. The correlated mixed strategy is efficient in the sense that neither player can be made better off without making the other worse off, and this is the way an economist like Alchian would have understood efficiency. So the correlated mixed strategy could be a cooperative solution to this game.

The controversies over interpretation of the Prisoner's Dilemma often assume that only one of these interpretations is true. But, as the Flood-Dresher experiment already showed, there could be a measure of truth (and falsehood) in each of them. Results from many Prisoner's Dilemma experiments (and other experiments) can be summed up as follows:

- *Real human rationality is **bounded rationality**.* People do not spontaneously choose the mathematically rational solutions to games, but think them through in complex and fallible ways. People tend to play according to heuristic rules, or "rules of thumb," such as Tit-for-Tat, which work well in many cases but are fallible. People can often find their way to the solutions of simple games, especially with some opportunity to learn through trial and error. However, they rarely find their way to more complicated solutions, such as the subgame perfect play on a Prisoner's Dilemma repeated 100 times. In many games, play approaches the equilibrium with experience and learning, but in the Prisoner's Dilemma, at least, learning can have the opposite effect, in that people learn to cooperate (as Alchian did in the Flood-Dresher experiment).

- Different people may approach the social dilemma with different motivations as well as different approaches to solving the problem. Some studies suggest at least three "types" of players:

  - *Self-interested types*, who try to maximize their own payoffs, as game theory assumes.

  - *Altruistic types*, who try to play in a way that benefits the whole group. This is not quite the whole story, since there could be more than one interpretation of altruism. One possibility is that the altruistic types try to maximize the total payoff. Table 20.2 shows what the Flood-Dresher game would look like to a player who is altruistic in this sense.

Table 20.2 | Total Payoffs in a Modified Prisoner's Dilemma

		John Williams	
		cooperate	defect
Armen Alchian	cooperate	1½	1
	defect	0	½

  - *Hypercompetitive types*, who try to maximize the difference of their own payoffs minus those of the opponent. Hyper-competitive play does not change the Prisoner's Dilemma, but can change some other games in crucial ways. Recall the Heave-Ho Game from Chapter 4. This is a coordination game with one equilibrium better (from the point of view of both players) than the other. It thus seems that "self-interested" types would be able to find the cooperative (heave, heave) strategy pair as a Schelling point, unless bad experiences lead them to expect something else. Table 20.3 shows how the Heave-Ho Game would look to two hypercompetitive types. It becomes a zero-sum game with a dominant strategy equilibrium of (don't, don't). To a

Table **20.3** | "Heave-Ho" as Seen by Two Hypercompetitive Types

		Karl	
		heave	don't
Jim	heave	0, 0	−10, 10
	don't	10, −10	0, 0

hypercompetitive type, all games are zero-sum. But this leads us back to the two interpretations: Is the hypercompetitive behavior actually something in the personality of the game player, or is it a misunderstanding of the possibilities of the games?

Other experimental studies have suggested a result that Flood and Dresher could not have obtained because everyone involved in that experiment was of the same gender. Some experimenters have found evidence of gender differences in Prisoner's Dilemma experiments. Somewhat cautiously, it seems likely that females are, on the whole, more likely to try for and arrive at the cooperative outcome than males are.

Some recent experiments by neurologists,[5] involving brain imaging, indicate that (in female experimental subjects) brain activity associated with cooperative play in Prisoner's Dilemma experiments is consistent with the hypothesis that cooperation is emotionally rewarding. This brain activity is observed when the other player is human, but not when the subject plays against a computer.

A Mixed Experiment

To illustrate the development of experimental game theory over the half-century following the Flood-Dresher experiment, let us consider one fairly general example, an experimental study[6] done in the late 1980s at the University of Iowa. The experimental subjects were business students. They were randomly matched to play the games and played them anonymously, via a computer network, without being able to see one another. This design assured that they were playing the one-off games the experimenters designed, and not some more complex repeated game. The payoffs were adjusted to offset risk aversion and similar considerations so that the numerical payoffs should correspond closely to subjective payoffs.[7] The authors write, ". . . there is strong support for the dominant strategy prediction . . . and the Nash equilibrium prediction. . . ."[8]

The games they played were, in many cases, designed to mix elements of a social dilemma with elements of a coordination game. An example is given as Table 20.4. The upper-left four cells in this game define a coordination game somewhat like Heave-Ho, in

5 Natalie Angier, "Why We're So Nice: We're Wired to Cooperate," *The New York Times*, Section F, (July 23, 2002), pp. 1–8.

6 Russell W. Cooper, Douglas V. DeJong, Robert Forsythe, and Thomas W. Ross, "Selection Criteria in Coordination Games: Some Experimental Results," *American Economic Review* v. 80, no. 1 (March 1990), pp. 218–233.

7 The actual payoffs were determined by a lottery with payoffs and probabilities based on game points, so that risk aversion should have no effect on the choice of strategies. The details are too advanced for this introductory text.

8 Cooper et al., p. 223.

that the two equilibria, (1, 1) and (2, 2) can be ranked in the same way by both players, (2, 2) better than (1, 1). In these circumstances, it has seemed that (2, 2) might be a Schelling point and therefore the equilibrium most likely to occur. However, (2, 2) is not the cooperative solution. Strategies (3, 3) make both players better off still. On the other hand, strategy 3 is dominated, as the cooperative strategies are in a social dilemma.

In these experiments, Nash equilibria were usually observed. A few players played the cooperative strategy, 3. But the most usual Nash equilibrium in the game in Table 20.4 was (1, 1), not the better equilibrium at (2, 2). The experimenters judged that (1, 1) was chosen because the subjects assigned a positive probability to the possibility that the other player would play the cooperative strategy 3. If Q plays the cooperative strategy, 3, and P plays 1, P makes a killing with 1,000 points. Or P might reason that Q will choose 1 because Q thinks P will choose 3! To test this hypothesis, the experimenters also tried a slightly different game shown in Table 20.5, in which (3, 3) is no longer the cooperative solution. In the Table 20.5 game, (2, 2) is the cooperative solution, so there is no conflict between cooperative and better-ranked Nash solutions. In this game, (2, 2) was almost always chosen.

The experimenters concluded that the cooperative solution can influence the choice of Nash equilibria, even though the cooperative strategies are dominated. This experiment is a good example of much experimental work in game theory, showing that many of the difficulties with the Flood-Dresher experiment can be addressed. It is consistent with many results that show that Nash and dominant strategy equilibria can be realized in experiments, especially when care is taken that the game is what it is meant to be and when the game is fairly simple and there is no conflict between Nash and cooperative outcomes. With respect to the Shelling point theory, the glass is at least half full, since the players found a Schelling point when they were not distracted by conflict between the cooperative and equilibrium solutions, and there really is no Schelling point when such a conflict exists.

For the rest of this chapter, however, we will focus on experimental results that raise issues for the theory of games and for noncooperative equilibrium concepts, on the principle that there is more to learn from negative results than from positive ones.

Table 20.4 An Experimental Three-Strategy Game

		Q		
		1	2	3
P	1	350, 350	350, 250	1000, 0
	2	250, 350	550, 550	0, 0
	3	0, 1000	0, 0	600, 600

Table 20.5 Another Experimental Three-Strategy Game

		Q		
		1	2	3
P	1	350, 350	350, 250	1000, 0
	2	250, 350	550, 550	0, 0
	3	0, 1000	0, 0	500, 500

Ultimatum Games

The **Ultimatum Game** shows the contrast between equilibrium and experimental results in an even stronger form. A certain amount of money (let us say, $50) is to be divided between two players. One player, the Proposer, offers to split the amount with the other player, the Responder. The Proposer suggests an amount that the Responder is to get, and the Responder can say only yes or no. There is no negotiation and no repetition.[9] If the Proposer and the Responder agree on the proportions in which the amount is to be split, then they each get the amount they have agreed upon. If they do not agree—that is, if the Responder answers no—then neither player gets anything.

Figure 20.1 | An Ultimatum Game

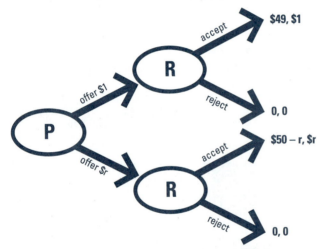

To keep things a little simpler, let's say that the Proposer can offer only whole-dollar amounts to the Responder. Then the Proposer has 51 strategies: 0, 1, . . . 50. Figure 20.1 shows just two of those strategies in a game in extensive form: "offer $1" and "offer r." The unknown amount r can stand in for any strategy other than "offer $1," so we can analyze the game with this diagram. We can see that, if the offer is $1, the Responder's best response is to accept, since $1 is better than nothing. First, suppose r is more than $1. If the Proposer offers $r, the Responder's best response is again to accept. Suppose, however, that r is 0. With an offer of 0, the Responder has nothing to lose by rejecting. If the probability of a rejection in that case is more than 2 percent, the Proposer will maximize his payoff by offering just $1—the minimum positive offer—and that is the subgame perfect equilibrium of this game.

The experimental results are quite different, however. On the one hand, Responders will usually reject offers of less than 30 percent. This is a sacrifice of self-interest, because, as we have pointed out, $1 or $5 is better than nothing, and nothing is what the Responder gets if he rejects the offer. Conversely, Proposers usually offer more than the minimum share to the Responders. That could, in principle, be rational self-interest. Knowing that rejections of small offers are probable, the Proposers might choose offers that maximize the expected value of their payoffs—just enough to balance the gain from making a smaller offer against the increased risk of a rejection resulting from it. But there is evidence that Proposers often give the Responders a bigger share than the share that would maximize the expected value of payoffs, and 50-50 splits are very common.

9 Some experimenters have studied repeated Ultimatum Games, but here we want to focus on the one-off game, which has a clear noncooperative equilibrium.

The Ultimatum Game has been studied in some nonwestern cultures, and there is evidence of differences of detail across cultures as well as differences between genders within Western cultures. In qualitative terms, however, the results are similar and are as described in the previous paragraph.

How can we account for these results? Altruism, in its simplest form, will not do it. An altruist who tries to maximize total payoffs would never turn down any offer, even a zero offer. On the other hand, if altruism is understood as a preference for fairness, that could be consistent with the experimental results. There is evidence that perceived fairness influences the outcomes in many games. A hypercompetitive player, on the other hand, would turn down any offer for less than one-half. It seems that we need to dig a little deeper.

A recent and rapidly growing group of studies are based on the hypothesis of **reciprocity**. The reciprocity hypothesis says that people will deviate from self-interest to return perceived favors or to retaliate for perceived slights. Thus, for example, a Responder in the Ultimatum Game who is offered $5 sees the offer as a wrong, since the Proposer keeps 90 percent of the payoff, and responds by sacrificing that $5 pay-

> ### Definition
>
> *Reciprocity*—When a player gives up a greater payoff in order to reward a perceived self-sacrifice by the other player, or to retaliate for perceived aggressiveness by the other player, this is called **reciprocity**. In the first case, reward, it is called *positive reciprocity*. In the second case, retaliation, it is called *negative reciprocity*.

off to retaliate by leaving the Proposer with nothing. This is called *negative reciprocity*. Sacrificing one's own payoffs to reward a good deed by the other is called *positive reciprocity*. The reciprocity hypothesis says that real human behavior will often deviate from self-interest in the direction of reciprocity, both positive and negative. On the whole, the results for the Ultimatum Game seem consistent with reciprocity.

Another example of the reciprocity hypothesis is found in experimental studies of the Centipede Game.

Centipede Games and Reciprocity

In Chapter 14, we used the **Centipede Game** as an example to illustrate subgame perfect equilibria. The simplest kind of Centipede Game is shown in Figure 20.2. Recall, the game begins with a payoff pot of 5 available. Player A can grab 4 of that, leaving 1 for player B, or can pass the pot to B. With the pot in his possession, B can grab or pass. Whenever the pot is passed it grows larger, so that B can grab 6, leaving 2, for a total of 8, but if the pot is passed a second time the two players split a pot of 10 equally, for (5, 5).

We recall that the subgame perfect equilibrium is to grab at the first play, and this is true

Figure 20.2 A Simple Centipede Game

Approximately repeats Figure 14.7, Chapter 14

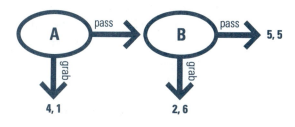

even if we extend the Centipede to 100 steps or more. In experimental studies, it is common for the pot to be passed to the end point of equal division, and grabs at the first step are uncommon. In experiments with more than two steps, there are some cases in which the pot is grabbed in late stages of the game.

Some studies explain these results by the reciprocity hypothesis, relying mainly on positive reciprocity. Player B understands that player A can grab the larger part of the pot, and if player A passes the pot, player B sees this as a favorable act, and is likely to reciprocate the positive act by passing as well, reducing his payoff from 6 to 5 but allowing player A a payoff of 5 rather than the 4 that player A has passed up. If player A is motivated by reciprocity, he might anticipate player B's self-sacrifice and will reciprocate an expected good turn on the part of player B. If both are motivated by reciprocity, we would see the pot passed to the end of the game. Even if player A is a "self-interested type," but believes player B is motivated by reciprocity, player A would pass in the expectation that the pass would be reciprocated by B. (However, a "self-interested type" might grab the pot at a later stage of a multistep Centipede).

Now it's your turn: Suppose that A and B play a four-stage Centipede Game with plays by A, B, A, and finally B. Suppose A is a "self-interested type" and A believes B is motivated by reciprocity. What is A's best strategy?[10]

Figure 20.3 | A Centipede Game with Retaliation

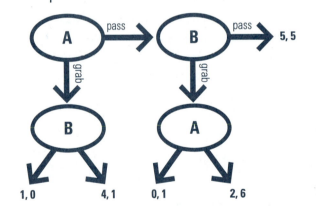

Thus, the Ultimatum Game gives a lead role to negative reciprocity, that is, costly retaliation, while the Centipede Game gives a lead role to positive reciprocity. But negative and positive reciprocity can reinforce one another. Consider the modified Centipede Game shown in extended form in Figure 20.3. After the "grab" stage, the other player has an opportunity to retaliate, by choosing "left," or not to retaliate, choosing "right." Retaliation makes both players worse off—the retaliator gives up even his smaller proportion of the pot, much

as a Responder who turns down a positive offer gives up his smaller proportion in the Ultimatum game. In both cases, in effect, the retaliators give up some of their own (potential) payoffs to punish the other player.

But does it make a difference in the Centipede Game? Notice that retaliation is never a best response in this game. Therefore, the option to retaliate is irrelevant to the subgame perfect equilibrium. (Grab, don't retaliate) at the first stage is the subgame perfect equilibrium. Therefore we would expect (based on the subgame perfect equilibrium) that there would be

10 The answer is on the last page of this chapter.

no difference, in experiments, between the games in Figure 20.2 and those in Figure 20.3. In actual experiments, however, "pass" strategies are more common in games like Figure 20.3 than in games like Figure 20.2. Evidently, the threat of self-sacrificing negative reciprocity reinforces the promise of self-sacrificing positive reciprocity in inducing players to pass rather than grab.

Work to Be Done (Framing)

Experimental game theory has adopted experimental approaches from other fields, particularly psychology and experimental economics, and in some cases has extended the results of those studies. One body of experimental studies (primarily in psychology) has focused on a phenomenon called framing. What these studies say is that human decisions may depend on the way the question is put. That is, the decision depends on the way the decision is framed. For example: Would you rather buy a product that is 95 percent fat free or one that is 5 percent fat? Of course, the two phrases mean the same thing, but when did you see a product advertised as 5 percent fat?

Framing is illustrated by a classical experiment by psychologists Amos Tversky and Daniel Kahneman. It is not a game theory experiment, but an experiment about risk perception, a closely related field. The experiment is based on a hypothetical disease threat: an epidemic of an obscure tropical disease is expected to kill 600 Americans if no precautions are taken. There are two programs of precautions that might be taken, but they are inconsistent, so only one of the two can be taken. Experimental subjects were asked to choose between the two programs.

One group of experimental subjects was told this:

- With program A, 200 people will be saved.

- With program B, there is a 1/3 probability that 600 will be saved and a 2/3 probability that none will be saved.

The other group was told this:

- With program A, 400 will die.

- With program B, there is a 1/3 probability that nobody will die and a 2/3 probability that 600 will die.

Notice that these two descriptions actually describe the same events, but the first one calls attention to the fact that, with program A, 200 people will live with certainty, whereas the second calls attention to the fact that 400 will certainly die with the same program. The choice is the same either way: a certain 200/400 split of living and dead, on the one hand, and an all-or-nothing risk with slightly bad odds on the other.

Despite the fact that the two descriptions add up to the same, the two experimental groups responded very differently. The ones who were told that 200 would live opted for program A by a 72–28 margin, while those who were told that 400 would die chose program B by a 78–22 margin! Evidently, the decisions depended very much on how the decision was framed—in a way positive or negative to program A.

Experimenters in game theory have only recently begun research on the role of framing in game theory. The reason for the delay probably is found in the roots of game theory in rational action theory. In traditional game theory models we assume rationality and common knowledge of rationality—so the only frame the decision needs is the fact that the other players are rational. But when decisions are influenced by perceived reciprocity, framing may be important, since the perception of reciprocity may depend on the way the game is framed. Self-interest, altruism, and bounded rationality, too, may give rise to decisions that depend on the way the decision is framed.

Hopefully, with further experimental work we will learn much more about the role of framing in games.

Where We Have Arrived

All in all, these experimental studies raise some deep questions about some models of noncooperative game theory *as a theory of human strategic behavior.* The following seems clear:

- Real human rationality is bounded, not unbounded as the common knowledge of rationality assumption implies.

- Real human behavior in games often approximates cooperative rather than noncooperative outcomes.

- Real human behavior in games is influenced by non-self-interested motives, such as reciprocity.

- It is probable that real human behavior in games is influenced by framing.

- Real human behavior in games can be complex and, for practical purposes, a considerable part of it is random.

   However,

- There are a wide range of experimental and observational cases in which noncooperative game models do describe observed behavior. Among these are coordination games, many games with more than two participants, and games in which people have plenty of opportunity to learn and refine their behavior.

- Noncooperative and cooperative game solutions together can explain a great deal of real human behavior.

- Game theory is only partly a theory of human behavior. It is also partly a "normative" theory, that is, a theory that explains how people would behave if they were (in one sense or another) rational.

- Whenever experimentalists conclude that the behavior they observe is irrational, they are using the normative concepts of rationality as the basis for the claim, and saying that observed behavior deviates predictably from normative rationality. Conversely, the observed behavior can be successfully explained as the sum of rational behavior plus the predictable deviation, and that will be useful for many practical purposes, even if it is not satisfactory to those seeking a deeper understanding.[11]

- While it is too soon to be certain, it may be that a noncooperative rationality theory, modified to allow for reciprocity, could account for most if not all of the predictable components of human strategic behavior, and provide that deeper understanding.

To summarize, there are two ways to interpret the disagreement between theory and experiment in some important, exemplary games. One way is to interpret it as evidence against the rationality hypothesis and the general applicability of game theory. The other is to interpret it as a step toward extending the theory beyond the rationality assumption to a more general and realistic theory of strategic behavior. The second interpretation seems preferable (to the author of this textbook) because it allows us to retain the wide range of games and applications in which theory, experiment, and observation agree well.

Business Application
Reciprocity in the Employment Relationship

Economists traditionally have taken the assumption of rational self-interest as given, and so there are few economic studies based on the reciprocity hypothesis. However, one study of the relationship between employers and employees by an economist[12] argued that reciprocal gifts are at the heart of successful employment relationships, and his thinking can be connected to one of the most famous experimental studies in business management.

---

11 This is sometimes criticized along lines suggested by the history of astronomy. Until Copernicus proposed an astronomic theory with the sun at the center of the solar system and the planets in orbit around it, astronomers had relied on the Pythagorean theory, which assumed, incorrectly, that the earth was at the center. Both theories assumed the orbits were circular, and the circular orbits did not fit the actual movements of the planets in the skies very well, so the Pythagoreans had adjusted the theory by adding smaller circles, so-called *epicycles*. Those who treat real human decisions as rationality plus an adjustment for irrationality are accused of "adding epicycles," which is supposed to imply that they are as wrong as the Pythagoreans were. But the critics might want to keep in mind that the Pythagorean theory, with its epicycles, actually fit the observations of the planets better than the Copernican theory, with its circular orbits around the sun. Thus, the Pythagorean theory remained the more useful one until Kepler proposed a theory with elliptical orbits around the sun. If anyone has a really new, Keplerian theory of human behavior, it would indeed be a big step forward. I believe some of the excitement about the reciprocity hypothesis reflects a hope that it might be getting us close to a Keplerian theory of real human behavior in games.

12 G. A. Akerlof, "Labor Contracts as a Partial Gift Exchange," *Quarterly Journal of Economics* v. 98, no. 4 (November 1982) pp. 543–570.

George Akerlof began from the observation that employers often pay more than the going wage in the labor market. This gives the employees something to lose if they should lose their jobs. After all, employees who are paid just what they can get in the market have nothing to lose by being dismissed—they can get other jobs at the same wages tomorrow.[13] The idea is that the higher wages increase productivity: Employees who have something to lose will work harder, and productivity and profits will be improved as a result. When employers pay above-market wages and this maximizes profits by enhancing productivity, the higher wage is called an *efficiency wage*, rather than a market wage.

But how does this increase in productivity happen? Akerlof argues that employees usually work harder than they really have to. Monitoring cannot be constant, and detailed observation in a case study indicated that employees worked more than the amount of work needed in order to avoid being *caught* shirking. Akerlof's reasoning is that the employees are responding to their employer's perceived generosity with positive reciprocity.

Akerlof drew from anthropological studies that had interpreted the observed behavior of people of various cultures as evidence of reciprocity. In many of these cases, reciprocity takes the form of mutual gift-giving. Akerlof saw a parallel to the anthropological studies in that the employees perceived their higher-than-market wages as a "gift" and responded with the "gift" of increased effort. But this is equally consistent with game theoretic experiments that point toward a tendency to sacrifice in order to return a perceived favor (or retaliate for a perceived slight).

Something like reciprocity in the workplace had been observed in one of the most famous experiments in the history of management science, experiments conducted between 1923 and 1932 in the Relay Assembly Test Room at the Hawthorne Works of Western Electric Company.[14] The experiments tested various changes of working conditions, such as lighting, for impacts on the productivity of the employees. What was found was that changes in the conditions tended to enhance productivity. In some cases, productivity was enhanced by opposite and inconsistent changes in the conditions, so that the productivity changes could not be attributed to the conditions themselves. One popular interpretation is that the test employees considered the experiments themselves as special treatment, something of a favor, and responded to it with increased effort. This would be consistent with the reciprocity hypothesis.

What this suggests is not a new idea, but nevertheless one that is often overlooked. It is that the employment relationship is more profitable if it is not simply a case of conflicting interests. Disgruntled employees are less profitable employees, so smart employers find ways (including, but not only, money) to "gruntle" their employees.

---

13 In more-developed countries, there are a very few labor markets in which this is literally true: Day labor markets and hiring-hall labor markets in which a person may work for a different employer every day. These are more common in less-developed countries. It is not clear what the growth of temporary employment might mean for this argument.

14 H. McIlvaine Parsons, "Hawthorne: An Early OBM Experiment," *Journal of Organizational Behavior Management*, v. 2, no. 1, (1992), pp. 27–44.

Summary

Games and experiments are similarly based on assumptions about the uniformity of that which is observed, and games lend themselves well to experimental work. Thus, there has been extensive experimental work in game theory, beginning in the earliest days of game theory at the RAND Corporation. In some ways, the earliest experiments (which gave rise to the Prisoner's Dilemma) gave a foretaste of what was to come. First, there can be ambiguity about just what is tested. For example, experiments with repeated play cannot be used to directly test hypotheses about simple one-off games. But even when all precautions are taken to remove ambiguity, the results clearly go beyond the limits of noncooperative equilibrium theory. Some equilibrium examples are confirmed by experiments, but in others the experimental results raise questions about both unlimited rationality and self-interest. When there is a conflict between the noncooperative and the cooperative solutions to an experimental game, the observed behavior is often pulled strongly toward the cooperative solution or otherwise influenced by it. It might be necessary to allow for a wide range of distinct non-self-interested and boundedly rational players, but it might also be that a wide range of human strategic behavior can be understood as a boundedly rational expression of self-interest modified by reciprocity.

Exercises and Discussion Questions

20.1 **Forward Induction.** Propose an experiment to study the hypothesis that game equilibria are influenced by "outside options" and forward induction as in Chapter 15. Your experiment should allow the subjects an opportunity to learn by experience but should not be influenced by "repeated play" considerations.

20.2 **Road Rage.** Recall the Road Rage Game from Chapter 14. Bob's strategies are (aggress, don't aggress) and Al's strategies are (if Bob aggresses) "retaliate" and "don't." The payoffs are shown in Table 20.E1.

In the subgame perfect equilibrium of this game, Bob aggresses and Al does not retaliate. However, drivers do not always aggress, and retaliation is sometimes observed when they do, even to the point (rarely!) of firing weapons at the aggressor. Explain these facts using concepts from this chapter. How would Bob and Al, respectively, play if they

Table **20.E1** The Road Rage Game

		Bob	
		aggress	don't aggress
Al	if Bob aggresses then retaliate; if not, do nothing	−50, −100	5, 4
	if Bob aggresses then don't; if not, do nothing	4, 5	5, 4

were altruists? Hypercompetitive? Motivated by reciprocity? The Washington State Police adopted a policy to discourage road rage by increasing the penalty for aggressive driving. Does this make sense in the light of the discussion in this chapter?

20.3 Payback Game. Player 1 gets a sum of money. He can keep all of it or pass all or some of it on to Player 2. If some of the money is passed on to Player 2, the experimenter matches the amount, so that the amount passed to Player 2 is double the amount given up by Player 1. Player 2 can then pay back to Player 1 all or part of the money Player 2 has received. Any money passed back is again matched by the experimenter, so that Player 1 receives 1.5 times the amount passed back. Thus, if Player 1 starts with $10 and passes it all, Player 2 gets $20, and if Player 2 passes all of it back, Player 1 gets $30.

What is the subgame perfect equilibrium of this game? How would an altruist (who maximizes the total payoff) play it? What about a hypercompetitive type? What if the players are motivated by reciprocity? Drawing on the information in this chapter, how would you expect the experiment to come out?

20.4 An Environmental Game. Prof. Greengrass is interested in the motives for conservation of environmental resources such as forest land and underground water. These resources may be of benefit to future generations, but any generation also has the option to use them up, for example, by cutting the forests or polluting the underground water. In that case, the resources are of less or no use to the future generations. For experimental purposes, Prof. Greengrass will set up a game along these lines: there are N participants, with N equal to two or more, and they will play in order. The first player is given a "resource" (a piece of paper) and may pass it to the second or return it to the experimenter. If it is passed, each player in turn has the same choices, and the game ends when the paper is returned to the experimenter. Each player who passes the paper to the next player gets one point, while the player who returns it to the experimenter gets two (unless he is the last in order, who can get only one point).

Draw the extensive form diagram for this game, assuming there are three players in the game. Assuming that the players are rational and self-interested, what would you expect would be the result? What do you think would happen? Why? What difference would it make if the number of players were larger?

20.5 Effort Dilemma. An effort dilemma, recall, is a social dilemma in which the cooperative strategy is to work (with a strong effort) and the noncooperative strategy is to shirk. The theory of indefinitely repeated games tells us that, if the probability of another play is large enough, cooperative play may occur. Design an experiment to test the influence of an increasing probability of repetition on the outcome of an effort dilemma.

*Answer to the exercise on page 328. Assume that, as in Figure 20.2, the cooperative payoff after four passes dominates the pay-offs if A grabs at the first stage. If A believes that B is motivated by reciprocity, then A will pass and, if B passes, pass again, anticipating that B will "return the favor" by passing, and so A will get the larger cooperative payoff. Thus, the knowledge that other players are not rational and self-interested leads the player who *is* rational and self-interested to act in ways that would not be rational otherwise.

21 Auctions

To best understand this chapter 21

To best understand this chapter you need to have studied and understood the material from Chapters 1–4, 7, 8, 14, 15, and 20.

In her biography of John Nash, *A Beautiful Mind*, (Simon and Schuster, 1998, p. 375), Sylvia Nasar writes, "The most dramatic use of game theory is [that] radio spectrum, T-bills, oil leases, timber, and pollution rights are now sold in auctions designed by game theorists. . . ." Game theorists have indeed played a key role in the design and conduct of auctions in the late twentieth century. This chapter introduces game theoretic analysis of auctions.

A Camera Auction

Definition

English Auction—An auction in which potential buyers call out sequentially higher prices, and the person who bids highest buys the item at the high bid price is called an **English auction**.

We begin, as usual, with an example. The most familiar kind of auction is the ascending-price **English auction**, the **auction type** in which people alternate in crying out their acceptance of a rising price. Usually the auctioneer will raise the price by some given amount between bids, until no one is willing to pay any higher price. Suppose Pat and Quincy are bidding on a camera in an auction of that kind, competing to buy a used camera for their own use, not for resale. Quincy has the high bid at 100, and bid increments are 5, so that the next bid is 105. From the viewpoint of game theory, how should Pat bid? What is his best response to this situation?

To answer this question, of course, we need to know a bit about Pat's payoffs, and about Quincy's payoffs, too. Pat's payoff depends on whether he gets the camera or not, but also on the price at which he gets it. The higher the price, the less the payoff. Certainly, if the price were very high, buying the item could make the buyer worse off. If, through some mistake, I bought a camera for my use for $100,000, I would feel worse off.[1] There must be an upper limit price, the highest price the person could pay and get the item and not feel worse off. This is the person's **value**, in the jargon of the economics of auctions.[2] If the person buys just at the

---

1 Of course, if I knew someone who was willing to pay me $150,000 for the camera, perhaps as a historic antique, that would be a very different matter. But it is also a complication we need to leave for a later section of this chapter. That's why we have assumed that Pat and Quincy are buying for their own use, not for resale.

2 The term *reservation price* is widely used in economics for the highest price a buyer is willing to pay or the lowest price a seller is willing to accept. In some auctions a seller can set a reservation price, which is the lowest price he is willing to accept *in the auction*. This is probably the original use of the term. The widespread use of the term *value* in discussions of auctions avoids confusion between the two related, but distinct, concepts.

value, then the purchase makes the person neither better off nor worse off. If the person buys at a higher price, she is worse off, and if she buys at a lower price, she is better off.

Accordingly, we assume that Pat's value is 114. He doesn't know Quincy's value, but thinks it might be 102 or 108. Pat can bid 105, 110, or pass —those are his strategies. Should he bid 110 and close Quincy out? There are no information sets, since Pat and Quincy know all the bids that have been made, although they don't know one another's values. Accordingly, we analyze the auction in extensive form, and this is shown in Figure 21.1. In this game, the first payoff is to Pat and the second to Quincy.

Now it's your turn: How many proper subgames does this game have? Which are basic? What is the subgame perfect equilibrium for this game?[3]

3 The answer is on the last page of this chapter.

Here are some concepts we will develop as this chapter goes along:

Auction Type: Auctions are of various types, including English and Dutch, and others. Whereas English auctions start with a low price and the price goes up until the item is sold, Dutch auctions start with a high price and the price drops until the item is sold.

Independent Private Value: The bidder's *value* for an item is the price she or he would pay rather than give up the item. If the value is independent of other bidders' values, the auction is said to be an *independent-private-value* auction.

Auction Frame: Auction strategy and outcomes will depend on characteristics of the bidders, as whether their values are given and independent (independent private values) or depend on an estimate of some objective fact such as resale value (pure common values). These characteristics constitute the *auction frame*.

Figure 21.1 | A Camera Auction

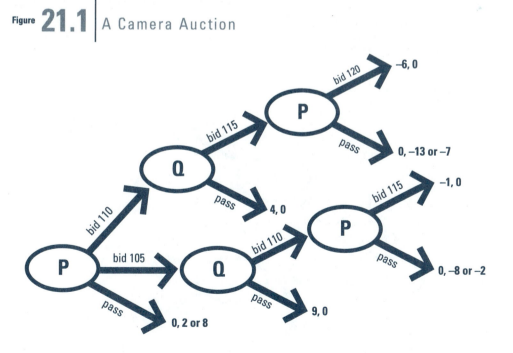

Figure **21.2** | A Basic Proper Subgame

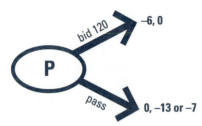

We analyze this game through backward induction. Let's see how that will go. The game has two basic proper subgames, Pat's rebids, shown in Figures 21.2 and 21.3. In each of these, Pat will pass for a payoff of 0 rather than bidding for a negative payoff. Thus, in each of these subgames, the equilibrium payoff pair is the lower one. Substituting the equilibrium payoffs for the subgames gives us the reduced auction game in Figure 21.4.

This game, in turn, has the two basic proper subgames shown in Figures 21.5 and 21.6. These are Quincy's bidding opportunities. In each case, Quincy's best response is to pass for a zero payoff rather than bid for a negative payoff. Thus, again, the equilibrial payoffs for these games are the lower ones. We can reduce the auction game another stage by substituting the equilibrium playoffs for the subgames, giving the reduced game shown in Figure 21.7. Clearly, the best bid for Pat is 105.

Figure **21.3** | Another Basic Proper Subgame

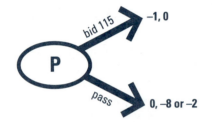

Thus, the subgame perfect equilibrium is for Pat to bid 105 and Quincy to pass. Indeed, it doesn't matter what Quincy's value is. The example would be more complicated if we were to allow for Quincy to have a value greater than 110, for example—but nevertheless, the conclusion would always be that Pat should raise the bid as long as the price does not go above his value.[4] This illustrates a general result: In an English auction, it is always subgame perfect to raise the bid

4 Of course, if Quincy has a value of 115 or higher, Pat will not get the camera. But then he is better off not to have it, since there is no price at which he can buy the camera that would be at or below his value. Buying the camera (at a price that Quincy will not overbid) would make Pat worse off in that case.

Figure **21.4** | The Camera Auction Reduced

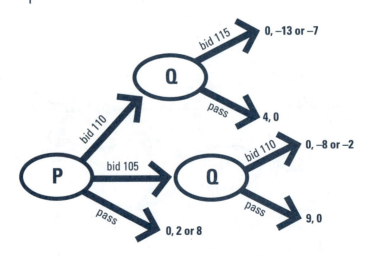

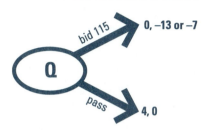

Figure 21.5 | A Basic Proper Subgame of the Reduced Game

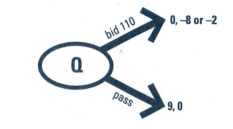

Figure 21.6 | Another Basic Proper Subgame of the Reduced Game

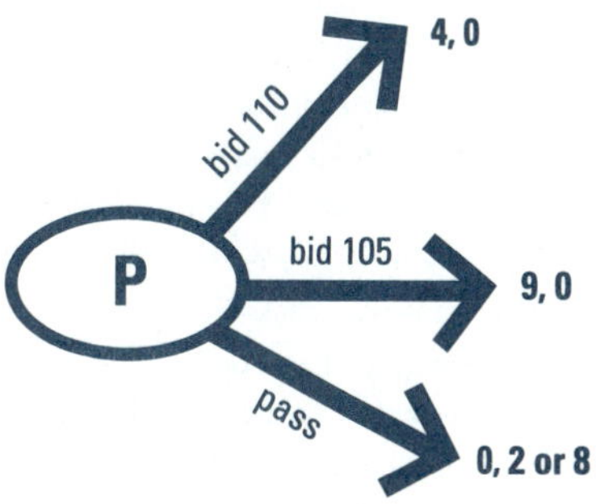

by the minimum increment so long as the bid does not go over your value. Notice that Pat doesn't need much information to know how to bid. All he needs know is his value and the bid increment. This is a major advantage of the English auction form.

Efficiency

We notice something else about this example: If both contestants bid rationally (i.e., if their bidding strategies are subgame perfect), then the person whose value is higher will always get the item at auction. And this is *efficient*.

Figure 21.7 | The Auction Game Reduced a Second Time

This is a general fact about values: It is always efficient for the person with the highest value to get the item. Here is the reasoning. Recall, an efficient situation is defined as a situation in which no one can be made better off without making someone else worse off. If someone can be made better off without making anyone worse off, that is an unrealized potential, and we have efficiency only when all of the potential for making people better off is realized. Suppose, then, that Sarah has some item—another used camera, let us say. Ruth's value is $100, and Sarah's value is $70. Then it would be possible to make both of them better off, and no one worse off, by transferring the item to Ruth at any price greater than $70 but less than $100. So long as the person with the lower value has the item, there is inefficiency that can be eliminated by shifting the item to the person with the higher value, at some price between their different values.

What we have learned, then, is that (in some examples such as this one) the English auction is *efficient*. This is important, because there are a number of different kinds of auctions. The choice—or design—of an auction form can be thought of as a case in social mechanism design, and efficiency is usually one of the criteria for social mechanism design. Thus, we will be concerned with the efficiency of different auction forms.

Although the English auction is efficient, in this example, auction rules may require that each bid raise the previous bid by some specific amount, the minimum bidding increment. In the Camera Auction, that minimum bidding increment is $5. This can introduce some inefficiency. Suppose that the two bidders' values had been different than the ones assumed in the Camera Auction example—specifically, suppose Quincy's value was 102 and Pat's was 104; and suppose also that Quincy had the high bid at $100. Then Pat would not be able to overbid Quincy, since he would have to bid $105 and lose $1 as a result. Quincy would get the camera, even though Pat sets a $2 greater value on it. This is inefficient. But there is a limit to the inefficiency from this source. The buyer's value can be less than that of someone who does not buy, but not by more than $5, the minimum increment. Good auctioneers reduce the minimum increment as the bidding slows down, so that the inefficiency might be quite small—but in practice there is usually a minimum bidding increment. Thus, it is probably better to say that, in practice, the English auction can be approximately efficient.

These details are usually ignored in game theoretic analyses, and probably approximate efficiency is all we can expect in the real world anyway.

Definition

Second-Price Auction—An auction in which the high bidder buys the item at the second highest price bid is called a **second-price auction**. It may be a sealed bid auction or an auction with sequential bidding of higher prices.

Now let us look at another example, a different and very important kind of auction.

The eBay Example

The eBay auction site is one of the most successful innovative new businesses to arise from the e-commerce boom of the late 1990s. If you were to visit the eBay auction site on the World Wide Web (*http://www.ebay.com*) and look at the page for a particular item such as a used book, you would see, at the bottom of the page, a box like Figure 21.8, where you may enter a bid if you wish.[5] The Web site explains how eBay bidding works as follows:

> Let's say you find something on eBay that you want . . . you're willing to pay $25.00 for it, but the current bid price is only $2.25. You could take the long route and sit at your computer, outbidding each new bid until you reach $25.00.
> Luckily, there's a better way. Here's how it works:
> 1. Decide the **maximum** you're willing to pay and enter this amount.
> 2. eBay will now confidentially bid **up** to your maximum amount. In this way, you don't have to keep an eye on your auction as it unfolds.
> 3. If other bidders outbid your maximum at the end of the auction, you don't get the item. But otherwise, you're the winner—and the final price might even be less than the maximum you had been willing to spend!
>
> *Remember:* eBay will use only as much of your maximum bid as is necessary to maintain your position as high bidder. Winning was never easier!

What eBay is describing is a bidding process known as a **second-price auction**.[6] In a second-price

---

5 Yes, I did place a bid on the book. I got it, too.

6 To be more exact, the eBay auction only *approximates* a second-price auction, for two reasons. First, since there is a minimum bidding increment, it is possible that the person with the highest value may not get the item. As we have seen, this can lead to inefficiency and would not occur in a pure second-price auction. Second, since the bidding continues over time, as it does in an English auction, it is possible for individuals to postpone bidding, hoping to place a bid late enough that others cannot get their bids in. This "sniping" with last-minute bids does occur on eBay and is not characteristic of a second-price auction. However, the advice eBay gives is based on the advantages of second-price auctions, as we will see.

auction, each bidder offers a price, and the bidder who offers the highest price is the buyer; but the price the buyer pays is the second-highest price bid. This allows the buyer to bid what he or she thinks the item is worth, and still get a benefit if other buyers don't think it is worth as much.

Second-price auctions are often conducted (off-line) as sealed-bid auctions. This is convenient, since the bidder does not have to be present in order to bid. EBay bidding is a second-price auction process modified by a minimum initial bid and bid increment. An earlier bid prevails over any later bid that does not raise the price by a minimal increment. Thus, unlike a **sealed-bid auction**, an eBay auction allows bidders to rebid, raising the bid as the auction goes on. But, as the eBay instructions tell us, it isn't necessary to do so—you can just bid your maximum, and if no one else's maximum is higher, you will get the item for what the second-highest bidder would be willing to pay for it.

> **Definition**
>
> **Sealed-Bid Auction**– An auction in which the bids are submitted simultaneously, so that no one bidder knows what the other bidders have bid, is called a **sealed-bid auction**.

Consider a bidding game along these lines between Ruth and Sarah for a unique item. Ruth's value for the item is 100 and Sarah's is 70, as before. The minimum bid is 50. But the bidders do not know one another's values. From Ruth's point of view, Sarah's value is an unknown: let us call it x. Ruth believes x < 100 with probability p, and x ≥ 100 with probability (1 − p). Sarah believes Ruth's value is less than 70 with probability q, and greater than 70 with probability 1 − q.

Ruth bids first, and her strategies are to bid 50, 100, or wait to bid at the third stage. Sarah can then bid 70 or pass. Ruth can then rebid, but only at a small (effort) cost of 3. (It

Figure 21.8 An eBay Bidding Window

> **Dudley Pope – Ramage & the Saracens 1st UK HB**
> Item # 1528568008
>
> Current bid: US $15.00
> Bid increment: US $0.50
>
> Your maximum bid: [   ]
>   *(Minimum bid : US $15.50)*
>   [Review bid]
>
> eBay will bid incrementally on your behalf **up to your maximum bid**, which is kept secret from other eBay users. The eBay term for this is _proxy bidding_ .
>
> **Your bid is a contract** – Place a bid only if you're serious about buying the item. If you are the winning bidder, you will enter into a legally binding contract to purchase the item from the seller.

may be argued that since rebidding can be automated, the effort cost should be very small, but it does not matter how small the effort cost is, as long as it is positive.)

The payoffs will then be as shown in Figure 21.9. The payoffs are shown in expected-value terms at the beginning of the game, as seen by Ruth; Sarah's bid is shown as unknown and the payoffs at the various points are weighted by the probability of getting there, as seen by the bidder. Nodes 1 and 4–6 are Ruth's strategy choices, while 2 and 3 are Sarah's. Since eBay does not show Ruth's maximum bid, Sarah does not know which bid Ruth has chosen, so long as Ruth bids. That is why node 2 is an information set. Nodes 4 to 6 are basic and can be reduced as follows:

Figure 21.9 | An eBay-Like Game in Extensive Form

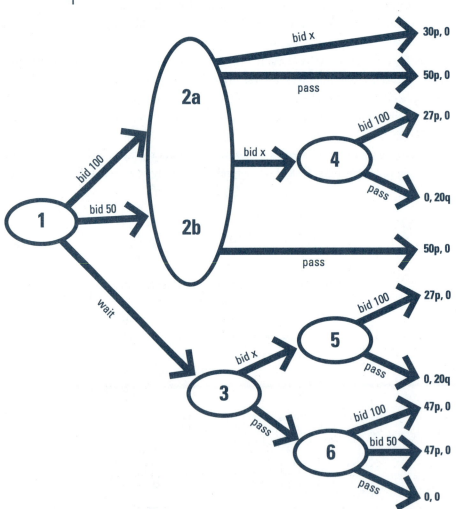

At node 4, shown in Figure 21.10 Ruth will bid 100. She gets the benefit of owning the item at a price of 70—the second-price bid by Sarah—net of her rebidding effort cost of 3.

At node 5, Ruth will bid 100, just as above at node 4. At node 6, Ruth is indifferent between bidding 50 or 100, but will bid, and will get the benefit of the item at a price of 50, net of the rebidding effort cost. With information from Figures 21.11 and 21.12, we can now reduce node 3 as shown in Figure 21.13.

At node 3, Sarah still does not know Ruth's value. So, in Figure 21.13, we show it as the unknown value y. The payoffs from bidding are shown as the expected values, based on the probability that Ruth's value is greater than 70, which means that in node 5 she will bid and win. In any case, as long as q is positive, Sarah's best response is to bid. That means node 6 is ruled out, and Ruth's payoff to waiting is at most 27p.

After reducing these nodes, we are left with the game in extensive form shown in Figure 21.14. This is still a rather complex game. On the one hand, there is the information set at 2, since Sarah does not know the upper limit Ruth has set if Ruth bid. On the other hand, Sarah has some information—she knows whether Ruth has bid at the first stage or not. To deal with this game, we shift to the representation in normal form. The reduced game in normal form is shown in Table 21.1.

We can proceed by simple elimination to find that the Nash equilibrium for this game is in the upper left: Ruth bids 100 and Sarah bids 70. First we will eliminate the right-hand side of the table. In either of the strategies in which Sarah passes when Ruth waits (strategies "otherwise pass,") Ruth's best response is to wait (the bottom row)—leaving Sarah with zero rather than 20q. So Sarah will never choose one of those strategies. Therefore, the equilibrium will never be on the right side of the table. Ruth can anticipate this. On the left-hand side of the table, her best payoff from a wait and rebid strategy is 27p, as we have already discovered, so Ruth will never choose "wait"—she can get at least 30p, better than 27p, by choosing a bidding strategy. Accordingly, we

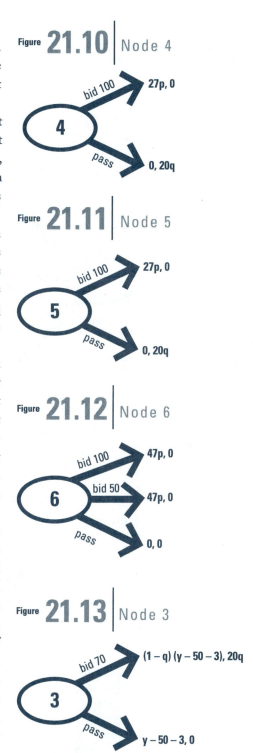

Figure 21.10 | Node 4

bid 100 → 27p, 0
pass → 0, 20q

Figure 21.11 | Node 5

bid 100 → 27p, 0
pass → 0, 20q

Figure 21.12 | Node 6

bid 100 → 47p, 0
bid 50 → 47p, 0
pass → 0, 0

Figure 21.13 | Node 3

bid 70 → (1 – q) (y – 50 – 3), 20q
pass → y – 50 – 3, 0

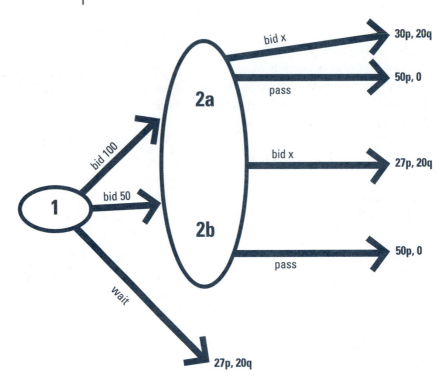

Figure 21.14 | The Reduced eBay Game

Table 21.1 | Payoffs for the Reduced eBay Game

		Sarah			
		if Ruth bids, then bid 70; otherwise bid 70	if Ruth bids, then pass; otherwise bid 70	if Ruth bids, then bid 70; otherwise pass	if Ruth bids, then pass; otherwise pass
Ruth	bid 100	30p, 20q	50p, 0	30p, 20q	50, 0
	bid 50	27p, 20q	50p, 0	27p, 20q	50, 0
	wait	27p, 20q	27p, 20q	47, 0	47, 0

can limit our attention to the four unshaded cells. Within them, it seems that Sarah will never pass on the first round, either—and Ruth, knowing that Sarah will bid, chooses to bid 100 for a payoff of 30p rather than bid 50 for a payoff of 27.

This is the subgame perfect equilibrium of the eBay game, then: Each bidder bids her value as soon as possible. What we have discovered in this game can be generalized. In a second-price auction, it is rational to bid the value as soon as possible—just as eBay advises its clients to do.

Like the English auction, the eBay auction does not require the bidder to have very much information. All the bidder needs to know is her value and the bidding increment—and unlike the English auction, she doesn't even need to monitor the bidding. It seems likely that these characteristics of its auction form are among the reasons for eBay's success.

Auctions
Kinds and Frames

Auctions have a long history and there are a number of well-known types. As we have seen, the English auction is the most common kind of ascending bid auction. There are also descending bid auctions. In a **Dutch auction**, the auctioneer begins the auction by

> **Definition**
>
> ***Dutch Auction***—An auction in which the seller initially posts a high price, and then lowers the price step by step until someone buys, is called a **Dutch auction**.

announcing a high price, and then lowers the price, step by step, until someone announces that the price is acceptable. That person is the buyer at that price. This is the form of auction that was used to sell tulips in the Netherlands and was used at the time of the famous *tulip bubble*—a boom-and-bust disaster for speculators in tulip bulbs in the 1630s.

Another family of auction types is the **sealed-bid auction**. In any sealed-bid auction, bids are submitted in writing to the auctioneer and are known only to him.

Sealed-bid auctions have these characteristics:

* *Single round first price:* The bidder who submits the highest price gets the item, and pays the price he has bid. This may seem obvious, but it isn't the only possibility.

* *Single round second price:*[7] In a second-price sealed-bid auction, each bidder offers a price, and the bidder who offers the highest price is the buyer; but the price the buyer pays is the second-highest price bid. This allows the buyer to bid what he or she thinks the item is worth, and still get a benefit if other buyers don't think it is worth as much. As we have seen, eBay combines the second-price sealed bid auction with some features of an ascending auction, and it is the second-price feature that makes it so easy for eBay bidders to bid with only a little information.

---

7 Nobel laureate economist William Vickrey (1914–1996) discovered the special advantages of the second-price auction, which is sometimes known as the Vickrey auction.

A Closer Look

William S. Vickrey (1914–1996)

Born in 1914 in Victoria, British Columbia (Canada), William Vickrey attended Yale, majoring in mathematics. His graduate work in economics was done at Columbia University. He joined the faculty in 1946, received his Ph.D. in 1947, and remained at Columbia for the rest of his life. He was a conscientious objector during World War II. His work was both theoretically innovative and applied, from his classic dissertation on progressive taxation through his work on auctions in the 1960s and on efficient pricing of public utilities and services. Vickrey was awarded the Nobel Memorial prize in economics in 1996, and died at the age of 82 only three days after the prize was announced.

- *Multiple round*—Sealed bid auctions can also be conducted with multiple rounds.

We have, then, a range of auction arrangements to choose among, for any particular transaction. One way to simplify this would be to discover that some of the types are equivalent. For example, William Samuelson writes, "It is easy to confirm that the [first-price] sealed bid and Dutch auctions are strategically equivalent; . . . Instead of waiting for the price to fall, each buyer could simply submit in writing the price at which it would first bid."[8] Thus, exactly the same strategies and equilibrium apply for these seemingly different auctions. But even if auctions are not "strategically equivalent," as these two auction forms are, other pairs of auction forms may yield the same revenue to the buyer (in expected value terms), and in that case we would say that they are *revenue equivalent*. English and Dutch auctions have very different equilibria, and so are not strategically equivalent, but in some cases they are revenue equivalent.

But everything so far rests on unstated assumptions about the bidders and the auction environment. Auction strategies and outcomes depend on the type of auction—the rules of the game—but also on the auction environment, that is, the payoffs and information available to the bidders. Another unstated assumption is that the bidders are symmetrical—that is, there are no known "strong" and "weak" bidders. Rather, every bidder has the same probability of being "strong" or "weak." But this will not always be so, and it can make a difference.

So far, in our examples, we have seen a single object sold for the buyer's personal use. We have also taken each bidder's value as given, depending only on the bidder's taste—by how much she or he wants the camera or book. But suppose, instead, that the auction were offering for sale a tract of land for oil exploration. No one knows whether there is oil under the land. If there is, then any one of the bidders can find it and profit equally. But no one knows what profit the exploration will yield. In this case, the values do not depend on individual tastes, known to the individual, but rather on objective circumstances, known to nobody! In the camera and eBay cases, we have assumed **independent private values**. To give some sense of the range of possibilities, we will consider two further examples.

> ### Definition
>
> ***Independent Private Values***—When each bidder's value for the item is independent of the values or bids of any other person, we have **independent private values**.

---

8 William Samuelson, "Auctions in Theory and Practice," in K. Chatterjee and W. Samuelson, *Game Theory and Business Applications* (Boston: Kluwer, 2001).

The Winner's Curse

The differences between auction frames matter a great deal. Here is an example, which is also important in itself. The example will illustrate a common value auction.

Three oil exploration companies are competing for the right to drill for oil in an undeveloped plot of land. They will compete in a sealed-bid auction. The three firms are Red Clay Exploration, Brown Drilling, and Black Gold, Inc.—Red, Brown, and Black, for short. They are all risk neutral, so they will balance the possible gains and losses and value the opportunity at its mathematical expectation. Each has done its due diligence and estimated the expected market value of the oil they might produce from it, taking account both the probability that there may be no oil and the probability that it might be a new bonanza. However, every estimate is subject to error, and each of the estimates has two components: the actual market value, which is $10,000,000, and a random error. Specifically, their estimates are as shown in Table 21.2.

Table **21.2**	Estimated Market Values by Three Firms

Red	7,000,000
Brown	11,000,000
Black	12,000,000

First, suppose the auction is a first-price auction. Suppose that Black simply bids his value. Then he will win the auction—and lose $2,000,000, since, as he will discover, the plot is worth only $10,000,000. This is the *winner's curse*. In a common value auction, if the bidders naïvely bid to their estimated values, the winner will be the one who most overestimates the common value.

What if the auction is a second-price auction?[9] We have seen that second-price auctions have some advantages of simplicity and efficiency in individual private value auctions. Because this is a common-value auction, we cannot apply the same analysis as before. Once again, it will *not* be rational simply to bid the expected value, as it would in a second price auction with individual private values. For suppose that each of the three firms did bid their respective expected values. The result is that Black wins the bid, but Black has to pay the second bid, Brown's bid of 11,000,000. Since the actual market value is 10,000,000, Black is going to lose $1,000,000 as a result of "winning" the bid. In a first-price sealed-bid auction, this would be an even bigger disaster for Black, but even in a second-price auction, with all its advantages in individual private value auction frames, the winner's curse can occur. If there are a large number of bidders, even the second highest is likely to be an overestimater, so the "winner" stands to lose money.

Of course, real bidders are not quite this stupid. A rational bidder will "put himself in the equation" and bid less than the value estimate. "For estimated statistical models of oil-lease

---

9 This auction form would probably *not* be used in an auction of oil drilling rights, but is chosen to point up the differences between individual private value and common value auctions.

bidding, the equilibrium strategies call for sealed bids in the range of 30 percent to 40 percent (depending on the number of bidders) of the firm's unbiased tract estimate."[10] This strategic reaction means that the best choice of auction forms is quite different with common values than what it would be with individual private values.

An Auction for Two Complementary Items

As we have seen, an auction of a single item can be complex. However, when multiple items are auctioned at the same time, we may see further complications. In the auctions of electromagnetic spectrum, for example, licenses were sold for the use of electromagnetic spectrum in different, adjoining regions or plots. A buyer who wanted to set up a cellular telephone service (for example) might place a higher value on a group of adjacent plots than he or she would place on the plots separately, since the adjacent plots together would make for a more profitable telephone service area. In this case the plots are *complementary*, since each enhances the value of the others.

Let's consider a case in which just two plot licenses are to be auctioned off. Plot X will be auctioned first and plot Y second. There are three bidders: firms A, B, and C. Firm A is interested in setting up a service for the two areas together, but the other two are not. Firm B is interested in adding plot X to a service it already offers in a nearby region, and Firm C is interested in plot Y, provided it can work out a merger with Firm D, which already serves areas adjacent to plot Y. The values the bidders set on plot X, plot Y, and a combination of plot X and Y, are shown in Table 21.3.

Table **21.3** | Value for Plots Offered in an Electromagnetic Spectrum Auction

Bidder	Plot X	Plot Y	Both
A	2	3	12
B	5	1	8
C	1	4, 8	5, 9

The table shows two values for Firm C in bidding for Plot Y because the value of Plot Y in this case depends on whether the merger takes place. Firm C values Plot Y at 4 if there is no merger and at 8 if the merger has taken place. At the time of the action, Firm C knows whether the merger has taken place, but the other bidders do not.

To keep things simple, we assume that Firm A will bid first in each auction, and that Firm A knows everything in the table. That is, firm A knows its values and those of Firm B, and knows Firm C's values except that Firm A does not know whether firm C's value for Plot Y, alone, is 4 or 8, or is 5 or 9 for both. We assume that Firm A assigns probabilities of 0.5 to each of the values 4 and 8—50-50, and similarly for values 5 and 9. Thus, we can focus only on Firm A's strategies and those of "nature" who determines which values are realized in fact.

10 William Samuelson, "Auctions in Theory and Practice," in K. Chatterjee and W. Samuelson, *Game Theory and Business Applications* (Boston: Kluwer, 2001), citing R. Wilson, "Bidding," in J. Eatwell, M. Milgate, and P. Newman, *The New Palgrave* (London: W. W. Norton, 1995).

Figure 21.15 Bidder A's Strategies in Extensive Form

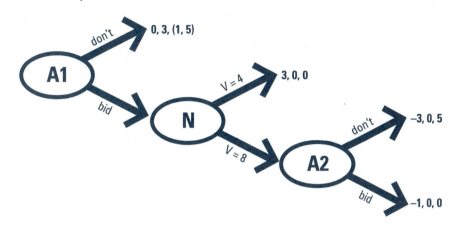

These are shown in extensive form in Figure 21.15. At the first node, A1, Firm A knows that it must bid at least 5 to get Plot X, since B will bid that high. If it chooses "don't"—meaning don't bid to 5—it will nevertheless bid to 2 in case B makes a mistake, so B gets the item for just over 2; and A will also bid to 3 on Plot Y, so that C gets it for just over 3, leaving payoffs in order A, B, C of 0, (just under) 3, and (just under) either 1 or 5, depending on the value of 4 or 8.[11] If Firm A chooses "bid" (to 5), then it will learn (from Firm C's bidding behavior) whether the merger takes place or not. We think of that as a play by "nature," who chooses a mixed strategy of (value) V = 4 with probability 0.5 and V = 8 with probability 0.5. On the upward fork, with Firm C's value at 4, Firm A can get the second plot with a bid of 4, get both plots, and earn a profit of 12 − 5 − 4 = 3, while the other two firms get 0. On the lower fork with V = 8, at node A2, A must choose, at the last node, whether to bid 8 and get Plot Y or not. If it does not bid, it is left with an item it values at 2, but for which it paid 5, for a payoff of −3, while Firm C gets plot Y for a bid of 3 and a profit of 5 (or possibly just under 5) and Firm B buys nothing for a payoff of 0. If Firm A chooses to bid 8, it gets both plots, which it values at 12, for a total price of 5 + 8 = 13 and a loss of 1. Other bidders get nothing and get payoffs of 0. Now we solve the game in Figure 21.15 by backward induction. The subgame at node A2 is basic. Since a loss of 1 is better than a loss of 3, Firm A will bid to 8 and assemble the plot. To evaluate its payoffs at N, we take the expected value 0.5(3) + 0.5(−1) = 1. Thus, the game reduces to a game shown in Figure 21.16. Since an expected value of 1 is better than nothing, Firm A will bid to obtain both properties.

Figure 21.16 The Bidding Game Reduced

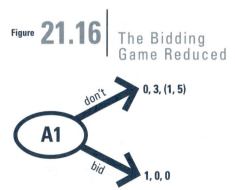

11 To really be complete, the diagram of the game in extensive form should include these decisions as well, but it is simpler to visualize if we treat them informally as we do here.

This example illustrates some important principles.

- Firm A may hesitate to bid above 2 on Plot X because it knows that it will be *exposed* to a loss if Firm C bids high on Plot Y. Indeed, if Firm A believes the merger will take place and therefore estimates a value of 8 for Plot Y, then Firm A will not bid above 2 on Plot X, because of the exposure. This exposure problem can limit both the efficiency and the sales revenue from auctions with complementary items.

- If the merger has, in fact, taken place, then the outcome is both unprofitable for Firm A and inefficient, since, in that case, the total value of the two plots in separate use is 13, and the combined use for a value of 12 is less efficient.

- In general, the efficiency of a sequential auction of complementary goods depends on the details of the example. Specifically, in this case, the outcome of the auction depends on the order in which the items are sold. Suppose, for example, that Plot Y were sold first. Then Firm C's bidding would tell Firm A all it needs to know about Firm C's valuation, and the result of the auction is efficient regardless whether Firm C values the item at 4 or 8.

Knowing that this sort of problem could occur, the game theorists who designed the spectrum auction actually did things in a different way. They did not sell the licenses in sequence. Instead, they allowed bidding on all the plots at the same time. If the auction in our example were conducted that way, then Firm A would be able to observe Firm C's bidding on Plot Y before committing to a high bid on Plot X.

But that's not the whole story. In addition to the problem of exposure, there is a converse *free rider* problem. Suppose Plot Y is auctioned first and the value of Plot Y to Firm C is 8. As long as the total price of the two plots is at least 12, Firm A cannot make a profit by bidding, and so Firms B and C will get the two plots. Firm C can restrict its bidding to 7, expecting that Firm B will bid 5 on Plot X, to give the total price of 12. Firm C is being a free rider on Firm B's bid, but, with Plot Y sold first, it does not matter—Firm B has no choice but bid its full value. However, if the two plots were auctioned simultaneously, both Firm A and Firm B might hold back from bidding their full values, each hoping to be a free rider on the other's bidding, and that could allow Firm A to assemble its inefficient combined plot. The advantage of a simultaneous auction thus will depend on the relative importance of the exposure problem and the free rider problem.

Multiple item auctions can be complex in other ways. Instead of being complements, for example, the items auctioned may be substitutes. This leads to a different set of problems.

Choosing Auction Forms

As we have seen, auction outcomes are sensitive to the details of auction frames. Common values, multiple items with complementarity or substitutability, and other aspects of the auction frame can change the results of each auction form and can change outcomes of different auction forms in different ways. This sensitivity, together with the wide range of auction frames, forms and objectives, means that the choice or design of an auction form for a particular purpose will be painstaking. If we are designing an auction for a particular purpose (such as selling Treasury bills or allocating electromagnetic spectrum) we might want to choose different auction forms for different environments. That is where equivalence results become important.

Our design might also have more than one objective. One obvious objective is to obtain the greatest possible revenue for the seller. When auctions are used for public policy purposes, such as allocation of electromagnetic spectrum, efficiency will also be an objective. Equity may also be an objective. In some of the U.S. government auctions to allocate electronic spectrum, one objective was to encourage small and female-headed businesses to bid. Since the success of each auction form (on each of these objectives) could vary from frame to frame, we may see the problem of auction design as one of fitting the form to the frame and the objectives. As we have seen, for example, the English auction scores well on efficiency in single item auctions with independent private values.

Some of the combinations have not yet been analyzed in game-theoretic terms, but remain unsolved problems. In some cases, such as the auction of complementary goods, the simple case we can solve alerts us to problems for which tentative solutions can be suggested. On the whole, we have a good deal of information on auction forms, including experimental evidence as well as game-theoretic analysis. We will continue the chapter by briefly summarizing some of the experimental results, without any details.

Some Experimental Findings
Individual Private Values

Designers of auctions are often concerned with efficiency and with the revenue to the seller. We have already seen that, with independent private values and best-response strategies, the English auction is efficient. It also yields the maximum expected value of revenue to the seller. The game analysis also tells us that all English, Dutch and sealed auctions are equivalent on both of these criteria—they all are efficient and maximize revenue. However, with Dutch and first-price sealed-bid auctions, mixed strategies will be used in equilibrium, so the seller's revenue might be riskier. Experimental evidence tells us, however, that sealed-bid auctions tend to yield more revenue than the others, and that the English auction tends to be highly efficient.

Pure Common Values

If we assume bidders are symmetrical and risk neutral, then, in theory, all auction forms are equally efficient for pure common values. However, the English auction has some advantages. Bidders are able to revise their estimates of the common value by observing how other participants bid, so they do not have to underbid their own estimates by quite so much to protect themselves against the winner's curse. As a result, the English auction returns the highest revenue to the seller. Experimental evidence suggests, though, that bids that are made are higher than the rational-action benchmarks. That is, bidders put too much confidence in their own estimates and do not allow enough either for errors or for information from observing the bidding of others. Sometimes a winner's curse is observed in actual markets. For example, there is evidence that returns to investments in offshore oil leases are less than the returns on competitive investments, consistent with a winner's curse in the auctions of offshore oil leases. The experimental evidence indicates that the English auction is more efficient, but yields less revenue, than the Dutch auction.

Summary

Auctions are increasingly the means of allocating scarce resources in market capitalism. They are also an area of substantial and growing game-theoretic knowledge and expertise.

In general, the payoffs of an auction participant depend on his value as well as the price paid. If the value is independent of any other person's information and bid, then we have an individual private value auction frame. However, if the value is the same for all bidders, but the bidders differ in their information, the value may depend on information that other bidders have, and we have a common value auction frame. Different auction frames may call for different kinds of auctions. In an individual private-value auction, a second-price sealed-bid auction is ideal in theory, but in a common-value auction it threatens a "winner's curse" and so may be inefficient and realize less revenue for the seller than a conventional English auction would realize. Unfortunately, here as in other fields of real-world application, real cases are complex, there is no "architectonic" theory, and there is much yet to be learned.

Exercises and Discussion Questions

21.1 EBay. Go to the eBay site on the Internet and find an auction with several days to run and with a few bids already shown. Antique art is a good category for this purpose and can be found at URL *http://listings.ebay.com/aw/plistings/list/all/category20126/index.html.*

Monitor this auction daily and determine whether the bids made are "rational" on the assumption that the auction frame is individual private value. Which ones, if any, would be irrational if the auction frame were common value? Why? How would you explain them?

21.2 A Collector's Dilemma. Rocco collects stamps from the Republic of Lower Fogravia. He would be willing to pay up to $500,000 to assure himself of a complete collection. Rocco has one rival in collecting Fogravian stamps: Sandor, who is sure to be at every auction where Fogravian stamps are offered. Sandor is just as determined to complete his collection as Rocco is. Both collectors are at an auction where a Fogravian inverted 36 Pfennig stamp is to be offered. Rocco knows that only a few of these were issued, and all but two are in museums. Rocco doesn't know whether Sandor has one or not. Is this an individual private auction frame? Supposing that Rocco observes that Sandor is not bidding on this stamp, what can he infer from that? Supposing that Rocco observes that Sandor is bidding; what can Rocco infer?

21.3 Auction Frames. Here are some examples of auctions. Indicate whether it seems best to analyze them as independent-private-value or common-value auctions, and say why:
a. An auction of unique antique artworks to collectors for their private collections
b. An auction of a tract of electronic spectrum in Dubuque, Iowa
c. An auction of the inventory of a bankrupt bookstore specializing in antique books

21.4 Absentee Bids. I have spent some time at old furniture auctions. One auctioneer would take absentee bids in writing and enter a bid for the absentee just above the going bid according to the increment, much in the way that eBay handles online bids. But I saw another (perhaps less experienced) auctioneer start the bidding at the absentee bid, so the absentee could not pay any less than that written bid. If you knew that the auctioneer was going to use this second approach, what effect would that have on your bidding strategy?

21.5 Another Online Exercise. Compare Spectrum Auctions (*http://www.spectrumauctions. com/spectrum-home.html*) with eBay Motors (*http://pages.ebay.com/ebaymotors/index.html*). Which would you use to buy a vintage Maserati? Why? Which would you use to sell a 1950s TR3 you just finished reconditioning?

Answer to exercise on page 637: There are three proper subgames, two of which are basic. As noted in the paragraph following the exercise, the subgame perfect equilibrium is bid 105, pass.

Evolution and Boundedly Rational Learning

To best understand this chapter

To best understand this chapter you need to have studied and understood the material from Chapters 1–8, 11, 14, 16, 17, and 21.

Think back to the Hawk vs. Dove Game in Chapter 5. In this example, two birds get into conflict and each bird has to choose between an aggressive strategy and a strategy of retreat. Yet birds are not the calculating rational creatures that we suppose human beings to be, in the context of game theory. In birds, much of the behavior we observe seems to be genetically determined. Hawks are aggressive, not because they choose to be, but because their genetic heritage makes them aggressive. Similarly, doves retreat because their genes have programmed them to retreat.

Nevertheless, game theory has had an influence on evolutionary biology. Biologists reason that evolution eliminates the strategies that do not work, so that game theory may be able to predict the result of this evolutionary process. The biologist John Maynard Smith, in particular, has proposed the concept of evolutionarily stable strategies (ESS) as a game theory approach appropriate for evolutionary biology.

But even in the case of human beings, the assumption of perfect rationality made in classical game theory may go too far. Many observers of human behavior would say that human rationality is *bounded*. Because human beings have limited cognitive capabilities, we may not really be able to come up with some of the more complicated computations for best-response strategies described in game theory. One possibility is that boundedly rational human beings usually act according to habit, routine, and rules of thumb. Even so, people learn. We are rational creatures in that we can learn and eliminate our mistakes. So, human learning might not be so very different from evolution, and the ideas the biologists have brought to game theory might be equally applicable to boundedly rational human beings.

This chapter explores the concept of evolutionarily stable strategies, along with its applications to both biology and boundedly rational learning.

Hawk vs. Dove

The game of Hawk vs. Dove was given in Chapter 5 as an example of a two-by-two game with two equilibria. The payoff table is shown as Table 22.1. The birds' payoffs are changes in their *inclusive fitness*, that is, changes in their rates of reproduction relative to the average rates of reproduction in their populations. In population biology, the assumption is that the two birds are matched at random and face a conflict in which each bird can, in principle, choose two strategies: aggressive (hawk) or evasive (dove.) Of course, the birds' strategies are determined by their genetic makeup, but if (for example) there are 25 percent hawks in the population and 75 percent doves, then the individual bird faces very much the same situation as if its opponent chose between the hawk and dove strategies with a mixed strategy, with 25 percent probability of choosing "hawk" and 75 percent probability of choosing "dove." In that case, a bird has three times the probability of being matched with a dove than with a hawk, so the payoffs to hawks are likely to be relatively high—with few fights and a lot of easy lunches.

Heads Up!

Here are some concepts we will develop as this chapter goes along:

Population Games: If members of a population are matched at random to play a game, with different types playing different strategies, the whole sequence of play is a *population game.*

Evolutionarily Stable Strategy: A Nash equilibrium that is stable under the replicator dynamics is an *evolutionarily stable strategy* equilibrium.

Replicator Dynamics: In a population game with *replicator dynamics*, each type increases or decreases relative to the total population in proportion as the payoff to the strategy played by that type exceeds or falls short of the average payoff.

Since the payoffs depend on probabilities, as with mixed strategies, we have to compute the expected values of payoffs. Suppose z is the proportion of hawks in the population (0.25 in the example in the previous paragraph). Therefore $(1 - z)$ is the proportion of doves (0.75 in the example). The expected value of the payoff for a hawk is

$$EV(hawk) = (-25z) + 14(1 - z) = 14 - 39z$$

since the hawk's payoff is −25 when matched with another hawk and 14 when matched with a dove. When z = 0.25, as in the example, EV(hawk) = 4.25. The expected value payoff for doves is

$$EV(dove) = -9z + 5(1 - z) = 5 - 14z$$

since the dove's payoff is −9 when matched with a hawk and 5 when matched with another dove. In the example, with z = .25, EV(dove) = 1.5.

Remember, these payoffs are proportional to rates of reproduction above replacement, so both populations will be growing. However, the population of hawks will be growing faster. The (weighted) average payoff is $1.5(1 - z) + 4.25z = 2.1875$. Thus, the population of hawks is growing 4.25/2.1875 = 1.94 times as fast—nearly twice as fast—as the population of birds as a whole, while the population of doves is growing only about two-thirds as fast.

Table 22.1 | Hawk vs. Dove

Repeats Table 5.9, Chapter 5

		Bird B	
		hawk	dove
Bird A	hawk	−25, −25	14, −9
	dove	−9, 14	5, 5

A Closer Look

John Maynard Smith 1920–

John Maynard Smith was born in 1920 in London. Originally educated as an aeronautical engineer at Cambridge, England, he studied zoology at University College, London. He was on the faculty of University College, London 1951–65 and then at the University of Sussex in England, where he retired in 1999. His contributions to game theory include applications to evolutionary theory, especially the concept of the evolutionarily stable strategy (ESS) as a factor in evolution.

These relative rates of reproduction determine what the population will be, in the long run. Figure 22.1 shows the expected-value payoffs to the two kinds of birds as the proportion of hawks varies. The proportion of hawks, z, is on the horizontal axis. The gray line shows the expected-value payoff for hawks, as z varies from 0 to 1, and the dark line shows the expected-value payoff for doves. At the intersection, the population is stable. The expected-value payoffs are equal—as in a mixed strategy Nash equilibrium. With a little algebra we can see that this equilibrium is at $z = 9/25 = 0.36$.[1]

This is an **evolutionarily stable strategy**, an ESS. According to Fernando Vega-Redondo, "a strategy . . . is said to an ESS if, once adopted by the whole population, no mutation . . . adopted by an arbitrarily small fraction of individuals can

1 $5 - 14z = 14 - 39z$
   $(39 - 14)z = 14 - 5$
   $25z = 9$
   $z = 9/25 = 0.36$

Figure 22.1 Relative Rates of Reproduction in a Hawk-Dove Game

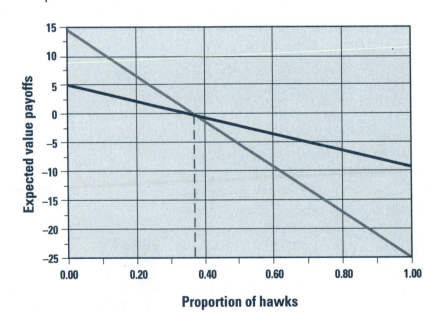

'invade,' (i.e., enter and survive) by getting at least a comparable payoff."[2] To apply this concept to the Hawk vs. Dove Game, we have to interpret the 9/25 equilibrium proportion as a mixed strategy—as if each individual bird adopted a mixed strategy with 9/25 probability of playing Hawk. We then ask, if a small population were to adopt a different probability, would they get higher payoffs? The answer is no. The mixed strategy with $z = 9/25$ is a Nash equilibrium, which means that each individual, and therefore every small population, is adopting its best response to the rest. Any mutation will not be a best response and will do worse still.

The dynamic idea underlying the ESS is the **replicator dynamics.** Again quoting Vega-Redondo, in the replicator dynamics, "the share of the population which plays any given strategy changes in proportion to its *relative* payoff (i.e., in proportion to its deviation, positive or negative, from the average payoff)."[3] In the discussion of the Hawk–Dove exam-

> ### Definition
>
> *Replicator Dynamics*—According to the **replicator dynamics**, the proportion of the population who play each strategy (in a population game) increases in proportion to the difference between the payoff to that strategy and the average payoff.

ple, we can apply the replicator dynamics, noting that (a) whenever $z < 9/25$, hawks have higher payoffs than the population average, and so their proportion, z, will increase, but (b) whenever $z > 9/25$, hawks have lower payoffs than the population average, and so their proportion, z, will decline. Visually, therefore, whenever z is different from 9/25 in Figure 22.1, z will be moving toward 9/25, and only $z = 9/25$ is stable under the replicator dynamics. Stable states under this dynamics are identical with evolutionarily stable strategies.

We may draw two conclusions.

1. *An ESS is a Nash equilibrium.* To say that "no mutation . . . adopted by an arbitrarily small fraction of individuals can 'invade' (i.e., enter and survive) by getting at least a comparable payoff" is to say that every creature is playing its best response when the population is at an ESS.

2. Not all Nash equilibria are ESS, since not all Nash equilibria are stable under the replicator dynamics.

A Sewage Game

Escherichi coli, E. coli for short, is a common sewage bacterium. According to *The New York Times*, three strains of E. coli play something like a Rock, Paper, Scissors Game.[4] In Rock, Paper, Scissors, two children choose among three strategies: Paper "covers" (defeats) rock, rock smashes (defeats) scissors, and scissors cut (defeat) paper. Since any predictable strategy

2 Fernando Vega-Redondo, *Evolution, Games and Economic Behavior* (Oxford, England: Oxford University Press, 1996), p. 14.
3 Ibid., p. 45.
4 Henry Fountain, "Bacteria's 3-Way Game," *The New York Times*, (July 30, 2002), Section F, P3.

can be exploited, a mixed strategy with probabilities of all strategies at 1/3 is the only Nash equilibrium.

The three strains of E. coli bacteria are as follows: Strain 1 produces both a lethal poison and a protein antidote to protect itself from its poison. Strain 2 produces only the antidote. Strain 3 produces neither. However, the production of each chemical costs the bacterium something, and slows down the reproduction of the bacteria, so that Strain 1 reproduces less rapidly than Strain 2, and (in the absence of the poison) Strain 2 reproduces less rapidly than Strain 3. What could an ESS look like?

First, a population of 100 percent of one strain will not be an ESS. Suppose, for example, that the population is all Strain 1. Then a mutation creating a small population of Strain 2 could invade, and outgrow the Strain 1 population and take over. Suppose the population were all Strain 2. Then a mutant population of Strain 3 could invade and become predominant. Finally, if the population were all Strain 3, a mutant population of Strain 1 could invade, kill off Strain 3 with the poison, and become predominant.

When the experimenters grew the bacteria on a plate, the bacterial culture formed small clumps of each type, with competition between strains only at the boundaries. Where Strain 1 competed with Strain 2, Strain 2 outgrew and crowded Strain 1 so that Strain 1 pulled back from those borders, while on borders where Strain 1 competed with Strain 3, Strain 3 retreated from the poison produced by Strain 1, so Strain 1 advanced. Predominant numbers of either two strains similarly led to advances and declines of their two sorts of competitors. Thus, the boundaries were constantly shifting.

However, the proportions of the three strains remained about the same, at 1/3 each. Here is why. Suppose that A is the proportion of Strain 1 in the population, B of Strain 2, and C of Strain 3. Then suppose A, B, and C are (40, 30, 30). Strain 3 will decline, since the probability that a Strain 3 bacterium will be matched with Strain 1 (where Strain 3 loses) is 1/3 larger than the probability that it will be matched with Strain 2 (where Strain 3 wins). But, for the same reason, Strain 2 will be increasing. From the point of view of Strain 1, both of these developments are bad news. Both the decline in Strain 3, which Strain 1 will beat, and the rise of Strain 2, which beats Strain 1, reduce the opportunities for Strain 1, so Strain 1 will begin to decline. The dynamics is complicated, but it leads to the conclusion that the population will be stable if, and only if, A/B = B/C = C/A. That means that each strain is 1/3 of the population—just as in Rock, Paper, Scissors.

All of this draws on the idea that the bacteria are randomly matched to play one-on-one games, and the shifting borders of clumps of each strain approximate that. If the matching is not random, then the result can be very different. In another experiment, the experimenters put their bacteria in a flask and mixed it thoroughly every day. This made it virtually certain that each Strain 3 organism would meet a Strain 1—and die of poisoning—very soon.[5] So Strain 1 wiped out Strain 3, setting the stage for Strain 2 to crowd out Strain 1, and only Strain 2

5 It may be, alternatively, that the stirring spread the poison throughout the flask. This would have the same effect.

remained. This is not stable in the long run, we know—if mutation were to recreate a small population of Strain 3, they could invade and displace Strain 2—but mutation is very unlikely on a short time scale, so this was not observed in the laboratory.

There are many other applications of game theory in evolutionary biology. It appears, then, that game theory can be usefully applied to nonhumans. But the key concepts for the biological applications—evolutionarily stable strategies and the replicator dynamics—can also be applied to human beings and the evolution of the strategies they habitually choose.

Bounded Rationality

In neoclassical economics and much of game theory, it is assumed that people *maximize*, or infallibly choose their *best response*. Others argue that real people cannot do that, but rather that real human rationality is **bounded**. There are several ways of expressing this, mostly derived from the work of Herbert Simon. One of the earliest suggested that, if

> ### Definition
>
> **Bounded Rationality**—According to some social scientists, people do not have sufficient cognitive capacity to choose rational strategies in the sense that they are best responses or that they maximize anything, but instead choose by means of heuristic rules. This sort of choosing is called **bounded rationality**.

people have a satisfactory solution to a problem, they will look no further—rather than maximizing, they *satisfice*. Another approach is expressed by the concept of *production systems*—that people act according to rules, though the rules may be very complex. This idea comes from studies in artificial intelligence,[6] but fits well with strategy rules like Tit-for-Tat. We can

put those ideas together, and say that people act according to rules that are not the ideal rules that would maximize their payoffs, but rather satisfactory rules. Such rules are known as **heuristics**. As we saw in Chapter 20, there is a good deal of evidence to support this idea.

> ### Definition
>
> **Heuristics**—**Heuristic** methods of problem solving are methods that are fast and usually reliable, but informal or inconclusive because they can fail in unusual cases.

This is not to say that people don't learn. Learning is important in games, and game theory includes some models of perfectly rational learning.[7] But a perfectly rational being would use all available information, would think in terms of probabilities, and would apply Bayes' rule to keep his estimated probabilities in line with the evidence. There are models in game theory based on that kind of Bayesian learning, but we will not attempt to cover them in this introductory book.[8] Here we are concerned with bounded rationality. Boundedly rational

---

6 Key works by Herbert Simon include H. A. Simon, "A Behavioral Model of Rational Choice," *Quarterly Journal of Economics* v. 69, no. 1 (February 1955), pp. 99–118 on satisficing, among many other writings, and Herbert A. Simon, "The Information-Processing Explanation of Gestalt Phenomena," *Computers in Human Behavior* v. 2 (1986), pp. 241–255 for an example of the production systems approach.

7 John Harsanyi, whose work spanned game theory, economics, and social philosophy, shared the Nobel Memorial prize with John Nash and Reinhard Selten because Harsanyi developed models of perfectly rational learning in games. That theory, important as it is, is beyond the scope of this introductory text.

8 Appendix B, Chapter 7, provides an example of Bayes' rule.

A Closer Look

Herbert Simon (1916–2001)

Herbert Simon was born in Milwaukee, Wisconsin, the son of an electrical engineer and inventor. He entered the University of Chicago in 1933, intending to become a mathematical social scientist, a field for which there were no curricula at that time. He received his Ph.D. in Political Science in 1942 from the University of Chicago for his study of administrative behavior. While a young professor of political science at Illinois Institute of Technology, he continued work in mathematical economics as well. In 1949, he was a founding faculty member of the Carnegie-Mellon University Graduate School of Industrial Administration, where he remained for the rest of his career. In collaboration with Allen Newell, he began to study human problem solving by computer simulation, thus becoming one of the originators of cognitive science. He received the Noble Memorial prize in 1978 for his work on decision making in organizations.

creatures learn much less systematically. Nevertheless, boundedly rational learning means that boundedly rational human beings do change their strategies on the basis of their experience, even if they do not use all available evidence and apply Bayes' rule. They will eliminate strategies that, in their experience, lead to lower payoffs. They can also learn by imitating one another. If I see that my neighbor plays Tit-for-Tat in social dilemmas and my neighbor gets better payoffs than I do when I always play cooperate, I can switch and begin to play Tit-for-Tat. Taking both of these points into account, we might think of boundedly rational learning as an evolutionary process in which the relatively unfit rules are eliminated and the fittest rules survive. The fittest rules are, of course, the ones that yield the highest payoffs on the average. We will explore this point with two examples.

Informationally (Almost) Efficient Markets

Many economists and financial theorists have argued that financial markets are informationally effieient. This means that the current price of a share in the XYZ corporation (for example) reflects all information about the profitability and risks of investment in XYZ that is available to the public. Because it reflects all available information, the stock price will change only in response to new information. That, in turn, means that the price of XYZ stock is not predictable—it will change in the future as a random walk. This is the "efficient markets theory." Thus, according to this view, there is no point in studying individual stocks to learn all you can about them. You may as well buy stocks at random—or buy an *index* fund, which is a bundle of all the stocks that make up some popular stock price index. And, in fact, index funds have become quite popular with small-scale investors in recent decades.[9]

While the efficient markets theory may be approximately true, Grossman and Stiglitz argue[10] that it cannot be exactly true. For if it were true, no one would bother to do any market research, and in fact the available information would not be reflected in the stock prices.

9 This idea was set out for the popular reader by Burton Gordon Malkiel in *A Random Walk Down Wall Street*, 7th edition (New York: W.W. Norton & Company), June 2000.

10 S. Grossman and J. Stiglitz, "On the Impossibility of Informationally Efficient Markets," *American Economic Review*, 70 (1980), pp. 393–408.

For, after all, *available* information is not *free*. Effort is required to read corporate annual reports and financial news reports, and effort is a cost. There may be money costs as well, for the best information. Why would anyone bear all that cost if he could just as well buy at random or imitate the decisions of others for no cost?

The efficient markets theory is a logically correct statement about the situation of an individual investor in a world in which other investors are informed. However, if all investors act as if they were in a world of informationally efficient markets, then the markets cannot be informationally efficient. Not only that. We know from observation that, while some investors buy index funds and do not do difficult market research, other investors commit a great deal of time and money to market research.

We might interpret this in game theoretic terms. An individual investor has at least two strategies: he can be informed or be uninformed.[11] As a first step, suppose there are only two investors, so that we have a two-by-two game. If at least one investor informs himself, both investors can get a rate of return of 8 percent on their investments. However, the effort and cost of getting the information is equivalent to a reduction of the rate of return by 1 percent, so the net payoff to the investor who chooses to be informed is 7 percent. If neither becomes informed, however, they both get a rate of return of only 4 percent. This gives rise to the payoffs in Table 22.2.

This game has two Nash equilibria in pure strategies—and each occurs where one investor is informed and the other is not. So, in this simplified game, we find an equilibrium at which just half the investors are informed, and those who are not informed come out with a higher payoff.

Table 22.2 | A Two-Person Investor Game

		George	
		informed	uninformed
Warren	informed	7, 7	7, 8
	uninformed	8, 7	4, 4

In the real world, there are many more than just two investors. If most of them are informed, then we would expect that the uninformed ones could do as well by investing at random or buying index funds. In this sort of world, a person who buys an index fund is, in effect, imitating the more informed investors, and doing it very cheaply. If there are enough informed investors, the uninformed may do as well this way as they could if they made the effort to become informed, or even better. In fact, while we don't know for certain, it seems likely that even a minority of informed investors could push the prices of the stocks to their efficient levels. After all, the decisions of the informed are likely to have more impact than the actions of the uninformed—the decisions of the informed are targeted, while the decisions of the uninformed are not.

11 R. Cressman and J. F. Wen, whose ideas suggested this example, point out that the investor can also choose from a range of mixed strategies, but we will ignore these for simplicity. See R. Cressman and J. F. Wen, (October 3, 2002) "Playing the Field: An Evolutionary Analysis of Investor Behavior with Mixed Strategies" working paper, GREQAM, Centre de la Ville Charite, 2 rue de la Charite, 13002 Marseille, France.

In place of the two-by-two game, in Table 22.2, it would be better to treat this game as a proportional game, like the commuter game in Chapter 11. Figure 22.2 shows payoffs for such a game, with the payoffs to uninformed investors shown by the solid curve. The payoffs in the figure are a little different from those in Table 22.2, in that the payoffs to an uninformed investor depend on how many investors are informed. An uninformed investor can get the maximum payoff of 8 only if he or she is the *only* uninformed investor in a population of informed investors.

At the other extreme, if all investors are uninformed, they make the 4 percent return available to the truly random investor. However, as the proportion of informed investors increases, the quality of information in the market increases rapidly, so that the returns to uninformed investors who invest at random or buy index funds rises quite steeply and then levels off when a quarter or more are informed.[12] Informed investors can always get a return of 7 percent, shown by the dashed horizontal line. Thus, it pays better to be informed whenever the proportion of investors who are informed is less than 31.6 percent, and it pays better to be uninformed when more than 31.6 percent of investors are informed.

Thinking of this as a proportional game, then, the equilibrium condition is that 31.6 percent of investors are informed. There are a large number of Nash equilibria—depending on which investors are informed and which are not—but every equilibrium has 31.6 informed and the rest uninformed.

12 The leveling off is an instance of *diminishing returns*. The idea is that when there are more informed investors, there is more information available for free to those who do not invest in market research, but the free information is subject to diminishing returns. It is computed as $4 + 4p^{0.25}$ where p is the proportion of investors who are informed and $p^{0.25}$ is the fourth root (square root of the square root) of p. This equation is an arbitrary one chosen for the sake of the example, but chosen to illustrate the diminishing returns to free information.

Figure 22.2 | Payoffs to Investors According to Proportion Informed

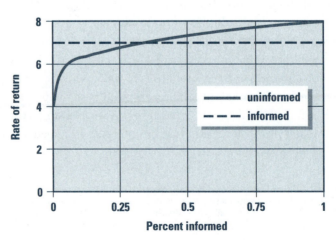

Is this evolutionarily stable? It is. The **replicator dynamics** says that the proportion choosing to be informed will increase, or decrease, in proportion with the relative payoff. Figure 22.3 shows the payoff to being informed, as a proportion of the average payoff for the whole population. With the replicator dynamic, this quotient will determine the change in the proportion informed from one period to the next. Clearly, whenever the proportion is different from the equilibrium at 31.6 percent, it will be moving in the direction of 31.6 percent. Figure 22.4 shows two paths toward equilibrium, beginning from proportions of 0.7 (dashed) and 0.1 (dotted) as the investors learn and revise their strategies.

Figure 22.3 Relative Payoff of Being Informed

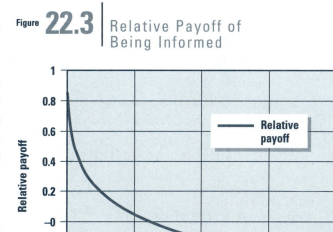

In equilibrium, then, we have two "kinds" of investors. One kind, the minority, does extensive market research and invests with care. They get a net payoff of 7 percent. The other kind buy index funds or invest at random. Because there are about 31.6 percent of investors

Figure 22.4 Two Paths to Equilibrium

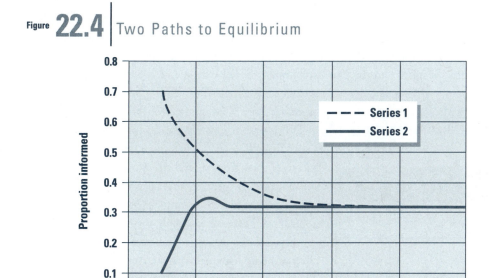

who do research, the prices in the marketplace are fairly highly efficient, and the inactive investors get a payoff of 7 percent. This sounds a bit like the real world we live in. Who is right, the investors who do research or the inactive ones? They both are, and in fact it doesn't matter who is inactive and who does research. There are no real differences between these "kinds" of investors except their strategies. All that is necessary for equilibrium is that 31.6 percent of them do research and are informed.

Evolution and a Repeated Social Dilemma

Table 22.3 | A Social Dilemma

		Q	
		C	D
P	C	3, 3	1, 4
	D	4, 1	2, 2

Suppose a population of agents play the social dilemma shown in Table 22.3. Two agents will be randomly matched on each round of play. The agents will play the game repeatedly with no definite number of repetitions. The discount factor, allowing for both time discount and the probability that there will be no next round of play, is 2/3.

The population who play this game are boundedly rational, in that they play according to one of three rules:

- always C
- always D
- Tit-for-Tat

The discounted present value payoffs for these three strategy rules are shown in Table 22.4.

At a given time, there is a small probability that an agent may switch strategies. Such an agent will shift from strategy R to strategy S with a probability that is proportionate to the payoff to strategy R relative to the payoff to strategy S. For example, if "always C" pays 2 on the average and "Tit-for-Tat" (TfT) pays 2.5, the ratio of the payoffs is 2.5:2 = 5:4, so the probability of a shift from C to TfT is proportionately greater than the probability of a shift from TfT to C. Then more will shift to TfT than will shift away from it, and the proportion playing TfT will increase. In general, the rules that give the higher payoffs will be played by an increasing proportion of the population. Thus, we can apply the replicator dynamics.

Since the agents are matched at random, the probability of being matched with a C player, a D player, or a Tit-for-Tat player depends on the proportions of C players, D players, and Tit-for-tatters in the population. This is complicated because we have two proportions to consider. However, "always C" is dominated, so we will keep

Table 22.4 | Strategy Rules and Payoffs in a Repeated Social Dilemma

		Q		
		always C	always D	Tit-for-Tat
P	always C	9, 9	3, 12	9, 9
	always D	12, 3	6, 6	8, 5
	Tit-for-Tat	9, 9	5, 8	9, 9

Table 22.5 | Some Tendancies in a Social Dilemma with Replicator Dynamics

Proportion of Tit-for-tatters	EV (always C)	EV (always D)	EV (TfT)	What happens
0.9	8.4	5.1	8.6	The population is increasingly dominated by TfTers and D players disappear.
0.8	7.8	5.2	8.2	ditto
0.5	6	5.5	7	ditto
0.2	4.2	5.8	5.8	Relative proportions of D and TfT players remain steady.
0.1	3.6	5.9	5.5	The population is increasingly dominated by D players and TfTers disappear.

it simple by considering only a few cases with the proportion of C players at zero with various proportions of Tit-for-tatters . The cases are shown in Table 22.5. Expected value payoffs for the three strategy rules are shown in the middle three columns. What we see is that the equilibrium depends on the starting point—if there are very few Tit-for-tatters at the beginning, then D will dominate and TfT disappear, but with any proportion of Tit-for-tatters above 0.2, Tit-for-Tat will win out and "always D" will disappear.

Thus, there are two stable equilibria with the replicator dynamics. One gives rise to cooperative outcomes and the other does not. The one that gives rise to cooperative behavior via a Tit-for-Tat rule is more probable than the other, in the sense that the population gets to it from more starting points. Thus, it seems that there is hope for boundedly rational learners to reach the cooperative equilibrium in some cases. Of course, the outcome of this example depends very much on the specific numbers and the probability of finding the cooperative equilibrium could be different if the numbers were different.

Tit-for-Tat, Reciprocity, and the Evolution of the Human Species

The forgiving trigger strategy known as Tit-for-Tat is based on rational self-interest, but, as we have seen, it can bring about cooperative solutions in many cases when mutually unprofitable noncooperative equilibria might occur otherwise. As we saw in Chapter 20, experimental evidence suggests that people do not always act in self-interested ways, and a number of studies are consistent with the idea that people often depart from self-interest in the direction of reciprocity. Some scholars believe that this tendency toward reciprocity may be part of the human genetic heritage—that our genes program us for some tendency to act with reciprocity, or to

learn to act with reciprocity. In this context, we notice that although Tit-for-Tat is consistent with self-interest in many cases, it is consistent with reciprocity in even more.

Why should our genes predispose or "program" us for reciprocity? The argument of some scholars in evolutionary psychology is that our human and pre-human ancestors have lived with social dilemmas for a long time, and that preagricultural humans and prehumans who were predisposed to reciprocity would solve those social dilemmas more readily, and so would be more likely to survive and reproduce.[13]

One argument is that teamwork is required by many of the hunting and gathering activities by means of which preagricultural people and prehumans survived. For example, some preagricultural people in Africa hunted antelope by chasing an antelope until he dropped dead of exhaustion. No one human could do that—antelope have more stamina and can run longer than humans. Running is the antelope's field of specialization. So the humans would hunt in teams, and a team of human hunters would post themselves at points equal distances apart around a large circle, with one hunter in reserve. Try to visualize them standing at their stations around the circle. We can call the points where the people stand station A, station B, and so on. It works like this: the person at station A chases the antelope toward station B, and then the person at station B takes over and chases the antelope to station C, and so on. The person who has chased the antelope from station A to station B now gets a long rest at station B, and the reserve person takes his place at station A. Once the antelope comes round to station A, the reserve person takes over and chases it to station B, and that first person takes another relay, following his rest. In that way, the humans could chase the antelope indefinitely, and certainly until it drops. This works best if everyone gives it an honest effort and nobody shirks—an age-old effort dilemma.

But even without teamwork, there are other reasons for hunting and gathering people to share food, as many of them routinely do. Hunting, after all, is risky, and even a good hunter may come home at the end of the day with no food for his family. In many preagricultural peoples, it is understood that the successful hunter shares his catch with those who are less successful.

---

13 Those who believe that human beings did not evolve, but, rather, were created as they are by an intelligent God, should have less difficulty in explaining why our heredity predisposes us to reciprocity or to other nonself-interested motives. It is evolution that poses the harder question, since evolution is inherently a selfish process—as biologist Richard Dawkins suggested by the title of his book, *The Selfish Gene* (Oxford University Press, 1976).

Here is an example to show what that means. Suppose we have two preagricultural hunters, known as Horse and Bull. Each is skillful, but on any given day, either of them may come home empty-handed. To keep the example simple, let us say that either Horse or Bull will be successful on any given day, and the other will not, and the probability that it is Horse is 0.5, and therefore the probability that Bull is successful is the same, 0.5. Table 22.6 shows the payoffs when Horse has been successful in the hunt, Bull has not, and each person chooses between the strategies "share" and "don't share." Since Bull has nothing to share, his decision makes no difference. The −20 payoff to Bull (if Horse does not share) reflects the possibility that Bull will be so weakened he will not be a successful hunter tomorrow, either, and that could threaten his life. Table 22.7 shows the payoffs if Bull is successful and Horse is not.

These are not social dilemmas, because they are so unsymmetrical—the unsuccessful hunter, having nothing to share, has nothing to lose by sharing. But, on any given day, no one knows which of these games they are playing. Accordingly, we calculate the expected-value payoffs, and they are shown in Table 22.8.

Table 22.8 is a social dilemma—both hunters are better off if they share, but refusing to share is a dominant strategy equilibrium. Of course, hunting people face this dilemma time and time again, with no definite limit. Accordingly, they might arrive at the cooperative solution by a self-interested Tit-for-Tat or similar trigger strategy. However, even with a trigger strategy, the cooperative outcome is only one of multiple stable outcomes; and when people make mistakes, or when there are more than two people, outcomes are even less certain. By contrast, human beings with some innate tendency to act with reciprocity would be all the more likely to share reciprocally, to return sharing when it is initiated, and to initiate sharing in the hope that it would be reciprocated—and thus all the more likely to survive in high-risk forms of hunting and gathering.

Thus, it seems that game theory and evolution have yet another connection: human beings may well have evolved to play certain kinds of games.

Table 22.6 A Sharing Dilemma When Horse Has Been Successful

		Horse	
		share	don't
Bull	share	5, 5	−20, 10
	don't	5, 5	−20, 10

Table 22.7 A Sharing Dilemma When Bull Has Been Successful

		Horse	
		share	don't
Bull	share	5, 5	5, 5
	don't	10, −20	10, −20

Table 22.8 The Expected-Value Payoffs of the Two Sharing Dilemmas

		Horse	
		share	don't
Bull	share	5, 5	−7.5, 7.5
	don't	7.5, −7.5	−5, −5

Summary

Game theory can be applied to the evolution of nonhuman animals if we think of the games as random matches of individuals from a population and interpret the payoffs of games as differences in the reproductive success of the "players" of the games. These ideas lead to the concepts of evolutionarily stable strategies (ESS) and the replicator dynamics. The replicator dynamics is a dynamics in which the proportion of the population playing a strategy increases in proportion to the relative payoff for that strategy in the game. A Nash equilibrium that is stable under this dynamic is an evolutionarily stable strategy. In this case, the strategy can be a *mixed strategy*—that is, the proportion of the population playing each strategy is the equalibrium probability in a mixed strategy equilibrium. These games sometimes have the same equilibria as familiar cases from basic game theory.

Recognizing that boundedly rational human beings may choose their strategies according to relatively simple, fallible rules, we might model boundedly rational learning by applying the ESS to a population of rules. This can lead to Nash equilibria and can narrow the range of Nash equilibria, in some cases, to cooperative or second-best solutions, depending on the details of the game.

Exercises and Discussion Questions

22.1 Frog Mating Game. Recall the Frog Mating Game from Exercise 6.2. The frogs are all males who can choose between two strategies for attracting females: the call strategy (call) or the satellite strategy (sit). On one hand, those who call take some risk of being eaten, while those who sit run less risk. On the other hand, the satellites who do not call may nevertheless encounter a female who has been attracted by another frog's call. So the payoff to the satellite strategy is better when a larger number of other male frogs are calling.

The payoff table for the three frogs is shown in Table 22.E1, with the first payoff to Kermit, the second to Michigan J, and the last to Flip. Suppose that a very large group of frogs are calling and sitting and the payoffs to callers and sitters depend on the proportion of frogs who call, that is, p. Suppose the payoff to frogs who call is

$$Y_1 = 12 - 13p - 6p^2 + 12p^3$$

while the payoff to sitters is

$$Y_2 = 1 + 4p - 8p^2 + 20p^3$$

Does this game have an ESS? What?

Table **22.E1** | Payoffs for Eager Frogs

Repeats Table 6.E2, Chapter 6

		Flip			
		call		sit	
		Michigan J.		Michigan J.	
		call	sit	call	sit
Kermit	call	5, 5, 5	4, 6, 4	4, 4, 6	7, 2, 2
	sit	6, 4, 4	2, 2, 7	2, 7, 2	1, 1, 1

22.2 El Farol. El Farol is a bar in Santa Fe, New Mexico, where chaos researchers from the Santa Fe Institute often hang out. It is said that El Farol is at its best when it is crowded, but not too crowded. We saw a three-person example a little like that in Chapter 6. Now suppose that there are 100 chaos researchers who choose between going to El Farol and staying home (those are the two strategies). Say the number of people who go to El Farol on a particular night is N and suppose the payoffs to each person who goes is $P = N - 0.013N^2$.

Does this game have an ESS? Is it efficient? Why or why not?

22.3 Maximizing Profits. Economists often assume that businesses maximize profits, an operation that can be expressed in terms of calculus. Yet it is well known that very few businesspeople use calculus in deciding how and when to change their prices and the outputs of their factories. Discuss this point in the light of concepts from this chapter. Can you think of some decisions that businesspeople might learn to make very accurately in an ESS? Any that would be difficult even in an ESS?

22.4 Silent Barter. Anthropologists report that a form of trade called *silent barter* is often observed among peoples who are at a fairly early stage of development, illiterate, and quite hostile. Silent barter works like this. Let us call the two groups the Easterners and the Westerners. At a customary time and place, groups from the two tribes meet, in sight of one another but at a distance too great for combat. The Westerners move forward while the Easterners stay back, out of reach of weapons. The Westerners put down the goods they want to sell in piles. Then they withdraw and the Easterners come forward. If an Easterner wants a pile of goods, he puts his own goods down in a pile beside it. Then the Easterners withdraw and the Westerners come forward again. If the exchange is satisfactory, the Westerners who have sold the goods will take the Easterners' pile, leaving their own, and go home. If the Easterners' offer is not sufficient, the Westerners may take a part of their own pile back, signifying a counteroffer at a price more favorable to themselves. This may continue for several rounds, until all piles are removed, either bartered or refused, without the two sides ever coming close enough to attack one another.

Explain this in terms of game theory, making reference to evolutionarily stable strategies and infinitely repeated games.

22.5 Butterflies. Some species of butterflies feed on plants that contain poisonous substances. Monarch butterflies, for example, feed on milkweed, and there are "cardiac glucosides in milkweed that monarch butterflies ingest. The glucosides are not bad for the butterflies, but they make birds that eat the butterflies sick, so birds do not eat them."[14] The fact that the butterflies are able to tolerate the glucosides is probably not without cost to the

14 James Gorman, "Did PCBs Save the Stripers? A Fish Story," *The New York Times* available at *http://www.nytimes.com/2003/03/25/science/life/25ESSA.html* as of March 27, 2003.

butterflies. There could be some metabolic cost, or a sacrifice from searching for milkweed and ignoring other food sources, that would be a disadvantage of relying on milkweed. Evidently, the advantage of reduced predation more than offsets any disadvantages from ingesting the glucosides.

Model this as an evolutionary game. Begin by constructing a two-by-two game between a bird and a butterfly, in which the bird and butterfly will be randomly matched. You will have to guess at the payoffs, but they should be in the right order to capture this problem—for example, ingesting glucosides should pay off for the butterfly only if the bird is a butterfly-eating predator. Next, apply the replicator dynamics and determine whether the equilibrium is one where butterflies specialize as milkweed-eaters and are avoided by predators, as we observe in nature.

This game has one other feature. Monarchs and other butterflies have bright coloration that makes it easy for birds to detect and avoid them. Extend your analysis to allow for this additional aspect of the strategy.

Glossary

A

A Public Good: *If a good or service has the properties that everyone in the population enjoys the same level of service, and it does not cost any more to provide one more person with the same level of service, it is what economists call a public good.*

Altruism: *Behavior is altruistic when it is not self-interested but considers benefits to others as well as those to oneself. In game theory, one possible interpretation is that the altruist tries to maximize the total payoffs.*

Approval Voting: *In approval voting there is no ranking of one alternative against another, but each voter simply votes "yes" or "no" for each alternative.*

B

Backward Induction: *Backward induction is a method for finding the subgame perfect Nash equilibrium of a game in extensive form. According to this method one must first solve all basic proper subgames, substitute the solution payoffs for the basic proper subgames, and apply the method again to the resulting "reduced" game, continuing in this way until there are no proper subgames. The resulting fully reduced game is then solved by any appropriate method for games in normal form.*

Basic Subgame: *A subgame is basic if it contains no other proper subgames within it.*

Bertrand-Edgeworth Equilibrium: *When two firms each set a price, and the firm with the cheaper price dominates the market, the price is the strategy and the resulting Nash equilibrium is a Bertrand-Edgeworth equilibrium.*

Best Response: *The best response for a player is the strategy that gives that player the maximum payoff, given the strategy the other player(s) has chosen or can be expected to choose. Notice that it is the best response to given strategies, not necessarily the best response to the situation on the whole.*

Borda Rule: *Proposed by the Chevalier de Borda, the Borda Rule has the voter assign points to each alternative in inverse proportion to preference ranking. Thus, in a three-way election, the first preference gets 3 points, the second preference 2, and so on. The alternative with the greatest sum of points wins.*

Bounded Rationality: *According to some social scientists, people do not have sufficient cognitive capacity to choose rational strategies in the sense that they are best responses or that they maximize payoffs, but instead choose by means of heuristic rules. This sort of choosing is called bounded rationality.*

C

Coalition: *A group of players who choose strategies jointly is called a coalition.*

Coalition Dominance: *In coalition structure A, suppose there is a group of people who can withdraw from their coalitions and form a new coalition, and be better off as a consequence. This results in a new coalition structure, structure B. In this case structure B dominates structure A. Note that, if the game has transferable utility, side payments may be made to assure that everyone in the new coalition is better off. If there is no coalition that dominates coalition C, coalition C is undominated.*

Coalition Structure: *A division of the players in a game into coalitions (including singleton coalitions) is called a coalition structure.*

Commitment Structure: *The set of proper subgames in a sequential game is the game's commitment structure.*

Complete Information Node: *In a game in extensive form, a complete information node is a choice node at which the decision maker knows all previous choices relevant to his decision.*

Completeness: *In voting, a voting scheme is complete if it leads to complete and consistent ranking of all alternatives.*

Complex Subgame: *If a subgame is not basic, it is a complex subgame.*

Condorcet Rule: *Proposed by the Marquise de Condorcet, the Condorcet Rule states that a* candidate who would win a two-way naïve vote against every other candidate should be the candidate selected.

Conjecture: *A conjecture is a judgment on a question of fact, based on whatever evidence seems relevant, but which is inconclusive and might prove wrong.*

Consistent Conjectures: *When two or more decision makers each base their decisions on conjectures about the decisions of others, and the conjectures lead each decision maker to make the decisions the others had conjectured she would—so that everyone turns out to be right—it is a case of consistent conjectures.*

Constant-Sum Game: *If the payoffs to all players add up to the same constant, regardless of which strategies they choose, it is a constant-sum game. The constant may be 0 or any other number.*

Contingency: *A contingency is an event that may or may not occur, such as the event that another player adopts a particular strategy.*

Contingency Plan: *A contingency plan is a plan to be put into operation only when it is known that the contingent event has occurred.*

Contingent Strategy: *A contingent strategy is a strategy to be adopted only when it is known that the contingent event has occurred.*

Contributory Negligence: *Contributory negligence refers to a legal rule in which a party cannot recover all damages from an accident if she could have taken action to prevent it, and did not do so.*

Cooperate: *In a social dilemma, to play the cooperative solution strategy is to "cooperate" with a hypothetical coalition to obtain the cooperative outcome.*

Cooperative Games and Solutions: *If the participants in a game can make binding commitments to coordinate their strategies then the game is cooperative. The solution with coordinated strategies is a cooperative solution.*

Cooperative Solution: *The cooperative solution of a game is the list of strategies and payoffs that the participants would choose if they could commit themselves to a coordinated choice of strategies—for example, by signing an enforceable contract.*

Coordination Game: *A game with two or more Nash Equilibria, including at least one in which the players are better off than they are in nonequilibrium outcomes, is called a coordination game, since it poses to the players the problem of coordinating their strategies to obtain a mutually advantageous equilibrium.*

Core of a Cooperative Game: *The core of a cooperative game consists of all coalition structures (if there are any) that are stable in the sense that there is no individual or group that can improve its payoffs (including side payments) by dropping out or reorganizing to form a new or separate coalition. If there are no coalition structures, the core is said to be empty.*

Correlated Equilibrium: *In a game with more than one Nash equilibrium in pure strategies, a group of players may form a coalition to choose their strategies jointly in such a way that one or more of the Nash equilibria are chosen with some probability. This is a correlated equilibrium.*

Cournot Equilibrium: *When two firms each put a certain quantity of output on the market, and sell at the price determined by the market, the output is the strategy and the resulting Nash equilibrium is a Cournot equilibrium.*

Cumulative Distribution Function: *For an uncertain variable x, the cumulative distribution function shows the answer to the question "How probable is it that the value I observe will be no greater than x?"*

D

Defect: *In a social dilemma, to play the non-cooperative equilibrium strategy is to "defect" from a hypothetical coalition to obtain the cooperative outcome.*

Demand Curve or Function: *The relationship between the price of a good and the quantity that can be sold at each respective price is a demand relationship. It can be shown in a diagram as the demand curve, or mathematically as the demand function.*

Density Function: *For an uncertain variable x, the density function shows the answer to the question "How probable is it that the value I observe will be in the neighborhood of x?"*

Differential Equations: *A differential equation is an equation in which the dependent variable is a rate of change.*

Differential Games: *Games expressed in differential equations are called differential games.*

Discount Factor: *In future plays of the game, payoffs are discounted both for the passage of time and the probability that the game will not be played so many times. The value of a future payoff is discounted for comparison with payoffs on the current play by multiplying it by a number between 0 and 1, inclusive, that reflects both time and uncertainty. This number is the discount factor, often symbolized by d.*

Dominant Strategy: *Whenever one strategy yields a higher payoff than a second strategy, regardless of which strategies the other players choose, the first strategy dominates the second. If one strategy dominates all other strategies (for a particular player in the game) it is said to be a dominant strategy (for that player).*

Dominant Strategy Equilibrium: *If, in a game, each player has a dominant strategy, and each player plays the dominant strategy, then that combination of (dominant) strategies and the corresponding payoffs are said to constitute the dominant strategy equilibrium for that game.*

Dominated Strategy: *Whenever one strategy yields a payoff strictly greater than that of a second strategy, regardless of which strategies the other players choose, the second strategy is strongly dominated by the first, and is said to be a strongly dominated strategy.*

Duopoly: *An industry in which just two firms compete for customers is called a duopoly.*

Dutch Auction: *An auction in which the seller initially posts a high price, and then lowers the price step by step until someone buys, is called a Dutch auction.*

E

Efficiency: *In voting or in the allocation of resources, the situation is efficient if there is no alternative that every person prefers to the existing alternative.*

Efficiency Wage: *When an employer pays more than the market wage in order to obtain greater productivity than would be obtained at the market wage that employer is paying an efficiency wage.*

Efficient (Pareto Optimum): *In neoclassical economics, the allocation of resources is said to be efficient, or Pareto optimum, if no one can be made better off without making someone else worse off.*

Empty-Core Games: *A game that has no allocations (coalitional strategies, payoffs and side payments) in the core is said to be an empty-core game.*

English Auction: *An auction in which potential buyers call out sequentially higher prices, and the person who bids highest buys the item at the high bid price is called an English auction.*

Evolutionarily Stable Strategy: *A Nash equilibrium that is stable under the replicator dynamics is an evolutionarily stable strategy equilibrium.*

Expected Value: *Suppose an uncertain event can have several outcomes with numerical values that may be different. The expected value (also known as mathematical expectation) of the event is the weighted average of the numerical values, with the probabilities of the outcomes as the weights.*

Extensive Form: *A game is represented in extensive form when it is shown as a sequence of decisions, commonly as a tree diagram.*

F

Focal Point: *See Schelling point.*

Folk Theorem: *The widely held intuition that noncooperative games played repeatedly may often have cooperative equilibria is called the folk theorem of game theory.*

Forgiving Trigger: *A forgiving trigger is a strategy that allows for a resumption of cooperative play after some period of retaliation, unlike the Grim Trigger. Tit-for-Tat is one example of a forgiving trigger.*

Forward Induction: *In some games, a player may be able to infer something from earlier decisions made by other players, because the game is nested or imbedded in a larger one. This is called forward induction.*

Framing: *When a decision (such as the choice of a strategy in a game) depends on the way the decision is stated, the decision is said to have been influenced by framing.*

G

Grand Coalition: *A coalition of all the players in the game is called the grand coalition.*

Grim Trigger: *A trigger strategy that responds to a defection by defection from that time on is a grim trigger. Other trigger strategies are forgiving triggers.*

H

Heuristic Methods: *Heuristic methods of problem solving (also called heuristics) are methods that are fast and usually reliable, but informal or inconclusive because they can fail in unusual cases.*

Hypercompetitive: *A player is hypercompetitive if, instead of acting in self-interest, he tries to maximize the difference of his own payoffs minus those of the opponent.*

I

Imbedded Games: *If a nested game is a proper subgame of the larger game, the nested game must be in equilibrium for the larger game to be in a subgame perfect equilibrium. The smaller game is then said to be imbedded in the larger.*

Indefinitely Repeated Games: *When a game is played repeatedly, but with no definite end point, it is treated as if it were repeated infinitely many times. Such games may also be said to be indefinitely repeated.*

Independent Private Values: *When each bidder's value for the item is independent of the values or bids of any other person, the values are independent private values.*

Index Fund: *A stock mutual fund that holds a bundle of all the stocks that make up some popular stock price index is called an index fund.*

Information Set: *A decision node with more than one branch included in it is called an information set. It indicates that the decision maker does not know some of the strategy choices another player has made, and therefore does not know which branch the other player is taking—it therefore indicates a lack of information.*

Informationally Efficient Markets: *A market is informationally efficient if prices determined in that market reflect all information about the profitability and risks of investment in shares on that market available to the public.*

Iterated Elimination of Dominated Strategies: *If a game has a dominated strategy, the game created by the elimination of that dominated strategy has the same Nash equilibria as the original game. This elimination can be done step by step until there are no more dominated strategies, and the resulting game has the same Nash equilibria as the original game.*

L

Liability: *In law, liability rules determine who is responsible for accidents or for the consequences of insufficient care. Different liability rules may lead to different Nash equilibria in some applications.*

Limiting Frequency: *Let an uncertain event be repeated again and again without limit. At each step, compute the proportion of all trials that have come out in one particular way. If this proportion settles down to a more-and-more predictable value, that value is the limiting frequency of the outcome, and is equivalent to the probability of that outcome on any single trial.*

M

Majority: *A candidate or alternative that receives more than half of the votes cast has a majority.*

Marginal Revenue: *A monopoly's marginal revenue is the additional revenue it will realize by cutting its price to sell one more unit (without price discrimination).*

Marginal Utility: *The additional utility a person obtains as a result of increasing the consumption of a good or service by 1 is called the marginal utility of the good or service. If measured in monetary units, it is called the marginal benefit.*

Market Equilibrium: *The price high enough so that the quantity offered by suppliers is equal to the quantity demanded is the market equilibrium price, and the quantity traded at that price is the market equilibrium quantity.*

Maximin: *The strategy that gives the biggest minimum is the maximin strategy.*

Maximum: *When a player chooses a particular strategy, the payoff depends on the strategies chosen by the other player or players. The largest of these payoffs is the maximum payoff.*

Mechanism Design: *Treating the desired outcome of the game as a given and trying to discover what rules will give that outcome as a Nash equilibrium is mechanism design.*

Median Voter: *If one voter's peak preference lies between one-half of the voters who prefer more and one-half who prefer less, that person is the median voter and his vote can be decisive.*

Minimax: *The strategy that gives the smallest maximum is the minimax strategy.*

Minimum: *When a player chooses a particular strategy, the payoff depends on the strategies chosen by the other player or players. The smallest of these payoffs is the minimum payoffs.*

Mixed Strategy: *A Nash equilibrium in which one or more players choose among two or more strategies according to given positive probabilities is called a mixed-strategy equilibrium, and every such decision rule is called a mixed strategy.*

N

Naïve Voting: *Naïve voting means voting for one's first choice regardless of the consequences.*

Nash Equilibrium: *In any noncooperative game, when each player chooses the strategy that is the best response to the strategies that the other players choose, that is a Nash equilibrium.*

Natural Uncertainty: *Natural uncertainty is uncertainty about the outcome of a game that results from some natural cause rather than the actions of the human players. In game theory we introduce natural uncertainty by allowing nature to be a player, and assuming that nature plays according to given probabilities.*

Nested Games: *If a game is part of a larger game, then equilibrium strategies in the smaller game may depend on the larger game. The smaller game is said to be nested within the larger.*

Neutral: *In voting, a voting scheme is neutral if the ranking of any two alternatives depends only on the preferences of the voters between those two alternatives.*

New Classical Economics: *The New Classical economics is a school of thought in macroeconomics that has restated and renewed traditional ideas of classical economics, especially on the role of money and efficient markets in the macroeconomy.*

Nonconstant-Sum Game: *If the payoffs in a game do not add up to a constant, but vary depending on which strategies are chosen, it is a nonconstant sum game.*

Noncooperative Games and Solutions: *If the participants in a game cannot make binding commitments to coordinate their strategies the game is noncooperative. The solution without coordination of strategies is a noncooperative solution. A Nash equilibrium is the most important concept of a noncooperative solution.*

Noncooperative Solution: *The noncooperative solution of a game is the list of strategies and payoffs that the participants would choose if there is no possibility to commit themselves to a coordinated joint strategy, so that each assumes the other will choose a best response strategy.*

Nondictatorial: *In voting, a voting scheme is nondictatorial if there is no one person whose preferences decide the election regardless of the preferences of others.*

Nontransferable Utility: *A game is said to have nontransferable utility (NTU) if it is impossible to make side payments, perhaps because the subjective payoffs are uncorrelated with money payments.*

Normal Form: *A game is represented in normal form when it is shown as a table of numbers with the strategies listed along the margins of the table and the payoffs for the participants in the cells of the table.*

N-Person Game: *A game with N players, usually implying the N is greater than 3, is an N-person game.*

O

One-off Game: *When a game is played just once—and not repeated—it is described as a one-off game.*

Opportunity Cost: *The opportunity cost of any good or service consists of the other goods or services that must be given up in order to obtain it. The money cost is the money measure of the opportunity cost. The marginal cost is the additional cost of selling one more unit. Generally, the marginal cost is the price on the supply curve.*

Ordinal: *A number expressed in terms of its order, such as first, second, third, and so on; rather than in terms of the quantity it expresses, is said to be an ordinal number.*

P

Payoff Dominant and Risk Dominant Equilibria: *If there are more than one Nash equilibria, and one of the equilibria yields a higher payoff to each player than the others do, it is said to be the payoff dominant equilibrium. If one of the equilibria gives the smallest maximum loss to each player, it is said to be the risk dominant equilibrium.*

Payoff Table: *A payoff table is a table with the strategies of two or three players along the margins and the payoffs to the players in the cells. Each strategy corresponds to a column or row and so the payoffs in a cell are the payoffs for the strategies that correspond to the column and row.*

Plurality: *A candidate or alternative that receives more votes than any other candidate or alternative has a plurality.*

Population Games: *If members of a population are matched at random to play a game, with different types playing different strategies, the whole sequence of play is a population game.*

Pork Barrel Politics: *Pork Barrel politics means that legislators collude to provide federal money to their own districts, regardless of the public interest.*

Preference Voting: *A scheme in which voters vote for more than one candidate or alternative, ranking them in order preference, is called preference voting.*

Price Discrimination: *Whenever a seller sells units of its product at different prices— whether the units are sold to different people or are sold to the same person at different prices— it is called price discrimination.*

Probability: *Probability is a numerical measure of the likelihood of one of the outcomes of an uncertain event. Probability measures have a certain kind of algebra that distinguishes them from other kinds of measures. For example, the probability that two events, independent of one another, both occur is the product of the probabilities that each one occurs.*

Product Differentiation: *When different firms sell products or services that are not perfect substitutes, and make the distinction among the products a basis of promotion or an aspect of market strategy, this is referred to as product differentiation.*

Proper Subgame: *A proper subgame is a subgame that includes only part of the complete game.*

Proportional Game: *In this book, a proportional game is an N-person game with large N, and with representative agents, in which the state variable is the proportion of the players choosing one strategy rather than another.*

Pure Strategy: *Every game in normal form is defined by a list of strategies with their payoffs. These are the pure strategies in the game.*

Pure Strict Liability: *Pure strict liability refers to a legal rule in which a party engaged in some activity, such as driving a car, is held responsible (liable) for any accident.*

Pursuit Games: *A pursuit game is a two-person game in which one of the players tries to capture the other or draw close enough to destroy the other. The objective of the player who is being pursued is to keep out of range as long as possible. In a typical pursuit game, each player's strategy is the rate and direction of travel. Since these can change continuously, pursuit games are expressed as differential equations.*

R

Randomize: *To choose a mixed strategy is to randomize one's strategy.*

Reaction Function: *In a Cournot Equilibrium, the profit-maximizing output for one firm can be expressed as a function of the output of the other firm. This is called a reaction function.*

Reciprocity: *When a player gives up a greater payoff in order to reward a perceived self-sacrifice by the other player, or to retaliate for perceived aggressiveness by the other player, it is called reciprocity. In the first case, reward, it is called positive reciprocity. In the second case, retaliation, it is called negative reciprocity.*

Refinement of Nash Equilibrium: *When a game has two or more Nash equilibria, we may be able to judge one more likely than others on the basis of some criterion of rationality additional to the best response. Such a limitation is called a refinement of the Nash equilibrium. Some important refinements are payoff dominance, risk dominance, the trembling hand assumption, and subgame perfect equilibrium. Stability against disturbance by coalition formation is also an important refinement of Nash Equilibrium.*

Repeated Games: *When a relatively simple game, such as a social dilemma, is played by the same players again and again so that a strategy in one repetition could, in principle, affect play in a later repetition, it becomes a repeated game. In that case, the sequence as a whole must be analyzed, and the subgame perfect equilibrium of the sequence is the equilibrium of the game.*

Replicator Dynamics: *In a population game with replicator dynamics, each type increases or decreases relative to the total population in proportion as the payoff to the strategy played by* that type exceeds or falls short of the average payoff.

Representative Agent: *In game theory, the simplifying assumption that every agent chooses from the same list of strategies and gets the same payoffs in given circumstances is called a representative agent model or theory.*

Revelation: *Successful mechanism design may require that people be given incentives to reveal information they have that the designer and authority lack.*

Revenue Equivalent: *Two auction forms are revenue equivalent if they yield the same expected value of revenue to the seller.*

Risk Aversion: *A person who will choose a safe payment over a risky payment with an expected value greater than that of the safe payment is said to be risk averse. A person who chooses a risky payment over a safe payment, even though the risky payment has a smaller expected value than the safe payment, is said to be risk loving. A person who will always choose the higher money expected value is said to be risk neutral.*

Runoff Election: *When there is no majority on the first round of voting, an election scheme that allows for a second round among the alternatives with larger votes on the first round, after alternatives that got fewer votes have been dropped out, is called a runoff election.*

S

Schelling Point: *If a game has two or more Nash equilibria, and some clue can lead the participants to believe that one equilibrium is more*

likely to be realized than the other, the more likely equilibrium is called a Schelling point.

Sealed-Bid Auction: *An auction in which the bids are submitted simultaneously, so that no one bidder knows what the other bidders have bid, is called a sealed-bid auction.*

Second-Price Auction: *An auction in which the high bidder buys the item at the second-highest price bid is called a second-bid auction. It may be a sealed-bid auction or an auction with sequential bidding of higher prices.*

Side Payment: *When part of the payoff is transferred from one member of a coalition to another, in order that no member of the coalition is worse off as a result of adopting the coordinated strategy of the coalition, this transfer is called a side payment.*

Single-Peaked Preferences: *If there is some dimension on which each voter's preference ranking first increases to a "best" and then decreases, the voter's preferences are said to be single-peaked.*

Singleton Coalition: *A single player who goes it alone in a cooperative game is called a singleton coalition.*

Social Dilemma: *A social dilemma is a game that has a dominant strategy equilibrium, and the dominant strategy solution is different from the cooperative solution to the game.*

Solution Set: *In a cooperative game with side payments, the solution set consists of all coordinated strategies and payoffs and side payments so that the total payoff to all participants in the game is as large as possible—that is, the total payoff is maximized.*

State Variable: *In differential games, a state variable means a single number, or one of a small list of numbers, that expresses the "state" of the game, so that a player who knows just the value of the state variable or variables has all the information he needs to choose a best-response strategy. In this book the term is extended to refer to all N-person games in which such variables may exist.*

Strategic Voting: *Strategic voting involves voting for something other than one's first preference in the hope of improving the outcome of the voting from one's own point of view.*

Strategically Equivalent: *Two auction forms are strategically equivalent if the same strategies and equilibria apply for both.*

Strongly Dominated Strategy: *Whenever one strategy yields a payoff strictly greater than of a second strategy, regardless of which strategies the other players choose, the second strategy is strongly dominated by the first, and is said to be a strongly dominated strategy.*

Subgame: *A subgame of any game consists of all nodes and payoffs that follow a complete information node.*

Subgame Perfect Equilibrium: *A game is in subgame perfect equilibrium if and only if every subgame is in a Nash equilibrium.*

T

Tacit Collusion: *When sellers of a particular good or substitutable goods keep their prices up to obtain a monopoly profit, they are*

said to collude. If they are able to do this without an explicit agreement, their collusion is tacit, that is, unspoken. This is then described as tacit collusion.*

Tattonement: *In economics, the French word tattonement refers to a process for the determination of a market price, as though a two-sided auction were conducted.*

Tit-for-Tat: *In game theory, Tit-for-Tat refers to a rule for choosing strategies of play in a repeated social dilemma or similar game. The rule is to play "cooperate" until the opponent plays "defect," and then to retaliate by playing "defect" on the following round.*

Tragedy of the Commons: *The tragedy of the commons is an illustrative example in environmental policy and related areas. The example is based on the medieval practice of keeping a common pasture on which the residents of the village would be allowed to pasture their animals. According to the example, they would have no incentive to limit the number of animals put to pasture on the commons, so that the pasture would be overexploited and rendered unproductive, The conclusion is that common property resources in general tend to be overexploited.*

Transferable Utility: *A game is said to have transferable utility (TU) if the subjective payoffs are closely enough correlated with money payoffs so that transfers of money can be used to adjust the payoffs within a coalition. Side payments will always be possible in a game with transferable utility but may not be possible in a game without transferable utility.*

Trembling Hand: *A player who might, with very small probability, choose a wrong strategy is said to play with a trembling hand. In games with more than one Nash equilibrium, some of the equilibria may be risky when the players have trembling hands. In some cases we refine the concept of Nash equilibrium by ruling out just those equilibria.*

Trigger Strategy: *A rule for choosing strategies in individual repetitions in an indefinitely repeated game is called a trigger strategy if the rule is that noncooperative play triggers one or more rounds of noncooperative play by the victim in retaliation.*

Tripwire: *A tripwire strategy in a game in extensive form is a strategy choice that commits the player to retaliation in some attack-retaliation subgame. This term was used with respect the the deployment of military forces by the United States during the Cold War (1949–1989), especially in the cases of West Germany and South Korea.*

U

Utility: *Utility is a numerical measure of the subjective benefits an individual derives from a particular good, service, income, or payoff.*

W

Weakly Dominated Strategy: *Whenever one strategy yields a payoff no less than a second strategy, regardless of which strategies the other players choose; and the payoff to the first strategy is strictly greater than the payoff to the second strategy for some strategies the other players might choose, the second strategy is weakly dominated by the first, and is said to be a weakly dominated strategy.*

Z

Zero-Sum Game: *A zero-sum game is a game in which the sum of the payoffs is always 0, that is, in which one player loses whatever the other players win. Zero-sum games are a class of constant-sum games.*